Studies in European Economic Law and Regulation

Volume 30

The series “Studies in European Economic Law and Regulation” is devoted to the analysis of European Economic Law. The series’ scope covers a broad range of topics within economics law including, but not limited to, the relationship between EU law and WTO law; free movement under EU law and its impact on fundamental rights; antitrust law; trade law; unfair competition law; financial market law; consumer law; food law; and health law. These subjects are approached both from doctrinal and interdisciplinary perspectives.

The series accepts monographs focusing on a specific topic, as well as edited collections of articles covering a specific theme or collections of articles. All contributions are subject to rigorous double-blind peer-review.

Fatmanur Cebeci Çorum

Application of Geo-Blocking to Copyright-Protected Digital Products

Springer

Fatmanur Cebeci Çorum
Faculty of Law
Ankara Yildirim Beyazit University
Ankara, Türkiye

ISSN 2214-2037 ISSN 2214-2045 (electronic)
Studies in European Economic Law and Regulation
ISBN 978-3-032-34506-6 ISBN 978-3-032-34507-3 (eBook)
https://doi.org/10.1007/978-3-032-34507-3

This Springer imprint is published by the registered company Springer Nature Switzerland AG
The registered company address is: Gewerbestrasse 11, 6330 Cham, Switzerland

To İpek and Hamza…

Preface

This study examines the practice of geo-blocking, which can be defined as the restriction of access to a digital product on the Internet based on the user's geographical location. With the increased use of the Internet, particularly the growing consumption of digital products, the issue of geo-blocking has become more prominent and integrated into daily life. This study analyses geo-blocking practices under the European Union copyright law, focusing specifically on the Geo-blocking Regulation. Although the Geo-blocking Regulation aimed to resolve the issue of cross-border access to online products, it did not cover copyright-protected products. Consequently, copyright-protected digital products within the European Union may still be subject to geo-blocking, despite the goal of creating a Digital Single Market in the European Union.

The geo-blocking debate is examined from various perspectives, exploring the most balanced approach that would support the proper functioning of the European Union internal market while respecting the interests of copyright holders, other rightsholders and users. This study assesses the need to include copyright-protected products within the scope of the Geo-blocking Regulation. To do so, it delves into the copyright law aspects of geo-blocking, particularly territorial licensing, the existing European Union legal framework regarding cross-border access to digital products, the competition law implications of this issue, and the circumvention of geo-blocking measures. In its final analysis, the study concludes that including copyright-protected digital products within the scope of the Geo-blocking Regulation would benefit users, copyright holders, and the internal market's proper functioning, albeit with certain limitations.

Ankara, Türkiye — Fatmanur Cebeci Çorum

Acknowledgements This book is the extended and updated version of my doctoral thesis, which I completed at Swansea University Faculty of Law. Bringing it into its current form has been a long journey, and I am deeply grateful to those who supported me along the way.

I would first like to express my sincere appreciation to Swansea University Faculty of Law for the academic environment, support and guidance that shaped this work throughout my PhD. I owe a particular debt of gratitude to Stefano Barazza for his supervision, thoughtful feedback and support during my research.

I am also grateful to the Turkish Ministry of National Education for the scholarship that made it possible for me to pursue my PhD abroad and to complete the research on which this book is based.

I would further like to thank Ankara Yıldırım Beyazıt University Faculty of Law for encouraging me to turn my thesis into a book, and for providing a friendly and supportive environment in which to continue my academic work and bring this project to completion.

I would like to thank my family for creating opportunities for me even in the midst of every difficulty. Your support has carried me further than words can express.

I dedicate this book to my husband, Hamza… I apologise for the time I had to take away from us during this process. Your understanding and steady support have carried me through this journey, and for that I am sincerely grateful. Sharing this journey with you, growing together, learning together, making sense of the world together has been one of my life's greatest joys.

I also dedicate this book to my daughter, İpek… Even before you arrived, you changed my life in the sweetest way. You made me stronger and more hopeful. I hope you are proud of me, and as you grow, I cannot wait to see the kindness, curiosity, and light you will bring into this world. If I am fortunate enough to watch you become the wonderful person you are meant to be, it will be my greatest happiness.

Fatmanur Cebeci Çorum

Competing Interests The author has no competing interests to declare that are relevant to the content of this manuscript.

Contents

Abbreviations

AG	Advocate General
AVOD	Advertisement-Based Video-On-Demand Services
B2B	Business-to-Business
CFR	Charter of Fundamental Rights
CJEU	Court of Justice of the European Union
CRM	Collective Rights Management
DMCA	Digital Millennium Copyright Act (in the USA)
DNS	Domain Name Servers
DRM	Digital Rights Management
DSM	Digital Single Market
ECHR	European Convention on Human Rights
ECS	European Copyright Society
ECtHR	European Court of Human Rights
EEA	European Economic Area
EEC	European Economic Community
EESC	European Economic and Social Committee
EST	Electronic-Sell-Through
EU	European Union
EULA	End-User Licence Agreement
FAST	Free Ad-supported Streaming Television Services
FRAND	Licensing on Fair, Reasonable and Non-Discriminatory Terms
GPS	Global Positioning System
ID	Identification
IP	Intellectual Property
IP	Internet Protocol
ISP	Internet Service Provider
JRC	Joint Research Centre
NGO	Non-Governmental Organisation
PC	Personal Computer
RELs	Rights Expression Languages
RMI	Rights Management Information

SMEs	Small and Medium-Sized Enterprises
SVOD	Subscription Video-on-Demand
TFEU	Treaty on the Functioning of the European Union
TPM	Technological Protection Measures
TRIPS Agreement	WTO Agreement on Trade-Related Aspects of Intellectual Property Rights
TTBER	Treaty on the Functioning of the European Union to Categories of Technology Transfer Agreements
TV	Television
TVOD	Transactional Video-on-Demand
UK	United Kingdom
UN	United Nations
US	United States
USA	United States of America
VAT	Value Added Tax
VBER	Vertical Block Exemption Regulation
VPN	Virtual Private Network
W3C	World Wide Web Consortium
WCT	WIPO Copyright Treaty
WHO	World Health Organization
WIPO	World Intellectual Property Organization
WPPT	WIPO Performances and Phonograms Treaty
WTO	World Trade Organization

Chapter 1
Introduction

Abstract Geo-blocking, understood as any measure restricting access to a digital product on the Internet on the basis of the user's geographical location, constitutes one of the principal obstacles to the effective functioning of the European Union Digital Single Market. Although the Geo-blocking Regulation, adopted on 3 December 2018, was intended to address such practices, its material scope remains limited: pursuant to Article 4(1)(b), it does not extend to electronically supplied services the main feature of which is the provision of access to and use of copyright-protected works or other protected subject matter, while audiovisual services are likewise excluded. In light of the evaluation mandate conferred upon the Commission by Article 9 of the Regulation, this study critically examines whether such electronically supplied services and audiovisual services (collectively, copyright-protected digital products) ought to be brought within its scope. Adopting a predominantly doctrinal methodology, the analysis addresses the justifications of geo-blocking, the territorial nature of copyright law and its harmonisation within the European Union, the principle of exhaustion and its possible digital extension, the existing acquis on cross-border distribution, the enforceability of territorial licensing arrangements under competition law, and the copyright-law implications of circumventing geo-blocking measures. On this basis, the study identifies the gaps in the current framework and formulates concrete policy recommendations to ensure that geo-blocking does not unduly hinder the realisation of a genuine Digital Single Market. The findings reflect the state of the law as of May 2026.

1.1 Introduction

Geo-blocking can be broadly defined as any measure taken to prevent access to a digital product on the Internet based on the user's geographical location. From a commercial perspective, it refers to practices used to restrict or block access to websites or online interfaces, redirect users to local stores, or provide less favourable or different terms to users based on their location for digital products. With the widespread use of the Internet, most users encounter geo-blocking measures that

F. Cebeci Çorum, *Application of Geo-Blocking to Copyright-Protected Digital Products*, Studies in European Economic Law and Regulation 30,
https://doi.org/10.1007/978-3-032-34507-3_1

prevent them from accessing digital products in a preferred manner. This inaccessibility is particularly problematic within the European Union, where the aim of the internal market has always been to ensure the free movement of goods, services, people, and capital, an objective pursued by the European Union since the 1950s. However, the traditional concept of an internal market has proven inadequate to guarantee these freedoms in the digital era. Therefore, the European Commission decided to establish a Digital Single Market. This initiative was meant to reflect the digitalisation of the economy and the impact of technology on modern economic systems. To this end, the European Commission introduced the 'Digital Single Market Strategy for Europe', which aims to guarantee the free movement of goods, services, people, and capital in the digital domain, while ensuring that individuals and businesses operate under fair competition, consumer protection, and data protection rules, irrespective of their nationality or place of residence.

The Digital Single Market Strategy particularly seeks to improve access to online goods and services for consumers and businesses across the European Union, thereby eliminating differences between the online and offline worlds. A key aspect of removing these differences is removing barriers to cross-border online activity. To achieve this goal, addressing unjustified geo-blocking was one of the primary targets set by the Digital Single Market Strategy.

Accordingly, on 3 December 2018, the European Union introduced a Regulation on tackling unjustified geo-blocking and other forms of discrimination based on customers' nationality, place of residence, or place of establishment within the internal market—the Geo-blocking Regulation. This regulation sought to promote the internal market by preventing unjustified geo-blocking and other forms of discrimination, directly or indirectly, based on customer nationality, residency, or place of establishment. However, it does not cover the activities listed in Article 2(2) of the Services Directive, such as audiovisual services, transport, and retail financial services. Moreover, the provisions of the Geo-blocking Regulation regarding electronically supplied services do not extend to access to and use of copyright-protected works, such as e-books, music, video games, and software, as mentioned in Article 4(1)(b) of this regulation. On the other hand, the Geo-blocking Regulation includes an evaluation article (Article 9), and the Commission plans to evaluate the Geo-Blocking Regulation as to whether this regulation shall apply to electronically supplied services, the main feature of which is the provision of access to and use of copyright-protected works or other protected subject matter, in the case the trader has the requisite rights for the relevant territories. As part of this evaluation article, the Commission also decided to analyse the potential consequences of inclusion of the audiovisual services to the scope of the Geo-blocking Regulation.

The primary focus of this research is to assess the need to include electronically supplied services, the main feature of which is the provision of access to and use of copyright-protected works or other protected subject matter and audiovisual services within the scope of the Geo-blocking Regulation, as part of this evaluation article, and examining possible justifications for such an inclusion. The principal research question is aimed at critically analysing gaps in the current framework applicable to geo-blocking in the European Union and evaluating potential reforms to strengthen the Digital Single Market. Ultimately, the goal is to offer concrete policy recommendations to ensure that geo-blocking does not hinder the effective functioning of the European Union Digital Single Market. The research will identify, evaluate, and propose solutions for critical issues and barriers that obstruct the creation of a digital market free from geo-blocking. Specifically, the study will address gaps and deficiencies in the existing Geo-blocking Regulation by offering concrete policy recommendations for its potential amendment. As such, the central research question revolves around the compatibility of geo-blocking with the Digital Single Market, the adequacy of the current normative framework, and the necessary amendments to existing legal structures.

The primary research question leads to several subsidiary questions, which the study will address:

- What is meant by geo-blocking, and what are the justifications and debates surrounding such practices?
- What is the relationship between copyright territoriality and geo-blocking, and what has been the European Union's response to copyright territoriality?
- What initiatives have been proposed by the European Union to improve the cross-border availability of copyright-protected products, and have these been successful?
- Does distributing copyright-protected digital products based on territorial licensing present problems, particularly in the context of competition law?
- Does circumvention of geo-blocking measures raise issues in terms of copyright infringement?
- Is there a need to propose amendments to the Geo-blocking Regulation, considering the justifications for geo-blocking, the territorial nature of copyright law, and the current demand for access to copyright-protected digital products?

To provide concrete answers to these questions:

First of all, the geo-blocking practice will be explained in detail. Therefore, Chap. 1 will define geo-blocking and evaluate justifications for its use, including arguments both for and against the practice.

From the perspective of copyright law, since the main reason of the application of geo-blocking practice in the copyright law domain is to comply with territorial copyright law and territorial licensing requirements, Chap. 2 will provide a brief overview of copyright law and its territorial nature, discussing the copyright harmonisation within the EU.

Chapter 3 will examine the principle of exhaustion, which is a response to copyright territoriality. Since the acceptance of the exhaustion principle in the digital domain could partially address the geo-blocking issue, this chapter will also assess the potential for digital exhaustion.

Chapter 4 will present the existing European Union regime on cross-border distribution and the availability of copyright-protected products in the European Union, supported by existing literature, so that gaps in current legislation can be pointed.

Since territorial licensing is central to the geo-blocking debate within copyright law, Chapter 5 will explore territorial licensing and assess the enforceability of such licences from the perspective of competition law.

Chapter 6 will focus on the potential consequences of circumventing geo-blocking measures from a copyright law standpoint, to assess the legality of circumvention of geo-blocking measures.

After setting out the debate on geo-blocking, Chap. 7 will conclude by discussing the need for the inclusion of electronically supplied services, main feature of which is the provision of access to and use of copyright protected works or other protected subject matter, and audiovisual services (altogether, will be referred as copyright-protected digital products) within the scope of the Geo-blocking Regulation in its next review, as part of Article 9 of this regulation, and will provide policy recommendations for European Union policy-makers accordingly.

This study primarily focuses on the copyright law aspects of geo-blocking practices. Any consequences affecting other areas of law will be considered only where explicitly stated. These findings reflect knowledge available as of May 2026.

In this study, doctrinal methodology was predominantly employed. The author of this study made library-based research, analysed case law, secondary sources and other relevant sources throughout this study. In some parts, the author also relied on surveys and studies conducted by other organisations or individuals/groups, yet the author did not involve in data collection.

Chapter 2
Geo-Blocking: Background, Definitions and the Debate on Geo-Blocking

Abstract The early vision of the Internet imagined a borderless environment in which information, goods, and digital products could circulate without geographical limits. Over time, however, widespread Internet use revealed significant legal, economic, and logistical barriers. States increasingly sought to control online activity to safeguard sovereignty, enforce national laws, and regulate the flow of information, often by imposing territorial restrictions through measures such as geo-blocking. These restrictions may serve purposes including censorship, compliance with court orders, or the implementation of policies such as the right to be forgotten. Private entities likewise began to rely on geo-blocking to control access to copyright-protected digital products. Rightsholders and distributors use territorial limitations mostly to manage distribution models, differentiate prices, comply with contractual obligations, or avoid the application of foreign legal systems. As a result, consumers may face redirected websites, altered catalogues or interfaces, different pricing, or refusal to access, stream, or download products, even those previously purchased. Geo-blocking has therefore become a central point of controversy. Supporters view it as a legitimate commercial tool, while critics argue that it restricts access to digital products and undermines user rights, including the ability to receive information freely and damage cultural diversity. The debate reflects broader tensions between territorial law, market integration, human rights aspects, and consumer expectations. Understanding these competing perspectives is essential for evaluating the justifications for geo-blocking and for considering potential approaches to the persistent unavailability of digital products on the Internet.

2.1 Introduction and General Overview

'This video is not available in your location', 'This content could not be purchased from that location', and many similar warnings, as illustrated in Fig. 2.1, have become a part of everyday life for Internet users. Individuals who wish to access, purchase, view, stream, or download information and products online often encounter difficulties due to the unavailability of these items in their geographical locations.

F. Cebeci Çorum, *Application of Geo-Blocking to Copyright-Protected Digital Products*, Studies in European Economic Law and Regulation 30,
https://doi.org/10.1007/978-3-032-34507-3_2

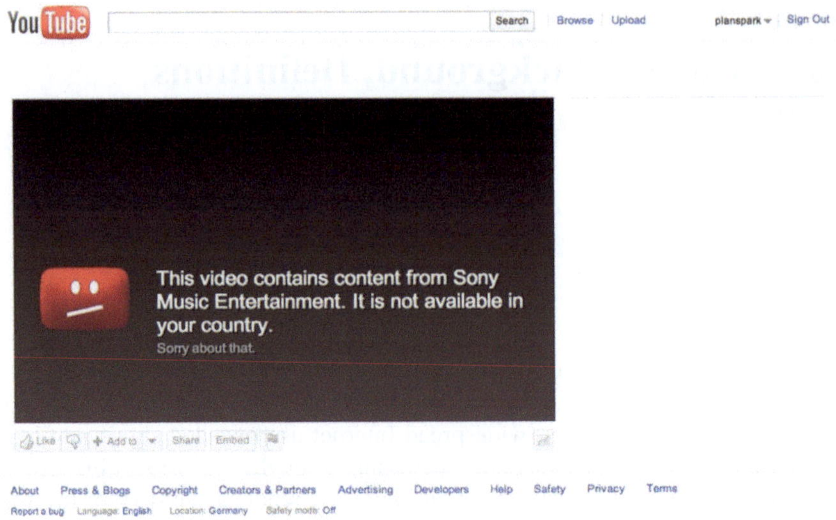

Fig. 2.1 An example of geo-blocking by Tim Bonnemann, https://www.flickr.com/photos/planspark/5285233192

When the Internet entered our lives and became a mass medium of many uses,[1] everyone thought that the Internet could be a free trade zone where information and products[2] flow borderless.[3] All basic needs have become accessible through the Internet, creating a distinct market for entrepreneurs who sell and promote these products online. However, many legal, economic, and logistical problems have also emerged. There has long been an assumption that the Internet has no geographical limitations or borders; for instance, sending an email to your neighbour requires the same effort as sending an email to someone in a different country.[4] Nevertheless, as time went on and Internet consumption increased, people started to experience difficulties online, and customers who wanted to access digital products encountered numerous barriers. Despite the main idea behind the Internet is to create a borderless environment and it is intended to be beyond the control of any state or third parties, legislators began to consider territorially limiting actions on the Internet within the last few decades as a result of this enormous consumption.[5] Notwithstanding, states and private entities[6] wanted to regulate online activity,[7] and they tried to impose territorial limits based on geographical location by blocking Internet users who wanted to access anything on the Internet.

[1] Trimble (2018, p. 55).

[2] Trimble (2012, p. 570).

[3] Trimble (2018, p. 55).

[4] Svantesson (2012, p. 474).

[5] Trimble (2024, p. 6).

[6] Trimble (2018, p. 55).

[7] Quinn (2021, p. 294).

States wanted to control the Internet, and all activities conducted online to maintain their sovereignty.[8] They used various restrictions to control the dissemination of goods, services, and digital products, or more broadly, the dissemination of information on the Internet. Territorial restrictions can be applied in the context of blocking or removing third-party content, emphasizing certain limitations.[9] The Internet, as a great source of power, has always been seen as both an opportunity and a danger by states. Every piece of information on the Internet is actually desired to be controlled by laws. Territorial restrictions imposed by states can be for a variety of reasons; however, the most common reasons for implementing territorial restrictions are for censorship purposes[10] and to comply with legal requirements, such as obeying the right to be forgotten[11] decisions. When an Internet intermediary is ordered to block or remove certain content from a specific geographical area, territorial restrictions can be used to remove the content from that location. For example, if a German court has ruled for Facebook to remove political and sensitive content from Germany, Facebook could use geo-blocking practices to prevent access to this content.[12] Some countries may also choose to apply restrictions on Internet websites within their territory due to cultural, religious, political, or other reasons that may impact their society. However, there are concerns that these restrictions could harm society by raising free speech issues,[13] as they could prevent access to important information. This study will not cover the government/states' requiring geo-blocking practices unless states implement geo-blocking for copyright-protected digital products.

Geo-blocking also wanted to be imposed by private entities for products on the Internet. Through these restrictions, the rightsholder can limit or block access to these products, which could result in redirecting the customer from the website or restricting access to these products. Additionally, these restrictions could affect

---

[8] Quinn (2021, p. 294).

[9] According to the article, written by Dan Jerker B. Svantesson, geo-blocking (he prefers to use the "geo-location blocking" term in his article) is defined as follows: "*Geo-location technologies may determine an Internet user's geographical location, for example, by reference to the user's IP address. Such technologies can, of course, be used to delineate the accessibility of Internet content. Indeed, such technologies can be used in various ways to achieve such a result, and I will consider both a "strict geo-location blocking" and a more nuanced "country lens" approach.*" For full article: Svantesson (2012, p. 473).

[10] Trimble (2018, p. 66).

[11] The right to be forgotten may be summarised as a person's right to request the deletion of data about their personal or family members which also includes the right to demand the exclusion from search engines. More information can be found here: Popovych et al. (2023, p. 42). Furthermore, in the Opinion of the Google v CNIL case (Case C-507/17 *Google LLC v Commission nationale de l'informatique et des libertés (CNIL)* (2019) Opinion of AG Szpunar para78) the Advocate General advised to use of 'geo-blocking' to comply with the right to be forgotten decisions: *In that context, that operator is required to take all steps available to him to ensure effective and complete de-referencing. That includes, in particular, the technique known as 'geo-blocking', from an IP address deemed to be located in one of the Member States subject to Directive 95/46, irrespective of the domain name used by the internet user carrying out the search.*

[12] Svantesson (2012, p. 157).

[13] Trimble (2024, p. 34).

consumers' choices, leading websites to show different catalogues, interfaces, or even prices. Furthermore, geo-blocking could result in refusing to open, play, stream, or download the product. Lastly, even if the products were purchased before, territorial restrictions could result in an 'after-sale' ban, preventing the play or stream of these previously downloaded or obtained products.[14] These restrictions may appear in cases where certain websites are not allowed to sell or stream the product in question, or they may appear in specific geographic locations, such as restricting the distribution of products to specific geographic areas. Furthermore, in the context of copyright-protected products, geo-blocking practices may be implemented as part of the business plan, such as price differentiation or making products available in different countries at different times.[15] The commercial or copyright law-related reasons will be outlined in great detail in that chapter.

In this part of the study, the author will first explain certain terms related to the study to clarify each term that will be used throughout the study. After that, the debate on geo-blocking for copyright-protected products will be explained from both perspectives.

2.2 Definitions

2.2.1 Digital Content

Very recently, the EU has defined the meaning of 'digital content' in the Supply of Digital Content and Digital Services Directive[16] and in the Contracts for the Sale of Goods Directive[17] by stating that: 'digital content' means data which are produced and supplied in digital form. Digital content also includes computer programmes, mobile applications, video and audio files in digital form.[18]

---

[14] Zarra (2016, p. 42).

[15] Kharb et al. (2023, p. 48).

[16] Directive (EU) 2019/770 of the European Parliament and of the Council of 20 May 2019 on certain aspects concerning contracts for the supply of digital content and digital services [2019] OJ L 136/1, Article 2(1).

[17] Directive (EU) 2019/771 of the European Parliament and of the Council of 20 May 2019 on certain aspects concerning contracts for the sale of goods, amending Regulation (EU) 2017/2394 and Directive 2009/22/EC, and repealing Directive 1999/44/EC [2019] OJ L 136/28, Article 2(6).

[18] Contracts for the supply of digital content and digital services (2019). In: EUR-Lex https://eur-lex.europa.eu/EN/legal-content/summary/contracts-for-the-supply-of-digital-content-and-digital-services.html.

2.2.2 *Digital Services and Electronically Supplied Services*

In the Supply of Digital Content and Digital Services Directive in Article 2(2) and the Contracts for the Sale of Goods Directive in Article 2(7), the meaning of digital services has also been defined. According to this definition, 'digital service' means (a) a service that allows the consumer to create, process, store or access data in digital form; or (b) a service that allows the sharing of or any other interaction with data in digital form uploaded or created by the consumer or other users of that service. Digital services also include cloud computing services and social media.[19]

'Electronically Supplied Services' defined in the Geo-blocking Regulation[20] Article 2(1) *as services which are delivered over the internet or an electronic network and the nature of which renders their supply essentially automated and involving minimal human intervention, and impossible to ensure in the absence of information technology.* Examples of electronically supplied services could be given as the supply of images, text, software and music.[21]

2.2.3 *Audiovisual Services*

According to the explanation provided by World Trade Organisation (WTO) website, audiovisual services include motion picture production and distribution services, motion picture projection services, radio and television services, radio and television transmission services, and sound recording.[22]

2.2.4 *Copyright-Protected Digital Products*

To start with, there is no exhaustive list of digital products; hence, digital products could be any goods and services which have the ability to be converted into a binary

---

[19] Contracts for the supply of digital content and digital services (2019). In: EUR-Lex https://eur-lex.europa.eu/EN/legal-content/summary/contracts-for-the-supply-of-digital-content-and-digital-services.html.

[20] Regulation (EU) 2018/302 of the European Parliament and of the Council of 28 February 2018 on addressing unjustified geo-blocking and other forms of discrimination based on customers' nationality, place of residence or place of establishment within the internal market and amending Regulations (EC) No 2006/2004 and (EU) 2017/2394 and Directive 2009/22/EC [2018] OJ L 60I. (hereinafter it will be referred as the Geo-blocking Regulation).

[21] More examples can be found at: 'Indicative list of electronically supplied services' https://taxation-customs.ec.europa.eu/document/download/23d6c227-514b-4742-8907-fbfc051005b3_en#:~:text=upgrades%20of%20software%3B-,•,•.

[22] Audiovisual Services. In: WTO https://www.wto.org/English/tratop_e/serv_e/audiovisual_e/audiovisual_e.htm#:~:text=Audiovisual%20services%20include%20motion%20picture,transmission%20services%2C%20and%20sound%20recording.

form, namely, to be digitised.[23] Examples include music, movies, software, videos, e-books, and pictures.

As mentioned in the introduction, the main aim of this study is to discuss the need to include electronically supplied services, main feature of which is the provision of access to and use of copyright protected works or other protected subject matter, and audiovisual services, within the scope of the Geo-blocking Regulation as a result of systematic and planned reviews to be conducted, as part of Article 9(2) of the Geo-blocking Regulation. To maintain consistency with this aim, the author has chosen to use the term 'copyright-protected digital products' to cover both electronically supplied services, main feature of which is the provision of access to and use of copyright protected works or other protected subject matter, and audiovisual services. Any reference to copyright-protected digital products in this study should be understood as inclusive of both unless otherwise stated.

2.2.5 *Geo-Location*

It is believed that geo-location technologies were invented by Ancient Greeks, who were making observations in order to take measurements of the stars of the sky.[24] Nowadays, geo-location technologies are used to determine the physical location of an internet-connected device.[25] Geo-location can be based on self-reporting, IP (Internet Protocol) addresses or a combination of information like WIFI signals or the Global Positioning System (GPS). Geo-location tools will be explained in more detail in Chap. 6.

Geo-location technology allows Internet content providers to determine the geographical location of visitors, allowing:

- content is to be available and variable for each user based on their geographic location, and this technology is used to detect the location of a device and adapt the content to the physical location of internet users.[26]
- search engines, social media platforms and websites produce content according to local regulations of countries.[27]
- users find products that are most relevant to their location, such as the international edition of the most important newspapers like the New York Times and users to be subject to localised advertisement.[28]

---

[23] Hui and Chau (2002, p. 73).

[24] Oikonomidis and Fouskas (2019, p. 1087).

[25] Trimble (2024, p. 8).

[26] Quinn (2021, p. 296).

[27] Quinn (2021, p. 296). *"For example, the technology can be used to prevent users located in Germany accessing dereferenced content through Google.com while it can still be accessible to users located in America using Google.com."*

[28] Trimble (2012, p. 570).

2.2.6 Geo-Blocking

As Trimble described in her article,[29] geo-blocking may broadly be described as any means of preventing access to a digital product[30] on the Internet based on the user's location. This definition is a broad definition and it covers all geo-blocking activities regardless of their aim; geo-blocking measures may be applied for political purposes (such as censorship),[31] for legal compliance[32] (such as the right to be forgotten decisions), for commercial reasons (such as price differentiation) as part of business strategy (such as making some products available in certain places in certain times)[33] and finally for compliance of territorial licences and territoriality of copyright. Besides, geo-blocking could be a useful tool to comply with some requirements, such as not making online gambling available in countries where they are not permitted.[34]

In this study, the term 'geo-blocking' will be used to refer to commercial practices applied as part of the business, distributor, or rightsholder's decision. This study will not focus on governmentally applied geo-blocking practices or those enacted for political reasons unless they are also related to copyright law considerations.

Geo-blocking practice relies on geo-location tools, and once the device's geographical location is determined, geo-blocking practice could be applicable.[35] Geo-blocking practice prevents users from accessing, buying, watching, seeing, downloading or streaming a digital product from the same location. Geo-blocking

---

[29] Trimble (2017, p. 46).

[30] Marketa Trimble, in her article, did not use the term 'digital products,' only the term 'internet content,' and did not include 'services' within the definition. In her very recent book, The EU Geo-Blocking Regulation Commentary (Trimble 2024, p 2), she still only used the term 'internet content' in her definition. The present author believes that not only digital content is geo-blocked, but also digital services. For example, some online content-sharing services are not available in certain countries due to geo-blocking. Therefore, the present author will use the term 'digital products' to cover both digital content and digital services.

[31] Opinion of the Google v CNIL case (Case C-507/17 *Google LLC v Commission nationale de l'informatique et des libertés (CNIL)* (2019) Opinion of AG Szpunar para71) the Advocate General Szpunar defined and explained geo-blocking as follows: *Geo-blocking is a technique that limits access to internet content depending on the geographic location of the user. In a system of geo-blocking, the user's location is determined with the help of geo-location techniques, such as verification of the user's IP address. Geo-blocking, which is a form of censorship, is deemed to be unjustified in the law of the EU internal market, where it is the subject, in particular, of a regulation designed to prevent professionals carrying out their activities in one Member State from blocking or limiting access by customers from other Member States wishing to carry out cross-border transactions on their online interfaces.* In that explanation, the Advocate General accepted that geo-blocking is a form of censorship.

[32] Trimble (2024, p. 7).

[33] Deeba Kharb et al. (2023, p. 48).

[34] Trimble (2024, p. 13).

[35] Annette Broocks et al. (2020) Geo-blocking: A Literature Review and New Evidence in Online Audio-visual Services. In: JRC Digital Economy Working Paper 2020–01 https://joint-research-centre.ec.europa.eu/reports-and-technical-documentation/geo-blocking-literature-review-and-new-evidence-online-audio-visual-services_en.

can be seen in different forms, like limiting/restricting or blocking access to websites from other countries or locations, or reroutes customers or subjects them to less favourable terms.

For the aim of this study, the geo-blocking practice may be defined as a commercial practice which is used to prevent access by restricting or blocking access to websites or online interfaces, or reroute to customers to local stores, or offering less favourable or different conditions for internet users based on their geographical locations for digital products. This definition also aligns with the Geo-blocking Regulation and activities mentioned in this Regulation. All legislative processes behind the Geo-blocking Regulation will also be outlined in this study later, in Chap. 4.

2.3 The Debate on Geo-Blocking: Views in Favour and Against

2.3.1 Introduction

With digitalisation, the increase in Internet consumption and the increase in products offered over the internet, access to these products has become more important than ever before for consumers. The consumption of the Internet and accessing information online has become part of daily life, and without accessing these products people may feel like they are missing important information, events or the chance of being part of the society. Therefore, the geo-blocking practice can easily be seen as an everyday problem, which results in two-sided debate.

First of all, when people cannot reach these products available on the Internet because of geo-blocking, without a doubt, geo-blocking receives numerous arguments against it. At the same time, there are also supporters of geo-blocking because implementing this practice is considered useful in terms of many aspects. In that part of the study, the debate on geo-blocking of digital products for commercial and copyright law purposes will be set from both sides of the points and will be evaluated deeply.

To summarise the opinions against geo-blocking practice:

- To start with, geo-blocking could be considered against some of the fundamental human rights.
  - First and foremost, geo-blocking is criticised for being contrary to the right to freedom of expression and access to information, which includes the right to receive and impart information and ideas without interference by public authority and regardless of frontiers.[36]

[36] Reda (2020, p. 82).

- Secondly, geo-blocking could be considered against 'equality' as an umbrella term; (or more specifically, could be against non-discrimination; cultural, religious and linguistic diversity; and finally, social equality) because the products are made unavailable in certain locations, and people who travel frequently, long term migrants or linguistic diversities could suffer from unavailability of these products, and this may lead to discrimination.[37]

- Furthermore, some argue that geo-blocking also results in cybertravel and digital piracy.[38] Digital piracy is one of the problems exacerbated by geo-blocking because when people encounter geo-blocking, they try to access or download the digital content illegally. Related to this, cybertravel is another issue. When people cannot reach these products in their location, they try to evade the geographical restriction by using Virtual Private Network (VPN) or any other circumvention tools. This issue and other aspects of circumvention of geo-blocking will be deeply evaluated in Chap. 6, therefore no further explanation will be provided here to avoid unnecessary repetition.
- From the economic perspective, not only consumers but also rightsholders or licensees can suffer from geo-blocking because rightsholders or licensees can lose profits due to content inaccessibility in the case when consumers are actually willing to pay a fair remuneration for lawful access to these products.[39]
- Besides, geo-blocking affects consumers looking to use the benefits of the common market within the EU to gain access to these products at more favourable conditions. Hence, this practice is considered contrary to the EU's Digital Single Market Strategy (the DSM Strategy), which is against the aim of better access for consumers and businesses to goods and services across Europe.[40]
- Lastly, since geo-blocking restricts cross-border transactions, this practice negatively affects competition by preventing competitive pressure from spreading across borders.[41] The close relationship between competition law and geo-blocking practice will mainly be explained in Chap. 5, therefore no further explanation will be provided here to avoid unnecessary repetition.

On the other hand, rightsholders or distributors may choose (or, in some situations, 'have to') not to make their products available in some locations, and therefore geo-blocking could be considered necessary or at least useful to achieve this aim. Geo-blocking is used for a variety of reasons, and there are lots of arguments to support geo-blocking practice.

- First and foremost, geo-blocking could be considered as a useful method to comply with the territorial nature of the IP Law and mainly copyright because copyright is a territorial right, and the copyright owner has an exclusive right over the

[37] Reda (2020, p. 86).

[38] Zahrádka (2020, p. 116).

[39] Yu (2019, p. 507).

[40] Trimble (2019, p. 495).

[41] Picht (2020, p. 244).

exploitation and making available of their work on the market.[42] Likewise, geo-blocking enables copyright owners to control over copying and distribution of their copyright-protected works. Furthermore, similarly, geo-blocking is employed to ensure that territorial licences granted for specific regions are effective, as these products are not available outside those particular locations.[43]

- Secondly, the commercial reasons behind the implementation of geo-blocking are pretty understandable. Sales strategies are one of the main reasons why sellers want to impose geo-blocking practices on the cross-border distribution of products. Sellers may maximise profits in a fragmented market for the same product at different locations and can differentiate the prices of products in different markets.[44] Furthermore, geo-blocking could be used by the sellers to customise localised services, and in that way, people can reach their countries' specific versions.[45] For example, when the consumer is in Germany and opens Amazon's website, Amazon shows the Amazon.de website and only makes available choices which can be delivered to Germany. Furthermore, geo-blocking is a useful way to avoid some requirements within specific locations and a way for the seller not to enter into any contractual relationship unless they want to.[46] For example, the seller may choose not to sell any product to specific countries to avoid any delivery cost that may occur during sales, foreign language requirements, some legal requirements such as privacy issues or avoid tax or VAT (Value Added Tax) obligations.[47]
- Additionally, geo-blocking could be supported by local industries because, in this way, they could have a chance to promote their cultural creativity, and they can be protected from foreign competition.[48]
- Finally, geo-blocking could be considered necessary for the freedom to conduct business, which covers the freedom to exercise an economic or commercial activity, the freedom of contract, free competition, freedom to choose with whom to do business and the freedom to determine the price of a product.

After presenting the whole debate, to explain them clearly and understand both views on geo-blocking, in this part of the research, the discussion mentioned will be elaborated thoroughly, and detail will be given for these arguments.

[42] Trimble (2019, p. 477).

[43] Zahrádka (2020, 102), Trimble (2019, p. 496).

[44] Yu (2019, p. 504), Trimble (2019, p. 478).

[45] Trimble (2019, p. 479).

[46] Trimble (2024, p. 14).

[47] Hamuľák et al. (2021, p. 156).

[48] Yu (2019, p. 506).

2.3.2 *Views Against Geo-Blocking*

2.3.2.1 Human Rights and Geo-Blocking

Due to the fact that geo-blocking practice enforces geographical boundaries on the Internet, there are some obstacles to accessing information freely. Therefore, it could be easily arguable that this practice limits the free flow of information.[49] This problem becomes more visible even in the EU since the EU has been established on the basis of a 'single internal market' understanding, where there is a free movement of goods, services, people and capital.[50] The Charter of Fundamental Rights of the European Union (the CFR)[51] promised to respect the right to access information within the EU by guaranteeing freedom of expression, including the right to receive and share information without borders. Consequently, if geo-blocking practice limits the access to content which should be moved freely in the EU and for people who have the freedom to move within the EU, despite the right to access information which is the fundamental right in the CFR, this practice should be regulated very carefully in terms of human rights.

Furthermore, the CFR in Article 21 has regulated the duty of non-discrimination, which means Member States should not combat any discrimination based on any ground, including nationality and language. Besides Article 22 of the CFR ruled that the Union shall respect cultural, religious and linguistic diversity within the EU. Unsurprisingly, some believe that geo-blocking practice is against these two important commitments, since as a result of geo-blocking people are discriminated against their nationality or place of residence and they cannot access their cultural products and their language.[52] Furthermore, it may be suggested that the unavailability of these products across borders may harm the cultural diversity within the EU.[53]

Therefore, territorial restrictions for digital products have been criticised because there could be a potential breach of human rights, namely the right to freedom of expression, access to information, and the right to equality, and may have a negative impact on cultural diversity within the EU.

2.3.2.1.1 Geo-Blocking and Right to Freedom of Expression and Access to Information

The right to freedom of expression and access information namely the right to access information on the Internet, has been subject to several regulations over time.

---

[49] Reda (2020, p. 82).

[50] Peers and Barnard (2023, p. 334).

[51] Charter of Fundamental Rights of the European Union [2010] OJ C83/53. (hereinafter it will be referred as the CFR).

[52] Reda (2020, p. 85).

[53] Reda (2020, p. 85).

The United Nations Universal Declaration of Human Rights (UDHR),[54] which was published in 1948, in Article 19 as '*Everyone has the right to freedom of opinion and expression; this right includes freedom to hold opinions without interference and to seek, receive and impart information and ideas through any media and regardless of frontiers. regulated the right to freedom of expression, also the right to access information without interference or any frontier.*' This was the first attempt[55] to regulate the right to access information and freedom of expression at the international level, although this declaration is not legally binding.[56] Following this development, the European Convention on Human Rights[57] (the ECHR) was presented in 1950 and was drafted by the Council of Europe. This convention is legally binding for the Council of Europe Member States as they should have ratified this convention to their national law.[58] The ECHR includes fundamental human rights, including the freedom of expression and the right to access information in Article 10, which specifically states the right to receive and impart information and ideas without interference by public authority and regardless of frontiers. In terms of European Union Law, the primary source for human rights in the EU is the CFR. Article 11 of the CFR has regulated the freedom of expression, including the right to freedom of receiving and imparting information without any frontier, as follows: '*Everyone has the right to freedom of expression. This right shall include freedom to hold opinions and to receive and impart information and ideas without interference by public authority and regardless of frontiers.*'

From the right to freedom of expression and access to information perspective, if there is a limitation, restriction or border to access any information, then it could be argued that there is a breach of this right. People who are against geo-blocking believe that implementation of geo-blocking practice could be detrimental due to the fact that the right to freedom of expression and access information could potentially be breached because of these restrictions; hence, basically, geo-blocking prohibits a person from restricting others from receiving information that they want to receive or may want to share.[59]

The freedom of expression and right to access information, mainly the right to receive and impart information regardless of any frontiers on the Internet, has also been subject to numerous regulations, guidance, declarations, recommendations and directives proposed by the EU. The EU gave a particular interest in the right to freedom of expression and access to information on the Internet, and one of the most

[54] Universal Declaration of Human Rights (adopted 10 December 1948 UNGA Res 217 A(III) (hereinafter it will be referred as UDHR).

[55] Bishop (2011, p. 11).

[56] Bishop (2011, p. 11).

[57] Convention for the Protection of Human Rights and Fundamental Freedoms (European Convention on Human Rights, as amended) (hereinafter it will be referred as ECHR).

[58] All EU Member States are also part of the Council of Europe. For more information regarding the relationship between the Council of Europe and the EU, please visit: https://www.coe.int/en/web/portal/european-union#:~:text=The%20Council%20of%20Europe%20and%20the%20European%20Union%20share%20the,different%2C%20yet%20complementary%2C%20roles.

[59] Reda (2020, p. 83).

critical pieces of legislation on that subject was the Directive on establishing the European Electronic Communications Code.[60] In that Directive, Article 61(2)[61] rules that digital radio and television broadcasting services and related complementary services should provide access to end-users without discrimination.

Besides, the EU adopted Regulation on laying down measures concerning open internet access[62] and in Article 3 of this regulation, it is stated that '*End-users shall have the right to access and distribute information and content, use and provide applications and services, and use terminal equipment of their choice, irrespective of the end-user's or provider's location or the location, origin or destination of the information, content, application or service,* via *their internet access service.'*

Overall, as explained here, the right to freedom of expression and access to information has a close and, most of the time, conflicting relationship with the geo-blocking practice. In a sense, geo-blocking is applied to restrict or block the access information available on the Internet, while everyone has the right to freedom of expression and access to information regardless of any frontiers on the Internet. On the other hand, Article 10 of the ECHR also rules that States may require the licensing of broadcasting, television or cinema enterprises.[63] Furthermore, Article 10(2) regulates that the exercise of freedom of expression and the right to access information may be subject to certain formalities, conditions, restrictions or sanctions necessary to protect the rights of others. Therefore, the right to freedom of expression and access to information can have some limitations to respecting others' rights, and geo-blocking could be assessed under this understanding, whether this limitation to this fundamental human right is necessary to respect the rights of others.

During the legislative process of the Geo-blocking Regulation, the possible impact of this regulation on the right to freedom of expression and access to information has not been a debated problem. In Recital 21, it is stated that this regulation does not have any intention to restrict the freedom of expression.[64] The Geo-blocking

[60] Directive (EU) 2018/1972 of the European Parliament and of the Council of 11 December 2018 establishing the European Electronic Communications Code [2018] OJ L 321.

[61] Article 61/2 (b): *to the extent necessary to ensure accessibility for end-users to digital radio and television broadcasting services and related complementary services specified by the Member State, obligations on operators to provide access to the other facilities referred to in Part II of Annex II on fair, reasonable and non-discriminatory terms.*

[62] Regulation (EU) 2015/2120 of the European Parliament and of the Council of 25 November 2015 laying down measures concerning open internet access and amending Directive 2002/22/EC on universal service and users' rights relating to electronic communications networks and services and Regulation (EU) No 531/2012 on roaming on public mobile communications networks within the Union [2015] OJ L 310.

[63] This is mainly because of the author's right to exploit their work and when there is a copyright-protected work, the freedom of expression and right to access to information should be carefully assessed in terms of the possible conflict with the right to property. Hence, to avoid forcing authors to exploit their work and to protect their right to property, the ECHR also included this provision.

[64] Recital 21 of the Geo-blocking Regulation includes this provision: *Nothing in this Regulation is intended to restrict the freedom of expression and the freedom and pluralism of the media, including the freedom of press, as they are guaranteed in the Union and in the Member States, and in particular under Article 11 of the Charter of Fundamental Rights of the European Union (the Charter).*

Regulation aimed to prohibit unjustified geo-blocking practices, which means this Regulation would ensure the free flow of information and would provide better access to products across borders. The impact of this Regulation and any potential positive impact of this regulation on the freedom of expression will deeply be evaluated in Chap. 4.

2.3.2.1.2 Geo-Blocking and Equality

Geo-blocking could be a real problem, especially for people who travel, since, as a result of geo-blocking, people who travel may not be able to access digital products when they are travelling, although they can reach them while they are in their home countries.[65] Furthermore, long-term migrants or people living in a country other than their home country may want to access the products available in their home countries but fail to do that because of geo-blocking. Finally, people who want to consume other countries' products may also suffer from geo-blocking due to product unavailability in their location. Hence, being not able to reach these products, geo-blocking is widely criticised since it could be against 'equality' as an umbrella term; more specifically, it could be regarded as a discriminatory practice, detrimental to cultural, religious and linguistic diversity, and finally, results in social inequality.[66]

Equality has been laid out in Chapter III of the CFR. Under this concept, in Article 21, the duty of non-discrimination has been regulated. According to this article, the Member States should not combat any discrimination based on any ground, such as sex, race, colour, ethnic or social origin, genetic features, language, religion or belief, political or any other opinion, membership of a national minority, property, birth, disability, age or sexual orientation. Likewise, Treaty on European Union (TEU)[67] Article 3 also regulated that the Union shall combat social exclusion and discrimination and promote equality and respect cultural and linguistic diversity.[68] On the other hand, geo-blocking could be considered against this non-discrimination principle due to this practice is used for limiting access to products based on the geographical locations of the users.[69] According to the latest studies, the EU has around 60 regional and minority languages, and these languages are spoken by around 50 million people.[70]

---

[65] Reda (2020, p. 85).

[66] Zahrádka (2020, p. 103).

[67] Consolidated version of the Treaty on European Union [2016] OJ C 202.

[68] Article 3 TEU '*...It shall combat social exclusion and discrimination, and shall promote social justice and protection, equality between women and men, solidarity between generations and protection of the rights of the child.*

It shall promote economic, social and territorial cohesion, and solidarity among Member States.

It shall respect its rich cultural and linguistic diversity, and shall ensure that Europe's cultural heritage is safeguarded and enhanced...'.

[69] Reda (2020, p. 85).

[70] Magdalena Pasikowska-Schnass, (2016) 'Regional and minority languages in the European Union'. In:Europarl https://www.europarl.europa.eu/EPRS/EPRS-Briefing-589794-Regional-minority-languages-EU-FINAL.pdf.

In the EU, there are some minorities such as Swedish language-speaking minorities in Finland[71] or Danish language-speaking minorities in Germany.[72] These minorities are usually too small for the creation of new markets and to have some investments which specifically serve their needs in the countries where they are regarded as minorities.[73] Unsurprisingly, like many other people, these people are also in need of accessing products which are created in their language, which reflect their cultural identity or which are produced in the countries where they have a special interest in their culture or language. These products could be cultural content, political content, educational materials or content that are produced by other countries or linguistic minorities. This practice could be regarded as discriminatory if people who travel between countries cannot reach them in their home language or if linguistic minorities cannot access the content in their language while they are abroad.[74] Therefore, people who try to reach products online can be discriminated against as a result of geo-blocking because of their nationality, their country of residence.

Accordingly, this practice could be associated with cultural, religious and linguistic diversity; since people who face geo-blocking are dominantly either people who travel and live abroad or people who try to reach the products and services which are mainly consumed in another country.[75] Article 22 of the CFR ruled that the Union shall respect cultural, religious and linguistic diversity within the EU. Despite this basic rule, within the EU, users may be geo-blocked to reach these products and services, and therefore, they are prevented from consuming other countries' products, so preserving cultural, religious and linguistic diversity within the EU could become questionable in the case of where people cannot reach products and services while they are abroad or people who are minorities in the country religiously or linguistically, they are at the risk of losing their cultural traditions or forgetting their language, cultural and historical backgrounds.[76]

For example, outside the UK, people cannot reach BBC iPlayer,[77] and therefore, they cannot rebroadcast, stream, or download the content available in BBC iPlayer while they are not in the UK. This exclusion becomes a problem for everyone who wants to access BBC's programs or services while they are abroad, but it becomes more prominent, especially for language minorities, like Scottish Gaelic.[78]

---

[71] Reda (2020, p. 86).

[72] POLITICO Europe (2016) 'Copyrights and Wrongs: Making a Single Market for Digital Content Work'. In: YouTube https://www.youtube.com/watch?v=qL5LSpEPDPQ.

[73] POLITICO Europe (2016) 'Copyrights and Wrongs: Making a Single Market for Digital Content Work'. In: YouTube https://www.youtube.com/watch?v=qL5LSpEPDPQ.

[74] Reda (2020, p. 85).

[75] Reda (2020, p. 85).

[76] Reda (2020, p. 84).

[77] According to the provision available in iPlayer help, *'Due to rights agreements, you need to be in the UK to stream and download programmes or watch BBC TV channels on BBC iPlayer'*. BBC iPlayer, 'iPlayer help home'. In: bbc.co.uk, https://www.bbc.co.uk/iplayer/help/questions/watching-outside-the-uk/outside-uk.

[78] Reda (2020, p. 86). In the case of Scottish Gaelic speakers who cannot reach the channels dedicated to their language, this is less likely to have any other channel or program which is made

As will be explained in the following chapters, so far, we have seen some attempts to regulate geo-blocking for online products and the Portability Regulation[79] was an important development in that field. The Portability Regulation has aimed to regulate the accessibility of the services for subscribers to portable online content services that are lawfully provided in their Member State of residence. They can access and use those services when temporarily present in a Member State other than their Member State of residence. Accordingly, mainly this Regulation has aimed to prevent geo-blocking to travellers, short-term migrants and tourists, and therefore beneficiaries of this Regulation are limited.[80] It created some criticism regarding creating social inequality since this regulation only provides an opportunity for people to reach their subscribed content for a limited period of time, for people who can return to their country, and people who cannot return to their country due to lots of different reasons are not subject to this Regulation.

On the other hand, as mentioned, the Geo-blocking Regulation does not cover copyright-protected digital products and does not have any provision for this issue or does not provide any exception either for linguistic minorities/long-term migrants or for cultural products and services. Nevertheless, in the 2023 review, the Committee on Legal Affairspublished its opinion[81] and accepted the problem for linguistic minorities. This report pointed out that cross-border availability of content and licensing in more areas would actually help linguistic minorities. If this availability exists, linguistic minorities will have the chance to watch and access these contents, which are available in their mother tongue. Furthermore, the European Parliament published a Resolution on the implementation of the 2018 Geo-blocking Regulation in the Digital Single Market on 13 December 2023.[82] The Resolution has also accepted that the circulation of audiovisual content and its availability is not at the desired level now, and there is more thing to preserve and reflect the richness and diversity of culture in the EU. This report also emphasised the need for linguistic minorities to access the contents in their mother tongue.

---

for Scottish Gaelic speakers. In this case, if the Scottish Gaelic speaker does not have any chance to return to the UK soon, they could be at risk of not consuming any content made in their language and eventually forgetting their language and culture.

[79] Regulation (EU) 2017/1128 of the European Parliament and of the Council of 14 June 2017 on cross-border portability of online content services in the internal market [2017] OJ L 168. (hereinafter it will be referred as the Portability Regulation).

[80] Kessen (2019) p. 567.

[81] Opinion of the Committee on Legal Affairs for the Committee on the Internal Market and Consumer Protection on implementation of the 2018 Geo-blocking Regulation in the digital single market (2023/2019(INI)). To access the full report please visit https://www.europarl.europa.eu/doceo/document/JURI-AD-749286_EN.pdf.

[82] European Parliament resolution of 13 December 2023 on the implementation of the 2018 Geo-blocking Regulation in the digital single market (2023/2019(INI)). To access the full adopted text please visit https://www.europarl.europa.eu/doceo/document/TA-9-2023-0473_EN.pdf.

2.3.2.2 Digital Single Market and Geo-Blocking for Digital Products

2.3.2.2.1 The Digital Single Market Strategy

The European Economic Community (now the European Union) was established to create European economic integration and one of the most important aims of this integration was to create a 'common market'. To reach that aim, in 1957, The Treaty of Rome (the European Economic Community Treaty, the EEC Treaty)[83] was signed by six member states of EEC,[84] and Article 2 of the Treaty of Rome mentioned establishing a common market.[85] Actually, in the 1970s 'common market' term was used instead of the European Community or European Union; when British people voted in a referendum to join the EEC, they were asked whether or not they wanted to be part of the common market.[86] For the terminology, the Treaty of Rome used the term common market, however, the Single European Act[87] of 1986 also used 'internal market' as a new term. The internal market is defined in Article 13 of the Single European Act as; *the internal market shall comprise an area without internal frontiers in which the free movement of goods, persons, services and capital is ensured in accordance with the provisions of the Treaties.* Free movement of goods, persons, services and capital can also be called the 'four freedoms'. The term 'single market' is also used to explain the same thing with the internal market; indeed, in political discussions, the term single market is often preferable.[88]

To clarify a point, the common market has a broader meaning than the internal market or the single market.[89] Nevertheless, the EU legislations and decisions, the terms of the common market, the internal market and the single market have been used interchangeably. Furthermore, the Court of Justice of the European Union (the CJEU) also used these terms instead of each other. To exemplify, according to Schul decision, '*The concept of a* ***common market*** *as defined by the court in a consistent line of decisions involves the elimination of all obstacles to intra-community trade in order to merge the national markets into* ***a single market*** *bringing about conditions*

[83] Treaty establishing the European Economic Community [1957] (Treaty of Rome, as amended).

[84] Belgium, France, Germany (West Germany), Italy, Luxembourg, and the Netherlands.

[85] Article 2 EEC Treaty mentioned the establishment of the common market as follows: "*The Community shall have as its task, by establishing a common market and an economic and monetary union and by implementing common policies or activities referred to in Articles 3 and 4, to promote throughout the Community a harmonious, balanced and sustainable development of economic activities, a high level of employment and of social protection, equality between men and women, sustainable and non-inflationary growth, a high degree of competitiveness and convergence of economic performance, a high level of protection and improvement of the quality of the environment, the raising of the standard of living and quality of life, and economic and social cohesion and solidarity among Member States.*"

[86] Peers and Barnard (2023, p. 336).

[87] Single European Act [1987] OJ L 169.

[88] Peers and Barnard (2023, p. 343).

[89] Peers and Barnard (2023, p. 343).

as close as possible to those of a genuine ***internal market.***'[90] Another example of this interchangeable use could be that the Lisbon Treaty[91] replaced all the references which are done to the common market with the term internal market.[92] From this attempt, it could be arguable that the EU did not make any distinction between these three terms and the main aim was to create an environment where the free movement of goods, persons, services and capital is ensured and establish an economic and monetary union by implementing common policies, without internal boundaries. In this study, the term 'single market' will be used to describe the EU's economic integration policy regarding the Digital Single Market Strategy, to be consistent with the terminology chosen by the EU.

From the historical development of the single market, it could be understandable that although creating a single market was mentioned even in the 1950s when the EEC was established, until the 1980s, there was no successful single market.[93] After the 1980s, the EEC accelerated the process of creating a single market, and the Single European Act[94] was signed in 1986. The Single European Act aimed to create a successful single market by 1992. Indeed, the creation of a single market has primarily been achieved until this day. On the other hand, establishing a single market across the EU is not a one-time goal as it is a dynamic process and is influenced by many different factors, such as technological developments. When it comes to the 2010s, the economy is becoming digital, and the EU was aware that the EU's single market did not fully benefit from the digital economic growth. At the same time, the EU also was aware that to maintain its position as a world leader in the digital economy,[95] the Union had to create a single market without borders even in digital, taking into account the level of digitalisation in the economy and the impact of technology on modern economic systems and to maximise the growth potential of European Digital Economy. In 2015, the European Council and the European Parliament mentioned that creating a Digital Single Market is the key priority of the EU, as well as for the European Commission, completion of the Digital Single Market was one of the top ten political priorities.[96] The Digital Single Market aims to ensure the free movement of goods, people, services and capital and to ensure that individuals and businesses operate their exercise within the scope of fair competition, and consumer and data protection regulations, regardless of nationality and place of residence for also digital activities.[97]

---

[90] Peers and Barnard (2023, p. 343).

[91] Treaty of Lisbon amending the Treaty on European Union and the Treaty establishing the European Community [2007] OJ C 306. (hereinafter it will be referred as the Lisbon Treaty).

[92] Peers and Barnard (2023, p. 343).

[93] Craig and Búrca, (2024, p. 656).

[94] Single European Act [1987] OJ L 169.

[95] Commission, 'A Digital Single Market Strategy for Europe' COM (2015) 192 final. (hereinafter it will be referred as the DSM Strategy).

[96] Commission, 'Commission staff working document - A Digital Single Market Strategy for Europe - Analysis and Evidence' COM (2015) 192 final, 3. (hereinafter it will be referred as the SWD for the DSM Strategy).

[97] DSM Strategy.

The Digital Single Market strategy could be beneficial to both consumers and businesses in terms of lots of aspects, and as a result of this win–win strategy, it is believed that the European Union could be a world leader in the digital economy.[98] All sectors have been affected by digitalisation, and now people are talking about not only the digital economy or digital market but also there is a 'digital society'.[99] Digitalisation affects the economy, employment, investments, businesses, consumers as well as daily lives. Nevertheless, a study, which was done in 2014, shows that consumers hesitated to shop online internationally; they preferred to shop domestically instead of cross-border.[100] DSM staff working document called that attitude 'home bias',[101] and this choice could have lots of reasons such as culture (language, brand etc.), as well as it could be because of lack of confidence to shop cross-border (delivery, payment or warranty issues). To overcome these problems and have a single market even in the digitalisation period, the European Commission decided to establish a Digital Single Market and published the Digital Single Market Strategy for Europe (the DSM Strategy), and this strategy has three essential principles[102]:

1. *Better access for consumers and businesses to online goods and services across Europe*

The DSM strategy tries to break down barriers to have better online activity and aims to remove differences between member states in terms of contract law and copyright law. To achieve this goal, DSM strategy has to establish an appropriate e-commerce framework and should give the same opportunity to consumers and businesses when they are trying to access content, goods and services online. There should be no discrimination in terms of nationality, residence, or place of establishment. Therefore, this strategy aimed to regulate the following subjects under this subtitle:

- Cross-border e-commerce rules that consumers and businesses can trust
- Affordable, high-quality cross-border parcel delivery
- Preventing unjustified geo-blocking
- Better access to digital content - A modern, more European copyright framework
- Reducing VAT-related burdens and obstacles when selling across borders.

2. *Creating the right conditions and a level playing field for advanced digital networks and innovative services*

This strategy wants to encourage innovation, and to achieve this aim, the EU is aware that it should also regulate cloud computing, big data tools or the Internet of Things. At the same time, this strategy has to build on trustworthy, high-speed and affordable networks and services to carry out the necessary investments to exploit innovations. To achieve this pillar of the DSM Strategy, the EU is also studying essential subjects, which are:

---

[98] DSM Strategy.

[99] SWD for the DSM Strategy, p. 4.

[100] SWD for the DSM Strategy, p. 6.

[101] SWD for the DSM Strategy, p. 6.

[102] DSM Strategy.

- Making the telecoms rules fit for purpose
- A media framework for the twenty-first century
- A fit-for-purpose regulatory environment for platforms and intermediaries
- Reinforcing trust and security in digital services and the handling of personal data.

3. *Maximising the growth potential of the European Digital Economy*

Economic activities are primarily dependent on digitalised, as well as any other sectors in the EU. Therefore, to have a maximum benefit from these transformations of the traditional economy to the digital economy. For this aim of the DSM Strategy, the EU is also studying essential topics, which are:

- Building a data economy
- Boosting competitiveness through interoperability and standardisation
- An inclusive e-society

To summarise, the aims of the DSM strategy are very comprehensive, and the EU is also aware of the importance of creating a single market in the digital domain. For example, creating a DSM can help consumers to have a more excellent choice with lower prices, which will help to have global competitiveness. Digital Single Market tries to establish a market in which the goods, persons, services, and capital move freely as well as where people and businesses can access and exercise online activities regardless of their nationality or place of residence.

2.3.2.2.2 Geo-Blocking and the Digital Single Market Strategy

To achieve a fully functional Digital Single Market within the EU, as explained above, there should be no boundaries or limitations on the cross-border movement of goods, services, capital and money. If there is a limitation on the cross-border availability of digital products in one or some Member States of the EU, with the help of geo-blocking practice, then it could easily be argued that geo-blocking is an obstacle to creating a Digital Single Market within the EU. Within the Digital Single Market, consumers should be able to enjoy the benefits of e-commerce,[103] which requires no unjustified discrimination between consumers. To avoid barriers in terms of cross-border transactions and prevent any barriers to e-commerce in terms of not only for consumers but also for businesses, the Commission actually announced an action plan to address these problems, and ending geo-blocking was one of the priorities of the EU.[104] Under the principle of better access for consumers and businesses to online goods and services across Europe, geo-blocking was counted as a subject to regulate. To achieve this aim, to end unjustified geo-blocking, the Geo-Blocking Regulation has been legislated. This regulation and its legislative process will be deeply analysed and critically evaluated in Chap. 4.

---

[103] SWD for the DSM Strategy, p. 21.

[104] SWD for the DSM Strategy, p. 21.

2.3.2.3 Geo-Blocking as a Potential Revenue Loss

Some commentators believe that the unavailability of products on the Internet could result in potential revenue loss, especially for copyright holders. Studies show that the primary reason for attempting to access digital products unlawfully, or piracy in a broader sense, is the inability to access the desired product even by paying for it.[105] Therefore, it is suggested that if there are people in a society who are willing to pay the necessary fees to rightsholders to consume a product, their demands should be met. Otherwise, it may be argued that instead of giving the necessary fee to legally access these products, which fee should go directly to the copyright holder, the same fee goes to VPN providers or other circumvention tool providers. That may result in potential revenue loss for the copyright holder.

2.3.3 Views in Favour of Geo-Blocking

2.3.3.1 Geo-Blocking to Comply with Copyright Territoriality and Territorial Licences

As will be deeply explained in the following chapter, intellectual property rights are territorial rights and the conferral, existence and exercise of this right will be under the national laws of individual states.[106] As a result of the territoriality principle of intellectual property rights, copyright protection is also territorial; since they are acquired country by country,[107] the scope of the copyright protection and enforcement of acquired rights could differ between the states. Although especially since the 1990s we have seen a good level of harmonisation of the copyright law within the EU, there are still disparities and some unharmonised aspects of the EU Copyright Law, which will be explained in the following chapter in detail.

The territoriality of copyright protection means that every state confers and enforces copyright protection within its territorial boundaries by virtue of its national legislation.[108] When considering the adverse effects of the territorial principle and the exclusionary nature of intellectual property rights, reconciling these with the free movement of goods and services becomes challenging.[109] To address this, the

[105] Zahrádka (2018, p. 195).

[106] Pila and Torremans (2019, p. 26).

[107] European Parliamentary Research Service, 'EU Copyright Reform: Revisiting the Principle of Territoriality' (Briefing, European Parliament, 2015) https://www.europarl.europa.eu/RegData/etudes/BRIE/2015/568348/EPRS_BRI%282015%29568348_EN.pdf.

[108] Bernt Hugenholtz, 'Copyright Territoriality in the European Union' (Note, European Parliament, 2010) https://www.europarl.europa.eu/RegData/etudes/note/join/2010/419621/IPOL-JURI_NT(2010)419621_EN.pdf.

[109] Aplin and Davis (2021, p. 36).

CJEU established the 'principle of exhaustion' in the 1971 case of Deutsche Grammophon v Metro.[110] The exhaustion principle means that if goods have been placed on the market with the intellectual property rightsholders or with their consent, the rightsholder can no longer control, resale, import, or export these goods.[111] Geo-blocking practice practically implements national borders on the Internet, therefore, it may be claimed that geo-blocking is a useful method to comply with copyright territoriality.[112] Some authors claim that geo-blocking could be a useful method to escape from the exhaustion principle since geo-blocking will de facto *restore*[113] the principle of copyright territoriality, where rightsholders may decide where and when they want to make available to the public their work regardless of the exhaustion principle. This issue will be explained in more detail in Chap. 3.

Furthermore, to disseminate copyright-protected products, licences are the most basic way granted by copyright owners to specific individuals, allowing them to perform certain activities. A licence can be described as permission to do something that would otherwise be prohibited without the copyright owner's consent[114] and they can be viewed as permission to undertake specific activities, and these licences may be limited geographically.[115] More explanation and deeper investigation regarding the nature of the territorial licences and its impact on competition law will deeply be examined in Chap. 5, therefore no further explanation will be provided here apart from its definition. Geo-blocking could be a useful tool to comply with territorial licences, in this way, copyright-protected products will not be accessible outside of the licensed area. This is the main reason, according to the European Commission's survey, to apply geo-blocking restrictions to copyright-protected products.

Geo-blocking is usually regarded as useful in terms of licensing practices because it is argued that in the absence of enforcement of the territorial licences, obtaining the EU-wide or global licences would be much higher and it would result in the exclusion of small and medium-sized enterprises from the competition.[116]

2.3.3.2 Commercial Reasons Behind the Geo-Blocking Practice

Traders, distributors or intermediaries usually tend to use geo-blocking as a part of their business strategy.[117] For instance, rightsholders may choose to make available

---

[110] Case C-78/70 *Deutsche Grammophon v Metro*, [1971] ECR 487. (hereinafter will be referred as the Deutsche Grammophon case).

[111] Bently et al. (2022, p. 14).

[112] Synodinou (2020, p. 136).

[113] Synodinou (2020, p. 136). In Synodinou's article, the geo-blocking practice is defined as follows: "*Geo-blocking is a technological protection measure which* de facto *restores the principle of copyright territoriality in the potentially borderless internet by restricting access to copyright-protected content on the basis of the user's geographical location.*"

[114] Bently et al. (2022, p. 326).

[115] Bently et al. (2022, p. 327).

[116] Trimble (2024, p. 52).

[117] Kharb et al. (2023, p. 46).

their products in some countries even if they clear all the rights or choose to make them available in different locations at different times. It could be because of maximising rightsholders' profits, not choosing to enter into any contractual relationship in some countries, or finally, because of the cultural, religious, or strategic needs of these locations, some products are not made available in certain locations.[118] Many businesses usually offer prices according to the affordability of the people in different countries. For example, Netflix Denmark's standard plan is offered for around €11.50,[119] while the same plan is offered for around €8 in Croatia[120] as of October 2024. In the legislative procedure of the Geo-blocking Regulation, the EU has also discussed whether price differentiation should be regarded as unjustified geo-blocking and prohibited. In the Regulation, it is made clear that traders remain free to choose their prices as long as they choose these pricing strategies in a non-discriminatory manner.[121]

Furthermore, geo-blocking is a useful tool to make some products available at different times in different countries. Some rightsholders may choose to apply this restriction to gain more revenue or they may decide to make available these products in different countries according to the demand.[122] This practice may help rightsholders to avoid taking unnecessary risks and they can plan and see the economic consequences of their choice better.

Geo-blocking could be a useful tool to avoid some requirements, especially those which can occur as a result of cross-border trades.[123] First of all, delivery costs (for tangible items) could be a massive concern for the seller in the case of cross-border sales. Therefore, if the seller does not want to sell their item internationally, they can apply geo-blocking and make unavailable their products in some locations. Likewise, for cross-border trades, countries may ask for extra requirements, especially for custom clearance and delivery purposes, such as an explanation of the item in other languages, or different VAT regulations, and sellers may have to deal with that requirement if they need to sell their products cross border.[124]

Furthermore, traders also may need to take some further actions to protect consumers or protect privacy. For example, according to the United Nations Guidelines for Consumer Protection[125] (UN Guidelines on Consumer Protection), businesses should take appropriate and necessary measures to protect their consumers' privacy. However, every country could ask for different requirements or could have different conditions in the context of e-commerce and privacy, such as conditions for commercial electronic mail messages, spam mail to consumers, and requirements for shopping or keeping confidential information. Again, according to the

[118] Trimble (2024, p. 9).

[119] Netflix Help Centre: Plans and Pricing. In: Netflix https://help.netflix.com/tr/node/24926/dk.

[120] Netflix Help Centre: Plans and Pricing. In: Netflix https://help.netflix.com/tr/node/24926/dk.

[121] Recital 10 of the Geo-blocking Regulation.

[122] Trimble (2024, p. 9).

[123] Kiss (2019, p. 103).

[124] Kiss (2019, p. 103).Trimble (2024, p. 14), Hamuľák et al. (2021, p. 156).

[125] To see guidelines please visit: United Nations Guidelines for Consumer Protection (2016). In: UNCTAD https://unctad.org/system/files/official-document/ditccplpmisc2016d1_en.pdf.

UN Guidelines on Consumer Protection, businesses must comply with national and international standards regarding alternative dispute resolution services and customer satisfaction laws for handling complaints. Therefore, traders may be under lots of obligation to deal with other law systems, and traders may have to deal with being sued outside of the trader's jurisdictions, and it could result in litigation expenses and other possible problems, such as going to court or hiring a lawyer.

2.3.3.3 Geo-Blocking to Avoid Foreign Influences

Some commentators and stakeholders believe that the geo-blocking practice is actually protecting local producers from foreign influences. For instance, the Australian Productivity Commission has pointed out that five Australian local producers were concerned about their cultural and local creative products because of the foreign influence in these sectors.[126] They believe that local industries cannot be shielded from competition with the more prominent actors in these areas, and it will have a negative impact on creativity, investment, and innovation, and it will damage the competitiveness of Australia in the digital economy. Likewise, one of the arguments by the commissioner in European Commission[127] situated in favour of geo-blocking during the Geo-blocking Regulation discussion was to geo-block Hollywood movies in Europe to maximise profit for the European movies. Furthermore, some music representatives in the EU have also suggested that music content from other countries actually decreases demand for local EU music content and this would be detrimental to promoting cultural diversity within the EU.[128]

2.3.3.4 Geo-Blocking and Freedom to Conduct Business

Another important subject to consider while speaking about territorial restrictions practices is the freedom to conduct business. Freedom to conduct business is regulated in the CFR in Article 16 and discussed in the *Sky Österreich*[129] decision; the scope of this freedom has been explained. According to this judgment, the freedom to conduct business covers the freedom to exercise an economic or commercial activity, the freedom of contract, free competition,[130] freedom to choose with whom to do business and the freedom to determine the price of service.[131] In a situation when there is an obligation to sell to consumers for traders, like in the Geo-blocking Regulation in which traders must not refuse to sell based on customers' nationality,

[126] Yu (2019, p. 506).

[127] Felix Reda (2016) How We Can End Geoblocking in the EU. In: YouTube, https://www.youtube.com/watch?v=MF8k5ooc4mw.

[128] Trimble (2024, 54).

[129] Case C-283/11 *Sky Österreich v. Österreichischer Rundfunk* [2013] OJ C 269.

[130] Case C-283/11 *Sky Österreich v. Österreichischer Rundfunk* [2013] OJ C 269. para 42.

[131] Case C-283/11 *Sky Österreich v. Österreichischer Rundfunk* [2013] OJ C 269. para 43.

place of residence or place of establishment, the potential breach of freedom to conduct business could be argued. In the case of traders who are forced to enter into a contractual relationship with the customers regardless of their nationality, place of residence or place of establishment, the freedom to conduct business could be other aspects to take into account.

2.4 Conclusion

Although the Internet was supposed to be border-free, governments and private entities want to regulate the Internet to control the activity done on the Internet, and it results in boundaries and national limits for the Internet. From the commercial perspective, to deal with these national law limitations, the traders, who use the Internet as a medium of trade, have started to impose some territorial restrictions, which is called geo-blocking, on the Internet to ensure control over the sale and distribution of their products to users. Also, because of this territorial nature of the law, to comply with the national laws or not to be a subject of other law systems, rightsholders, distributors or sellers have started to use this practice as a means of compliance with the necessary law. Geo-blocking has become a part of the business plan for many traders/businesses since there could be different commercial aims behind this practice. Finally, to comply with the contracts signed between rightsholders and distributors/sellers, a geo-blocking practice has been used. Rightsholders can restrict online access to digital products via geo-blocking practices.

Geo-blocking, on the other hand, was subject to ongoing debate. While some stakeholders think that geo-blocking is a useful tool and should not be prohibited, some stakeholders and especially most of the users think that geo-blocking limits the accessibility of digital products and this limitation is against some of the basic human rights. Potential solutions to the geo-blocking debate will be central to this study, therefore the author chooses to explain the geo-blocking debate and set the whole scene in the first chapter. Some conflicting opinions and the interdisciplinary nature of the geo-blocking practice will be explained from different perspectives in this study. Related to this, to offer any recommendation to solve the geo-blocking debate, some background information and further debates related to that issue will be provided in the following chapters. This study will critically analyse the geo-blocking practice deeply, and it will try to find appropriate justifications and limitations to this practice. In the following chapters, this study will also evaluate the historical evolution of geo-blocking as a territorial restriction and drafts and debates for the Geo-Blocking Regulation, as well as other EU initiatives, and the scope of these legislations will be critically explained. Furthermore, the necessary copyright law background will be provided, especially the territoriality of copyright and the exhaustion principle will be deeply evaluated. Furthermore, the competition law aspects of the geo-blocking practice will be evaluated, subsequently. After these observations, the circumvention of the geo-blocking practice will critically be evaluated. Finally, the last chapter will be dedicated to the potential recommendations for the unavailability of digital products on the Internet, namely the geo-blocking problem. This chapter will also include some recommendations for EU policymakers in the context of the Geo-blocking Regulation.

The next chapter will be dedicated to explaining copyright law aspects of the geo-blocking practice; therefore, this chapter will provide some background information on copyright law and evaluate related debates in that regard related to this study.

References

Aplin T, Davis J (2021) Intellectual property law, 4th edn. Oxford University Press, Oxford

Bently L et al (2022) Intellectual property law, 6th edn. Oxford University Press, Oxford

Bishop CA (2011) Access to information as a human right. LFB Scholarly Publishing, New York

Craig P, de Búrca G (2024) EU law, 8th edn. Oxford University Press, Oxford

Hamulák O et al (2021) "This content is not available in your country": a general summary on geo-blocking in and outside the European Union. Int Comp Law Rev 21:153–183

Hui KL, Chau PYK (2002) Classifying digital products. Commun ACM 45:73–79

Kharb D et al (2023) Circumvention of geo-blocking measures in audio-visual sector: related copyright issues. NTUT J Intellect Prop Law Manag 12:44–60

Kiss LN (2019) A general summary on geo-blocking in the EU. Eur Stud Rev Eur Law Econ Polit 6:95–107

Oikonomidis T, Fouskas K (2019) A literature review of smartphone geolocation technologies. In: Kavoura A, Kefallonitis E, Giovanis A (eds) Strategic innovative marketing and tourism. Springer proceedings in business and economics. Springer, Cham. https://doi.org/10.1007/978-3-030-12453-3_125

Peers S, Barnard C (2023) European Union law, 4th edn. Oxford University Press, Oxford

Picht PG (2020) The EU geo-blocking regulation from a competition law perspective. J Eur Compet Law Pract 11:244–256

Pila J, Torremans P (2019) European intellectual property law, 2nd edn. Oxford University Press, Oxford

Popovych T et al (2023) The right to be forgotten as a special digital right. Law State Telecommun Rev 15:42–53

Quinn J (2021) Geo-location technology: restricting access to online content without illegitimate extraterritorial effects. Int Data Priv Law 11:294–306

Reda J (2020) Geoblocking: at odds with the EU single market and consumer expectations. In: Szczepanik P et al (eds) Digital peripheries: the online circulation of audiovisual content from the small market perspective. Springer, Cham, pp 81–100

Svantesson D (2012) Time for the law to take internet geolocation technologies seriously. J Priv Int Law 8:473–487

Schmidt-Kessen MJ (2017) EU digital single market strategy, digital content and geo-blocking: costs and benefits of partitioning the EU's internal market. Colum J Eur L 24:561–576

Synodinou TE (2020) Geoblocking in EU copyright law: challenges and perspectives. GRUR Int 69:136–150

Trimble M (2012) The future of cybertravel: legal implications of the evasion of geolocation. Fordham Intell Prop Media Ent LJ 22:567–657

Trimble M (2017) The role of geoblocking in the internet legal landscape. IDP Rev Internet Derecho Politica 2017:45–58

Trimble M (2018) Geoblocking and "legitimate trade." In: Heath C et al (eds) Intellectual property and obstacles to legitimate trade. Wolters Kluwer, Alphen aan den Rijn, pp 55–81

Trimble M (2019) Copyright and geoblocking: the consequences of eliminating geoblocking. Scholarly Works 2019:476–502

Trimble M (2024) The EU geo-blocking regulation: a commentary. Edward Elgar Publishing, Cheltenham

Yu PK (2019) A hater's guide to geoblocking. B U J Sci Technol Law 25:507–529

Zahrádka P (2018) Geo-blocking: protection of author's rights, of cultural diversity, or of an outdated business model? Annu Rev Law Ethics 26:191–208

Zahrádka P (2020) The Czech and Slovak audiovisual market as a laboratory experiment for the Digital Single Market in Europe. In: Szczepanik P et al (eds) Digital peripheries: the online circulation of audiovisual content from the small market perspective. Springer, Cham, pp 101–124

Zarra A (2016) Geo-blocking and price discrimination by online marketplaces in the EU. Master thesis, Università Commerciale Luigi Bocconi

Chapter 3
Geo-Blocking as a Copyright Phenomenon: Territoriality of Copyright

Abstract Copyright can be defined as one of the intellectual property law subjects which regulates the creation and use of cultural products, and it protects original literary, dramatic, musical and artistic works once they are fixated in a material form. Historically, copyright gives a territorial right, meaning that the conferral, legal effects and enforcement of copyright protection depend on the national laws of each state. This territoriality reflects the 'principle of sovereignty', and the rationale was to reward and encourage intellectual creations, skills and time for the benefit of the state. With the advent of the printing press and the Internet, the circulation of information has become relatively easy, and territoriality has created difficulties for copyright owners, resellers, distributors, end users and society. From the nineteenth century onwards, states began to consider harmonising aspects of copyright law to ensure more unified protection, and in the EU this harmonisation process continues, albeit slowly. Because of territorial differences and territorially limited licences, rightsholders often apply geo-blocking practices and make works available only in particular countries. The historical development of copyright reveals a system built on a range of justifications for protection and shaped by international agreements that continue to influence EU law. Copyright's territoriality principle, rooted in national sovereignty, has produced significant practical consequences, particularly as markets expanded and digital technologies enabled the seamless cross-border circulation of protected works. Divergent national rules have increasingly conflicted with the EU's objective of creating a genuinely integrated internal market, prompting decades of regulatory and legislative activity aimed at harmonising copyright law. From the 1980s onwards, the EU has issued a broad set of directives, regulations, recommendations and communications to reduce fragmentation, with the DSM Directive standing out as a major intervention in the digital landscape. Despite scholarly support for further unification, recent years have seen limited progress, leaving substantial tension between the territorial structure of copyright and the demands of a borderless digital economy.

F. Cebeci Çorum, *Application of Geo-Blocking to Copyright-Protected Digital Products*, Studies in European Economic Law and Regulation 30,
https://doi.org/10.1007/978-3-032-34507-3_3

3.1 Introduction

Copyright can be broadly defined as one of the intellectual property law subjects which regulates the creation and use of cultural products,[1] such as books, movies, paintings, plays, etc. The subject matter protected by copyright is referred to as 'works'.[2] Copyright law protects original literary, dramatic, musical and artistic works. Copyright protection automatically arises when an original work is fixated in a material form, and it gives a limited term exclusionary right over the work.[3] At the same time, historically, copyright gives a territorial right, which means conferral of copyright protection depends on the national laws of each state, and therefore, the legal effects and enforcement of those rights are also limited to the territory where the copyright protection is conferred.[4] Territoriality of intellectual property rights is the reflection of the 'principle of sovereignty' understanding, and the rationale behind the protection of intellectual property was rewarding and encouraging these intellectual creations, skills and time behind it to be of benefit to the state.[5]

With the advent of the printing press and the Internet,[6] the circulation of information has become relatively easy, and therefore, the territoriality of the copyright has created some problems for the copyright owners, resellers, distributors, end users and finally, society. During the nineteenth century, states started to think about harmonising some of the aspects of the copyright law and having more unified protection for the protection of copyright works, and since then, there are still some ongoing works on this subject.[7] Especially in the EU, the harmonisation process is still ongoing, albeit slowly. Because of these differences in the copyright law and having territorially limited licences for copyright-protected works, the rightsholders usually choose to apply geo-blocking practices and make these works available in only particular countries to comply with the copyright law.[8]

In this part of the study, firstly, the historical development of copyright law and justifications for copyright will be explained. Then, the legal requirements for the subsistence of copyright and related rights protection under the EU Law context, with reference to relevant international agreements and conventions, will be considered. This consideration will be mainly straightforward and brief since this research aims to discuss copyright-protected digital products and their availability on the Internet; therefore, only the necessity and basic information will be given, and more detail will be provided in the relevant parts if necessary.

After the brief explanation of history, justifications and subsistence of copyright protection, the territoriality principle of copyright law will be deeply evaluated. The

---

[1] Aplin and Davis (2021, p. 55), Bently et al. (2022, p. 37).

[2] Bently et al. (2022, p. 37).

[3] Pila and Torremans (2019, p. 221).

[4] Pila and Torremans (2019, p. 26).

[5] Pila and Torremans (2019, p. 26).

[6] Karapapa and McDonagh (2019, p. 6).

[7] Karapapa and McDonagh (2019, p. 9).

[8] Zahrádka (2020, p. 102), Trimble (2019, p. 496).

territorial nature of copyright law will be explained with reference to the historical development of the territoriality principle, the results of copyright territoriality and finally, responses to copyright territoriality. In that part of the study, particular interest will be given to responses to copyright territoriality, especially the harmonisation process of the copyright law within the EU law.

3.2 Copyright Protection

3.2.1 Historical Development of Copyright and Justifications for Copyright Protection

3.2.1.1 Historical Development of Copyright

The idea of intellectual property and authorship can be traced back to the classical Roman period, where the person who painted the canvas acquired ownership of that canvas.[9] Nevertheless, copying or reproducing the same work was not quite a problem until the fifteenth century, since until the printing press had been invented, copying required a relatively long time as everything had to be done by hand. As a result of the invention of the Gutenberg printing press[10] and, therefore, with the easement of copying, the creative skill products were at risk of reproduction. The time needed to make further copies has decreased, and at the same time, more accurate copies have been made. Hence, there was a need for a legal response to prevent unauthorised copies.

The first piece of copyright legislation in the world was drafted in the UK, and it was the Copyright Act 1709 (The Statute of Anne), which gives 14 years of publication and re-publication rights for book authors, with the possibility of extension for the additional 14 years if the author is still alive.[11] However, during the nineteenth century, when copyright protection had expired for most of the books published, there was a need to have new attempts to publish an act that extended the term protection more.[12] At the same time, British authors did not have any protection in foreign countries for the same book that they had published in the UK, which means their books could be easily reproduced in other countries.[13] Likewise, other nationals in the UK did not receive any copyright protection, unlike UK citizens.[14] With the increase in trading relationships, the disparities between law systems on copyright had created

[9] Pila and Torremans (2019, p. 9).

[10] Karapapa and McDonagh (2019, p. 6).

[11] Karapapa and McDonagh (2019, p. 6).

[12] Aplin and Davis (2021, p. 56).

[13] Karapapa and McDonagh (2019, p. 9).

[14] Karapapa and McDonagh (2019, p. 9).

problems, and an international level of harmonisation was needed.[15] Only the most important and relevant international regulations about copyright law will be outlined in this study.

The first attempt at an international level was the Berne Convention for the Protection of Literary and Artistic Works[16] (the Berne Convention), signed in 1886. The Berne Convention did not regulate the standard level of protection that every contracting state should obey; instead, this convention only announced the minimum level of protection that contracting states should take into account while drafting legislation.[17] The most important thing that the Berne Convention regulated for copyright protection was the 'principle of national treatment'.[18] According to the principle of national treatment, the same protection should be given to the works which are originating in one of the contracting states, as its own nationals. Hence, the other countries' citizens should be given the same opportunity as the citizens of the contracting states when it comes to the protection of copyright owners' rights. In other words, states should grant the same protection to the works of foreigners as is given to their own nationals.[19] Berne Convention has been amended several times up to today, and it was an essential milestone in copyright law history for harmonisation at the international level, with 181 contracting states as of 2023.[20]

Another significant development in copyright law was the Rome Convention for the Protection of Performers, Producers of Phonograms and Broadcasting Organisations[21] (the Rome Convention) signed in 1961. The Rome Convention (so-called Neighbouring Rights Convention) has regulated the minimum level of protection for the performances for performers, in phonograms for producers of phonograms and in broadcasts for broadcasting organisations.

Subsequently, the member states of the World Trade Organisation (WTO) signed the WTO Agreement on Trade-Related Aspects of Intellectual Property Rights[22] (TRIPS Agreement), which came into effect on 1 January 1995. TRIPS Agreement

---

[15] Karapapa and McDonagh (2019, p. 9).

[16] Berne Convention for the Protection of Literary and Artistic Works (adopted 14 July1967 entered into force 29 January 1970) 828 UNTS 221. (hereinafter it will be referred as the Berne Convention).

[17] For example, Article 7 of the Berne Convention requires minimum 50 years of protection for Copyright, however it is a minimum level, therefore contracting states are free to extend that period within their national law.

[18] Article 5 of the Berne Convention regulates the national treatment principle as follows: *"(3) Protection in the country of origin is governed by domestic law. However, when the author is not a national of the country of origin of the work for which he is protected under this Convention, he shall enjoy in that country the same rights as national authors."*

[19] Lundstedt (2016, p. 85).

[20] To see the contracting states, please visit: https://treaties.un.org/pages/showdetails.aspx?objid=08000002801115ec9.

[21] International Convention for the Protection of Performers, Producers of Phonograms and Broadcasting Organisations (adopted 26 October 1961 entered into force 18 May 1964) 496 UNTS 43. (hereinafter it will be referred as the Rome Convention).

[22] General Agreement on Trade-Related Aspects of Intellectual Property (adopted 15 April 1994 entry into force 1 January 1995) 1869 UNTS 3; 33 I.L.M. 1197. (hereinafter will be referred as the TRIPS Agreement).

was the most comprehensive treaty until that date, which regulates copyright and related rights, trade mark, geographical indications, industrial designs, patents, new varieties of plants, and undisclosed information, including trade secrets and test data and trade aspects of these intellectual property rights.

In 1996, the World Intellectual Property Organization (WIPO) published two essential legislations, which are: (i) the WIPO Copyright Treaty[23] (WCT) and (ii) the WIPO Performances and Phonograms Treaty[24] (WPPT). The WCT deals with the protection of works and the rights of their authors in the digital environment, while the WPPT deals with the rights of performers and producers of phonograms, particularly in the digital environment.

The historical development within the EU in terms of copyright harmonisation will also be explained later in this part with a deeper analysis.

3.2.1.2 Justifications for Copyright Protection

To decide whether there should be protection for intellectual property, the different interests need to be taken into account. Firstly, there are different actors involved in the creation and exploitation of intellectual property, and affected by the creation and exploitation of these, which are creators, users, intermediaries (sellers or distributors), society and governments.[25]

i. *Creators* are at the centre of the creation and exploitation process of intellectual property, and they have a variety of interests to receive protection for this property. First of all, creators should receive a reward for their creativity, and this reward could have some economic consequences.[26] At the same time, in most cases, creators are also making some investment to produce an intellectual creation, such as buying painting materials for paintings or having a course to learn how to paint. Hence, creators want to recoup that investment.[27]
ii. *Users* also have an interest in the exploitation of these products because that way, they can access or benefit from this intellectual creation.
iii. *Intermediaries (sellers or distributors)* may want to make these products available on the market in the best possible way. Intermediaries also benefit from the increasing intellectual creation within society because they can make a profit from making these works available to the users.

---

[23] WIPO Copyright Treaty (adopted 20 December 1996 entry into force 6 March 2002) 2186 UNTS 121; 36 I.L.M. 65. (hereinafter will be referred as the WCT).

[24] WIPO Performances and Phonograms Treaty (adopted 20 December 1996 entry into force 20 May 2002) 2186 UNTS 203; 36 I.L.M. 76. (hereinafter will be referred as the WPPT).

[25] This explanation regarding the different interests at stake belongs to lecture notes: Stefano Barazza, 'Principles and Justifications for Intellectual Property Rights' (Swansea University Undergraduate Lectures, 12 October 2022).

[26] Brown et al. (2023, p. 45).

[27] Pila and Torremans (2019, p. 304).

iv. *Society* also benefits from the protection of intellectual creations since if the protection is given to the outcome of intellectual creativity, society will make more efforts to produce these kinds of creations. At the same time, as a result of intellectual creation, technological[28] and cultural development will be faster.
v. *Governments or states also have* their own interests in the protection and exploitation of intellectual products. Especially from the economic perspective, governments can use these intellectual properties as an economic instrument, and they can use them to gain a competitive advantage over the other states. At the same time, intellectual creations help the development of that state; in some sectors, states can be fundamental and gain economic advantages.[29]

Related to these interests, there is a very important question to ask: *why should there be copyright protection for the work that the author created?* Throughout the history of copyright, this question has been subject to lots of debates, and there are some arguments given to the justifications of copyright protection. The main arguments could be summarised as follows:

i. *Natural rights and Personality-based theory—Hegelian theory:* The supporters of this argument claim that these works result from intellectual creativity, and there should be protection for this since it is the right thing to do.[30] According to this understanding, the intellectual product is the equivalent of the tangible product, and the unauthorised copy of this work is equivalent to a thief. According to this theory, there should be protection for the work that the author creates because this work reflects the personality of that author.[31] The work is an embodiment of the author, and it deserves a right to protect the creation of their own intellectuality. This theory is reflected in the moral rights that the copyright owner has.[32]
ii. *Reward and Labour theory—Lockean theory:* It is suggested that because the labour is invested in order to create this product, the creator should have a right over the product over their intellectual labour.[33]According to that theory, protection should be given to the creator as a reward for their effort and investment.[34]
iii. *Economic justifications:* The rationale behind the economic justifications is mainly the need to provide incentives for the creation of intellectual products and recoup the investment for future creations.[35]

---

[28] This situation is especially very prominent in the patent law domain, with the inventions, technological development will be fostered.

[29] It could be as a result of patent protection for inventions, or copyright protection and design can also be a tool for this: for example, museums can have special exhibitions or buildings can attract tourist attention and states can benefit from it economically.

[30] Bently et al. (2022, p. 42).

[31] Aplin and Davis (2021, p. 60).

[32] Bently et al. (2022, p. 42).

[33] Karapapa and McDonagh (2019, p. 14).

[34] Bently et al. (2022, p. 43).

[35] Aplin and Davis (2021, p. 59), Bently et al. (2022, p. 45).

3.2.2 *The Subsistence of Copyright*

The subject matter of copyright is called work. According to the latest decisions[36] given by the CJEU, the requirements for the definition of the work in the context of copyright law can be outlined as (i) the work in question should be original and the author's own intellectual creation, and (ii) the work should include elements that are the expression of such creation, meaning that the subject matter of the work is identifiable with sufficient precision and objectivity.

There is an informal distinction between subject matters: (i) authorial works and (ii) entrepreneurial works.

- *Authorial works* are, generally speaking, reflecting the author's own intellectual creations,[37] the author's personality, free and creative choices,[38] and there is a personal touch of authors.[39] Author's right (or copyright) exists any authorial works created by authors such as books, films, poems or drawings. To receive copyright protection, these authorial works should be original.
- *Entrepreneurial works* usually refer to works created by entrepreneurs,[40] such as broadcasts and sound recordings. Entrepreneurial works are derivative works and usually rely on technical or organisational skills rather than the author's intellectual creativity skills.[41] These works are protected by related rights (or can be called 'neighbouring rights'), and these rights are given to the people who make the necessary financial or organisational background of these works.[42]

3.2.2.1 Subject Matter of Copyright (and Related Rights) in the International Law

Copyright is one of the intellectual property rights and protects original literary, dramatic, musical and artistic works. Berne Convention Article 2(1) requires that the Berne Union should recognise and protect the following by copyright:

- literary and artistic works, including literary, scientific and artistic domains, whatever may be the mode or form of its expression—such as books, pamphlets and other writings, lectures, addresses (any form in writing)

---

[36] Case C-310/17 *Levola Hengelo BV v Smilde Foods BV* [2018] OJ C 269, paras 35–40. The same definition also confirmed in the Case C-683/17 *Cofemel – Sociedade de Vestuário SA v G-Star Raw CV* [2019] OJ C 383, paras 29–34.

[37] Case C-5/08 *Infopaq International A/S v Danske Dagblades Forening* [2009] ECR 2009 I-06569. (hereinafter will be referred to as the Infopaq Case) para 37.

[38] Joined Cases C-403/08 and C-429/08 *Football Association Premier League and Others* [2011] ECR I-0000, para 98.

[39] Case C-145/10 *Eva-Maria Painer v Standard VerlagsGmbH and Others* [2011] ECR 2011 - 00,000, para 92.

[40] Bently et al. (2022, p. 38).

[41] Bently et al. (2022, p. 38).

[42] Bently et al. (2022, p. 38).

- dramatic or musical works; choreographic works and entertainments; musical compositions with or without words
- cinematographic works
- drawing, painting, architecture, sculpture, engraving and lithography; and
- photographic works, works of applied art, illustrations, maps, plans, sketches and three-dimensional works relative to geography, topography, architecture or science.

In addition to this provision, the Berne Convention Article 2(8) excludes news of the day or miscellaneous facts having the character of mere items of press information from copyright protection. Article 10 of the TRIPS Agreement rules that *computer programs* shall be protected as literary works.

Berne Convention Article 2(2) rules that if works have not been fixed in some material form, then they shall not be protected. Copyright protection subsists automatically when an *original work* is *fixated* in a material form, and therefore, the copyright owner will receive limited-term exclusionary rights over the exploitation of this work.[43] After these requirements are fulfilled, copyright protection will subsist automatically upon the creation of the work without any formalities.

Furthermore, the TRIPS Agreement Article 9(2) also proposes the so-called idea/expression dichotomy and rules that copyright protection shall extend to expressions and not to ideas, procedures, methods of operation or mathematical concepts as such. This means that copyright protection does not subsist in ideas but only subsists in the expressions of these ideas.

Related rights have also been subject to several instruments in international law. Rome Convention is a substantial source for the related rights, which regulates the minimum standards for the protection in respect of (i) performances,[44] (ii) producers of the phonograms,[45] and (iii) broadcasting organisations.[46] All these standards have also been regulated and extended in TRIPS Agreements and WPPT in relevant articles.

3.2.2.2 Subject Matter of Copyright in the EU Acquis

According to Protocol 28 On Intellectual Property of the EEA Agreement,[47] the EU and member states of the EU need to comply with the Berne Convention. Hence, the

[43] Pila and Torremans (2019, p. 221).

[44] Rome Convention Article 3: (a) "performers" means actors, singers, musicians, dancers, and other persons who act, sing, deliver, declaim, play in, or otherwise perform literary or artistic works".

[45] Rome Convention Article 3: (b) "phonogram" means any exclusively aural fixation of sounds of a performance or of other sounds.

[46] Rome Convention Article 3: (f) "broadcasting" means the transmission by wireless means for public reception of sounds or of images and sounds.

[47] Protocol 28 On Intellectual Property (1994). In: EFTA https://www.efta.int/sites/default/files/documents/legal-texts/eea/the-eea-agreement/Protocols%20to%20the%20Agreement/protocol28.pdf.

requirement for the Berne Union regarding the protection of the works written above with copyright protection is also valid and binding for the EU and its member states.

For the TRIPS Agreements, since both the EU and each of the EU countries are members of the WTO, the EU needs to comply with all the provisions outlined in these agreements. Apart from the Berne Convention, the TRIPS Agreement Article 9(1) also requires that its contracting parties should comply with Articles 1-21 of the Berne Convention.

For treaties produced by WIPO, as a result of the decision taken by the Council of the EU in 2000,[48] the EU has become a part of the WIPO treaties in the field of copyright and neighbouring rights, such as WCT and WPPT.

In summary, provisions mentioned in international law related to the subject matter of copyright will also be valid for the EU. At the same time, the EU has also enacted their own legislation in accordance with the relevant international law.

Furthermore, according to CFR Article 17 the right to property has been regulated as follows:

1. *Everyone has the right to own, use, dispose of and bequeath his or her lawfully acquired possessions. No one may be deprived of his or her possessions, except in the public interest and in the cases and under the conditions provided for by law, subject to fair compensation being paid in good time for their loss. The use of property may be regulated by law in so far as is necessary for the general interest.*
2. *Intellectual property shall be protected.*

This means that, intellectual property should be protected as part of the property right and can only be limited in the public interest and in the cases and under the conditions provided for by law, subject to fair compensation being paid to copyright holders.

The most important provision for the subject matter of copyright in the EU Acquis is the Directive 2001/29/EC of the European Parliament and of the Council of 22 May 2001 on the harmonisation of certain aspects of copyright and related rights in the information society[49] (the InfoSoc Directive). According to Article 2 of the InfoSoc Directive, copyright and related rights protection should be given:

- for authors, of their works;
- for performers, of fixations of their performances;
- for phonogram producers, of their phonograms;
- for the producers of the first fixations of films, in respect of the original and copies of their films;

[48] EUR-lex, 'Accession to the World Intellectual Property Organisation Treaties' (2019) https://eur-lex.europa.eu/EN/legal-content/summary/accession-to-the-world-intellectual-property-organisation-treaties.html.

[49] Directive 2001/29/EC of the European Parliament and of the Council of 22 May 2001 on the harmonisation of certain aspects of copyright and related rights in the information society [2001] OJ L 167. (hereinafter will be referred as the InfoSoc Directive).

- for broadcasting organisations, of fixations of their broadcasts, whether those broadcasts are transmitted by wire or over the air, including by cable or satellite.

Furthermore, in the numerous directives, some works are also deemed protectable by copyright, such as:

- In the Term Directive[50] and Rental and Lending Right Directive[51]—photographs, films, moving images;
- In the Database Directive[52]—databases;
- In the Software Directive[53]—computer programs;

Also, in the numerous directives, some works are also deemed protectable by related rights, such as:

- In the Term Directive[54]—previously unpublished works' first publishment or communication to the public after the expiry of their copyright.
- In the Database Directive[55]—databases—for the maker of databases, who made a substantial investment.

Apart from them, there are several judgments given by the CJEU to discuss whether some subject matters can be protected by copyright or related rights, such as the taste of cheese[56]; however, these judgments will not be explained in detail in this part of the study in further detail.

In this study, the 'copyright' term will be used in a broader term, which also covers 'related rights' therefore, any reference made to 'copyright' should be understood as 'copyright and related rights' unless otherwise mentioned.

Finally, this study focuses on an assessment within the EU Law; therefore, after that, the whole examination will be done on the basis of the EU Law unless otherwise stated.

---

[50] Directive 2006/116/EC of the European Parliament and of the Council of 12 December 2006 on the term of protection of copyright and certain related rights [2006] OJ L 372, Article 6. (hereinafter will be referred as the Term Directive).

[51] Directive 2006/115/EC of the European Parliament and of the Council of 12 December 2006 on rental right and lending right and on certain rights related to copyright in the field of intellectual property, [2006] OJ L 376, Article 6. (hereinafter will be referred as the Rental and Lending Right Directive).

[52] Directive 96/9/EC of the European Parliament and of the Council of 11 March 1996 on the legal protection of databases [1996] OJ L 77, Article 4. (hereinafter will be referred as the Database Directive).

[53] Directive 2009/24/EC of the European Parliament and of the Council of 23 April 2009 on the legal protection of computer programs [2009] OJ L 111, Article 1. (hereinafter will be referred as the Software Directive).

[54] Article 4, Term Directive.

[55] Article 7, Database Directive.

[56] Case C-310/17 *Levola Hengelo BV v Smilde Foods BV* [2018] OJ C 269. In this case, the Court ruled that (para 40) taste of the cheese cannot be protectable by copyright since a taste of something cannot be identifiable with sufficient precision and objectivity.

3.2.2.3 The Rights Conferred by Copyright

This part of the study will briefly summarise the consequences of copyright subsistence in the work. As a result of copyright protection, copyright holders can enjoy some exclusionary rights, which provide a limited-term monopoly over the work. These rights are:

- The reproduction right
- The right of communication to the public
- The right of distribution
- The right of rental and lending
- The resale right

The reproduction right is the most basic right conferred by copyright, and it is regulated under Article 2 of the InfoSoc Directive. According to this right, the copyright owner has an exclusive right to reproduce the work, and they can prohibit direct or indirect, temporary or permanent reproduction of the work by any means. There are some exceptions in this right, especially the 'temporary act of reproduction' exception has particular relevance with downloading and streaming online; therefore, this exception and other relevant exceptions will be analysed deeply in Chap. 6.

The right of communication to the public is regulated in Article 3 of the InfoSoc Directive, and this is the right to make available to the public the copies of the work by wire or wireless means, and the public shall have access to them from a place and at a time individually chosen by them. This right has become very important, especially with the Internet and the increase in broadcasting; therefore, deciding the scope of this right and any infringement related to this has been subject to several judgments and opinions given by the CJEU. These decisions and the scope of this right in terms of copyright-protected digital products will be explained in the next chapter, where the exhaustion is outlined.

The right of distribution is regulated in Article 4 of the InfoSoc Directive, and this right gives an exclusionary right to the copyright owner over the distribution of these works in any form to the public by sale or otherwise. To ensure the free movement of goods and services within the EU and to control the distribution right of the authors within the EU, the exhaustion principle was accepted and later regulated in Article 4(2) of the InfoSoc Directive. The exhaustion principle will be explained in Chapter 3 in great detail.

The right of rental and lending is regulated in the Rental and Lending Right Directive under Article 3, and this right is to make available the copyright-protected works for use for a limited period of time and for direct or indirect economic or commercial advantage.

The resale right is regulated under the Resale Directive,[57] and according to this right, member states should provide a right for the rightsholders to benefit from

[57] Directive 2001/84/EC of the European Parliament and of the Council of 27 September 2001 on the resale right for the benefit of the author of an original work of art, [2001] OJ L 272. (hereinafter will be referred as the Resale Directive).

receiving a royalty based on the sale price obtained for any resale of the work subsequent to the first transfer of the work by the author. This is an unassignable and inalienable right and cannot be waived. This right is also known as 'droit de suite'.

3.3 The Territoriality Principle of Copyright

3.3.1 The Principle of Territoriality

The territoriality principle is one of the most basic principles of international law, which could be understood as states having jurisdiction over acts in case the actions have occurred within the territory of the states and historically, this principle has an essential link with the principle of sovereignty of nation states over their territory.[58] The principle of territoriality is one of the basic principles of intellectual property law, and according to the territoriality principle in intellectual property law, intellectual property rights are limited to the territory of the state in which the rights have been conferred.[59] In other words, the territoriality principle of intellectual property rights permits nation-states to control and decide their own laws, which are more convenient for the needs and overall understanding of their law system and legislature within their territory.[60]

International intellectual property law has emerged and established its rules according to the principle of territoriality. As explained in the historical development part, the protection of intellectual property has been perceived as a protection of domestic manufacture for the benefit of the state. In light of this aim, the first patent statute from Venice during the fifteenth century expresses that *'every person who shall build any new and ingenious device in this City ... will have a ten-year monopoly over its manufacture in our territories and towns'*.[61] The same principle is also valid for copyright (as also outlined in the historical development part); the Statute of Anne regulated that any author publishing and depositing the book in Britain will have 14 years renewable right over the exploitation, importing and printing of this book in that territory.[62]

Economic interests and benefits of the states have also played a significant role in the territoriality of intellectual property law. Especially for international trade, having protection for scientific products or creative works within the country became very important to foster exports and gain more profit from them. Therefore, countries wanted to have protection for these products within their territory so that they could control the sale and exportation of these products. For example, the French Patent

[58] Oke (2018, p. 316).

[59] Lundstedt (2016, p. 28).

[60] Lundstedt (2016, p. 28).

[61] Pila and Torremans (2019, p. 26).

[62] Pila and Torremans (2019, p. 27).

Law of 1791 regulated that if the product was patented in France, the inventor could not apply for another patent in another country, whereas the same law allowed an invention from abroad to be patented, even if it was protected by a foreign patent.[63]

These disparities in the intellectual property law created problems between states, especially with globalisation and the invention of the printing press, emerging new technologies and increasing transnational trade; the need for the states to protect other nationals' rights in their territory and their citizens abroad has increased. Hence, it leads states entering into bilateral and multilateral treaties to have a harmonised understanding of the intellectual property law and mutually protect and enforce the intellectual property rights of foreigners in their states and territories and their citizens living in other countries.[64] To that end, the Paris Convention for the Protection of Industrial Property of 1883 (Paris Convention)[65] was signed.

The Paris Convention was the first attempt to regulate industrial property in the widest sense, including patents, trademarks, and industrial designs. As also stated in the previous section, the Berne Convention deals with copyright, i.e. protection of works and the rights of their author. Both the Paris Convention and the Berne Convention regulated the national treatment principle and according to this principle, "*Nationals of countries outside the Union who are domiciled or who have real and effective industrial or commercial establishments in the territory of one of the countries of the Union shall be treated in the same manner as nationals of the countries of the Union*". Some argue that although the national treatment principle does not explicitly require a territoriality principle, this principle de facto creates copyright territoriality; hence, Article 5(2) of the Berne Convention could be understood as national copyright law will apply to the situations as a result of the national treatment principle, and therefore, the territoriality of the intellectual property law is the consequence of this principle.[66] On the other hand, according to another opinion which points that the national treatment principle only requires that the protection of copyright should be alike for both foreign and nationals, and therefore, this should not be understood as a direct application of the law of any country, or choice of a law which is deriving from the principle of territoriality.[67] The territoriality of copyright has been stated in the *Lagardere* ruling decided by the CJEU in 2005, and in this decision, the territoriality of copyright is mentioned as one of the principles of the EU copyright law as well.[68]

---

63 Pila and Torremans (2019, p. 27).

64 Oke (2018, p. 316), Lundstedt (2016, p. 85).

65 Paris Convention for the protection of industrial property of March 20, 1883, 828 UNTS 305. (hereinafter will be referred as the Paris Convention).

66 Torremans and Keosomphan (2021, p. 1088).

67 Lundstedt (2016, p. 98).

68 European Parliamentary Research Service (2015) EU Copyright Reform: Revisiting the Principle of Territoriality. In: Europarl. https://www.europarl.europa.eu/RegData/etudes/BRIE/2015/568348/EPRS_BRI%282015%29568348_EN.pdf. According to the paragraph 46 of the Case C-192/04 Lagardère Active Broadcast v Société pour la perception de la rémunération équitable (SPRE) and Gesellschaft zur Verwertung von Leistungsschutzrechten mbH (GVL) [2005] ECR 2005 I-07199 judgment: '*At the outset, it must be emphasised that it is clear from its wording and scheme that*

This study will focus on the territoriality principle and the consequences of this only within the EU Copyright Law.

There are some consequences of the principle of territoriality. Due to the territoriality principle, copyright rules may vary among the Member States. When the supranational nature and the supremacy of the EU Law are considered, this territoriality principle becomes more problematic and questionable within the EU Member States. As explained the main aim of the EU was to create an internal market where there are no borders or differences within the EU, where goods, services, persons, and capital move freely. Yet, the territorial nature of the copyright results in 27 different copyright legislation within the EU. This results in disparities and differences between the Member States and unharmonisation of the intellectual property law and copyright laws per se. The territorial nature of copyright has some practical consequences; for example, the differences between the notion of a 'subject matter of protection' or different interpretations of 'work of authorship' could result in unharmonised copyright legislation in some respects.[69]

As a result of the territorial nature and country-by-country enforcement of the copyright, the exceptions and limitations may vary among the Member States, although these are mostly regulated under different Directives.[70] Some copyright exceptions and limitations allow people to use a fair amount of copyright-protected works without the permission of the copyright owner, which is set out in Article 9 (2) of the Berne Convention. According to the three-step test, exceptions and limitations can only be permitted if:

i. It occurs in only specific cases,
ii. It does not conflict with a normal exploitation of the work,
iii. Finally, this act does not unreasonably prejudice the author's legitimate interests.

According to these three conditions, it should be decided that the act should be within copyright limitation or exception. Hence, all the countries make their interpretation according to their own national legislation when they decide on copyright exceptions and limitations; this results in different consequences of the three-step test, resulting in substantial differences in the interpretation of the copyright law. To simplify, for example, if a temporary act of copying is excepted as an exception to copyright as a

Directive 92/100 provides for minimal harmonisation regarding rights related to copyright. Thus, it does not purport to detract, in particular, from the principle of the territoriality of those rights, which is recognised in international law and also in the EC Treaty. Those rights are therefore of a territorial nature and, moreover, domestic law can only penalise conduct engaged in within national territory.'

[69] In 2006, the Supreme Court of the Netherlands held that under the Dutch Copyright Act, in the Lancôme v Kecofa case, since there was no exhaustive list of work in the InfoSoc Directive that can be copyrightable, a smell can be protectable by copyright since it may be perceived by humans. On the other hand, in the same year, the French Court de Cassation in the Bsiri-Barbir case, the French Supreme Court held that a fragrance does not constitute a tangible form of expression and a nose cannot be regarded as the author; therefore a smell of perfume cannot be protectable by copyright.

[70] European Parliamentary Research Service (2015) EU Copyright Reform: Revisiting the Principle of Territoriality. In: Europarl. https://www.europarl.europa.eu/RegData/etudes/BRIE/2015/568348/EPRS_BRI%282015%29568348_EN.pdf.

result of the application of the three-step test in Latvia, the same action may not be considered an exception in Poland since the three-step test is applied differently.

The territoriality principle links the private international law rule when it comes to copyright infringement of copyright; hence, according to Article 8 of the Rome II Regulation, where the protection has been acquired, the country's law will deal with copyright infringement. This could be understood as, for example, Greek law will be applicable if there is a copyright claim concerning Greece. This rule becomes problematic and creates legal uncertainty regarding online copyright infringement, as online works could be accessed from every Member State; therefore, different rules have been needed with the emergence of the Internet and online works.

The territoriality of copyright also results in economic consequences, increasing the transaction, licensing, and enforcement costs.[71] As a result of the territoriality principle, rightsholders tend to sign territorial licence agreements because of cultural and linguistic differences. Therefore, the fragmented nature of copyright law can result in increased licensing costs across the EU, if someone would like to acquire the licence for multiple countries.

Territoriality of copyright can also result in the practice of geo-blocking activities in order to comply with the copyright law. This issue was also explained in the first chapter in detail.

3.3.2 *Response to Territoriality: Harmonisation of Copyright Law Within the EU with EU Legislations*

When the EU was established, the primary understanding was copyright law, and the EU law was different from each other since the former one could have been regulated under the national sovereignty.[72] There were three main legal bases to support this argument[73]:

- In the Treaty of Rome, in Article 36, there was no exclusive reference to the copyright law although there was a reference for industrial and commercial property,[74]

[71] European Parliamentary Research Service (2015) EU Copyright Reform: Revisiting the Principle of Territoriality. In: Europarl. https://www.europarl.europa.eu/RegData/etudes/BRIE/2015/568348/EPRS_BRI%282015%29568348_EN.pdf.

[72] Synodinou (2021, p. 41).

[73] Synodinou (2021, p. 41).

[74] Article 36 of Treaty of Rome states that *'The provisions of Articles 30 to 34 shall not preclude prohibitions or restrictions on imports, exports or goods in transit justified on grounds of public morality, public policy or public security; the protection of health and life of humans, animals or plants; the protection of national treasures possessing artistic historic or archaeological value; or the protection of industrial and commercial property. Such prohibitions or restrictions shall not, however, constitute a means of arbitrary discrimination or a disguised restriction on trade between Member States.'*

- Article 22 also rules that this treaty shall in no way prejudice the rules in the Member States governing the system of property ownership, and copyright has a property-related nature.
- Finally, copyright was considered to have a unique nature which regulates the moral and economic rights of the authors.

As a result of those explained difficulties because of the territoriality of copyright and since the emergence of the Internet and global technologies where there is no border, the territoriality of copyright has also been problematic. Especially since copyright-protected digital products have become a primary medium of digital sale, and their cross-border exploitation has increased,[75] the territoriality approach and its benefits have been debated.

After these developments, the potential positive aspects of harmonising and approximating the copyright law in the EU were considered. First of all, it was suggested that copyright harmonisation would bring better protection of copyright and authors' rights with the help of the internal market.[76] Furthermore, it was outlined that this unification would have attracted more stakeholders because harmonisation would bring better competition within the EU.[77] Thirdly, according to some commentators, copyright reform may ensure greater fairness and remedy some market imbalances.[78]

To avoid substantially different copyright legislation throughout the EU, the European Parliament and the Council of the EU have decided to harmonise copyright legislation within the EU. To that end, the EU has started to work on a harmonisation process since the 1980s and has adopted numerous directives, regulations and recommendations since 1991. As a response to the territoriality of copyright, to comply with the idea of creating a single market within the Community, the EU wanted to harmonise copyright law. At the same time, the CJEU has established the principle of exhaustion to deal with copyright territoriality and ensure the free movement of goods and services within the EU. The exhaustion principle will be explained in Chap. 3 of this study.

With the White Paper[79] published by the Commission in 1985, the harmonisation progress started. Accordingly, Green Paper,[80] published in 1988, also admits the importance of emerging technologies and challenges for the copyright.

i. *Completing the Internal Market, White Paper from the Commission to the European Council, Milan, 28–29 June 1985, 14 June 1985:* The European Council

[75] Synodinou (2021, p. 41).

[76] Rosati (2023, p. 10).

[77] Rosati (2023, p. 10).

[78] Rosati (2023, p. 10).

[79] Commission, 'Completing The Internal Market: White Paper From The Commission To The European Council' [1985] COM_1985_0310_FIN. (hereinafter will be referred to as the White Paper).

[80] Commission, 'Green Paper on Copyright and the Challenge Of Technology Copyright Issues Requiring Immediate Action' [1988] COM 88 final (hereinafter will be referred to as the Green Paper).

has published this white paper to finalise the most significant aim of the EU which is to create an internal market throughout the EU. To achieve this aim, the road map has been decided, and by 1992 the creation of an entirely beneficial internal market should have been finished. Additionally, more than 300 different legislations have been planned. For the intellectual property law domain, the Council of the EU decided to remove the differences in intellectual property laws as they have a direct and negative impact on intra-community trade and on the ability of enterprises to treat the common market as a single environment for their economic activities. Nevertheless, the main focus was on the patent and trade mark domain.

ii. Green Paper on 'Copyright and the Challenge of Technology' by the European Commission in 1988: Just after the Warner Brothers[81] decision, which expands the exhaustion principle for video rental, the European Commission decided to publish a paper which explains and points out the challenges in the field of copyright arising from global technologies. This paper immediately points out that copyright cannot restrict the free movement of goods.[82] With the recent impact of the Warner Brothers decision, this paper also stipulates the importance and complexity of video rentals, sound recordings and imported films. This paper mainly focused on the importance of the modernisation of existing copyright protection systems at both the national and Community level and to that end, it consulted and covered piracy, the copying of sound and audiovisual works, the distribution and rental rights for sound and video recordings, to the legal protection of computer programs and finally legal problems of databases.

After these papers, the EU initiated to harmonise all aspects of copyright and, to that end, has published recommendations, directives and regulations since 1991. In that part of the study, the most important incentives for harmonisation of copyright law throughout the EU will be explained briefly.

i. *Council Directive 91/250/EEC of 14 May 1991 on the legal protection of computer programs* **which is replaced by**: *the Directive on the legal protection of computer programs ('Software Directive'), 23 April 2009:* As the aforementioned green paper, after the technological advances and the challenges to the copyright, including the aim of creating a single market, the EU has decided to regulate the legal protection of computer programs. This Directive mainly covers the legal protection of computer programs by copyright, as stated in the Berne Convention for the Protection of Literary and Artistic Works.

[81] Case 158/86 *Warner Brothers Inc. and Metronome Video ApS v Erik Viuff Christiansen* [1988] ECR 1988-02605. (hereinafter will be referred as the Warner Brothers case). This decision will be explained in the exhaustion part, in Chapter 3 with more detail.

[82] Green paper, p. 1. '*As elsewhere in the field of intellectual property rights, the European Court of Justice quickly established the principle that, where goods are lawfully placed on the market in a Member State, copyright cannot be relied upon to restrict the free circulation of those goods elsewhere in the Community.*'

ii. *Council Directive 92/100/EEC of 19 November 1992 on rental right and lending right and on certain rights related to copyright in the field of intellectual property* **Which is replaced by** *the Directive on rental rights and lending rights and on certain rights related to copyright in the field of intellectual property ('Rental and Lending Directive'), 12 December 2006:* These directives aimed to create rental and lending right as a part of copyright protection and also regulated protection for the related rights of performers, phonogram and film producers and broadcasting organisations.[83]

iii. *Directive on the coordination of certain rules concerning copyright and rights related to copyright applicable to satellite broadcasting and cable retransmission*[84] *('Satellite and Cable Directive, SatCab Directive'), 27 September 1993:* To harmonise copyright rules, especially to deal with copyright territoriality, Article 1(2)(1) of this Directive regulates that '*The act of communication to the public by satellite occurs solely in the Member State where, under the control and responsibility of the broadcasting organisation, the programme-carrying signals are introduced into an uninterrupted chain of communication leading to the satellite and down towards the earth.'* Accordingly, only if there is a signal from the country of the origin of this satellite broadcast will it be considered a communication to the public; hence, only obtaining a licence from the home country of the satellite broadcast will be needed. This practice called as country-of-origin principle and this will be further explained in the part of the territorial licences, in Chap. 7 of this study.

iv. *Directive on the legal protection of databases ('Database Directive'), 11 March 1996:* This Directive covers the legal protection of databases by copyright, to protect the intellectual effort and creation of the author.

v. *Directive on the harmonisation of certain aspects of copyright and related rights in the information society ('Information Society Directive—InfoSoc Directive'), 22 May 2001:* According to Recital 4 of this Directive, a harmonised legal framework on copyright and related rights will provide increased legal certainty and a high level of protection of intellectual property while encouraging significant investment in innovation. According to Recital 4 of this Directive, a harmonised legal framework on copyright and related rights will provide increased legal certainty and a high level of intellectual property protection while encouraging significant investment in innovation. It will also enable the development and competitiveness of European industry on a large scale, both in the area of content delivery and information technology and in the industrial and cultural sectors in general. The main aim of this Directive

[83] According to Recital 3 of the Rental and Lending Rights Directive, "*The adequate protection of copyright works and subject matter of related rights protection by rental and lending rights as well as the protection of the subject matter of related rights protection by the fixation right, distribution right, right to broadcast and communication to the public can accordingly be considered as being of fundamental importance for the economic and cultural development of the Community.*"

[84] Council Directive 93/83/EEC of 27 September 1993 on the coordination of certain rules concerning copyright and rights related to copyright applicable to satellite broadcasting and cable retransmission [1993] OJ L 248. (hereinafter will be referred as the SatCab Directive).

was to harmonise copyright and related rights within the EU when creating a single market aim was taken into account. To that end, the InfoSoc Directive was an important milestone for the process of harmonisation of copyright and related rights in the European Union.

vi. *Directive on the resale right for the benefit of the author of an original work of art*[85] *('Resale Right Directive'), 27 September 2001:* Article 14ter of the Berne Convention regulates the right droit de suite. According to this Article, the author, or after his death the persons or institutions authorised by national legislation, shall, with respect to original works of art and original manuscripts of writers and composers, enjoy the inalienable right to an interest in any sale of the work subsequent to the first transfer by the author of the work. This Directive has been regulated by the EU to remove differences between the Member States to comply with both the Berne Convention and internal market requirements and regulates the resale right, which gives the opportunity to authors to receive royalties on their works when they are resold.

vii. *Directive on the enforcement of intellectual property right*[86] *('IPRED') (Enforcement Directive), 29 April 2004:* To remove differences in the enforcement of IP Rights within the Member States, this Directive aimed to approximate legislative systems so as to ensure a high, equivalent and homogeneous level of protection in the internal market.

viii. *Commission Recommendation of 18 May 2005 on collective cross-border management of copyright and related rights for legitimate online music services*[87]*:* According to this non-binding recommendation, the aim was to grant community-wide licences for the online use of the music; and rightsholders should have the right to entrust the management of any of the online rights necessary to operate legitimate online music services, on territorial scope of their choice, to a collective rights manager of their choice, irrespective of the Member State of residence or the nationality of either the collective rights manager or the right-holder.

ix. *Directive on the term of protection of copyright and certain related rights amending the previous 2006 Directive ('Term Directive'), 27 September 2011:* This Directive aimed to harmonise the term of protection for copyright and related rights within the EU.

x. *Directive on certain permitted uses of orphan works*[88] *('Orphan Works Directive'), 25 October 2012:* Orphan works are copyright-protected works whose authors cannot be identified or found. When cultural heritage has been taken into account to harmonise the copyright law within the EU regarding orphan

[85] Directive 2001/84/EC of the European Parliament and of the Council of 27 September 2001 on the resale right for the benefit of the author of an original work of art [2001] OJ L 272.

[86] Directive 2004/48/EC of the European Parliament and of the Council of 29 April 2004 on the enforcement of intellectual property rights [2004] OJ L 157.

[87] Commission Recommendation of 18 May 2005 on collective cross-border management of copyright and related rights for legitimate online music services [2005] OJ L 276.

[88] Directive 2012/28/EU of the European Parliament and of the Council of 25 October 2012 on certain permitted uses of orphan works Text with EEA relevance [2012] OJ L 299.

works, this Directive has been published. According to Article 1 of this Directive, the aim of the Orphan Works Directive concerns certain uses made of orphan works by publicly accessible libraries, educational establishments and museums, as well as by archives, film or audio heritage institutions and public-service broadcasting organisations, established in the Member States, in order to achieve aims related to their public-interest missions.

xi. *Directive on collective management of copyright and related rights and multi-territorial licensing of rights in musical works for online use in the internal market*[89] *('CRM Directive'), 26 February 2014:* This Directive has been established to ensure collective management of copyright works across national borders and also impose some requirements on the collective management organisations that license the online use of musical works on a multi-territorial basis.

xii. *Directive on certain permitted uses of certain works and other subject matter protected by copyright and related rights for the benefit of persons who are blind, visually impaired or otherwise print-disabled*[90] *(Directive implementing the Marrakech Treaty in the EU),13 September 2017; Regulation on the cross-border exchange between the Union and third countries of accessible format copies of certain works and other subject matter protected by copyright and related rights for the benefit of persons who are blind, visually impaired or otherwise print-disabled*[91] *(Regulation implementing the Marrakech Treaty in the EU), 13 September 2017:* This Directive and Regulation were established to implement the Marrakech Treaty for the blind, visually impaired or otherwise print-disabled persons, including a copyright exception that permits the cross-border exchange of accessible format copies of certain works and subject matter that are ordinarily protected by copyright and related rights.

xiii. *Regulation on cross-border portability of online content services in the internal market ('Portability Regulation'), 14 June 2017:* The EU has adopted the Regulation on cross-border portability of online content services to provide a common approach in the Union to the cross-border portability of online content services, by ensuring that subscribers to portable online content services which are lawfully provided in their Member State of residence can access and use those services when temporarily present in a Member State other than their

[89] Directive 2014/26/EU of the European Parliament and of the Council of 26 February 2014 on collective management of copyright and related rights and multi-territorial licensing of rights in musical works for online use in the internal market Text with EEA relevance [2014] OJ L 84. (hereinafter will be referred as the CRM Directive).

[90] Directive (EU) 2017/1564 of the European Parliament and of the Council of 13 September 2017 on certain permitted uses of certain works and other subject matter protected by copyright and related rights for the benefit of persons who are blind, visually impaired or otherwise print-disabled and amending Directive 2001/29/EC on the harmonisation of certain aspects of copyright and related rights in the information society [2017] OJ L 242.

[91] Regulation (EU) 2017/1563 of the European Parliament and of the Council of 13 September 2017 on the cross-border exchange between the Union and third countries of accessible format copies of certain works and other subject matter protected by copyright and related rights for the benefit of persons who are blind, visually impaired or otherwise print-disabled [2017] OJ L 242.

Member State of residence. This Regulation will be explained later in this study, in depth.

xiv. *Regulation (EU) 2018/302 of the European Parliament and of the Council of 28 February 2018 on addressing unjustified geo-blocking and other forms of discrimination based on customers' nationality, place of residence or place of establishment within the internal market: ('Geo-blocking Regulation')* As mentioned in previous chapters, this Regulation aims to prevent unjustified geo-blocking within the EU based on customers' nationality, place of residence or place of establishment. This Regulation will be explained in this study later, in-depth.

xv. *Directive on copyright and related rights in the Digital Single Market*[92] *('DSM Directive'), 17 April 2019:* According to Article 1 of the DSM Directive, the aim was to harmonise the EU Law in terms of copyright and related rights with regard to the aim of having a single market, especially for the digital and cross-border uses of copyright-protected products. To achieve this objective, this Directive also brings some exceptions and limitations to copyright and related rights on the facilitation of licences. This Directive was a really important development in that field and tried to solve lots of copyright-related problems in the EU's digital single market; however, the DSM Directive will not be covered in that study since it does not have a direct link with the geo-blocking practice.

xvi. *Directive on the exercise of copyright and related rights applicable to certain online transmissions of broadcasting organisations and retransmissions of television and radio programmes*[93] *('Satellite and Cable II, the SatCab II Directive'), 17 April 2019:* It does some amendments to the Satellite and Cable Directive dated 27 September 1993 and includes online transmissions of broadcasting organisations and retransmissions of television and radio programmes within the SatCab Directive.

Very importantly, the Treaty of Lisbon introduced the legal basis for the EU-wide copyright law consideration and unification of intellectual property law with Article 118. This Article points that:

> In the context of the establishment and functioning of the internal market, the European Parliament and the Council, acting in accordance with the ordinary legislative procedure, shall establish measures for the creation of European intellectual property rights to provide uniform protection of intellectual property rights throughout the Union and for the setting up of centralised Union-wide authorisation, coordination and supervision arrangements.

---

[92] Directive (EU) 2019/790 of the European Parliament and of the Council of 17 April 2019 on copyright and related rights in the Digital Single Market and amending Directives 96/9/EC and 2001/29/EC [2019] OJ L 130. (hereinafter will be referred as the DSM Directive).

[93] Directive (EU) 2019/789 of the European Parliament and of the Council of 17 April 2019 laying down rules on the exercise of copyright and related rights applicable to certain online transmissions of broadcasting organisations and retransmissions of television and radio programmes, and amending Council Directive 93/83/EEC [2019] OJ L 130. (hereinafter will be referred as SatCab II Directive).

That development points out that if the EU would like to unify the intellectual property laws despite the territoriality principle. After this legal basis, the EU published the DSM Strategy for the EU in 2015, to have a unified understanding of the Digital Single Market within the EU where there is a free movement of goods, services, capital and people in also digital environment. The DSM Strategy was explained in detail in Chap. 1, therefore no further explanation will be provided here.

3.3.3 *The Latest Discussions About the Harmonisation of Copyright Law Within the EU*

After the DSM Strategy, the EU published numerous assessments and stakeholder reviews[94] for the harmonisation of the copyright law in the context of the DSM Directive to harmonise the EU Law in terms of copyright and related rights with regard to the aim of having a single market, especially for the digital and cross-border uses of copyright-protected products. Before the acceptance of the DSM Directive, the EU updated the SatCab II Directive and most interestingly for this research, the EU regulated different aspects of the portability of the subscribed online content-sharing services with the Portability Regulation and territorial restrictions to copyright-protected products with the Geo-blocking Regulation. The Portability Regulation and the Geo-blocking Regulation will be explained in the next chapter.

Just after the DSM Strategy, the European Parliamentary Research Service published a Briefing[95] called 'EU copyright reform: Revisiting the principle of territoriality' and in that Briefing, it was accepted that unified copyright law would replace disparities between national copyright law and could remove territorial barriers in copyright law. On the other hand, the Briefing also mentioned that unified copyright law in the EU should be seen as a long-term project and that the Commission should initiate some assessments on the impact of the unified copyright law.[96] The Commission published an impact assessment on the modernisation of the copyright

---

[94] The procedure for the DSM Directive with the opinions and proposals can be seen here: https://eur-lex.europa.eu/legal-content/EN/HIS/?uri=CELEX:32019L0790.

[95] European Parliamentary Research Service, 'EU Copyright Reform: Revisiting the Principle of Territoriality' (Briefing, European Parliament, 2015) https://www.europarl.europa.eu/RegData/etudes/BRIE/2015/568348/EPRS_BRI%282015%29568348_EN.pdf.

[96] European Parliamentary Research Service, 'EU Copyright Reform: Revisiting the Principle of Territoriality' (Briefing, European Parliament, 2015) https://www.europarl.europa.eu/RegData/etudes/BRIE/2015/568348/EPRS_BRI%282015%29568348_EN.pdf. '*The full harmonisation of copyright in the EU, in the form of a single copyright code and a single copyright title, would require substantial changes in the way our rules work today. Areas that have so far been left to the discretion of national legislators would have to be harmonised. Uniform application of the rules would call for a single copyright jurisdiction with its own tribunal, so that inconsistent case law does not lead to more fragmentation.*'

law for the DSM Directive Proposal.[97] Nevertheless, no work or assessment for the feasibility of unified copyright law was published until the July 2024. On the other hand, very importantly this Briefing accepted that a common copyright legislation should be introduced so that cultural, intellectual and scientific productions move freely within the EU.

Right now, in the EU, there are important European copyright working platforms, usually consist of distinguish academics, the reCreating Europe and the European Copyright Society (ECS) are two of them. Both groups have published important studies recently for copyright harmonisation within the EU. Firstly, reCreating Europe published their extensive study's result in terms of the outcome of copyright modernisation in certain areas in the EU[98] and offered medium-term and long-term solutions for the most debated copyright law problems, especially for the Digital Single Market. Secondly, the ECS sent a letter[99] to the European Commission in 2023. In that letter, the ECS asked for optimising the level of harmonisation achieved thus far, reflecting clear general principles on future European copyright law, and most importantly introducing a unitary title. Nonetheless, so far as of July 2024, no further update or step on harmonisation has been provided by the EU.

Finally, it is worth mentioning that copyright law has also been harmonised and shaped with the help of the CJEU decisions, especially after the Infopaq case. Indeed, with the effect of the preliminary ruling mechanism[100] the CJEU harmonised different aspects of the copyright law within the EU, such as definition of work[101] or the scope of the exceptions and limitations.[102] In that study, harmonisation through case law of the EU will not be discussed in detail, since it may require a very detailed analysis, and this detailed analysis will not be particularly relevant with the study. Therefore, only case law relevant to the particular subjects in distinct parts of the study will be provided in detail.

Although a good level of harmonisation has been provided with the help of the CJEU judgments, legislations and especially with the current effort since the DSM Strategy, territoriality still remains as a main obstacle to fragment the Digital Single Market and especially for the rightsholders, it becomes harder to manage their rights

---

[97] Commission (2016) Impact Assessment on the modernisation of EU copyright rules. In: Shaping Europe's digital future https://digital-strategy.ec.europa.eu/en/library/impact-assessment-modernisation-eu-copyright-rules.

[98] reCreating Europe Consortium, 'Recreating Europe Final Conference Booklet'. Zenodo, 27 March 2023 https://zenodo.org/records/7774557.

[99] European Copyright Society (2023) Letter to Commissioner for Internal Market European Commission 'Future agenda in the field of copyright law'. In: European Copyright Society https://europeancopyrightsociety.org/wp-content/uploads/2023/04/ecs-letter-to-commissioner-breton-april-2023.pdf.

[100] Rosati (2023, p. 27).

[101] For example, with the judgments aforementioned Levola Hengelo BV v Smilde Foods case, Cofemel case, Infopaq case, FAPL and Murphy cases, Painer case.

[102] Infopaq case provided five requirements that must be met for the temporary copy exception, which will be explained in Chapter 7 in more detail.

across borders.[103] Therefore, to have a fully functional Digital Single Market within the EU, removing borders especially in the copyright law will be a good step, albeit this will require more time and effort and should not be seen as a short-term project.

3.4 Conclusion

This chapter mainly focused on the copyright protection, subsistence and subject matter of copyright-protected work as well as the territorial nature of the copyright law. The territoriality of copyright law stems from national sovereignty understanding and countries would like to legislate this delicate area according to their culture, law systems and their needs. On the other hand, in the EU, where the main aim is to create a fully functioning internal market, disparities in national laws created some problems, especially with the increase in cross-border trade and exploitation of copyright-protected digital products. Therefore, the EU was in the need to answer this territoriality principle, and the main response was to harmonise the copyright law in the EU.

Since the 1980s the EU worked to harmonise lots of aspects of copyright law in the EU and published numerous regulations, directives, recommendations, and other types of communications in that field. The last and one of the most important ones in that field was the DSM Directive, which tried to harmonise lots of aspects of digital copyright law. Nevertheless, after that legislation, the EU did not make more effort to harmonise and unify copyright law across the EU, even though scholars were mainly in favour of this unification.

The other important response to the territoriality principle was the 'Exhaustion Principle' and this important principle will be explained in detail in the next chapter.

References

Aplin T, Davis J (2021) Intellectual property law, 4th edn. Oxford University Press, Oxford
Bently L et al (2022) Intellectual property law, 6th edn. Oxford University Press, Oxford
Brown A et al (2023) Contemporary intellectual property, 6th edn. Oxford University Press, Oxford
Oke EK (2018) Territoriality in intellectual property law: examining the tension between securing societal goals and treating intellectual property as an investment asset. Scripted 15(2):313
Karapapa S, McDonagh L (2019) Intellectual property law. Oxford University Press, Oxford
Lundstedt L (2016) Territoriality in intellectual property law. Department of Law, Stockholm University, Stockholm
Pila J, Torremans P (2019) European intellectual property law, 2nd edn. Oxford University Press, Oxford

[103] European Copyright Society (2023) Letter to Commissioner for Internal Market European Commission 'Future agenda in the field of copyright law'. In: European Copyright Society https://europeancopyrightsociety.org/wp-content/uploads/2023/04/ecs-letter-to-commissioner-breton-april-2023.pdf.

Rosati E (2023) Copyright and the Court of Justice of the European Union, 2nd edn. Oxford University Press, Oxford

Synodinou TE (2021) The desirability of unification of European copyright law. In: Rosati E (ed) The Routledge handbook of EU copyright law. Routledge, London

Torremans P, Keosomphan K (2021) Towards a European copyright law: territoriality and limitations and exceptions as major outstanding issue. In: Stamatoudi I, Torremans P (eds) EU copyright law: a commentary, 2nd edn. Edward Elgar Publishing, Cheltenham, pp 1087–1103

Trimble M (2019) Copyright and geoblocking: the consequences of eliminating geoblocking. Scholarly Works 2019:476–502

Zahrádka P (2020) The Czech and Slovak audiovisual market as a laboratory experiment for the digital single market in Europe. In: Szczepanik P et al (eds) Digital peripheries: the online circulation of audiovisual content from the small market perspective. Springer, Cham, pp 101–124

Chapter 4
Geo-Blocking as a Copyright Phenomenon: The Exhaustion Principle

Abstract The exhaustion principle functions as a response to the exclusive and territorial nature of intellectual property rights. Intellectual property law grants rightsholders the power to prevent others from using protected goods, yet such exclusivity may conflict with the EU's commitment to the free movement of goods and services. The CJEU addressed this tension in Deutsche Grammophon v Metro, holding that the use of national copyrights to limit the importation of goods within the Union was incompatible with internal market objectives. Under the exhaustion doctrine, once goods are placed on the market by the rightsholder or with their consent, control over their resale, import or export is no longer permitted. The EU applies community exhaustion, ensuring that distribution rights are exhausted across the EU and EEA. While this framework supports the circulation of tangible goods, digital products remain regulated more strictly, as the EU has not recognised digital exhaustion. The momentum generated by UsedSoft was curtailed by Tom Kabinet. Current discussions consider whether exhaustion principles could address certain geo-blocking practices, but digital exhaustion is not accepted in the EU, although there are numerous arguments in favour of it.

4.1 Introduction

Intellectual property law creates an exclusive right[1] which prohibits others from using the same thing in a particular area; for example, in the patent domain, patents give the right to holders to prohibit selling or making the same invention, and in the copyright domain, it provides the right to holders to prohibit the reproduction of copyright works. To solve the apparent contradiction between the protection of intellectual property rights and the free movements of goods and services,[2] CJEU has established the 'principle of exhaustion' in the case Deutsche Grammophon v Metro decision in 1971. In this decision, the Court ruled that preventing the importation of records within the European Union based on national copyrights contradicted the

[1] Bently et al (2022, p. 9).

[2] Aplin and Davis (2021, p.36).

F. Cebeci Çorum, *Application of Geo-Blocking to Copyright-Protected Digital Products*, Studies in European Economic Law and Regulation 30,
https://doi.org/10.1007/978-3-032-34507-3_4

Union's provisions on the free movement of goods in the common market. This case is significant as it established the exhaustion principle within the Community.

The exhaustion principle means that, as also explained in the first chapter, if goods have been placed on the market by the intellectual property rightsholders or with their consent in the first place, the rightsholder can no longer control, resale, import, or export these goods.[3] In other words, the exhaustion principle prohibits intellectual property rights owners from relying on their rights to oppose further agreements on those particular goods.[4] This principle applies to all types of intellectual property rights.[5] At the same time, this principle is also known as 'the first sale doctrine'.[6]

The principle of 'regional (or community) exhaustion' has been adopted in the European Union[7] not to affect the single market and not harm competition. This means that when the product is put on the market with the permission of the rightsholder in any country of the EU, the distribution right is exhausted in the whole EU region and the countries in the European Economic Area (EEA). This issue can be exemplified as follows: if an author sells their book in France, a third party can buy it from France and sell it in Italy without obtaining further permission from this author. In the Deutsche Grammophon case and following cases related to exhaustion (such as the Membran[8] and Patricia[9] cases), the Court confirmed the supremacy of creating the internal market within the EU over the interests of the copyright holder,[10] which also shows the rationale behind the accepting community exhaustion within the EU.[11]

The acceptance of the exhaustion principle in traditional copyright law helps to circulate physical copies freely within the EU. However, digital versions are subject to restrictive copyright rules, as the concept of 'digital exhaustion' has not been accepted yet. These restrictions are enforced through geo-blocking, limiting the availability of digital products in accordance with copyright licences. Therefore, this chapter will analyse the potential effects of digital exhaustion on the geo-blocking debate, as well as consider the possibility of the acceptance of digital exhaustion with the latest developments in these field.

In this part of the study, to start with, justifications of the exhaustion doctrine will be explained. Then, all legislation in the EU that covers the exhaustion doctrine will be explained. Subsequently, the landmark decisions related to exhaustion, which help

---

[3] Bently et al (2022, p. 14).

[4] Aplin and Davis (2021, p.37).

[5] Bently et al (2022, p. 14).

[6] Perzanowski and Schultz (2011, p. 889).

[7] Deutsche Grammophon case confirms the community exhaustion for the distribution of copyright protected works, please see para498.

[8] Joined Cases 55 and 57/80 *Musik-Vertrieb membran GmbH and K-tel International v. GEMA–Gesellschaft für musikalische Aufführungs- und mechanische Vervielfältigungsrechte* [1981] ECR 1981–00,147.(hereinafter will be referred as the Membran case.

[9] Case C-341/87 *EMI Electrola GmbH v. Patricia Im- und Export and Others*, [1989] ECR 1989–00,079. (hereinafter will be referred as the Patricia case).

[10] The Membran case para 15; the Deutsche Grammophon case p 498; the Patricia para 8.

[11] Mezei (2022, p. 48).

the development of this doctrine within the EU, will be evaluated. Finally, the debates on the applicability of digital exhaustion will be deeply and critically covered.

4.2 The Historical Development of the Exhaustion Principle

4.2.1 Justifications of the Exhaustion Principle

As explained above, the exhaustion principle limits the distribution right by controlling the further sale of these products after rightsholders put these on the market with their consent. To prevent monopolies over the works, exclusive rights might have some limitations.[12] This limitation could be justified by stating that once the rightsholder puts their product on the market, they are free to decide on the price of that product, in most cases. Therefore, these rightsholders were already rewarded as a result of their cultural creativity.[13]

Furthermore, copyright law is designed to protect also society's interest, which is to access cultural products and access important knowledge.[14] By doing this, copyright law should seek the right balance between the author's and the public's rights and interests, since authors should also be encouraged to have incentives to create these works.[15] Therefore, availability and affordability of these products are very central to this debate, and by protecting copyright holders' interests, this doctrine will help facilitate innovation and foster competition.

Finally, the existence of the exhaustion principle for the products will help rightsholders avoid lots of follow-up negotiations and it will fasten the market economy.[16] Otherwise, without the exhaustion principle, market operations would be overly complicated.[17]

4.2.2 Early Decisions on the Exhaustion by the CJEU

In order to protect commercial and industrial property, the Articles between 34 and 36 Treaty on the Functioning of the European Union (TFEU)[18] have allowed limiting the free movement of goods within the EU in the case when these restrictions do not limit the trade between states and do not constitute arbitrary discrimination. In the

[12] Mezei (2022, p. 8).

[13] Geiregat (2022, p. 2).

[14] Mezei (2022, p. 8).

[15] Mezei (2022, p. 8).

[16] Geiregat (2022, p. 2).

[17] Geiregat (2022, p. 2).

[18] Consolidated version of the Treaty on the Functioning of the European Union [2016] OJ C 202/51. (hereinafter will be referred as TFEU).

Phil Collins case,[19] the CJEU confirmed that commercial exploitation of copyright results in the same problems as any other industrial and commercial property right and, as such, ruled that copyright law forms a part of a property.[20] Furthermore, in the Patricia case,[21] the Court found that the free movement of goods (the Court only used the term 'goods' and did not include 'services') was a barrier to the exercise of copyright law.[22] As explained in Chap. 1, the main aim of the EU was to create a single market where there are no internal frontiers and barriers to trade. In principle, quantitative restrictions on imports shall be prohibited between the Member States[23] unless it is necessary to protect commercial property.[24] Nevertheless, preventing the importing of goods between the Member States with the use of intellectual property rights could be considered a quantitative restriction.[25] Competition law aspects of geo-blocking and further explanation regarding this will also be deeply evaluated in Chap. 5.

In the EU, the landmark decision related to the exhaustion principle is the Deutsche Grammophon v Metro case. The subject of the lawsuit arose when the company Metro, which bought the records produced by the German Deutsche Grammophon music company from the distributor of this company in France, imported these records to Germany. In addition, it started to sell the imported records below the minimum sales prices determined by the Deutsche Grammophon for Germany. Thereupon, the Deutsche Grammophon stated that the company named Metro infringed the copyright, as the right granted by the German Copyright Law had not been exhausted since the said records had not yet been put up for sale in Germany by the Deutsche Grammophon. The Court of Justice stated that for a music production company to prevent, based on national copyrights, the importation into its country of records released by itself or by a third party with its consent in another Member State would be inconsistent with the Union's provisions on the free movement of goods in the common market.[26] The importance of the case is that this is the landmark case in which the Court of Justice has established the doctrine of exhaustion within the European Community. Following this development, in other decisions such as the Membran and the Patricia, the Court confirmed the doctrine of exhaustion for the goods and the supremacy of the internal market over the copyright holders' interest by establishing community exhaustion.

[19] Joined cases C-92/92 and C-326/92 *Phil Collins v. Imtrat Handelsgesellschaft mbH and Patricia Im- und Export Verwaltungsgesellschaft mbH and Leif Emanuel Kraul v. EMI Electrola GmbH* [1993] ECR 1993 I-05145. (hereinafter will be referred as the Phil Collins case).

[20] Mezei (2022, p. 36).

[21] The Patricia case para8.

[22] Mezei (2022, p. 36).

[23] According to the Article 34 TFEU.

[24] According to the Article 36 TFEU.

[25] Bently et al (2022, p. 13).

[26] The Deutsche Grammophon case paras. 12–13.

Subsequently, the Coditel[27] case is very significant in terms of evaluation of the exhaustion principle and to decide the limits of this principle. In this case, plaintiff Ciné Vog Films obtained the exclusive rights to show Le Boucher publicly in Belgium, including film performances and TV broadcasts. The original producers of Le Boucher also authorised the German public television broadcasting station to broadcast the work on the territory of the FRG. Coditel, a Belgian cable television network, received the signals of the program on 5 January 1971, broadcast in Germany and retransmitted the signals to its subscribers via cable. Ciné Vog Films considered this action a violation of its exclusive rights over the content. This is the case where the CJEU has established the boundaries of the doctrine of exhaustion. In short, it concluded that the exhaustion principle does not apply to service-like uses and affirmed the scope of this principle.[28] Notably, the Court also made it clear that the geographically limited licences to broadcast movies cannot be considered as an arbitrary discrimination or disguised restriction.[29]

The other important case that explains the scope of the principle of exhaustion is the Warner Brothers case. This legal dispute originated from video rental practices. The defendant, who managed a video rental store in Copenhagen, legally acquired a copy of the plaintiff's film, 'Never Say Never Again' in the UK and imported it to Denmark. Danish copyright law conferred an exclusive rental right to authors and producers of audiovisual works; these rights were held by Metronome Video ApS for the plaintiff's movie. The plaintiff asked for an injunction for this use, and the Court ruled that[30] (i) the market for hiring the video cassettes reaches the wider public than the sale of these cassettes and potentially provides more revenue than the traditional sale method, (ii) if the makers of these films were allowed to collect royalties only from the sale, even though these cassettes are also available as a rental, they would not receive fair remuneration from the exploitation of their works. Therefore, the CJEU not only ruled out the application of exhaustion in the context of video rental but also set a precedent for the harmonization of rental rights more broadly.

These decisions are the fundamental decisions to decide the scope and the applicability of the exhaustion principle within the EU. In this part, the provisions related to exhaustion legislated by the EU will be explained.

4.2.3 Exhaustion Under the EU Law Legislations

In the European Union Acquis, there are four different legislations which cover exhaustion principle.

---

[27] Case 262/81 *Coditel SA, Compagnie générale pour la diffusion de la télévision, and others v Ciné-Vog Films SA and others* [1982] ECR 1982 -03,381. (hereinafter will be referred as the Coditel case).

[28] Mezei (2022, p. 35).

[29] The Coditel case paras 14–17.

[30] The Warner Brothers case paras 14–15.

1. The first legislation related to exhaustion is included in the InfoSoc Directive. According to Article 4(2) of that Directive, the distribution right shall not be exhausted within the Community in respect of the *original or copies of the work*, except where the *first sale or other transfer* of ownership of that object is made by the rightsholder or with her consent.
   - Recital 28 of this Directive explains the term 'original or copies of the work' and clarifies that exhaustion will only be applicable in the case of the control of the distribution of the work in tangible form.
2. The other directive that the exhaustion principle has been regulated is the Rental and Lending Directive.
   - According to Article 9 of the Rental and Lending Directive, the distribution right will not be exhausted within the Community for an item, unless the initial sale of that item in the Community is carried out by the rightsholder or with their permission.
3. The other legislative act that has regulated the exhaustion is the Software Directive.
   - According to Article 4 of the Software Directive, the distribution right of a copy of a program is exhausted after the initial sale by the rightsholder or with their consent, except for the right to control further rental of the program or a copy thereof. Under this Article, upon the first sale of a computer program copy in the Community by the rightsholder or with their consent, the right to distribute the relevant computer program shall be exhausted.
4. Finally, the Database Directive has also regulated the exhaustion principle.
   - According to Article 5, the first sale in the Community of a copy of the database by the rightsholder or with his consent shall exhaust the right to control the resale of that copy within the Community.

Alongside that, the same principles have also been regulated in international treaties. Most importantly, the WCT (Article 6(2)) and the WPPT (Article 8(2)) have included the exhaustion principle[31] and ruled that the exhaustion principle will be applicable after the first sale or other transfer of ownership of the *original* or a *copy of the work.* The Agreed Statement concerning the WCT clarifies that the meaning of the 'original' and 'copies' should be understood as fixed copies that can be circulated as tangible objects.[32] Given that these WIPO legislations were drafted almost thirty

[31] WCT Article 6(2) and WPPT Article 8(2): *Nothing in this Treaty shall affect the freedom of Contracting Parties to determine the conditions, if any, under which the exhaustion of the right in paragraph (1) applies after the first sale or other transfer of ownership of the original or a copy of the work with the authorization of the author.*

[32] Agreed statements concerning the WIPO Copyright Treaty (1996) In: wipo.int < https://www.wipo.int/wipolex/en/text/295456. Concerning Articles 6 and 7: *As used in these Articles, the expressions "copies" and "original and copies", being subject to the right of distribution and the right*

years ago and these EU legislations are also from the early 2000s, some commentators[33] believed that the understanding of exhaustion should align with technological developments. Therefore, there have been questions about objects disseminated in intangible mediums, considering the significant consumption of digital products. Consequently, over the last few years, the potential application of this principle to digital products has been a subject of debate. In the following part of the study, this issue will be further explained.

4.3 The Digital Exhaustion Debate in Case Law

Perzanowski and Schultz[34] introduced the term 'digital exhaustion' in 2011 to address and question the applicability of the first sale doctrine[35] within the digital marketplace and in relation to digital works. The emergence of this issue gained prominence as the consumption of digital products increased and the digital marketplace expanded. As outlined earlier in this study, the exhaustion principle serves as an exception to the distribution right, limiting the control of rightsholders over subsequent sales of goods. Nevertheless, in the digital environment, the circulation of products, the medium used for this dissemination, the nature of the contract, and, finally, the duration of that transfer is significantly different from traditional methods. Moreover, unlike tangible copies that can deteriorate with use, digital copies remain unaffected by the passage of time and use. In contrast to tangible copies, where ownership entails relinquishing possession, the digital domain presents its own challenges in this regard. Due to these distinctions, the applicability of digital exhaustion has been a topic of extensive debate, influenced by both traditional and literal interpretations of the exhaustion principle.

In this part of the study, the main judgments made by the CJEU regarding digital exhaustion will be critically explained. Secondly, the main arguments in favour and against digital exhaustion will be covered. The critical analysis of the possible effects resulting from the application of digital exhaustion on geo-blocking will be explained in the final part of the study, along with other possible solutions for enhancing the accessibility of digital products in the EU without territorial restrictions.

---

of rental under the said Articles, refer exclusively to fixed copies that can be put into circulation as tangible objects.

[33] Mezei (2022, p. 177), Sganga (2021, p. 7).

[34] Perzanowski and Schultz (2011, p. 889).

[35] Perzanowski and Schultz (2011, p. 889).

4.3.1 *Decisions Given by the CJEU Related to Digital Exhaustion*

4.3.1.1 The UsedSoft Decision

The CJEU has been subject to numerous applications to clarify the applicability of digital exhaustion. The first judgment made by the CJEU on this topic was the UsedSoft[36] decision, which was held in 2012. Oracle was a developer of computer software and also marketed it.[37] This software was distributed by downloading from the Internet, from Oracle's website in most cases.[38] Oracle also offered group licences for a maximum of 25 users and according to the licence agreement, the user of this software can store a copy of the program on the server permanently, and this was a non-transferable and non-exclusive right.[39] UsedSoft was marketing used software licences, including Oracle's, and made Oracle's used licence available on the Internet via downloading[40] (which means there was not a physical form of this software such as CD or DVD).

Oracle brought proceedings against UsedSoft, claiming that this licence cannot be transferable and that this act by UsedSoft infringes on Oracle's exclusive right to reproduce its software.[41] German Courts decided to stay the proceedings and refer three questions to CJEU for a preliminary ruling, including the question: *'Can a person who has acquired a "used" software licence for generating a program copy as "lawful acquirer" under Article 5(1) and the first half-sentence of Article 4(2) of Directive 2009/24 also rely on exhaustion of the right to distribute the copy of the computer program made by the first acquirer with the rightholder's consent by downloading the program from the internet onto a data carrier if the first acquirer has erased his program copy or no longer uses it?'*[42] To answer that question, the Court analysed whether downloading a program from the Internet may be regarded as a 'first sale' with reference to Article 4(2) of the Software Directive.[43] In that case the Court provided the definition of the sale and according to that definition, *a 'sale' is an agreement by which a person, in return for payment, transfers to another person his rights of ownership in an item of tangible or intangible property belonging to him.*[44] According to that definition, the Court stated that those who acquire the program will have the right to use the program for an unlimited period, whether they buy it in the

---

[36] Case C-128/11 *UsedSoft GmbH v Oracle International Corp.*, [2012] OJ C 194. (hereinafter will be referred to as the UsedSoft case).

[37] The UsedSoft case, para 20.

[38] The UsedSoft case, para 21.

[39] The UsedSoft case, paras 22–23.

[40] The UsedSoft case, para 25.

[41] The UsedSoft case, para 27.

[42] The UsedSoft case, para 34.

[43] The UsedSoft case, para 38.

[44] The UsedSoft case, 42.

physical form or download it from the Internet.[45] Also, from an economic point of view,[46] the sale of computer programs via material mediums and downloading from the Internet is the same since the functionally main aim is the same, and this Directive did not distinguish between tangible and intangible forms of the copy while referring the sale of the computer program. The Court adopted a functional definition for the sale and ruled that if there is a permanent transfer and if the given fee corresponds to the value of that item, this way of circulation is economically equivalent to the sale. Notwithstanding, even though there was a teleological and functional definition for the sale, the Court used the *lex specialis* shortcut[47] and ruled that exhaustion of the distribution right under Article 4(2) of the Software Directive also covers the copy of the computer programs if the copyright holder had authorised the downloading of the copy from the Internet in the first place.[48] Therefore, the exhaustion principle will also apply to the digital sale of computer programs if they are marketed by the copyright holder or with the copyright holder's consent.

The UsedSoft decision was very significant. Not only was it the first decision to discuss digital exhaustion, but it also adopted a teleological and functional definition to solve the digital exhaustion debate. Yet, the Court used the *lex specialis* argument, and the whole discussion could not result in any substantial evaluation of digital exhaustion, and most of the questions remained the same on this subject. After this decision, the Court was subject to other preliminary requests, and more references related to digital exhaustion were made until 2019, until the very significant the Tom Kabinet case.[49]

4.3.1.2 The Art& Allposters V Stichting Pictoright Decision

The Art& Allposters v Stichting Pictoright decision[50] was also significant in this field. Pictoright is a copyright collecting society in the Netherlands which looks after the interest of foreign artists in the Netherlands, particularly by licensing and taking action in the case of infringement against copyright holders.[51] Allposters markets posters and other reproductions of the works of famous painters and offers images on canvases and to create an image on canvas, they transfer the images from posters to canvas, and to do that, firstly, the lamination process is applied to paper; then,

---

[45] The UsedSoft case, 44.

[46] The UsedSoft case, 61.

[47] Sganga (2021, p. 7). 'Lex specialis' is a Latin term, which means that more specific rules will prevail over the less specific or more general rules.

[48] The UsedSoft case, para 72.

[49] Case C-263/18 *Nederlands Uitgeversverbond and Groep Algemene Uitgevers v Tom Kabinet Internet BV and Others* [2019] OJ L 376/28. (hereinafter will be referred as the Tom Kabinet case).

[50] Case C-419/13 *Art & Allposters International BV v Stichting Pictoright* [2015] OJ C 325. (hereinafter will be referred as the Art & Allposters International BV v Stichting Pictoright case).

[51] The Art & Allposters International BV v Stichting Pictoright case, para 14.

the paper is converted to a canvas via a chemical process, followed by the canvas is stretched over a wooden frame.[52]

Pictoright brought an action against the sale of the canvas since there was no consent of the copyright holders.[53] Allposter argued that the distribution right had been exhausted on that image, therefore, there was no unlawful use.[54] The Court in the Netherlands decided to stay the proceedings and mainly asked the Court of Justice whether exhaustion could apply even though the reproduction had subsequently undergone an alteration in respect of its form and is again brought into circulation in that form.[55]

In this decision, the Court made a strictly literal approach and ruled that the transfer of that reproduction from a paper poster onto a canvas is a significant alteration of the medium, it is placed on the market again with this new form, as such, the exhaustion principle does not apply here under the Article 4(2) of the InfoSoc Directive.[56] Even though this decision is not particularly about digital exhaustion, in this decision, the Court stated that the exhaustion of the distribution right applies to tangible objects.[57]

4.3.1.3 The Ranks & Vasiļevičs Decision

The Ranks & Vasiļevičs decision[58] was also significant which gives reference to the UsedSoft judgment. Mr Ranks and Mr Vasiļevičs were charged in Latvia for selling some counterfeits of copyright-protected computer programs published by Microsoft, such as Microsoft Windows and Microsoft Office.[59] During the re-examination of this case, the Latvian Criminal Court decided to stay the proceedings and asked the Court whether the lawful acquirer of the tangible copy of the computer software could rely on exhaustion of the right to distribute a copy of that computer program if the original disk is damaged and if the first purchaser has erased his copy and no longer uses it.[60] In this decision, the court recalled the UsedSoft decision and ruled that while an original buyer of a computer program, who holds an unlimited user licence, cannot give their back-up copy to the new buyer even if the original medium containing the program has been damaged, destroyed, or lost, unless they have permission from the copyright holder.[61]

---

52 The Art & Allposters International BV v Stichting Pictoright case, para 15.

53 The Art & Allposters International BV v Stichting Pictoright case, para 16.

54 The Art & Allposters International BV v Stichting Pictoright case, para 20.

55 The Art & Allposters International BV v Stichting Pictoright case, para 21.

56 The Art & Allposters International BV v Stichting Pictoright case, para 49.

57 The Art & Allposters International BV v Stichting Pictoright case, para 40.

58 Case C-166/15 *Aleksandrs Ranks and Jurijs Vasiļevičs v Finanšu un ekonomisko noziegumu izmeklēšanas prokoratūra and Microsoft Corp.* [2016] OJ C 205. (hereinafter will be referred as the Ranks & Vasiļevičs case).

59 The Ranks & Vasiļevičs case, paras 10–13.

60 The Ranks & Vasiļevičs case, para 17.

61 The Ranks & Vasiļevičs case, paras 55–57.

4.3.1.4 The Vob & Stichting Decision

Furthermore, the Court has been asked to clarify the Rental and Lending Directive in terms of the exhaustion principle in the Vob & Stichting case.[62] Vob represents the interests of all public libraries in the Netherlands, and public libraries lend physical books and, in return, make a payment to Stichting, the foundation designated to collect loan payments.[63] The public libraries make e-books available on the internet[64] and allow a copy to be downloaded by only one person during the loan period, and after that period the copy will not be usable.[65] Also, it is not possible to lend the same book to more than one person at the same time.[66] In this case, the CJEU sought an answer to the question of whether the concept of lending include the digital copy of a book and digital lending of e-books by libraries could be evaluated within the scope of the Rental and Lending Directive.[67]

First of all, the Court stated that, the Rental and Lending Directive does not make any specification regarding whether 'copies of copyright works' also cover the digital copies of that work.[68] Yet, Agreed Statement to Articles 6 and 7 WCT limits 'copies' and 'originals' terms to tangible copies also in the case of rental, as mentioned before.[69] Furthermore, the Court made reference to Recital 4 of the Rental and Lending Directive, which states copyright protection must adapt to new economic developments, such as new forms of exploitation, and ruled that exclusion of digital lending from this Directive could be detrimental to the general principle requiring a high level of protection for the authors.[70] As such, the Court concluded that public lending of a digital copy also falls within the scope of the Rental and Lending Directive in the case the borrower downloads a digital copy of the book to their own computer from the public library servers and when the loan period expires, the borrower's access to the relevant copy disappears.[71] Although the Court has not explicitly evaluated whether e-books are subject to the principle of exhaustion, ruled that EU Law does not preclude to member states to apply exhaustion principle to digital copies.[72]

---

[62] Case C-174/15 *Vereniging Openbare. Bibliotheken v Stichting Leenrecht* [2016] OJ C 213. (hereinafter will be referred as the Vob & Stichting case).

[63] The Vob & Stichting case paras 17–18.

[64] The Ranks & Vasiļevičs case, para 24.

[65] The Ranks & Vasiļevičs case, para 27.

[66] The Ranks & Vasiļevičs case, para 27.

[67] The Ranks & Vasiļevičs case, para 26.

[68] The Ranks & Vasiļevičs case, para 28.

[69] Sganga (2021, p. 9).

[70] The Ranks & Vasiļevičs case, paras 45–46.

[71] The Ranks & Vasiļevičs case, para 54.

[72] The Ranks & Vasiļevičs case, para 65.

4.3.1.5 The Tom Kabinet Decision

After all of these judgments, the CJEU has been asked to clarify whether the right to circulation of e-books could be exhausted. The Tom Kabinet decision was very significant in terms of clarification on the applicability of digital exhaustion. Since in the UsedSoft decision, the Court used the *lex specialis* shortcut, and likewise, in other decisions, they have not discussed the conditions of digital exhaustion, the Tom Kabinet decision was the perfect opportunity for the Court to discuss the applicability of digital exhaustion.

The Tom Kabinet was a Dutch company, and it created a reading club called Tom Leesclub.[73] Tom Kabinet operated as a secondary marketplace for e-books, from where reading club members could buy second-hand e-books, which were bought either by Tom Kabinet or donated to Tom Kabinet by reading club members.[74] NUV and GAU are Dutch associations in the Netherlands for publishers, and they defend the interests of publishers in terms of copyright infringements.[75] NUV and GAU applied for an injunction against Tom Kabinet, claiming that Tom Kabinet was making an unauthorised communication of e-books to the public because they did not receive any consent from the e-books' authors.[76] When this decision was before the District Court of the Hauge, this Court stopped the proceedings and asked to clarify whether the doctrine of exhaustion also applies to digital products other than the software for a preliminary ruling.

In this decision, firstly, the CJEU needed to clarify whether making available an e-book for an unlimited period by download at a price fall within the scope of the right to distribution in the sense of Article 4(1) of the InfoSoc Directive or within the scope of communication to the public within the meaning of InfoSoc Directive Article 3(1).[77]

First of all, the Court stated that the UsedSoft v Oracle decision regarding the applicability of digital exhaustion for computer programs has its basis in the Software Directive, where the sale of the computer program via an intangible medium is accepted as a sale and for the e-book in question, there is no way to implement the same provisions of the Software Directive.[78] Contradictory, the InfoSoc Directive drew a clear line between tangible and intangible copies of works.[79]

---

[73] Tom Kabinet case, para 24.

[74] Tom Kabinet case, para 24.

[75] Tom Kabinet case, para 22.

[76] Tom Kabinet case, para 27.

[77] Tom Kabinet case, para 33.

[78] Tom Kabinet case, paras 53–54.

[79] Tom Kabinet case, para 42. Explanatory memorandum of Proposal for a European Parliament and Council Directive on the harmonization of certain aspects of copyright and related rights in the Information Society, p 22. *"At the same time, this proposal gives an opportunity to provide for a coherent level playing field for the electronic and tangible distribution of protected material and to draw a clear line between them."* It can be found at: https://aei.pitt.edu/6216/1/6216.pdf.

Secondly, the Court also stated that the sale of a computer program in a material form or sale by downloading is functionally the same.[80] Nevertheless, the Court found that the sale of a physical book and the supply of an e-book is not functionally the same since the digital copies of the books do not deteriorate with use and used copies are therefore perfect substitutes for new copies.[81] Additionally, because exchanging e-book copies does not require any additional effort, the second-hand e-book market can negatively affect the copyright holder's right in terms of fair and appropriate reward.[82]

After this assessment, the Court finally clarified whether the transfer of e-books amounts to an act within Article 3(1) of the InfoSoc Directive, which is the communication to the public.[83] The Court found out that there was an act of communication to the public because the protected work was made available to the new public, and they could have individual access from different places and at different times.[84] Furthermore, the Court also suggested that there was no technical measure to check that e-books were downloaded only by one user at a time, and the copy would not be accessible by other users and deleted from the users' computers after they sold it to the club.[85]

Therefore, the Court concluded that the act of making these e-books available to new users in such a way that the members of the public may access them from a place and at a time individually chosen by them constitutes a communication to the public and, therefore, the exhaustion principle will not be applicable.[86]

4.3.1.6 Other Referrals

Alongside all of these decisions, the CJEU has clarified that in the Nintendo case, video games are not subject to the Software Directive but subject to the InfoSoc Directive because of their complex matter.[87] Therefore, the first sale (distribution) of video games will not be subject to exhaustion. This decision has been critical for analysing the applicability of the principle of exhaustion to mixed works, especially for computer programs which include graphic user interfaces. With this decision, it has been confirmed that only works which are sole computer programs will be subject to exhaustion.

---

[80] Tom Kabinet case, para 57.

[81] Tom Kabinet case, para 58.

[82] Tom Kabinet case, para 58.

[83] Tom Kabinet case, para 65.

[84] Tom Kabinet case, para 67.

[85] Tom Kabinet case, para 67.

[86] Tom Kabinet case, para 72.

[87] Case C-355/12 *Nintendo Co. Ltd and Others v PC Box Srl and 9Net Srl* [2014] OJ C 295, para 23. (hereinafter will be referred as the Nintendo case).

Furthermore, in the European Commission v French Republic[88] decision, e-books have been considered as a service in terms of VAT regulations. That means e-books are services and cannot be subject to exhaustion. This was also confirmed in the Tom Kabinet decision, as explained above.

4.3.1.6.1 The Capitol Records, LLC v. ReDigi Decision in the USA

The Capitol Records, LLC v. ReDigi Inc. case[89] is the most important decision in the digital exhaustion subject in the US.

The Capitol Records (the plaintiff) is a company which holds copyrights or licences in sound recordings, and it distributes these recordings in digital forms or compact discs through authorised agent services such as Apple iTunes.[90] ReDigi has created a marketplace for the resale of lawfully purchased digital music files from iTunes, which has been done through the 'Music Manager' software program.[91] This program should be installed onto the user's computer (who is looking to resell the music file) and after this program is installed, the program looks and verifies whether the file was lawfully purchased from iTunes.[92] If this was lawfully purchased, it is deemed an 'eligible file', and it could be resold and the eligible file should be transferred to Redigi's remote server, known as the 'Cloud Locker'.[93] The ReDigi has developed a new method, which was called 'data migration', and in this method, the digital music files are broken into small blocks (roughly four thousand bytes in length), and after that, the system creates a 'transitory copy'.[94] After all files have been transmitted, ReDigi's software delete the copy of the music files from the initial purchaser's computer, and the eligible copy has been entirely removed from the initial user's device.[95] As such, the file will never exist in two places at the same time.[96] In 2012, the plaintiff claimed that ReDigi's acts should have been considered an act of copyright infringement since there was an unauthorised reproduction and distribution of the plaintiff's copyright-protected works.[97]

In this decision, the Court has started to discuss the applicability of the first sale doctrine in this case. The Court referred to section 109(a) of the Copyright Act, that regulates the first sale doctrine, which helps to control the further distribution of

---

[88] Case C-479/13 *European Commission v French Republic* [2015] OJ C 344, para 40. (hereinafter will be referred as the European Commission v French Republic case).

[89] Capitol Records, LLC, v. ReDigi Inc., 934 F.Supp.2d 640 (No. 16–2321) (2013). (hereinafter will be referred as the Capitol Records, LLC v. ReDigi Inc. case).

[90] The Capitol Records, LLC v. ReDigi Inc. case, p. 3.

[91] The Capitol Records, LLC v. ReDigi Inc. case, p. 4.

[92] The Capitol Records, LLC v. ReDigi Inc. case, p. 4.

[93] The Capitol Records, LLC v. ReDigi Inc. case, p. 5.

[94] The Capitol Records, LLC v. ReDigi Inc. case, p. 5.

[95] The Capitol Records, LLC v. ReDigi Inc. case, p. 6.

[96] The Capitol Records, LLC v. ReDigi Inc. case, p. 7.

[97] The Capitol Records, LLC v. ReDigi Inc. case, p. 10.

the particular copy of the work. The Court ruled that, in this case, Cloud Locker produces a new phonorecord on ReDigi's server when the user uploads their copy to this server, hence, there was no distribution of 'the particular copy' of that work.[98] As such, the new copy could not be able to benefit from the first sale doctrine.

4.4 A Critical Analysis of Digital Exhaustion

As explained above, the exhaustion principle limits the distribution right by controlling the further sale of the products after rightsholders put these on the market with their consent. Nevertheless, in the digital domain, the circulation of these digital products has differed from the circulation of tangible items. As such, the definition of the exhaustion principle, the limitations and the conditions have been scrutinised to analyse whether the current law regime is suitable for digital exhaustion.

That means, there have been numerous arguments suggested in favour and against digital exhaustion. To start with the arguments against the digital exhaustion principle, it has been suggested that there is a need to (i) clarify what the nature of this transaction is (to clarify the distinction between sale and licence), (ii) clarify the scope of goods (to explain the difference between goods and services), and finally, to (iii) explain the dichotomy between the distribution right and the communication to the public right. Another main argument is that since the distribution of a particular copy is technically impossible in the digital domain, many commentators believe that the exhaustion principle will not be applicable to this new copy (the new copy argument). Related to this, some scholars and decisions have pointed out the ease of creating new copies for digital products (ease of creating new digital copies). Also, some commentators suggested that in the UsedSoft decision, the applicability of digital exhaustion has been accepted since, in the Software Directive, there is a specific provision which allows the exhaustion of the copy of a computer program (the lex specialis argument). As a result of the Tom Kabinet judgment, some commentators also questioned the applicability of the one-user-at-a-time argument to the digital exhaustion debate (the single-user argument). In the Tom Kabinet decision, the Court also mentioned the deterioration of tangible items by use by contrast, the digital products and some scholars suggested looking at the issue from the 'reward theory' and pointed out that fair remuneration for authors should be at the centre of this debate (the deterioration and fair remuneration for authors argument).

From the other side of this debate, there are some arguments in favour of the digital exhaustion principle. First of all, as a result of the UsedSoft judgment, some commentators suggested to apply the functional equivalence understanding and suggested equal treatment argument. Related to this, since the Court has also made obiter dicta in UsedSoft decision to the applicability of the exhaustion principle as downloading the computer program from the Internet is functionally equivalent to the physical distribution of the same computer program, some commentators also

[98] The Capitol Records, LLC v. ReDigi Inc. case, p. 20.

suggested the same logic for other digital products (the functional equivalence argument) and related to this, some commentators also suggested finding a technology-neutral solution for the distribution of digital and tangible items (the equal treatment argument). Apart from that, some commentators have highlighted the potentially misleading nature of the 'buy now' button for digital products (the 'buy now' button argument). Also, some scholars have thought of a potential way to allow digital exhaustion and suggested some technological measures to follow the specific copy of that digital product, such as forward-and-delete and appointing a User-ID for each digital product (forward-and-delete and User-ID arguments). As a natural outcome of the applicability of digital exhaustion, the secondary market for digital products will rise, and some commentators have started to question the potential benefits and risks of the secondary market for digital products (the secondary market for digital product argument). Related to this, some scholars also believed that the introduction of digital exhaustion would have a positive economic impact, such as fostering competition and triggering innovation (economic arguments). Also, it has been argued that accepting digital exhaustion would enable easy access to copyright-protected products and could preserve the privacy of any further transactions on this product (enabling easy access to copyright-protected products and preserving privacy argument). Some commentators also pointed out the different interpretations of the provisions of the InfoSoc Directive regarding exhaustion, and they suggested streamlining the interpretations of provisions of the InfoSoc Directive regarding the exhaustion principle to assess the current situation of the EU Acquis better (the interpretation of the InfoSoc Directive Argument). Finally, some commentators took into account the case law of the CJEU, which accepted the superiority of the internal market within the EU compared to the copyright holders' interests and questioned the potential changes in the near future for this debate from the case law of the CJEU point of view (the superiority of the internal market argument).

All of these arguments and debates mentioned above will be critically but briefly analysed in this part of the study. The author will also mention about her view for these arguments where appropriate.

4.4.1 Arguments Against the Applicability of Digital Exhaustion

4.4.1.1 The Difference Between the Legal Nature of Transactions: The Sale vs Licence

Provided that there is no tangible medium that plays a role in the circulation of digital products, the nature of this transaction has been subject to some questions: is it a sale or a licence?[99] In international treaties and EU Directives, exhaustion has always been accepted in the case of the *sale or other transfer of ownership* of the item, as

[99] Karapapa (2020, p. 498).

already explained in this chapter. Thus, there is a need to explain what constitutes a sale or other transfer of ownership and how to call the legal transaction of the transfer of digital content.

*A **licence*** gives permission to the licensee to do specific acts which would otherwise constitute a copyright infringement, such as to communicate to the public, to perform or to reproduce the work, and in the digital domain, the rightsholders or distributors usually exploit their works by granting licences.[100] Besides, these works usually have an end-user licence agreement (EULA) or user licence, and these licences usually limit these acts to be done when there is access to those works, such as only giving permission to watch the movie, not to download or record it.[101] This practice was also confirmed by the Court in the Tom Kabinet decision by stating that the user licence of the e-book only gives permission to read the e-book from the equipment.

The definition of the ***sale*** has been described in the UsedSoft case, as mentioned in the summary of this decision, and to point out again, a sale means that 'if someone transfers to another person his rights in return for a payment of ownership in an item of tangible or intangible property belonging to him.' This definition clearly accepts the concept of the sale in the case of intangible items.

In the UsedSoft decision, as explained above, the Court adopted a functional definition and ruled that if there is a permanent transfer and if the given fee corresponds to the value of that item, this way of circulation is functionally equivalent to the sale, and considered the licence agreement between Oracle and UsedSoft as a sale. Therefore, it could be understood that if there is a one-time payment which provides fair remuneration to the author of the work and if the copy of the work is permanently transferred to the end user (like in the case of downloading), this way of legal transaction could be functionally equivalent to the sale. This explanation could be justified because of three reasons:

- (i) firstly, the case law states that IP rights do not provide the possible highest remuneration but should provide a fair remuneration for rightsholders.[102] So, if the one-time payment for this digital content corresponds to the economic value of the item, then the author would receive the appropriate reward for this creative idea.
- (ii) secondly, the exhaustion principle protects free trade as long as the rightsholder receives the reward.[103] Thus, if there is an appropriate reward, then the exhaustion principle should find its application in the context of the sale of digital products as well.

[100] Stokes (2019, p. 166).

[101] Geiregat (2022, p. 72).

[102] Geiregat (2022, p. 6).

[103] Geiregat (2022, p. 3), Mezei (2022, p. 145).

- (iii) finally, if this transfer leads to the use of these works for an indefinite period of time,[104] this usage could be excluded from the scope of the licence and considered a sale-like transaction.

In the UsedSoft decision, the court also clearly stated that[105] to be protected from the exhaustion principle, labelling the contract as a 'licence' even though it is a sale would not safeguard the subject matter from the free movement principle. As such, the labelling of the contract by the distributor or rightsholder does not provide the legal transaction of this transfer, there is a need to scrutinise the specifications of this contract to call them either sale or licence in the case of the digital content dissemination.

The present author argues that if the fee corresponds to the value of the intangible item in question by providing fair remuneration for the author of that work, and there is a permanent transfer of this work which results in indefinite use of the work, regardless of the labelling of that transaction, this transaction may be called as a sale. This functional definition could better serve the needs of the internal market by considering the recent developments and increases in the context of digital transactions. According to Recital 3 of the InfoSoc Directive, there should be a free movement of four freedoms within the internal market with respect to the law of property, freedom of expression and the public interest. Additionally, a fair balance between these interests and freedoms should be set out by reassessing the new electronic environment, as stated in Recital 31 of the InfoSoc Directive. When there is a reassessing of the new electronic development, there is no doubt that technology and digitalisation have enormously increased since the InfoSoc Directive was drafted in the early 2000s. In the light of the InfoSoc Directive, the present author also argues that, in the context of the sale, there is a need to leave the traditional understanding and give more consideration to the digital transfer of these contents. Therefore, as happens in the traditional type of sale, when there is a permanent transfer of ownership and exchange of the fee, regardless of the medium or place, this transaction may be called a sale. The same observation was also made by the CJEU in the UsedSoft judgment, and the Court accepted Oracle's licence agreement as a sale, as explained above. Accordingly, if the possibility of sale has been accepted in the context of the digital content, then, theoretically, the sale can fall under the distribution right and subject to the exhaustion principle if other conditions are met.[106]

[104] Mezei (2022, p. 145).

[105] The UsedSoft case, para 72.

[106] Mezei (2022, p. 149).

4.4.1.2 The Difference Between Goods and Services

The definition of the goods and services have not been made by the treaties, and the Court usually made its assessment on a case basis rather than providing a clear definition which could have been used in all cases.[107] Usually, the copies in physical forms have been accepted as goods, and electronic copies of the works have been assessed as services.[108] The Court usually describes 'goods' as products or objects which are in tangible forms.[109] Therefore, the distinction between goods and services is more complicated in intangible products because, until recently, the line between goods and services has been drawn as tangible products are goods, whereas intangible products are services. The E-commerce Directive,[110] with a debatable choice, accepted the online sales of goods as services.[111] Also, in the European Commission v French Republic, the Court accepted the supply of e-books as a service, as mentioned before. The Consumer Rights Directive[112] offered a hybrid definition,[113] and in Recital 19, dissemination of digital content has been described as "neither as sales contracts nor as service contracts". This development has been considered useful for accepting meta-criteria for the goods and services dichotomy, considering the high amount of consumption of digital content and online forms of commercialisation.[114]

According to Article 57 TFEU, the services are also subject to the free movement principle within the EU, where these services are normally provided for remuneration. These services could include cable and air broadcasting of TV shows, information society services or other Internet-supplied services.[115] Furthermore, the Portability Regulation[116] and the Geo-blocking Regulation[117] have been drafted to ensure that people within the EU should benefit from the free movement of services. Nevertheless, while the goods have been subject to a strict interpretation of the understanding of free movement, the free movement of services has been in a grey area so far.[118] Alongside that, the free movement of services can have some limitations with reference to copyright law, as affirmed by the Court with the Coditel and Warner Brothers judgments, which ruled that the principle of exhaustion does not find its

[107] Sganga (2021, p. 14).

[108] Karapapa (2020, p. 492).

[109] Sganga (2021, p. 14).

[110] Directive 2000/31/EC of the European Parliament and of the Council of 8 June 2000 on certain legal aspects of information society services, in particular electronic commerce, in the Internal Market [2000] OJ L 178. (hereinafter will be referred to as the E-commerce Directive).

[111] The E-commerce Directive, Recital 18.

[112] Directive 2011/83/EU of the European Parliament and of the Council of 25 October 2011 on consumer rights [2011] OJ L 304. ((hereinafter will be referred to as the Consumer Rights Directive).

[113] Sganga (2021, p. 15).

[114] Sganga (2021, p. 15).

[115] Geigerat (2021, p. 1220).

[116] Recital 1 of the Portability Regulation.

[117] Recital 1 of the Geo-blocking Regulation.

[118] Oprysk (2020, p. 174).

application in services. Related to that, the InfoSoc Directive has pointed out in Recital 29 that the question of exhaustion does not arise in the case of services and online services in particular.

The present author supports that the distinction between goods and services should not be on the basis of tangibility, and as it happened in the Consumer Rights Directive, a more pragmatic and consistent approach to the internal market and copyright law should be adopted. The critical point is that the discussion is not about the subject matter but the medium used for the dissemination of the work.[119] Therefore, if the intangible medium has been used to disseminate the digital content, labelling that as a service and excluding them to the scope of exhaustion could be detrimental to the copyright holders' rights and interests because, as a result of accepting digital exhaustion, copyright holders actually may receive further remuneration for their digital products, they could increase their revenue, they could have benefited from competition. Also, excluding services from the free movement principle could be detrimental to the internal market within the EU. Additionally, as many argued, the distinction between goods and services is not a technologically neutral approach.[120]

4.4.1.3 The Difference Between the Distribution Right and the Communication to the Public Right

As explained above, the exhaustion principle has been used to control the further distribution right of the copyright owner by limiting the monopoly of this right owner over the exploitation of this work. Thus, only the distribution right will be exhausted, whereas the right to make available to the public by communication is not subject to exhaustion. As such, drawing the line between these two rights is essential to deciding the applicability of the exhaustion principle. The definitions of the distribution right and the communication to the public right have already been made; therefore, in this part of the study, only the differences between them will be deeply explained.

The right to communicate the work to the public is traditionally accepted in the context of intangible objects.[121] On-demand transmissions, which do not entail the permanent reproduction or retention of the copy, are usually characterised as communication to the public, and this right only provides the possibility to access the work from a place and a time decided by the user and after the transmission, the user should not retain any copy of the work.[122] In the InfoSoc Directive, Article 3, this right has been defined as *including the making available to the public of their works in such a way that members of the public may access them from a place and at a time individually chosen by them* and according to Recital 23, this right *should*

---

119 Mezei (2022, p. 164).

120 Sganga (2021, p. 15).

121 Geiregat (2022, p. 5).

122 Sganga (2021, p. 12).

cover any such transmission or retransmission of a work to the public by wire or wireless means, including broadcasting.

A considerable discussion is still ongoing about the nature of communication to the public right, and scholars and Courts are trying to analyse the main questions about this issue, such as what constitutes 'communication' and how to decide a 'public'. It can be said that if there is a transmission of broadcast or Internet-based streaming of these broadcasts, showing work to some members of the public constitutes 'communication'.[123] The question of what constitutes a public has been discussed by the Court in the joined cases the FAPL v QC Leisure and Murphy v Media Protection Services case.[124] The Court ruled that if copyright-protected works were made available to the new public, the public different from that the rightsholders intended in the first place, then there is a possibility of communication to the public under Article 3(1) of the InfoSoc Directive. The Court stated that *Where a broadcast work is transmitted, in a place accessible to the public, for an additional public which is permitted by the owner of the television set to hear or see the work, an intentional intervention of that kind must be regarded as an act by which the work in question is communicated to a new public.*[125] Also, in the Svensson judgment, the Court confirmed that if there is a 'clickable link' which enables access to copyright-protected works, this act must be considered to be 'making available and act of communication to the public'.[126]

In the Tom Kabinet case, the Court ruled that the dissemination of e-books is not the act of distribution, but it constitutes a communication to the public if these works are made available to the public on the website.[127] The Court in the UsedSoft case has also considered the transfer of the ownership of a copy of a computer program as a sale, as explained above, and even though this act concluded on the Internet, the act of dissemination was accepted as a distribution.[128] This could be understood as the Court differentiated between the uses which hold a permanent copy of the work and others.[129] From this logic, it could be supported that the dissemination of music files on a permanent basis for a fixed price on the Internet could be considered an act of distribution, while on-demand streaming on a subscribed basis (such as Netflix)

---

[123] As regulated under the InfoSoc Directive, SatCab Directive, Rental and Lending Directive.

[124] Joined Cases C-403/08 and C-429/08 *Football Association Premier League Ltd and Others v QC Leisure and Others; and Karen Murphy v Media Protection Services Ltd* [2011] ECR 2011 I-09083. (hereinafter will be referred to as the FAPL and Murphy cases).

[125] The FAPL and Murphy cases, para 198.

[126] Case C-466/12 Nils Svensson, Sten Sjögren, Madelaine Sahlman, Pia Gadd v Retriever Sverige AB [2014] OJ C 379, para20. (hereinafter will be referred to as the Svensson case).

[127] The Tom Kabinet case, para65: In the present case, it is common ground that Tom Kabinet makes the works concerned available to anyone who is registered with the reading club's website, that person being able to access the site from a place and at a time individually chosen by him or her. Accordingly, the supply of such a service must be considered to be the communication of a work within the meaning of Article 3(1) of Directive 2001/29, irrespective of whether that person avails himself or herself of that opportunity by actually retrieving the e-book from that website.

[128] Mezei (2022, p. 150).

[129] Mezei (2022, p. 150).

will be labelled as communication to the public.[130] The same logic was followed by the Canadian Supreme Court in 2012 in the ESA ruling.[131] The Supreme Court of Canada pointed out that there is no difference between buying a copy of the work from the store and downloading an identical copy from the Internet[132] and ruled that downloading a video game would not constitute an act of communication to the public.

The Agreed Statement on WCT provides a definition of the distribution right, which limits the distribution right only to tangible objects, which also discussed before. Furthermore, Article 4 of the InfoSoc Directive also defines the distribution right in line with the WCT. Notwithstanding, in the UsedSoft decision, the Court only looked at the effect of the transfer[133] and ruled that if there is a transfer of the right of ownership of the copy, this act should be called a distribution, and the Court did not make any reference to tangibility and intangibility of the item.[134]

The present author argues that there is a need to update and clarify the differences between Article 3 and Article 4 of the InfoSoc Directive and the need to decide whether the dissemination of intangible objects constitutes the act of communication to the public whenever they make their works available to the public. This clarification is also important in terms of the exhaustion and the fair remuneration of the authors. In the case of distribution, when the authors put their works into the market by their consent in the first place, they are (usually) free to decide the 'appropriate' remuneration for their works and after they freely put their works to the market, now they need to accept the consequences of this transfer.[135] On the other hand, since the act of communication can repeat indefinitely (such as broadcasting or streaming movies), the author of these works can expect subsequent remuneration each time the work has been communicated to the public, and the communication to the public does not give rise to exhaustion as Court has pointed out in the Coditel and the FAPL and Murphy judgment.[136] As Sganga pointed out,[137] the Tom Kabinet was the perfect opportunity to draw a clear border between the communication to the public and the distribution right and clarify whether the distinction between these two rights is actually based on the tangibility of the item. Furthermore, in the case of downloading, when the ownership of the intangible item has been permanently transferred, and therefore, the user can retain any copy of the work, this way of transfer does not fit any of the definitions. The present author argues that, in the case of downloading, which gives the possibility of keeping the copy of the digital content permanently,

[130] Mezei (2022, p. 150).

[131] Case 33,921 *Entertainment Software Association v. Society of Composers, Authors and Music Publishers of Canada* [2012] 2 SCR 231(hereinafter will be referred to as the ESA case).

[132] The ESA case, para 5.

[133] The ESA case, para 52.

[134] Sganga (2021, p. 12).

[135] Geiregat (2022, p. 5).

[136] Geiregat (2022, p. 6).

[137] Sganga (2021, p. 14).

this way of circulation could be considered as an act of distribution rather than an act of communication to the public.

4.4.1.4 The New Copy Argument

The exhaustion principle applies to the particular copy which has been marketed by the rightsholders or with their consent in the first place, and this principle will not cover the creation of new copies from this particular copy. As such, the exhaustion principle will limit the further distribution of the exact same copy.[138] The Art & Allposters case also mentioned this limitation, in which the Court adopted a restrictive approach by saying if the work had been altered in a way and ruled that the exhaustion principle would not be applicable in different objects other than those marketed in the first place.

On the other hand, in the digital domain, the reproduction of the digital file is unavoidable in the case of file transmission[139] and, therefore, technically speaking, since there is no physical carrier involved in that transmission, the one that the rightsholders marketed on the Internet will be reproduced and a 'new copy' will be circulated after that transmission.[140] This aspect of the discussion has also been stressed by the Courts in the USA in the ReDigi judgment, where the Court ruled that since the sound recordings that have been sold were not the exact copy of the recordings marketed in the first place, the first sale doctrine will not be applicable to the new copies. Interestingly, although the same question has been referred to the CJEU for clarification in the Tom Kabinet case, the CJEU has remained silent and did not touch upon this problem. In the UsedSoft case, the Court has dealt with the issue where the used licence keys were distributed and there was no transfer of digital files in that case. Therefore, the UsedSoft decision was also compatible with the 'new copy theory'.

The present author suggests that with the help of technological advancements, this condition of the exhaustion principle could be partially met, such as forward and delete technology and ID applications, the subject of which will be explained below in the same chapter and the subtitle is 4.2.3.

4.4.1.5 The Ease of Creation of New Digital Copies Argument

One of the main arguments against digital exhaustion is that digital copies can easily be reproduced by losing zero quality,[141] and the creation of digital copies requires less energy, time, labour, and money in most cases compared to tangible copies. This statement has its own justifications in the case of accepting digital exhaustion

[138] Karapapa (2020, p. 492).

[139] Geiregat (2022, p. 68).

[140] Kaiser (2020, p. 493).

[141] Mezei (2022, p. 183).

without the help of technological measures, such as digital rights management and technological protection measures, specifically forwarding and deleting technology and the acceptance of IDs for every digital product. Under these circumstances, all copyright-protected works will be under the risk of reproducing easily compared to tangible items. To minimise that risk and to benefit from the possible outcomes of the acceptance of the digital exhaustion principle, the present author suggests technological protections against any possible reproductions of these works. It could be argued that if authors are ensured that their work will not be reproduced without notice or remuneration with the help of technological means, this argument against digital exhaustion would be rendered pointless. Furthermore, for tangible items, the exhaustion only limits the distribution right, and therefore, the user will only be able to transfer this product without reproduction since unlawful reproductions are still not permitted. This transfer also does not require extra money or effort compared to the transfer of digital products, provided that the subsequent buyer and the initial purchaser are at the same place. Therefore, unlawful copies and reproductions of these digital products would be prohibited even though the doctrine of digital exhaustion was accepted.

4.4.1.6 The Lex Specialis Argument

In the UsedSoft decision, the Court stated that the principle of exhaustion was accepted in the case of computer programs since the Software Directive includes a specific provision which regulates the principle of exhaustion in the context of computer programs. Although the Court had made a teleological interpretation of the context of the sale and licence dichotomy, this analysis has been weakened by relying on the lex specialis argument, according to many scholars. According to Sganga,[142] the main aim of the WCT was not to distinguish between the different subject matter of copyright-protected works; this Treaty only requires the extension of the copyright protection to the software and databases with the Software Directive. Therefore, the Software Directive should not have to create a specific provision for the computer program in the case of digital exhaustion because there was no evidence that, at that time, the market for computer programs needed to have specific measures for exhaustion in 1991.[143] Furthermore, Mezei[144] claimed that the argument that the Software Directive is lex specialis because this Directive has special provisions different from those of WCT is misleading. He stressed that the WCT had been accepted in 1996, and all of the new provisions were adopted by the InfoSoc Directive in 2001; therefore, the InfoSoc Directive includes all of the provisions regarding the general exhaustion principle.

142 Sganga (2021, p. 18).
143 Sganga (2021, p. 18).
144 Mezei (2022, p. 12).

This present author also agrees with these opinions because there is no evidence to prove that computer programs should have different provisions regarding the exhaustion principle. Also, as Mezei suggested, the InfoSoc Directive aimed to regulate WCT's provisions,[145] therefore, the InfoSoc Directive do not differentiate between different subject matters. In the case where this provision does not exist, probably the Court in the UsedSoft judgment would reach the same argument because (i) the legal nature of this transaction has been found as functionally equivalent to the sale, and (ii) there was only circulation of the licence key, there was no new copy of digital products. Therefore, this present author also agrees that relying on the lex specialis argument has weakened the teleological interpretation of the exhaustion principle.

4.4.1.7 The Single-User Argument

The other argument against digital exhaustion is that the owner of this copy needs to give up their possession of a tangible copy; therefore, the copyright holder could be sure that their work is only possessed by one person at a time.[146] Considering the easement of reproducing the new exact same digital copy, the copyright holder may not be sure that (i) the copy of the digital content is only possessed once and (ii) the digital object that is circulated is the exact same copy of the work that the author puts into circulation in the first place. The same observation has also been made in the Tom Kabinet case, where the Court pointed out that there is no guarantee for the authors that their works have been accessible by one user at one time. The main counter-argument against this could be the application of technological protection measures, where the copy of the work can be tracked. This could be thanks to forward-and-delete technology and the application of the Unique ID model for each product. This will be explained later in this chapter in the subtitle 4.2.3.

4.4.1.8 The Deterioration of Tangible Items and Fair Remuneration for Author's Arguments

Tangible objects are subject to wear and tear by use and can deteriorate over time,[147] therefore, the creation of a secondary market for tangible objects has been justified without any questions. Because, in that way, the objects which are already used and lost their quality and marketability when they were first marketed can be sold for a lower price. On the other hand, digital works do not deteriorate by use and do not lose their value or quality over time. Therefore, it is argued that the secondary market for digital products which have not lost their quality by use or with time could have some

[145] Recital 15 of the WCT.

[146] Sganga (2021, p. 2).

[147] Sganga (2021, p. 2).

negative consequences for the copyright holder because they may not be entitled to appropriate remuneration for their work.[148]

So far, with technological advancements, there have been some attempts to adopt a technology which helps the deterioration of digital files over time. For example, IBM had a patent on the 'Aging File System', which gives digital data the opportunity to age by use as normal paper.[149]

This argument is a very strong argument against the applicability of digital exhaustion. As explained above, in the Tom Kabinet decision, the Court stressed this as well. On the other hand, so far two counter-arguments have been expressed against this.

First of all, in terms of fair remuneration concern, when the copyright owner makes available their work by putting the market in the first place, they can also decide on a 'fair price' for their work to let the users download this content. Furthermore, the distributors or information society services ask different prices for the 'rent' and 'buy' options of digital content. In most cases, the rent option only gives limited-time access to that content; the buy option gives permanent access to this content.

For example, Paramount + is asking for $6.99 to buy the Titanic movie (which gives permanent access to that movie), while the same platform is asking for $3.99 for the rental option (which only allows watching the video within 48 h once it is stream in the 30 days of the payment) as of November 2023. Furthermore, the DVD version of the Titanic movie is also advertised as £6.99 on Amazon UK as of November 2023.This may be understood from this example, although users paid almost the same amount for the DVD version and downloading version of the Titanic where both users can keep the permanent copy of the work, the users are free to sell the used version of this DVD and other users are not allowed to sell the Paramount + versions of their copy. This example could show that when the amount that has been paid for the downloaded version of the Titanic movie has been almost the same as the DVD version, where the author decided 'fair remuneration' for this tangible copy, therefore, 'fair remuneration' argument will not be valid and will prove otherwise. In terms of justification for the exhaustion principle with reward theory, the exhaustion principle will be applicable when authors freely decide on fair and adequate remuneration for their works and after they decide when and how they are going to market their works.[150] In that case, if the value freely decided by the author for the digital product is (almost) the same as the tangible versions, then this argument would not be considered convincing. Some commentators suggested that if reward theory had been accepted in traditional copyright case law so far, the same theory could also be a valid argument in digital copyright case law as well.[151] Furthermore, it may be suggested that if a consumer buys the DVD version of the Titanic movie, this DVD could be broken or scratched, but the quality of the movie most of the time will not be affected, other than these mediums have been unusable. This is the same for video games and computer programs when they are also sold

[148] Sganga (2021, p. 2).

[149] Sganga (2021, p. 2).

[150] Geiregat (2022, p. 2).

[151] Mezei (2022, p. 146).

in tangible objects such as CDs. Therefore, if traditional copyright law accepts the exhaustion of the distribution rights for these objects, the non-deterioration of the digital products argument will lose its points.

Secondly, the present author would like to express her disagreement with the argument suggesting that digital products never lose their marketability over time. Especially for computer programs, it is possible to argue the opposite. For example, the file that allows the installation of Windows 95 does not have the same marketability, interest from customers, or value as it had during the early 2000s.[152] Furthermore, the movies, songs, e-books, and video games, which were marketed quite a long time ago, will most probably not have the same marketability, interests, and value over time. For example, Grand Theft Auto V (a very popular video game) was marketed for approximately $60 when it was first released in 2013,[153] while a few years later, the same video game was distributed for free to download through Epic Games' internet platform.[154] Therefore, it could be argued that digital products would easily lose their value, marketability and interest from society, and these products could be sold for lower prices than their initial prices. Overall, if the reward theory has been accepted and used for the remuneration of the authors for their works, then there is no point in limiting the same theory in the digital domain as long as authors are fairly remunerated.[155]

4.4.2 *Arguments in Favour of the Applicability of Digital Exhaustion*

4.4.2.1 The Functional Equivalence and Equal Treatment Arguments

The functional equivalence argument has been suggested in the UsedSoft judgment by the Court, which pointed out that the sale of computer programs via material mediums and downloading from the Internet is functionally the same since the outcome of these transactions is the same.

In UsedSoft judgment, the Court pointed out that in paragraph 61:

> It should be added that, from an economic point of view, the sale of a computer program on CD-ROM or DVD and the sale of a program by downloading from the internet are similar. The on-line transmission method is the functional equivalent of the supply of a material

---

152 Mezei (2022, p. 184).

153 Marc Graser, 'Grand Theft Auto V' Earns $800 Million in a Day, More than Worldwide Haul of 'Man of Steel'' (Variety, 18 September 2013) < https://variety.com/2013/digital/news/grand-theft-auto-v-earns-800-million-in-a-day-more-than-worldwide-haul-of-man-of-steel-1200616706/.

154 Rockstargames, 'GTAV: Premium Edition Available Free on the Epic Games Store Until May 21st' (14 May 2020) < https://www.rockstargames.com/newswire/article/o349k55255a257/GTAV-Premium-Edition-Available-Free-on-the-Epic-Games-Store-Until-May-.

155 Peter Mezei, 'Meet the unavoidable – the challenges of digital second-hand marketplaces to the doctrine of exhaustion' in Taina Pihlajarinne and others (eds) *Online Distribution of Content in the EU* (Edward Elgar Publishing (2019), p. 9).

> medium. Interpreting Article 4(2) of Directive 2009/24 in the light of the principle of equal treatment confirms that the exhaustion of the distribution right under that provision takes effect after the first sale in the European Union of a copy of a computer program by the copyright holder or with his consent, regardless of whether the sale relates to a tangible or an intangible copy of the program.

This observation from the Court has created some question marks. First of all, it has been argued that this interpretation of the Court has been reflected as broader than what the Court actually aimed for.[156] The second paragraph could easily be understood to mean that digital exhaustion should be accepted as a result of the equal treatment principle, although the Court did not accept the same logic after the UsedSoft judgment, especially in the Tom Kabinet decision.[157] Some commentators interpreted this Paragraph by saying the Court only limited this observation to the computer programs and excluded other digital files such as audiobooks and music.[158]

Related to this argument, also an important question could be asked: if downloading is the functional equivalent of the supply of a material medium, then why should the online and offline markets be treated differently?[159] This question is also a result of the expectation of the principle of equal treatment. Some scholars argued that there is a need to find a technology-neutral solution and apply the equal treatment principle to the digital exhaustion case.[160] This has been found necessary by the Court[161] to keep the right balance between copyright and technological advancements. The author of this study also suggests reducing, if not removing, differences in the applicability of copyright law practices between online and offline markets. Also, this author strongly agrees with the decision from the Canadian Supreme Court (the ESA case), which pointed out that there was no practical difference between buying a tangible object from the store and downloading the same object from the Internet. Since the CJEU has also accepted (for now limited to computer programs) the functional equivalence theory, it could be assumed that in the near future, if the economic value of the same products is equivalent to the tangible version and there is a permanent transaction, the same functional equivalent would be applicable for all digital

---

[156] Linklater (2014, p. 18).

[157] Linklater (2014, p. 18).

[158] Mezei (2022, p. 164).

[159] Linklater (2014, p. 17).

[160] Mezei and Sganga (2024, p. 149).

[161] Case C-433/20 *Austro-Mechana Gesellschaft zur Wahrnehmung mechanisch-musikalischer Urheberrechte Gesellschaft mbH v Strato AG* [2022] OJ C 414. Paragraph 26 and 27 states that '*In that regard, the Court has already pointed out, in the light of the mandatory exception referred to in Article 5(1) of Directive 2001/29, that the exemption provided for in that provision must allow and ensure the development and operation of new technologies, and must safeguard a fair balance between the rights and interests of rightholders and of users of protected works who wish to avail themselves of those technologies. Such an interpretation, which is consistent with the principle of technological neutrality, according to which the law must specify the rights and obligations of persons in a generic manner, so as not to favour the use of one technology to the detriment of another (see, to that effect, judgment of 15 April 2021, Eutelsat, C-515/19, EU:C:2021:273, paragraph 48), must also be accepted with regard to the optional exception referred to in Article 5(2)(b) of Directive 2011/29, as the Advocate General observed, in essence, in point 36 of his Opinion.*'

products. This acceptance could also be a technology-neutral solution, which helps the main aims of the copyright law within the EU, especially considering the Austro Mechana case and the mentioned Recital 31 of the InfoSoc Directive.

4.4.2.2 The 'Buy Now' Button Argument

As explained in the Titanic example above, some information society services are advertising their digital products by putting a 'buy now' button. For example, Amazon is advertising their Kindle Books via read now and buy now options. The 'read now' option is for Kindle Unlimited subscribers who pay monthly subscription fees, and the 'buy now' option is for every Kindle user, which gives permanent access to this book via the Kindle platform.

YouTube also advertises some movies and TV series, and like Paramount + does, it has rent and buy options. The rent option only provides 30 days of access, and when the movie or TV series starts within that time frame, the user only has 48 h to stream it. The buy option also gives access indefinitely via the YouTube program.

Some commentators believe that if users are presented with these options, they may think that the 'buy now' option actually stands for the sale of the content and that the user can have the same options with the tangible products that they usually buy.[162] To prove this point and to understand the expectations of the consumers regarding the buy now button, an empirical MediaShop study has been conducted by Perzanowski, and the results showed the same observation. Furthermore, Mezei also suggested that consumers can interpret the meanings of the contract more favourably.[163]

Notwithstanding, it could be easily arguable that the EULA or user licences usually consist of lots of information, and people who want to access these contents do not read these licences to learn their permitted activity. To prove this point, there is a study conducted by Ober and Oeldorf,[164] they created a fake social networking website, and in the licence agreement, for payment, they included this term[165] 'for exchange for service, all users of this site agree to assign their first-born child to NameDrop, Inc immediately'. Out of 543 participants, only 9 of them realised and informed the licensee about this clause, which means 98.3% of participants were not aware of this clause.[166] This study showed that most people actually do not read the terms and conditions written in the licence agreement. Therefore, some commentators supported that even though the licence agreement does not allow some activities, overall users may not be aware of this situation and could assume that they have any right to do the same activities (such as resale or rent) that they can do with tangible objects even they received these products in the intangible medium.

[162] Mezei (2022, p. 180).

[163] Mezei (2022, p. 180).

[164] Obar Oeldorf-Hirsch (2018, p. 128).

[165] Obar Oeldorf-Hirsch (2018, p. 40).

[166] Obar Oeldorf-Hirsch (2018, p. 44).

Yet, the present author does not support this argument, which has been stipulated in favour of digital exhaustion. Although the author strongly agrees with the conclusion of these surveys and accepts the misleading nature of the 'buy now' button, she believes that licence agreements for these products should have been read by the end-users and any restricted activity should not be done under the *ignorantia juris non excusat*[167] principle. The general behaviour of the consumers is not strong evidence to prove the necessity of the acceptation of the digital exhaustion principle.

4.4.2.3 The Forward-and-Delete and Unique-ID Arguments

To overcome opinions against digital exhaustion, one of the main solutions that supporters of digital exhaustion are to ask for the help of technological advancements. The main suggestion is to apply forward-and-delete technology to track each copy of the copyright-protected works.[168] Some commentators suggested that technological advancements could help copyright owners ensure that their work does not get reproduced illegally in the digital domain. Apple and Amazon already had some initiatives on the resale of digital content; for example, both of them had patents on techniques which allow the user to transfer their digital file, and after that transfer, the user would not have the opportunity to access this content any more.[169] Kindle could be another example to prove this point because Amazon has the ability to delete and make unavailable some books from the user's account.

The author of this study suggests that technological advancements could help overcome this negative effect and help the resale of digital content. Therefore, the solution could be to adopt the 'forward-and-delete' approach in the case of downloading by providing a unique ID number for each digital content, as Mezei[170] and Karapapa[171] also suggested. Implementation of technological protection measures and digital rights management for copyright-protected work to avoid illegal copies and to ease tracking each work disseminated online would really solve the question of digital exhaustion and could help copyright owners to ensure that:

- Their work is not reproduced illegally.
- Their work is only accessible by one user at a time.
- They could track the copy of the work, which could help them to collect royalties.

---

[167] The Latin way of saying: Ignorance of the law could not be accepted as an excuse.

[168] Mezei (2022, p. 157), Karapapa (2020, p. 497).

[169] Mezei (2022, p. 159).

[170] Mezei (2022, p. 158 and 191).

[171] Karapapa (2020, p. 497).

4.4.2.4 The Need for a Secondary Market for Digital Products and Potential Economic Benefits Arguments

Allowing the applicability of digital exhaustion would naturally result in the creation of a secondary market for digital products. Therefore, the potential results of this digital secondary market have been evaluated by the commentators. The creation of a secondary market for digital products could only be possible when the user receives a permanent copy of the work and would like to resell it. Therefore, the discussion on potential outcomes of the creation of a digital secondary market will only be explained in the case where the end-user obtained the digital file permanently without the tangible medium. Transferring contractual relationships which give the right of temporary access to digital products (such as subscriptions to streaming services) will not be discussed here since the temporary access does not raise the exhaustion problem.

First of all, it has been suggested that the digital secondary market could have a negative impact on streaming platforms if the downloaded products (such as music files or movies) were available in the secondary market for indefinite use.[172] This present author does not agree with that opinion because, for example, Netflix has over 13,000 content[173] as of August 2023, and it should be cheaper to access all of these products with a monthly subscription fee (as of January 2024, the cheapest subscription fee for Netflix is £5.99 for the advertised version in the UK) unless the end-user wants to have indefinite access for only one content. Furthermore, one of the main reasons that Netflix was successful in the first place was to accept the exhaustion doctrine, where these streaming channels relied on the exhaustion doctrine and did not seek any approval from movie studios.[174]

Secondly, some argued that the prices of digital products would increase if the possibility of resale of these products were permitted.[175] However, as a counter-argument, it would be suggested that even though higher prices are set, the willingness to buy these products would increase for the initial purchaser since the first user would have the option to resell these products.[176]

Additionally, some scholars have mentioned the possibility of negative consequences for distributors or rightsholders, such as the elimination of price differences between different markets.[177] As explained in Chapter 1, price differentiation is a widely used tool by rightsholders, distributors, or traders to maximise profit from this fragmentation and better serve the affordability of different markets. In the Geo-blocking Regulation, price differentiation activity between different Member States has been found justified as long as it does not discriminate on the basis of nationality

---

[172] Stevens (2016, p. 189).

[173] How much is Netflix (2023). In Littlebirdie, https://www.littlebirdie.co.uk/post/how-much-is-netflix-uk.

[174] Karapapa (2020, p. 489).

[175] Mezei (2022, p. 178).

[176] Kerber (2016, p. 156).

[177] Kerber (2016, p. 158).

or place of establishment. Therefore, not accepting the digital exhaustion principle actually helps these actors to discriminate prices between different markets. This argument is hard to prove or disprove. On the one side, the acceptance of digital exhaustion could really have a negative impact on rightsholders, distributors, or traders, especially in some Member States where they market their products higher prices than other Member States.[178] On the other side of the point, this secondary market would actually increase the affordability of users from lower-income countries and could have an increase in revenue.[179] This dilemma could only be solved by empirical economic research that potentially takes into account all aspects of this change. The present author also supports and strongly advises conducting this empirical economic research and having a dialogue with different stakeholders.

It could also be argued that the creation of a secondary digital market would be beneficial to combat piracy in the digital domain.[180] Some studies have shown that the availability of e-books at a lower price has actually reduced the illegal activities to access these products. Therefore, it could be easily suggested that if the availability exist, some people are actually ready to pay and legally access these products. Also, as Mezei[181] suggested, the availability of used digital products for an affordable price would actually attract users' attention, and they could buy these products legally.

Finally, some economic benefits of the secondary markets have been suggested by scholars.[182] As explained at the beginning of the exhaustion part, the rationale behind the exhaustion principle was to ensure the availability and affordability of copyright-protected works as well as to foster competition and facilitate innovation. Acceptance of the secondary market for digital products could help to foster competition for digital products. In the current situation, for digital products, only first-hand sales are permitted, and there is no secondary market; if there were a secondary market, the competition in that area would be higher, and the prices may be positively affected. Also, from the secondary marketplaces and distributors' point of view, they may have incentives to innovate because they would have more opportunities to recoup the investment that they had.

4.4.2.5 Enabling Easy Access to Copyright-Protected Products and Preserving Privacy Arguments

It could be argued that the acceptance of the digital exhaustion principle would be beneficial in terms of enabling easy access to copyright-protected products, especially with the help of the creation of a secondary market for digital products.[183] This could be even more important for digital products which are out of commerce or for orphan

[178] Kerber (2016, p. 158).

[179] Kerber (2016, p. 158).

[180] Mezei (2022, p. 188).

[181] Mezei, (2015, p. 55).

[182] Mezei (2022, p. 188), Sganga (2021, p.19), Karapapa (2020, p. 488), Kerber (2016, p. 6).

[183] Sganga (2021, p. 20).

works.[184] Digital exhaustion could really help to reduce the monopoly of the author's power to control the dissemination of their digital products after they first marketed them. The possibility of resale them could enable easy access to copyright-protected works because the availability of these products will be increased.

Furthermore, it is also suggested that the privacy of the subsequent buyers would be protected if digital exhaustion is accepted.[185] In the absence of digital exhaustion, the buyers could be profiled and tracked as a result of every buying, and this would result in controlling consumers' behaviours.[186] Therefore, it could be suggested that if the rightsholders or distributors cannot see and track the consumption of these products, it would have a positive impact on privacy. On the other hand, this author also wants to highlight the contradiction between the forward-and-delete and unique-ID numbers argument and this privacy argument. The forward-and-delete and unique-ID numbers argument has been suggested to track every transaction so that the rightsholders can ensure that their work does not get reproduced and is accessible by one user at a time. As a natural result of this technology, the subsequent buyers will be identifiable, and every transaction will become trackable. Therefore, the present author does not agree with the privacy statement since the forward-and-delete technology could be a good tool to allow digital exhaustion, but it does not guarantee privacy and, indeed, could be criticised against privacy concerns.

4.4.2.6 Streamlining the Interpretations of Provisions of the InfoSoc Directive Regarding the Exhaustion Principle Argument

Sganga[187] has pointed out that the methods of interpretation of Article 4(1) of the InfoSoc Directive, which regulates the right of distribution, and Article 4(2) of the InfoSoc Directive, which regulates the exhaustion principle, have differed historically. She suggests that Article 4(1) has been subject to flexible and teleological interpretation by the Courts, while Article 4(2) is strictly interpreted by a literal approach.

The teleological interpretation method is the main method[188] that the CJEU uses in its judgments; while deciding on cases, it takes into account the main aims of the treaties and needs of the EU Law and rules accordingly. On the other hand, in the Tom Kabinet decision especially, it could be easily arguable that the Court only made a strictly literal interpretation, even though the Court should have used a teleological interpretation. From the teleological interpretation perspective, taking into account Recitals 3 and 31 of the InfoSoc Directive, this approach would be more consistent

[184] Sganga (2021, p. 20).

[185] Mezei (2022, p. 167).

[186] Sganga (2021, p. 20).

[187] Sganga (2021, p. 17).

[188] European Parliament Briefing (2017) The EU as a community of law Overview of the role of law in the Union, https://www.europarl.europa.eu/RegData/etudes/BRIE/2017/599364/EPRS_BRI(2017)599364_EN.pdf.

with the EU's aims and striking the correct balance between the internal market, copyright holders and the needs of the public and especially end users, the result of the Tom Kabinet case would be different.

4.4.2.7 The Superiority of the Internal Market Within the EU Argument

In the EU, the traditional approach for balancing rights was usually decided in favour of the supremacy of the internal market over the copyright holders' interest, as confirmed by the Membran and the Patricia cases. Therefore, the CJEU, in the context of copyright law, actually does not use an end-user-centred approach or do not rule in favour of supremacy of the copyright holders' interests. This would mean that, in its decisions, with the help of the teleological interpretation method and recitals of the InfoSoc Directive, the EU is trying to preserve the internal market within the EU and considering the increase in digital transactions and the trend in digital consumption, the principle of digital exhaustion would find applicability within the EU in the very near future.

On the other hand, recently, the European Court of Human Rights (ECtHR) ruled in Safarov v Azerbaijan.[189] In that case, the applicant is the author of a book related to the ethnicity of Irali, and he published his book in 2009. In 2010, an NGO (non-governmental organisation) called Irali Public Union made an electronic version of this book available on their website, and this book has been downloaded more than 400 times. The author went to court to claim his damages since he did not receive any royalties, and this NGO did not seek any permission prior to making available their work in the digital format. The Azerbaijani Court rejected this claim, given that the main aim of this NGO was to provide information related to the history of Azerbaijan; therefore, the court ruled that this NGO could benefit from the library exception in Azerbaijani Law. The author made the claim before the ECtHR, and the Court ruled that the domestic court failed to provide legal reasoning in terms of the applicability of this exception in the present case therefore, the State failed to obey its positive obligations to protect the copyright of the citizens by violating Article 1 of Protocol No 1 of the ECHR. With this judgment, the ECtHR confirmed that intellectual property rights are within the scope of Article 1 of Protocol No. 1, which regulates the right to peaceful enjoyment of possession, and accordingly, countries have a positive obligation to take appropriate measures to protect the right to property, including intellectual property.[190] Furthermore, in this judgment, the Court also ruled that exhaustion only occurs by sale as tangible objects.[191]

Accepting the digital exhaustion doctrine would actually be regarded as contrary to that argument since this judgment clearly limits the exhaustion principle with tangible objects. Nevertheless, this approach is understandable since this Court only tried to

---

[189] *Safarov v. Azerbaijan* (2012) 885 EHRR 12.

[190] Geigerat (2023, p. 204).

[191] *Safarov v. Azerbaijan* (2012) 885 EHRR 12, para 35.

analyse and interpret the existing legislation and made a literal and strict interpretation regarding the applicability of the exhaustion principle. The present author strongly suggests that there is a need to adopt a teleological and functional interpretation approach which would serve the needs of all parties better. Furthermore, traditionally, the CJEU also adopts a teleological approach. Therefore, there is no need to depart from this understanding on the subject of digital exhaustion for the CJEU.

4.4.3 How to Solve This Debate: A Balanced Approach to Digital Exhaustion

Since 2011, with Perzanowski and Schultz's article regarding this subject, the debate on digital exhaustion has become a very interesting topic to discuss, and especially after the UsedSoft judgment in the EU, the applicability of this principle in the digital domain has subjected lots of discussions. As explained above, in the UsedSoft judgment, the Court pointed out that the transfer of the licence keys to download used computer programs permanently in exchange for money is functionally and economically equivalent to the sale. This observation creates some questions about other types of digital products; for example, if licence keys for video games are transferred, would the Court make the same observation? Furthermore, if the same transactions which do not require the transfer of the file (to avoid reproductions and new copies) would be done for other copyright-protected products, such as accessing the same products via clouds or transfer of user ID/e-mails and passwords, would these transfers be functionally and economically equivalent to the sale? The present author thinks that the answer should be 'yes'. To answer this question without any hesitation, the author suggests changing copyright legislation to regulate these areas, especially in the InfoSoc Directive as Sganga also suggested.[192]

Apart from all the debates, the most important thing, according to the author of this study, is to find an appropriate balance between different stakeholders in that question: copyright owners and other rightsholders, distributors, traders, end-users, the internal market and finally, the society. The interests of the copyright owners are really significant to consider in this debate since, as a result of accepting digital exhaustion, the rightsholders' exclusive rights will have some boundaries.[193] On the other hand, the reasonable expectations of the end-users and society should be met. As explained at the beginning of this Chapter, the principle of exhaustion is indeed a valuable tool to guarantee access and affordability of protected works, foster competition, and facilitate innovation; the same arguments could also be suggested in the context of digital exhaustion by the rising secondary market for digital contents as well.[194] The creation of a secondary market for used digital products would provide cheaper access to the product, and this activity could ensure that low-budget end-users

---

192 Sganga (2021, p. 28).

193 Oprysk (2020, p. 176).

194 Sganga (2021, p. 19).

will also have the same access to digital products. If the secondary market opens, the prices would be expected to be more competitive for the first-hand digital products to attract consumers to buy them instead of the already-used products. This market would be beneficial for society and end users, and since there is a free movement of goods and services, the internal market within the EU could also benefit from this application. The new market could also be beneficial for the distributors and traders because the market could have more potential to make more profit over the further exploitation of these works. Nevertheless, to understand the outcome of this extension, there is a need to set out the results of comprehensive empirical economic research.

From the copyright holders' and rightsholders' perspective, if the forward-and-delete and the unique ID numbers options for each digital product were enabled, these rightsholders may also be offered royalties over the further exploitation of their works. Furthermore, the availability of digital products for more affordable prices would decrease piracy and illegal copies of these works, and this would also serve the rightsholders' interests.

The exhaustion principle was accepted in the 1970s when the needs of the market and the expectations of end-users were really different at that time. To meet reasonable expectations in the context of the dissemination of the works online, the present author firmly suggests the application of digital exhaustion and suggests the legislative changes in the InfoSoc Directive and other related instruments (i) to clear the line between the sale and licence, (ii) to provide clear and up-to-date definitions for goods and services, (iii) to find a meta-criteria for contents disseminated online which provides permanent access and finally (iv) offer the technological protection measures for the contents which are subject to resale by accepting forward-and-delete by providing a unique ID number for each digital product. Furthermore, blockchain technology would also be a very strong tool to track and identify each copy of digital products because every transaction is recorded on that platform; therefore, in the future, the blockchain could be a very useful tool for copyright-protected works.[195] More information on the blockchain technology will be provided in the final chapter of this study. Nevertheless, considering the very low understanding of the use of blockchain today, suggesting blockchain technology to access all of the copyright-protected products would not be an end-user-centred solution for this debate. Therefore, the present author accepts and strongly agrees with all of the positive and potential outcomes of blockchain technology; nevertheless, she believes that it is still early to provide a solution solely based on blockchain technology in this debate.

The author also strongly believes that the rise of the secondary market for digital products would be beneficial for end-users and society, which would easily provide more products with lower prices, and it could be even more beneficial for rightsholders provided that the author of the digital product could also receive further remuneration, such as by collecting royalties for each work disseminated again.

[195] Mezei (2022, p. 188).

Furthermore, it should be noted that the exhaustion principle should not contradict the general exhaustion principles of the given countries and territorial scope.

However, with the Safarov v Azerbaijan decision in 2022, there could be an expectation from the CJEU to prioritise the copyright holders' interests as part of the property right. In the very near future, it may be expected that the CJEU will provide a ruling in the context of exhaustion, and there is a possibility that the CJEU will follow this trend. On the other hand, as stated above, the author of this study believes that the ECtHR made a strictly literal interpretation in the Safarov v Azerbaijan. However, the CJEU use the teleological interpretation method. If the CJEU continue to make teleological interpretations, with reference to the Recitals of the InfoSoc Directive, the different outcomes that could be expected from the CJEU, especially the interpretation in favour of the technological advancements, the outcome of this interpretation could be in favour of accepting digital exhaustion.

Finally, from the perspective of geo-blocking practice, it is the first time suggested that the acceptance of digital exhaustion could solve the geo-blocking debate in the case of the permanent transfer of digital products in exchange for the given value of the digital product. If these products were subject to digital exhaustion after the first transfer of these products, the rightsholders would not be able to control the further dissemination of these products, and there would not be any fragmented markets where rightsholders price discriminate. Therefore, there would not be any need to implement the geo-blocking practice for these products.

However, accepting digital exhaustion would only address the issue of geo-blocking for digital products that are downloaded or owned on a permanent basis. This is because, if digital exhaustion were to be established, there would be no need to apply geo-blocking measures. Once the copyright holders exercise their exclusive right to distribute the content, their distribution rights would be exhausted, and they would no longer have the option to impose any further restrictions on the content's distribution. While the author believes that digital exhaustion could resolve the geo-blocking issue for these products, it would only provide a partial solution for content that is distributed but not communicated to the public. Therefore, the examination of digital exhaustion was necessary to offer a solution for products acquired on a permanent basis. However, digital exhaustion will not be a broad solution for access to copyright-protected digital products unless the EU accepts the digital exhaustion principle for works that are communicated to the public. This seems very unlikely after the Tom Kabinet decision.

4.5 Conclusion

The exhaustion principle is a valid response to the territoriality principle of copyright law. With the help of exhaustion, the absolute monopoly over the work can be prohibited and the rightsholders can no longer control, resale, import, or export these goods once they put the market by their consent. Furthermore, the exhaustion principle creates a good balance between the needs of the society and rightsholders.

With the help of the exhaustion principle, the availability and affordability of the products increase, while there is also an incentive for the rightsholders to innovate. The traditional understanding of the exhaustion principle is well established with the help of the decision made by the CJEU and the legislation created by the EU bodies.

On the other hand, digital exhaustion is a non-exhausted debate[196] for now and both sides of this debate have very distinct yet understandable arguments. Especially after the UsedSoft decision, the CJEU found itself at the centre of this debate, and were subject to numerous preliminary requests to clear some aspects of this debate. Nevertheless, although the UsedSoft decision was very interesting and thought-provoking, other decisions, especially Tom Kabinet, resulted from a strictly literal interpretation, which closes the door to the development of digital exhaustion in the EU, at least for now. This decision pointed out that the circulation of e-books constitutes communication to the public and is not subject to the exhaustion principle.

For the geo-blocking problem, acceptance of digital exhaustion could solve the geo-blocking issue for products distributed and acquired on a permanent basis. On the other hand, since digital products are usually acquired on a temporary basis and through communication to the public, acceptance of digital exhaustion would not solve the geo-blocking problem as a whole.

References

Aplin T, Davis J (2021) Intellectual property law, 4th edn. Oxford University Press, Oxford

Bently L et al (2022) Intellectual property law, 6th edn. Oxford University Press, Oxford

Geiregat S (2022) Supplying and reselling digital content. Edward Elgar Publishing, Cheltenham

Geiregat S (2023) A state's positive obligation on the protection of intellectual property rights. GRUR Int 72:199–206

Kaiser A (2020) Exhaustion, distribution and communication to the public: the CJEU's decision C-263/18—Tom Kabinet on e-books and beyond. GRUR Int 69:489–495

Karapapa S (2020) Exhaustion of rights on digital content under EU copyright: positive and normative perspectives. In: Aplin T (ed) Research handbook on intellectual property and digital technologies. Edward Elgar Publishing, Cheltenham, pp 483–505

Linklater E (2014) UsedSoft and the Big Bang Theory: is the e-exhaustion meteor about to strike? JIPITEC 5:12–22

Mezei P (2015) Digital first sale doctrine ante portas: exhaustion in the online environment. JIPITEC 6:23–71

Mezei P (2022) Copyright exhaustion, 2nd edn. Cambridge University Press, Cambridge

Mezei P, Sganga C (2024) The need for a more balanced policy approach for digital exhaustion. In: Mezei P et al (eds) Harmonizing intellectual property law for a trans-Atlantic knowledge economy. Brill, Leiden, pp 133–153

Obar JA, Oeldorf-Hirsch A (2018) The biggest lie on the Internet: ignoring the privacy policies and terms of service policies of social networking services. Inf Commun Soc 23(1):128–147

Perzanowski A, Schultz J (2011) Digital exhaustion. UCLA Law Rev 58:889–946

Sganga C (2021) Digital exhaustion after Tom Kabinet: a non-exhausted debate. In: Synodinou T et al (eds) EU internet law in the digital single market. Springer, Cham, pp 141–176

[196] This phrase is used thanks to the Caterina Sganga's Book Chapter's name 'Digital exhaustion after Tom Kabinet: a non-exhausted debate'.

Stevens J (2016) The secondary sale copyright conundrum: why we need a secondary market for digital content. Aust Intellect Prop J 26:179–194

Stokes S (2019) Digital copyright: law and practice. Bloomsbury Publishing, London

Wolfgang S (2016) Exhaustion of digital goods: an economic perspective. MAGKS Joint Discussion Paper Series in Economics, No. 23-2016

Chapter 5
Cross-Border Availability of Copyright-Protected Digital Products to Users: The European Union's Initiatives

Abstract The EU's digital single market (DSM) strategy aimed to remove internal barriers in the digital environment and ensure that Europeans could access online content services irrespective of their location. Existing directives such as the Television Without Frontiers Directive, the Services Directive, the SatCab instruments and the AVMSD had not solved the problem of cross-border access to copyright-protected digital products, and stakeholder consultations showed a clear and growing demand for such access. As a response, the Commission proposed the Portability Regulation in 2015, marking the first use of a regulation in EU copyright law in order to guarantee uniform application and avoid the structural limitations associated with directives. In parallel, the Geo-blocking Regulation was adopted as another core element of the DSM Strategy. However, due to lobbying pressures and compromise, its scope excluded both audiovisual content and copyright-protected non-audiovisual digital products, thereby creating the widely criticised 'copyright gap'. The 2020 early review of the Geo-blocking Regulation did not support extending the Regulation to copyright-protected services.

5.1 Introduction

With the digital single market (DSM) strategy, the European Commission aimed to create a fully established single market in the digital realm within the EU. This strategy sought to eliminate barriers within the EU, fostering innovation and enhancing the functioning of the internal market by granting freedom to both receive and provide services. Especially since the 2010s, there has been a significant increase in the use of online content services, leading Europeans to expect access to these services regardless of their location.[1] However, cross-border access to these services was only available to a limited extent. Until that time, the cross-border availability of copyright-protected services was only regulated under the Television Without

[1] SWD for the DSM Strategy, 2.

F. Cebeci Çorum, *Application of Geo-Blocking to Copyright-Protected Digital Products*, Studies in European Economic Law and Regulation 30,
https://doi.org/10.1007/978-3-032-34507-3_5

Frontiers Directive,[2] the Services Directive,[3] the SatCab Directive (and the SatCab II Directive) and finally, under the Audiovisual Media Services Directive[4] (the AVMSD). These initiatives will be mentioned briefly in that part of the study.

Even though these directives existed, they were not successful in solving the problem of the cross-border access to copyright-protected digital products. Studies highlighted the substantial demand for cross-border accessibility to online content, particularly evident from stakeholder consultations between 2013 and 2015.[5] Recognising the increasing need for cross-border access to online content services, the Commission devised a roadmap to address any obstacles to accessing these services, prioritising this issue within the EU. While representatives of rightsholders and service providers often preferred non-binding recommendations, the Commission believed that a binding instrument would be more effective in achieving the desired outcomes.[6]

Therefore, the first initiative, as part of the DSM strategy published in 2015, was to create a legal instrument for the cross-border portability of online content services, which would be proposed later in the same year (the Portability Regulation Proposal).

Since the publication of the White Paper in 1985, the EU has been actively trying to harmonise copyright law in various aspects, and until 2015, directives[7] have been the sole legislative tool used in the field of copyright for this purpose. However, for the first time in the copyright domain, the legislative activity has been preferred through regulation.[8] The Portability Regulation Proposal states that this preference

---

[2] Council Directive 89/552/EEC of 3 October 1989 on the coordination of certain provisions laid down by Law, Regulation or Administrative Action in Member States concerning the pursuit of television broadcasting activities [1989] OJ L 298. (hereinafter will be referred to as the Television Without Frontiers Directive).

[3] Directive 2006/123/EC of the European Parliament and of the Council of 12 December 2006 on services in the internal market [2006] OJ L 37. (hereinafter will be referred to as the Services Directive).

[4] Directive (EU) 2018/1808 of the European Parliament and of the Council of 14 November 2018 amending Directive 2010/13/EU on the coordination of certain provisions laid down by law, regulation or administrative action in Member States concerning the provision of audiovisual media services (Audiovisual Media Services Directive) in view of changing market realities [2018] OJ L 303. (hereinafter will be referred to as the AVMSD).

[5] Proposal for a Regulation of the European Parliament and of the Council on ensuring the cross-border portability of online content services in the internal market, COM (2015) 627 final, 5. (hereinafter will be referred to as the Portability Regulation Proposal).

[6] The Portability Regulation Proposal, p. 4.

[7] Directives in EU law are the secondary legislation types that set out specific objectives and a framework that (addressed) EU member states must achieve this transposition until the deadline specified in the Directive. While regulations are directly applicable and binding on all member states, directives need to be implemented into national law by each member state. Member states are free to choose their methods while adopting their own laws to comply with the directive's requirements. For more information please see: Berry et al. (2019, p. 113).

[8] Regulations in EU law are the secondary legislation types that are directly applicable to all Member States. They are binding entirely and become applicable across all Member States without the need for additional implementation measures, as they take effect automatically. For more information please see: Berry et al. (2019, p. 113).

is due to its direct applicability in EU member states and simultaneous entry into force date. Additionally, it is emphasised that through regulation, the uniform application of portability rules among Member States and ensuring that rightsholders and online service providers are subject to exactly the same rules will be guaranteed.[9] This choice is further explained in the European Parliament Policy Department's Study,[10] by stating the rapid technological advancements have made the directive-based harmonisation method inadequate to address emerging challenges. Furthermore, in this study, it has been stated that structural deficiencies, partial harmonization effects, national discrepancies, legal uncertainty, and high costs could lead to some negative consequences in this area, and the limited potential of directives to provide a harmonised copyright law for a digital single market has been noted.[11] Due to the reasons explained, it has been decided and justified to use regulation as a legislative tool for the first time in the field of copyright law. The Portability Regulation Proposal has become the first proposed Regulation in the field of copyright law. An in-depth analysis of this Regulation will be provided in this chapter and its impact will be evaluated subsequently.

The other important legislative act covering the cross-border availability of products was the Geo-blocking Regulation. As part of the DSM Strategy, the Commission announced an action plan to address ending geo-blocking as one of the priorities of the EU. Because of the same reasons explained above, the EU chose a regulation as their legislative instrument. Nevertheless, the Geo-blocking Regulation does not apply to copyright-protected digital products, and this copyright law gap created lots of criticism among commentators. The legislative history and short-term reviews of this Regulation will be explained in detail, however, the copyright gap and potential solutions to this gap will be covered in Chap. 7, where the author will share her opinion and recommendations for this debate for the EU policymakers. This chapter will focus on the EU's initiatives regarding the cross-border availability of copyright-protected services and the main scene will be set in this area. Therefore, the main aim of this chapter is to show the current framework in this field and try to emphasise current needs in these legislations. After explaining current critics and gaps in this field, and after giving the necessary information regarding the geo-blocking problem for the cross-border circulation of the copyright-protected products, the last chapter, Chap. 7, will be dedicated to offering some recommendations for the EU policymakers. As such, the author will share her critics about these regulations, nevertheless will hesitate to offer any policy change in this chapter.

---

9 The Portability Regulation Proposal, p. 4; The Portability Regulation Proposal, Recital 35.

10 European Parliament, 'EU Portability Regulation: In-depth Analysis of the Proposal' (2016), https://www.europarl.europa.eu/RegData/etudes/IDAN/2016/571369/IPOL_IDA(2016)571369_EN.pdf.

11 European Parliament, 'EU Portability Regulation: In-depth Analysis of the Proposal' (2016), https://www.europarl.europa.eu/RegData/etudes/IDAN/2016/571369/IPOL_IDA(2016)571369_EN.pdf, p. 5–6.

5.2 EU Initiatives Before the Portability Regulation

The Television Without Frontiers Directive was the first important initiatives which regulate cross-border availability of the broadcasting.[12] The main aim of this directive was to ensure the free movement of television programming, in a traditional way. This directive also admitted that the free movement of broadcasting and distribution of television services have a strong link with the freedom of expression.[13] This directive regulated the country-of-origin principle, according to this principle only one member states will have the jurisdiction over the media service providers.[14] This directive's latest revision is the AVMSD. The AVMSD was also subjected to numerous updates, and the latest revision is available as of November 2018. This directive includes provisions for the quotas for the European productions to better promote European works across the EU and protection of minors, as the Television Without Frontiers Directive had.[15] The most important change that the 2018 revision of the AVMSD included is including provisions in line with the technological developments, such as the provisions related to non-linear audiovisual services.[16] This directive also included country-of-origin principle for the jurisdiction, and according to that they will be bound by the jurisdiction of the country *in where their central administration is located and where management decisions are taken on programming or selection of content.*[17] Nevertheless, both the Television Without Frontiers Directive and the AVMSD did not solve the problem of the cross-border availability of these services from the copyright law aspects.[18]

In 2006, the Services Directive have been legislated. The main aim of this legislation was to provide free movement of services, by ensuring the non-discrimination principle for the recipient.[19] According to that provision, *'Member States shall ensure that the general conditions of access to a service, which are made available to the public at large by the provider, do not contain discriminatory provisions relating to the nationality or place of residence of the recipient, but without precluding the possibility of providing for differences in the conditions of access where those differences are directly justified by objective criteria.'* That means, member states should provide these services to recipients without any discrimination on the grounds of nationality or place of residence. Nevertheless, audiovisual services were excluded

---

[12] Mylly and Herrero (2022, p. 1044).

[13] Television Without Frontiers Directive, Preamble.

[14] Memo/06/419 (2006) 'The modernisation of the Television without Frontiers Directive: Frequently asked questions, https://ec.europa.eu/commission/presscorner/detail/en/memo_06_419.

[15] Mylly and Herrero (2022, p. 1045).

[16] AVMSD, Recital 9.

[17] General Principles of the AVMSD (2024). In: Shaping Europe's digital future, https://digital-strategy.ec.europa.eu/en/policies/general-principles-avmsd#:~:text=Country%20of%20Origin%20principle&text=If%20any%20EU%20country%20adopts,to%20providers%20in%20that%20jurisdiction.

[18] Mylly and Herrero (2022, p. 1046).

[19] Article 20 of the Services Directive.

from the scope of the Services Directive, according to the Article 2(2) and freedom to provide services does not apply to copyright-protected services according to Article 17(11). Regardless of this, the EU also aware that the non-discrimination principle is not applied properly within the EU and recipients are still unfairly discriminated.[20]

Lastly, the SatCab and SatCab II Directives also regulated the cross-border availability of copyright-protected digital products. The SatCab Directive also proposed the country-of-origin principle (which is also called as the emission principle[21]) and according to that principle, a legal fiction created, and broadcasters will only need to clear the rights from the country-of-origin of the broadcasting signals.[22] With this legal fiction, the copyright related act will be regarded as occurred in the country where the signals received, according to Article 1(2)(b) of this directive. Nevertheless, Recital 16 of the SatCab Directive regulated that under the contractual freedom, the exploitation of these rights may be limited. The FAPL and Murphy cases discussed the limitation of contractual freedom under that provision, which will be explained later in that study in Chap. 5. With the SatCab II Directive, the EU wanted to extend the country-of-origin principle in the licensing system beyond the satellite broadcasting and the cable retransmission; however, only a limited extend it was successful. Article 3 regulated the application of the country-of-origin principle to ancillary online services, yet only (a) radio programmes; and (b) television programmes which are: (i) news and current affairs programmes; or (ii) fully financed own productions of the broadcasting organisation were included in the scope of this directive.

As these developments show that until the Portability Regulation, the cross-border availability of the copyright-protected digital products were regulated to a limited extent. This part of the study will focus on how Portability Regulation and the Geo-blocking Regulation legislated the cross-border availability of these products across the Union.

5.3 The Portability Regulation

5.3.1 The Portability Regulation Proposal

The main aim of this Regulation was to address the issue of inability to access online service providers due to territorial restrictions of copyright law and to provide a specific exception that would enable the portability of online services for lawful subscribers by granting access to these copyright-protected works.[23] To that end, in December 2015, the Commission published the Portability Regulation Proposal.

[20] Trimble (2024, p. 65).

[21] Trimble (2024, p. 106), Mylly and Herrero (2022, p. 1046).

[22] Mylly and Herrero (2022, p. 1046).

[23] EU Portability Regulation: In-depth Analysis of the Proposal (2016), https://www.europarl.europa.eu/RegData/etudes/IDAN/2016/571369/IPOL_IDA(2016)571369_EN.pdf.

The Portability Regulation Proposal aimed to enable cross-border portability of online content that consumers already legally access in their home country while temporarily travelling to any other EU Member State.[24] With this aim, the Commission published an eight-article Proposal in December 2015.

Article 1 of this Proposal articulates the primary objective of this regulation, which is to introduce a unified approach to guaranteeing that subscribers to online content services delivered on a portable basis can access these services when temporarily present in any other EU member state.

Article 2 included some key definitions, such as the meanings of 'subscriber', 'consumer', and 'online content services'. According to these definitions, a *subscriber* is someone authorised by a contract with a provider to access and use online content services within their home Member State; a *consumer* is any individual not engaging in business-related activities under contracts regulated by this Regulation. An *online content service* is also defined as a lawful service provided by a service provider within the resident Member State on a portable basis, as defined by Articles 56 and 57 of the Treaty on the Functioning of the European Union. This encompasses audiovisual media services under the Audiovisual Media Services Directive, or services primarily offering access to works, protected subject matter, or broadcasting organization transmissions, whether linear or on-demand.

It is important to note that this Proposal covered all types of copyright-protected content that can be provided online, not only audiovisual content.[25] Furthermore, the beneficiaries of this legislation have also been stated as providers of online content services and their customers. Furthermore, this Proposal does not distinguish between online content service providers; any technologies which allow streaming and downloading (and any new technologies that may go beyond these) will be subject to these terms.[26] In Article 2, also the definition of 'temporarily present' meaning has been explained as the *presence of a subscriber in a member state other than the member state of residence,* and yet, this explanation does not specify how long a stay would be considered a temporary residence.

Article 3 regulates a platform obligation to enable cross-border portability of online content services. However, platforms do not have to guarantee the quality of these services unless otherwise expressly agreed by the provider. Furthermore, according to Recital 18, platforms of online content services should offer the portability of the same range of content that is available in the subscriber's home country. Additionally, the quality of service may decrease as providing the same level of service quality would incur disproportionate costs for the platforms; therefore, platforms will not be held liable if the service delivery quality is lower, as stated in Recital 19.

In the proposed regulation, there is no provision which prevents rightsholders from asking for extra money from the subscribers for offering portability.[27]

---

[24] The Portability Regulation Proposal, 2.

[25] Rauer and Kaase (2020, p. 505).

[26] Rauer and Kaase (2020, p. 506).

[27] Shapiro (2016, p. 359).

This Proposed Regulation was actually built on a so-called 'legal fiction', which was stated in **Article 4**:

> The provision of an online content service to, as well as the access to and the use of this service by, a subscriber, in accordance with Article 3(1), shall be deemed to occur solely in the Member State of residence including for the purposes of Directive 96/9/EC, Directive 2001/29/EC, Directive 2006/115/EC, Directive 2009/24 and Directive 2010/13/EU.

According to this legal assumption, a subscriber residing in one EU Member State and temporarily present in another EU Member State when accessing and using an online content service under this Regulation, the act will be deemed to have occurred in the Member State where the subscriber habitually resides.[28] This is not the first time that the EU has used this legal assumption in the copyright law domain; in the SatCab Directive this assumption was also used.[29]

A valid subscription in the subscriber's Member State of residence will automatically oblige the service providers to offer portability of these online content services. This means that when a subscriber is in another Member State, they have the right to access and use the same content provided by online content service providers in their home Member State. This legal fiction has been justified in Recital 21 as follows:

> In order to ensure that providers of online content services comply with the obligation to provide cross-border portability of their services without acquiring the relevant rights in another Member State, it is necessary to stipulate that those service providers which lawfully provide portable online content services in the Member State of residence of subscribers are always entitled to provide such services to those subscribers when they are temporarily present in another Member State. This should be achieved by establishing that the provision, the access to and the use of such online content service should be deemed to occur in the Member State of the subscriber's residence.

To summarise, online content service providers are permitted to offer their services to subscribers temporarily present in a Member State other than their own without obtaining the relevant rights in that Member State. All relevant acts under the copyright law domain (such as accessing and using the service by the subscriber) will fictionally take place in the same place, which is the habitual residence of the subscriber.[30] In the absence of the multi-territorial licences, this legal fiction will help online content services to fulfil their obligation to provide a portable service across the EU.[31] The rights acquired in the subscriber's Member State of residence will be adequate to provide an EU-wide portability and this activity will not infringe copyright thanks to this legal fiction.[32]

Article 5 regulates that any contractual provisions which are contrary to these provisions will be unenforceable.

---

[28] Rauer and Kaase (2020, p. 510).

[29] Rauer and Kaase (2020, p. 511).

[30] Rauer and Kaase (2020, p. 513).

[31] Karmel (2020, p. 418).

[32] Shapiro (2016, p. 354).

For the processing and protection of personal data, **Article 6** only states that '*The processing of personal data carried out within the framework of this Regulation including, in particular, for purposes of verification under Article 5(2), shall be carried out in compliance with Directives 95/46/EC and 2002/58/EC.*' In this proposal, no other provision or explanation has been made regarding how the subscriber's location will be verified, how the data obtained from this verification will be used, and how and for how long this data will be stored.

Article 7 made clear that this Regulation will be applicable to any contractual relationship, even if it is concluded before the date of this Regulation, as long as it is relevant to the provision.

Finally, **Article 8** includes provisions for the entry into force date (which is the twentieth day following its publication in the Official Journal of the European Union) and states that this Proposal should apply six months after its publication.

5.3.2 The Debates on the Proposed Regulation and the Final Version of the Portability Regulation

During the legislative process of this Regulation, some important discussions were held, and the following issues have been discussed, such as (i) the lack of a clear definition of 'temporary present', (ii) the process of verifying the residence of Member States, and the collection and privacy of personal data, (iii) the position of free online service providers, and finally, (iv) the timeframe provided to Member States for implementation. In line with the objectives of this study, the author will particularly and only focus on the 'temporary presence' debate with detail. The discussion concerning the applicability of portability regulations to the circulation of copyrighted works, including the duration and conditions under which they can be enforced, can be regarded as the most relevant and crucial debate for the purpose of this doctoral study. Other discussions mainly pertain to procedural matters and the use of personal data. These discussions will only be briefly explained to provide a general understanding for the reader.

5.3.2.1 Definition of 'Temporary Present'

Due to the absence of a clear definition precisely describing what 'temporary present' entails, the Council and some stakeholders raised certain questions and concerns. According to them, it has been noted that the lack of this definition and the absence of a definitive framework could pose certain legal certainty issues, as well as the provisions in this Regulation could be interpreted broadly, potentially leading to abusive use of the Regulation.[33] On the other hand, other stakeholders stated that a

[33] Rauer and Kaase (2020, p. 516).

flexible approach could be more beneficial and would serve the aims of this Regulation better.[34] The Commission clearly states in the Impact Assessment (2015)[35] that there will be no clear explanation and detail in the term 'temporary presence' and it justifies this choice as follows:

> "No concrete indication as to the length of such temporary presence would be provided in the intervention. Several factors explain the choice of this approach.
>
> Specification of duration of temporary presence is not required, as the main defining feature is that such presence does not change the habitual residence of the subscriber. The definition needs to accommodate temporary presences of various length and for various purposes, such as leisure, travel, work and study. This will benefit consumers without generating extra cost for service providers or undermining right holders' content distribution practices. Also, online content services are developing dynamically and are characterised by a variety of offers, which makes it difficult to set a uniform duration. Furthermore, the objective of the intervention is to keep the possible verification of the MS of residence within what is reasonable and necessary. This objective would not be served by a fixed period of temporary presence which would imply checks of the exact duration of consumers' presence in MS other than his or her MS of residence."[36]

After receiving the comments and suggestions about this definition, the Commission chose to keep open the length of the stay and no additional explanation or specific timeframe has been provided. On the other hand, they have updated and added the phrase 'limited period of time' to the definition of temporary presence as follows:

> (4) 'temporarily present in a Member State' means being present in a Member State other than the Member State of residence for a limited period of time;

This vague definition has also been criticised by academics, and they have suggested improving and further clarifying the definition of this concept, although it may not necessarily require specifying a certain number of days since it may be too restrictive.[37] Additionally, it has been argued that due to the lack of a clear definition or further explanation, even in the recitals, to guide on this matter, the ambiguity regarding what period of time should be considered as a 'temporary presence' could create some complexity for both subscribers and platform providers.[38] This situation has been stated as extremely important because of the legal certainty.[39] It is also stated that this ambiguous definition may result in some liability risks for providers especially considering the verification process for the subscriber's Member State of residence.[40]

---

[34] Rauer and Kaase (2020, p. 516).

[35] Commission Staff Working Document Impact Assessment Accompanying the document Proposal for a Regulation of the European Parliament and of the Council to ensure the cross-border portability of online content services in the internal market SWD (2015) 271 final. (hereinafter will be referred to as the SWD for the Portability Regulation Regulation).

[36] SWD for the Portability Regulation Regulation, p. 25.

[37] Shapiro (2016, p. 358), Rauer and Kaase (2020, p. 537), Engels and Nordemann (2018, p. 184).

[38] Rauer and Kaase (2020, p. 537).

[39] Rauer and Kaase (2020, p. 537).

[40] Engels and Nordemann (2018, p. 184).

Commentators also stated that since there is no limitation in the Regulation for the time a person can spend abroad, any contractual provision envisaged by service providers to impose such a restriction will not be enforceable.[41] On the other hand, in practice, the pay-tv provider Sky TV has set their limit as 37 days per stay,[42] and the German Media Association has set their limit as 45 days.[43]

The author of this study strongly agrees with the opinions of numerous authors in this field. First and foremost, to establish a common practice in this field and avoid creating an unfair situation for both subscribers and platform providers, a clear and more defined explanation about the nature of being temporarily present in another country should have been provided. Secondly, while the Commission portrays leaving this definition flexible for activities of varying purposes and durations as a reason for not imposing restrictions and providing further explanations, the durations of these activities could vary significantly. For instance, an educational activity could span approximately 9–10 months or a full year, whereas a tourist activity might be limited to just a few days. Therefore, if this Regulation is overly flexible, it could lead to the misuse of the regulation and create legal uncertainties, especially for service providers. Additionally, in practice, as the given example above, different service providers may set different periods and conditions for their services. This situation creates variations in practice and makes it impossible to fully benefit from the Regulation in line with its intended purpose. For these reasons, the author of this study suggests providing a clearer definition and more explanation regarding the limit of temporary presence to eliminate all these risks; however, the author also agrees with other authors that adopting a very strict approach on the number of days could actually hinder the purpose of this Regulation.

5.3.2.2 The Process of Verifying the Member States of Residence and Protection of Personal Data

In the Proposed Regulation, only two articles were dedicated to the process of verifying the Member States of residence and, accordingly, protection of the collection of personal data. Article 5(2) regulates the verification process, and according to this provision, online content service providers may verify that the service is provided in conformity with Article 3(1) through verification, and the tools used for verification should be reasonable and not exceed what is necessary to achieve their purpose.

As a result of this verification, lawmakers realised that an extensive amount of personal data may be collected. For the protection and processing of these personal data, Article 6 has been regulated as follows:

---

[41] Rauer and Kaase (2020, p. 539).

[42] Rauer and Kaase (2020, p. 539). Sky TV also requires subscribers to log in to their system in their Member State of residence at least once between journeys.

[43] Rauer and Kaase (2020, p. 539).

> The processing of personal data carried out within the framework of this Regulation including, in particular, for purposes of verification under Article 5(2), shall be carried out in compliance with Directives 95/46/EC and 2002/58/EC.

Furthermore, in Recital 17, the Proposed Regulation indicated some possible ways to determine the subscriber's member state of residence. According to this proposed recital 17, regarding the verification of the subscriber's Member State of residence, information such as payment of a licence fee for services provided in the Member State of residence, the existence of a contract for internet or telephone connection, IP address, or other means of authentication can be used if they provide the provider with reasonable indications about the Member State of residence of its subscribers.

In Article 5, the Proposed Regulation rules that the verification method should be 'reasonable' and 'not go beyond what is necessary to achieve the purpose'. This, obviously, created some questions such as 'what is reasonable and proportionate?[44] Because there is no clear answer and no indication about this 'reasonable and proportionate verification' it has been suggested that more explanation and clarity should have been provided.[45] Related to this, consumer associations were in doubt that rigid verification may result in extensive collection of personal data and this issue has not been taken into account by the Commission in the first place.[46] As such, the verification methods and protection of personal data have been the main topics that have been discussed during the readings.

As a result of these discussions, in the final draft, two extensive and detailed articles have been suggested. In Article 5, the Regulation suggested reasonable, proportionate and effective methods to verify the Member states of residence of the subscriber and listed exhaustive methods to verify this country. Additionally, when the service provider has reasonable doubts about the subscriber's Member State of residence in the course of the duration of the contract for the provision of an online content service, the Regulation allows that the provider may repeat the verification of the Member State of residence of the subscriber. From the personal data point of view, Article 8 and Recital 30 regulate detailed provisions regarding the collection of data, use of data and destroying data, yet these discussions will not be detailed in this study.

5.3.2.3 The Positions of Services Provided for Payment of Money vs Without Payment of Money

According to Proposed Regulation Recital 16, this *Regulation should apply to online content services which are provided against payment of money*. Furthermore, Recital 17 pointed out that *online content services which are provided without payment of money are also included in the scope of this Regulation to the extent that providers verify the Member State of residence of their subscribers.* On the other hand, since

---

[44] Shapiro (2016, p. 358).

[45] Shapiro (2016, p. 367).

[46] Rauer and Kaase (2020, p. 516).

online content services, which are offered without payment of money, do not have a registration process, therefore, agreed text chooses to exclude these free services from the scope of this Regulation. Also, these free services may also choose to opt for this Regulation. Therefore, a voluntary system for online services provided without payment of money has been adopted. Also, the agreed Regulation made clear that the payment of a mandatory fee for public broadcasting services should not be regarded as a payment of money for an online content service. That means they are also not in the scope of this Regulation, such as national broadcasters. Again, these services may also choose to opt for this Regulation, as Belgium national broadcaster RTBF did, or they can continue not to opt for it as the UK's BBC did.[47]

Furthermore, as stated above, the proposed regulation did not contain a provision preventing rightsholders from charging subscribers extra for offering portability. The agreed text correctly made clear that in Article 3(2), service providers cannot charge subscribers extra for access to and use of the online content service.

Finally, it should be noted that this Regulation does not require online content service providers to be based in the EU or to have corresponding establishments there. On the contrary, any content service provider entering into contracts within the EU with EU consumers is naturally expected to comply with EU laws, without exception, including the Portability Regulation.[48]

5.3.2.4 The Implementation Period of the Regulation

The Proposed Regulation sets a six-month implementation period deadline. Nevertheless, it has been criticised as being too short because the legal and technical background needed to be adjusted.[49] The agreed text was adopted in June 2017 and the provisions of the Regulation became binding as of 1 April 2018. The lawmakers chose to extend this period to enable rightsholders and providers to amend their terms for the use of their services.[50]

5.3.3 *After the Portability Regulation—Reviews and Some Question Marks*

In June 2022, the European Commission published a Commission Staff Working Document, which is a report on the application of the Portability Regulation of

[47] Karmel (2020, p. 417).

[48] Engels and Nordemann (2018, p. 185). This is particularly important for the big actors from the US such as Netflix, Disney and Amazon Prime.

[49] Rauer and Kaase (2020, p. 517).

[50] Engels and Nordemann (2018, p. 199).

online content services in the internal market.[51] One of the most important pieces of information in this report was that the beneficiaries of this Regulation only amount to approximately 5% of the total subscribers.[52] While it may fall under the intention of the Regulation, it is worth noting that there were extremely tight travel restrictions, especially between 2020 and 2022, due to the Covid-19 pandemic. On the other hand, just before the pandemic, some scholars also expressed doubts about the effectiveness of this Regulation by pointing out that only a very small portion and a privileged segment of EU consumers would benefit from it.[53]

Secondly, the report stated that consumer protection organizations and authorities received very few or no complaints, indicating that there were no major problems with the implementation of this Regulation.[54] Actually, this is quite an optimistic estimate, as the reason for receiving so few complaints could be attributed to the lack of any enforcement mechanism until 2020. Consumers did not know where or how to file a complaint in the case where a provider failed to offer portability.[55] In January 2020, the Portability Regulation were covered by the updated Regulation 2017/2394 on cooperation between national authorities responsible for the enforcement of consumer protection laws and repealing Regulation, and its enforcement will be done according to this Regulation 2017/2394.[56]

In terms of verification and protection of data, the report outlined that more than half of the SMEs (small and medium-sized enterprises) found this Regulation challenging since verification and data protection provisions actually led to significant additional costs.[57] Privacy and verification have been at the central of the debates since the proposal, especially with the increased popularity of the GDPR (the General Data Protection Regulation). As explained above, this study will not cover privacy and data protection debates extensively as it goes beyond the scope of this research.

The report also mentioned the interpretation of 'temporary presence'.[58] This report suggests that a case-by-case assessment determines the time frame for being temporarily present in another Member State, and service providers are prohibited from pre-defining any time limit under Article 7(2) of the Regulation. The report also mentioned that they were aware that some service providers actually impose some pre-defined time limits, and the Commission's services will remind these providers that they are not allowed to impose any time limits. The author of this study has already explained her opinion above so no further comment will be made in this part of the study.

---

[51] Commission Staff Working Document Report on the application of the Regulation on cross-border portability of online content services (2022) SWD (2022) 173, 6. (hereinafter will be referred to as SWD on Portability Regulation 2022).

[52] SWD on Portability Regulation 2022, p. 6.

[53] Reda (2020, p. 86).

[54] SWD on Portability Regulation 2022, 6.

[55] Karmel (2020, p. 420).

[56] Karmel (2020, p. 421).

[57] SWD on Portability Regulation 2022, 8.

[58] SWD on Portability Regulation 2022, 12.

One important point that the study did not address is subscribers who share the same plan. The Regulation assumes that all subscribers have individual plans and does not account for joint or family plans where multiple users access the same account. No explanation or provision has been provided regarding this matter. For instance, Netflix, as one of the providers obligated to comply with this regulation, offers family plans where up to four different users can access the same subscription simultaneously. As mentioned in Karmel's article,[59] the course of action in situations where one of these users temporarily moves to a different Member State remains unclear. After a certain period, will providers fulfilling their obligations under the Portability Regulation be able to terminate access to such subscriptions simply because one or a few users do not reside in the Member State of the subscription? Alternatively, will the IP address of the user or information obtained through verification methods suffice to ensure that the service is provided in the country of subscription? Neither the Regulation nor subsequent studies provide answers to these questions.

5.3.4 Conclusion

The Portability Regulation[60] is the first regulation in the copyright field, and it is the first attempt to comply with the strategy of Digital Single Market. This Regulation aims to provide a uniform approach throughout the EU in terms of the portability of online content services across borders. This is particularly important from the territoriality of copyright aspect since Article 4 of this Regulation creates a so-called legal fiction. According to this provision, any act regarding the access and the use of the online content services shall be deemed to occur solely in the Member State of residence. This provision helped service providers to ensure that they do not infringe copyright while they are making available these protected works outside the licensed area. This legal fiction was a good step in the right direction towards a more modern and uniform EU Copyright Law by enabling easy access to copyright-protected digital works.

On the other hand, there has been some criticism about this Regulation. To start with, this Regulation does not clearly explain what 'temporarily present in a Member State' means, and this unclarity results in some differences in practices. Furthermore, only a very limited number of EU citizens can benefit from this Regulation. This Regulation provides prevention in geo-blocking to travellers, short-term migrants and tourists, with the number of beneficiaries of around 2.5 million EU citizens by 2020, which means only about 0.5% of the EU population.[61] Also, this Regulation has

[59] Karmel (2020, p. 425).

[60] Just to inform the reader, the Portability Regulation does not apply to UK since in the UK the regulation has been revoked, with the effect of Brexit. For more information please visit: Guidance on Cross-border portability of online content services, https://www.gov.uk/guidance/cross-border-portability-of-online-content-services#:~:text=The%20EU%20Portability%20Regulation%20no,in%20an%20EEA%20Member%20State.

[61] Schmidt-Kessen (2017, p. 567).

resulted in some debates on privacy and protection of personal data, and still, there are some question marks about this issue. Furthermore, this Regulation has some negative effects on SMEs. Finally, the Regulation did not cover some important points, such as joint subscriptions.

The EU has adopted the Regulation on cross-border portability of online content services to provide a common approach in the Union to the cross-border portability of online content services by ensuring that subscribers to portable online content services which are lawfully provided in their Member State of residence can access and use those services when temporarily present in a Member State other than their Member State of residence. As stated, this is a small yet important step in the right direction to regulate the circulation of copyright-protected works within the EU. Nevertheless, the number of beneficiaries of this Regulation was quite low. The next step was to regulate the cross-border access for products within the EU by eliminating unjustified geo-blocking based on nationality, place of residence or place of establishment of consumers. The next chapter will explain this initiative in depth.

5.4 The Geo-Blocking Regulation

The EU aimed to regulate a broader framework for e-commerce where there is no discrimination in terms of nationality, place of residence or place of establishment of consumers. Discrimination could occur if online distributors refuse to sell their products to different nationals or different locations, if these require different conditions to sell their products, or rerouting the consumers to their national website of sellers without the prior consent of the consumers. The EU tried to find a name for this discriminatory practice and after finding an appropriate name for this, there were still some disparities in definitions. The term 'geo-blocking' was used for the first time in EU's legal documents, in the Communication published in 2012 by the Commission as follows: *'distribution of content is often limited to one or a few Member States (e.g. using geo-blocking), with service providers (online platforms) or rights holders electing to impose cross-border sales restrictions.'*[62]

Subsequently, in the European Parliament study dated 2013 called Discrimination of Consumers in the Digital Single Market, the discriminatory practice has been defined as *'simple refusal to sell, automatic re-routing, and unjustified diversifying of sale conditions'.*[63] However, this definition was not called 'geo-blocking'. In the Commission Staff Working Document for a Digital Single Market Strategy for

---

[62] Communication From the Commission On content in the Digital Single Market COM (2012) 789 final.

[63] European Parliament Study (2013) Discrimination of Consumers in the Digital Single Market, p. 8.

Europe on 6 May 2015, the same definition has been used[64] with reference to the European Parliament study; this time, this discriminatory practice is called 'geo-blocking'. In the same year, geo-blocking is defined in the DSM Strategy. DSM Strategy defines geo-blocking as: *'Geo-blocking refers to practices used for commercial reasons by online sellers that result in the denial of access to websites based in other Member States.'*[65] This definition explains that geo-blocking occurs if there is only denial of access to websites and according to this explanation, geo-blocking can be seen in only one form, which results from the denial of access to websites. Although in the previous study by the European Parliament, geo-blocking was defined broadly, which includes *"refusal to sell, automatic re-routing and unjustified diversifying"*, when they were transposing it, apparently European Council decided to keep the definition short, and they wanted to explain other scenarios with the examples.[66]

As decided in the DSM Strategy, to prohibit these unjustified practices so that EU consumers and businesses can take full advantage of the single market in terms of choice and lower prices, the European Commission started to work to publish a regulation which will prevent unjustified geo-blocking. The first staff working paper on preventing unjustified geo-blocking[67] was published on 25.5.2016, only 20 days later from the DSM Strategy, and it included a different definition of geo-blocking, *"i.e. practices used for commercial reasons by online sellers that result in the denial of access to websites based in other Member States, or to the products or services sought for; or where different prices or conditions are automatically applied on the basis of geographic location."* In this definition, geo-blocking is explained broadly, and in the Commission Staff Working Document Impact Assessment, geo-blocking was intended to be explained as a whole with the definition, not with the examples as done in the DSM Strategy. In the Geo-blocking Regulation Proposal,[68] geo-blocking was also explained as follows: *'That occurs where traders operating in one Member State block or limit the access to their online interfaces, such as websites and apps, of customers from other Member States wishing to engage in cross-border commercial transactions (a practice known as geo-blocking). It also occurs when certain traders apply different general conditions of access to their goods and services with respect to such customers from other Member States, both online and offline'*. The Geo-Blocking Regulation is explaining geo-blocking as the same as the Proposal. It is

[64] Commission Staff Working Document, A Digital Single Market Strategy for Europe - Analysis and Evidence in SWD (2015) 100 final 21.

[65] Commission Staff Working Document, A Digital Single Market Strategy for Europe - Analysis and Evidence in SWD (2015) 100 final 21, 4.

[66] DSM Strategy, point 2.3.

[67] Commission Staff Working Document Impact Assessment Accompanying the document proposal for a Regulation of The European Parliament and Of the Council on addressing geo-blocking and other forms of discrimination based on place of residence or establishment or nationality within the Single Market SWD (2016) 173 final.

[68] In Proposal for a Regulation on Addressing Geo-blocking and Other Forms of Discrimination Based on Customers' Nationality, Place of Residence or Place of Establishment within the Internal Market and Amending Regulation (EC) No 2006/2004 and Directive 2009/22/EC, COM/2016/0289 final. (hereinafter will be referred to as the Geo-blocking Regulation Proposal).

clear that, after the DSM Strategy, the definition has been developed and evolved, the more comprehensive and broad explanations are accepted, and both online and offline sales are covered by the Geo-Blocking Regulation. The Geo-Blocking Regulation addresses the following forms of geo-blocking: (1) it prohibits traders from blocking access to their online interfaces and re-routing customers involuntarily on the basis of their place of residence; (2) it prohibits discrimination on the basis of residence in cross-border transactions; and (3) it particularly prohibits discrimination regarding payments, (however this definition is not called as geo-blocking, but called 'other types of discriminations').

Besides, the European Commission's 'Questions and Answers on the Geo-blocking Regulation in the Context of E-commerce',[69] which was published in 2018, also describes geo-blocking as follows: *"Geo-blocking refers to practices used by online sellers to restrict online cross-border sales based on nationality, residence or place of establishment... 'Geo- discrimination' also takes place when buying goods and services off-line, e.g. when consumers are physically present at the trader's location but are either prevented from accessing a product or service or from being offered different conditions due to their nationality or residence."* In this publication, there is another classification regarding geo-blocking, and the European Commission explains geo-blocking as a commercial practice which is used for online sales and explains geo-discrimination as an offline sales practice. This is a new approach taken by the European Commission, hence, there is not a single explanation regarding geo-discrimination, and the term 'geo-discrimination' has not been used in the Geo-Blocking Regulation.

Finally, the JRC Report[70] dated November 2020 regarding Geo-blocking: A literature review and new evidence in online audio-visual services, geo-blocking is also defined as follows: *"Geo-blocking is enabled by geo-location tools that allow websites to identify the physical location of their visitors through their IP addresses and other sources of information. Geo-location technologies allow localised advertising and search and as such are valued by companies. Although geo-blocking can be legitimate as a means to respect trade restrictions in national legislation, geo-location tools can also be used for commercial reasons to erect commercial barriers to cross-border online transactions."* This report explains geo-blocking with different words when it is compared to other European Commission publications. Besides, although there are two different reports and three related works[71] that were published in November 2020 with regards to the short-term review of the Geo-Blocking Regulation, none of them explained or mentioned geo-discrimination, which is explained in the European Commission's publication for questions and

---

[69] Commission (2018) Questions & Answers on the Geo-blocking Regulation in the context of e-commerce, https://digital-strategy.ec.europa.eu/en/news/geo-blocking-regulation-questions-and-answers.

[70] Broocks et al. (2020) Geo-blocking: A literature review and new evidence in online audio-visual services, JRC Publications Repository, https://publications.jrc.ec.europa.eu/repository/handle/JRC120267 (hereinafter will be referred to as the JRC Report).

[71] To access reviews please visit: https://digital-strategy.ec.europa.eu/en/news/commission-publishes-its-short-term-review-geo-blocking-regulation.

answers for geo-blocking in 2018. To summarise, in the Geo-blocking Regulation, geo-blocking was defined to include (i) the block or limit of access to websites and interfaces and (ii) traders applying different general conditions of access to their goods and services.

In 2015, there was a study regarding identifying the main cross-border sale obstacles to the Digital Single Market and where they matter most.[72] According to this study, consumers faced obstacles when attempting to do cross-border shopping online. The primary responses from consumers regarding problems were rerouting the seller's website in their own country, refusing the sale in their country of residence, only displaying limited content, and refusing the payments. Furthermore, in 2015, there was a consultation[73] related to geo-blocking in the case of online shopping. The first finding[74] in this consultation was that shoppers want to shop cross-border and remove any existing barriers, especially discrimination based on nationality and temporary location. Such discriminations pose significant obstacles to achieving a fully integrated digital single market within the EU.

Consequently, the EU has prioritised addressing this issue, recognising that discrimination linked to place of residence or establishment discourages cross-border shopping, potentially leading to price disparities for identical services. To explain the issue more precise, according to the given example in the staff working document for the DSM strategy, if a consumer residing in the UK is looking for a car rental company, this consumer will see more expensive prices (up to 53%) compared to consumers who are residing in Poland, Slovenia and Romania who are looking for the same car rental company. All these differences are indeed barriers to establishing a single market where there are no borders or geographical limitations. To this end, as part of the extensive Digital Single Market Strategy, the European Commission has deemed it necessary to take measures to prevent unfair geographical limitations. Furthermore, to achieve this goal, preventing unjustified geo-blocking was one of the subjects that the DSM Strategy targeted to regulate. According to the road map of the DSM Strategy, the proposal for preventing unjustified geo-blocking should

---

[72] European Commission (2015) Directorate-General for Justice and Consumers. Provision of two online consumer surveys as support and evidence base to a Commission study: identifying the main cross-border obstacles to the Digital Single Market and where they matter most. In: Publications Office of the European Union https://op.europa.eu/en/publication-detail/-/publication/1ee5f89c-812c-11e5-b8b7-01aa75ed71a1/language-en.

[73] The European Commission's 2015 Public Consultation on Geo-Blocking and Other Geographically-Based Restrictions When Shopping and Accessing Information in the EU (2015). In: Shaping Europe's digital future https://digital-strategy.ec.europa.eu/en/consultations/public-consultation-geo-blocking-and-other-geographically-based-restrictions-when-shopping-and#:~:text=This%20consultation%2C%20an%20initiative%20of,borders%20in%20the%20European%20Union.

[74] The European Commission's 2015 Public Consultation on Geo-Blocking and Other Geographically-Based Restrictions When Shopping and Accessing Information in the EU (2015). In: Shaping Europe's digital future https://digital-strategy.ec.europa.eu/en/consultations/public-consultation-geo-blocking-and-other-geographically-based-restrictions-when-shopping-and#:~:text=This%20consultation%2C%20an%20initiative%20of,borders%20in%20the%20European%20Union, p. 15.

have been published within 2015; however, the Geo-blocking Regulation Proposal was published in May 2016.

5.4.1 Geo-Blocking Regulation Proposal and Related Documents

The Geo-blocking Regulation Proposal was published in May 2016, and on the same date, the Commission Staff Working Document Impact Assessment on addressing geo-blocking[75] (the staff working document) was also published. This staff working document explains the background of the Geo-blocking Regulation Proposal and analyses the aims of this proposal.

To start with, this proposal aims to address geo-blocking and other forms of discrimination based on customers' nationality, place of residence or place of establishment within the internal market. Although the topic of the Geo-blocking Regulation Proposal does not include the term 'unjustified' (unlike the Geo-blocking Regulation, which is titled 'Addressing Unjustified Geo-Blocking', Geo-blocking Regulation Proposal name did not include the 'unjustified' term), the staff working document explains under which circumstances this discrimination will be considered as an 'unjustified'[76]:

1. First, the staff working document points out that if cross-border sales will result in substantial extra costs or complications for businesses, and if a business does not want to sell cross-border, this practice is most likely to be considered justified.
2. Furthermore, the staff working document adds that case-to-case analysis would create more accurate results to decide whether or not this cross-border sale restriction was justified.
3. Nonetheless, the staff working document analysed some of the cases where local and foreign customers were in a similar position, and this document identified the following scenarios as unjustified:

    a. When a foreign customer is willing to pick up the parcel from the location, the trader has already made cross-border delivery; however, the trader prevents this customer from buying this physical good.
    b. When a foreign customer is prevented from buying electronically supplied service when there is no delivery cost issue or VAT or taxation problem.
    c. When a foreign customer is prevented from accessing electronically supplied non-audiovisual copyright-protected content services, even though the trader has required licence or relevant rights in the relevant territories.

[75] Commission Staff Working Document Impact Assessment Accompanying the document proposal for a Regulation of The European Parliament and Of the Council on addressing geo-blocking and other forms of discrimination based on place of residence or establishment or nationality within the Single Market SWD/2016/0173 final. (hereinafter will be referred to as SWD for the Geo-blocking Regulation Proposal).

[76] SWD for the Geo-blocking Regulation Proposal, p. 10.

d. When a foreign customer moves to another country, s/he is charged differently than any domestic customers for the services.

After these evaluations, the staff working document also analysed in which stages of the purchasing process the unjustified restrictions can be seen.[77]

- Firstly, this document identified the lack of transparency as a problem because, under the Consumer Rights Directive, consumers should see the delivery restrictions (if there are any) and accepted means of payment at the beginning of the purchasing process. Therefore, not obeying this provision could result in a problem for the customers since they could continue to shop and look at the products until the very end of this purchasing process.
- Secondly, traders can prevent access to the website from specific locations/outside of the specific locations or can reroute the consumers to their local stores.
- Thirdly, unjustified geo-blocking can also occur in the case of a customer is offered different conditions, such as a higher price or if a seller refuses to sell the product in three specifics[78] cases (explained in a, c and d scenarios) because of their nationality, place of residence or establishment. Furthermore, the staff working document also regulates that an unjustified practice can occur in the payment phase of purchasing, such as refusal of foreign means of payment (such as the country of credit card issuance). Lastly, refusal to deliver is also considered an unjustified practice, and it is the last scenario that unjustified geo-blocking could occur.

To prevent (unjustified) geo-blocking, it was clear that accepting a new policy was necessary. To this end, with regard to the DSM Strategy action plan, the European Commission wanted to adopt a proposal for preventing (unjustified) geo-blocking. Nevertheless, the scope of this legislative act was also controversial because there was a necessity to accept the scope of objectives and to choose the best policy options.

Firstly, the staff working document provides four main policy objectives, which are improving transparency for customers, preventing unjustified differences in accessing goods and services, improving public enforcement in relation to unjustified geo-blocking, and finally, increasing legal certainty for businesses for cross-border transactions. These policy objectives were accepted cumulatively, and the Commission actually had to decide which policy could be ideal to solve and address the problem of geo-blocking. The staff working document outlined seven different policy options which are:

1. *Option 0: No EU policy change*: this option was the baseline scenario, and it focused on other Directives and Regulations that can help to remove unjustified geo-blocking.
2. *Option 1: Improving transparency and enforcement:* in this option, traders will have to explain the reasons why this restriction is applied, and with regard to the

[77] SWD for the Geo-blocking Regulation Proposal, pp. 9–12.

[78] SWD for the Geo-blocking Regulation Proposal, p. 12.

Consumer Rights Directive, they will inform the consumers about restrictions for delivery or payment beforehand.

3. *Option 2: Banning blocking of accessing:* this option focused on banning denial of access to a website, and rerouting could be subject to the customer's consent.
4. *Option 3: Banning blocking of access + equal treatment in specific situations (shop like a local):* this option focuses on banning denial of access to a website, and rerouting could be subject to the customer's consent. Plus, traders should also provide equal treatment for both foreign and local customers.
5. *Option 4: Banning blocking of accessing + list of justifications deemed not to be based on objective criteria:* this option focused on banning denial of access to a website and rerouting could be subject to the customer's consent plus to explain situations why they are not justified.
6. *Option 5: Banning blocking of accessing + equal treatment in specific situations (shop like a local) + obligation to serve customers across the EU:* this option focused on banning denial of access to a website and rerouting could be subject to customer's consent plus traders should also provide equal treatment for both foreign and local customers, and furthermore, companies should not refuse to deliver cross border as a general rule.
7. *Option 6: Other policy options,* such as publishing soft law, guidelines, and recommendations.

After considerations and comparisons, in the staff working document, the preferred option was Option 3, which means banning denial of access to a website and rerouting could be subject to the customer's consent, and traders should also provide equal treatment for both foreign and local customers. To achieve this goal, the Commission also had to choose the legal instrument which would be appropriate to reach these aims. To this end, legislating a regulation seemed to be the best option as, firstly, it is enforceable in all the countries, and secondly, the directive leaves some room for the Member States to choose their form and way to implement these objectives in their national legislation, and it creates a risk as rules can change between countries and objectives could not be achieved for a long time. Therefore, the regulation could also meet these criteria. As a result, the staff working document suggested that the Commission should adopt a proposal for Regulation, and it should choose option 3; this Geo-blocking Regulation should ban denial of access to a website, should require consent from customers to reroute them to a local store and traders should provide equal treatment for both foreign and local customers. To achieve these objectives, on 25 May 2016, the Geo-blocking Regulation Proposal was published.

The Geo-blocking Regulation Proposal explains its aim in an explanatory memorandum, and, according to this proposal, the Geo-blocking Regulation will:

- Prohibit the blocking of access to website and other online interfaces
- Prohibit rerouting the consumer from one country version to another
- Prohibit discrimination against customers for reasons related to nationality, place of residence and place of establishment of the customer in four specific cases:
  - Accessing online interfaces

- Accessing goods and services in these scenarios:
  - Selling of physical goods when the trader is not involved in the delivery of this good
  - Accessing electronically supplied service
  - Providing different services by the trader which is different from the customer's residence
- Non-discrimination for reasons related to payment
- Agreements on passive sales.

Furthermore, according to the explanatory memorandum, this proposal will not address pricing as such, and traders remain free to choose their prices as long as they choose these pricing strategies in a non-discriminatory manner. This proposal explains that the most affected sectors by geo-blocking are clothing, footwear and accessories, physical media (books), computer hardware and electronics, aeroplane tickets, car rental, digital content such as streaming services, computer games and software, e-books, and MP3. Nevertheless, although audiovisual services are one of the most affected sectors, they are not considered in the scope of this regulation as they are provided on the basis of exclusive territorial licences. Besides that, transportation sectors also excluded subject matter of the Geo-blocking Regulation proposal, such as discrimination with respect to sales of tickets for the transport of passengers since common rules related to transportation have already been regulated by the EU before.[79]

The Geo-blocking Regulation Proposal has eleven articles. Article 1 explains the objective and scope of this proposal, while Article 2 clarifies some definitions, where geo-blocking has not been defined. Articles 3, 4, 5, and 6 explain unjustified geo-blocking practices while articles 7 and 8 explain enforcement of these provisions by Member State authorities and require the designation of a body to deal with consumers' and traders' disputes. Article 9 remarkably regulates a necessary review provision in terms of the scope of the Geo-Blocking Regulation. This review clause firstly requires that 2 years after the entry into force of this Geo-Blocking

[79] Regulation (EC) No 1008/2008 of the European Parliament and of the Council of 24 September 2008 on common rules for the operation of air services in the Community; Regulation (EU) No 1177/2010 of the European Parliament and of the Council of 24 November 2010 concerning the rights of passengers when travelling by sea and inland waterway and amending Regulation (EC) No 2006/2004; Regulation (EU) 2017/2394 of the European Parliament and of the Council of 12 December 2017 on cooperation between national authorities responsible for the enforcement of consumer protection laws and repealing Regulation (EC) No 2006/2004 (this regulation has been excepted after this proposal, before that regulation the other Regulation name was: Regulation (EC) No 2006/2004); Regulation (EU) No 181/2011 of the European Parliament and of the Council of 16 February 2011 concerning the rights of passengers in bus and coach transport and amending Regulation (EC) No 2006/2004; Regulation (EC) No 1371/2007 of the European Parliament and of the Council of 23 October 2007 on rail passengers' rights and obligations.

Regulation, and every 5 years thereafter, the Commission should indicate an evaluation report.[80] Furthermore, Article 9 also regulates that Article 4(1)(b)[81] should be assessed whether *the prohibition of Article 4(1)(b) should also apply to electronically supplied services, the main feature of which is the provision of access to and use of copyright protected works or other protected subject matter, provided that the trader has the requisite rights for the relevant territories.*

Finally, articles 10 and 11 also regulate amended regulations and final provisions. After this proposal was published in May 2016, the Council of the European Union and the European Parliament started to analyse this proposal deeply, and they published numerous types of documents analysing these provisions. In the following part of this study, the documents published by the Council of the European Union and the European Parliament during the legislation procedure, until the main Regulation is published, will be evaluated, and which parts of the Geo-blocking Regulation proposal have been discussed and why and how these provisions were controversial will be explained in the following subtitle.

5.4.1.1 Assessment of Proposal by the EU Institutions and Proposed Changes

Geo-blocking has a very close relationship with the internal market, which requires the free movement of goods, services, capital and people.[82] On the other hand, the EU Law treaties also regulate that traders should be free to choose to conduct business with consumers.[83] Therefore, the new legislation regarding geo-blocking should have balanced these rights.

A very short time after the publication of the Geo-blocking Regulation Proposal, the European Economic and Social Committee (EESC) published an Opinion on 19 October 2016.[84] In this Opinion, the EESC welcomed the new proposal as geo-blocking conflicts with one of the very basic principles of the internal market since it prevents the free movement of goods and services across the border. At the same time,

---

[80] The first report was published in November 2020, 2 years after the Geo-Blocking Regulation entered into force. This study will also analyse this report in this chapter.

[81] Article 4(1)(b): *where the trader provides electronically supplied services, other than services the main feature of which is the provision of access to and use of copyright protected works or other protected subject matter.*

[82] European Parliament Study (2017) The Geo-blocking Proposal: Internal Market, Competition Law and Regulatory Aspects, p. 7 https://www.europarl.europa.eu/RegData/etudes/STUD/2017/595362/IPOL_STU(2017)595362_EN.pdf.

[83] European Parliament Study (2017) The Geo-blocking Proposal: Internal Market, Competition Law and Regulatory Aspects, p. 11 https://www.europarl.europa.eu/RegData/etudes/STUD/2017/595362/IPOL_STU(2017)595362_EN.pdf.

[84] Opinion of the European Economic and Social Committee on the 'Proposal for a Regulation of the European Parliament and of the Council on addressing geo-blocking and other forms of discrimination based on customers' nationality, place of residence or place of establishment within the internal market and amending Regulation (EC) No 2006/2004 and Directive 2009/22/EC' (2016) OJ C 34. (hereinafter will be referred to as the Opinion of the EESC for the Geo-blocking Proposal).

the EESC was aware that geo-blocking can also be justified as companies and, notably SMEs can have well-founded reasons to implement geo-blocking practises because of delivery cost, competition, and language requirements as such. Besides, this Opinion made it clear that the proposed regulation does not oblige any requirement to traders to deliver goods outside of national states or any other states where the customer is residing.

To clarify key points from the competition law perspective, the European Parliament published a study called 'The geo-blocking proposal: Internal Market, Competition Law and Regulatory Aspects'[85] on 11 September 2017, and made clear the importance of looking for Article 101 and 102 TFEU as export ban may be under the exemption of Article 101(3) and may not infringe Article 101(1) TFEU. Actually, the Commission was also willing to give some space to traders and ready to tolerate some geo-blocking activities especially if it costs much for a trader. From the competition law point, the European Parliament study only found that Article 6 of the proposed directive is problematic, which regulates agreements on passive sales. This article provides that *agreements imposing on traders obligations, in respect of passive sales, to act in violation of this Regulation shall be automatically void.*[86] The Parliament suggested that forbidding passive sales could not be the best option as a ban on active and passive sales has been designed to balance the rights of traders and changing this could mean possible harm to competition. The Parliament proposed to remove Article 6 from the Regulation.

Finally, this study also analysed the scope of the proposed Regulation. To start with, this study points out that this proposed Regulation only focused on the gaps that the Services Directive failed to regulate. Therefore, this study found the scope of this proposed Regulation was very limited. Besides, there are some gaps in the proposed Regulation; firstly, this proposed Regulation Article 1(3) provides a list of exclusions by reference to Article 2(2) of the Services Directive. Financial services, electronic communications, transport services and healthcare services are excluded from the Geo-blocking Regulation. Furthermore, there are some gaps related to these legislations and finally, there is a very debatable and significant gap which is the copyright gap. To explain briefly why and how they are considered as a gap in the proposed directive[87]:

1. Financial services: The Geo-blocking Regulation Proposal did not consider regulating financial services under this Regulation because, in the impact assessment of the Geo-blocking Regulation Proposal, it is explained that legislation is designed to address discrimination in access to certain financial services (such as mortgages or opening a bank account).

[85] European Parliament (2017) Directorate-General for Internal Policies of the Union, The geo-blocking proposal: internal market, competition law and regulatory aspects. In: Publications Office of the European Union https://op.europa.eu/en/publication-detail/-/publication/5784bfbc-9768-11e7-b92d-01aa75ed71a1 (hereinafter will be referred to as the European Parliament study for the Geo-blocking Proposal).

[86] The European Parliament study for the Geo-blocking Proposal, p. 22.

[87] The European Parliament study for the Geo-blocking Proposal, pp 27–29.

2. Electronic communications: The Roaming Regulation actually provides a prohibition to discriminate when providing internet access services which has a direct impact on the ability of service providers to geo-block in terms of roaming charges especially.
3. Transport services: As it is explained before, the Geo-blocking Regulation Proposal decided not to regulate transport services since common rules related to transportation have already been regulated by the EU before.
4. Healthcare services: Hence some cross-border mobility has already been facilitated by Directive 2011/24/EU of the European Parliament and of the Council of 9 March 2011 on the application of patients' rights in cross-border healthcare, the Commission decided not to include healthcare services under the Geo-blocking Regulation Proposal.
5. The SME gap: This proposed Regulation excludes certain undertakings from Article 4(2) due to the costs linked with registration for VAT purposes.[88]
6. The book sales gap: This exclusion is regulated under Article 4(3), which rules that *with respect to sales of books, the prohibition set out in paragraph 1 shall not preclude traders from applying different prices to customers in certain territories in so far as they are required to do so under the laws of Member States in accordance with Union law.*
7. The B2B (business-to-business) gap: This situation was regulated in Recital 12 of the Geo-blocking Regulation and regulated that preventing geo-blocking should not extend to customers purchasing a good or service for resale as this prohibition could have an effect on distribution systems.
8. The copyright gap: The proposed regulation included Article 4(1)(b), which regulates the electronically supplied service and made clear that traders are prohibited from imposing varying general conditions of access to their goods or services when offering electronically supplied services, except for services primarily focused on providing access to and using copyright-protected works or other protected subject matter. Furthermore, this regulation also excluded services regulated under Article 2(2) of the Services Directive, audiovisual services, including cinematographic services, whatever their mode of production, distribution and transmission, and radio broadcasting. Therefore, copyright-protected digital products have been excluded from the scope of this Regulation, and this limitation created lots of criticism. This debate will be evaluated later in this study.
9. The applicable law and after-sale services[89]: In this proposed Regulation, the wording of the applicable law, which is regulated in Article 1(5), is not clear, and it should be amended more clearly, and after-sale services such as return costs, compensation, warranty are not specifically explained and covered in the proposed Regulation.

---

[88] Article 4(2): The prohibition set out in point (b) of paragraph 1 shall not apply to traders that are exempted from VAT on the basis of the provisions of Chapter 1 of Title XII of Directive 2006/112/EC.

[89] Opinion of the EESC for the Geo-blocking Proposal.

To fill these gaps and have a broader and more consistent regulation, both the European Parliament and the Council of the EU have proposed some changes. To explain and outline some significant proposed amendments:

1. Firstly, the title of this Regulation was subject to amendment as both the Parliament and the Council proposed to add an 'unjustified' word to this topic; this change means that the title should change from '…addressing geo-blocking…' to '…addressing **unjustified** geo-blocking…'.
2. Secondly, the other main amendment was done by both the Parliament and the Council, which was to change from 'customer' to 'consumer', regarding the proposal to limit this Regulation's scope as it was considered that this limitation could be proportional for both parties.
3. Furthermore, changing the 'place of establishment' term to a 'temporary location' was also proposed to ensure that a non-discriminatory prohibition also covers temporary location.
4. Article 4 was one of the most significant discussions for both Parliament and the Council because of these points:

    a. Firstly, as mentioned before, the proposed Regulation provides for postponing the enforceability of Article 4(1)(b) for 2 years, which regulates electronically supplied service. Nevertheless, both the Parliament and the Council proposed to remove this exclusion.
    b. Secondly, the Parliament also offered to add electronically supplied services such as e-books, e-music games, and software to Article 4 of this Regulation to ensure that they are included in the scope of this Regulation if traders have requisite rights in the relevant territories for these copyright-protected works.

5. Also, both the Parliament and the Council proposed to clarify that this Regulation does not apply to purely internal situations in which there is no cross-border element included.
6. Furthermore, the Parliament proposed to remove Article 6 from the Regulation.
7. Finally, there are some amendments related to grammar and the proposal's language.

After all these assessments and proposed amendments, just before the voting which should be done in the Council of the European Union, on 19.02.2018, Luxembourg made a statement and criticism about the proposed Geo-blocking Regulation because Luxembourg believed that this proposed regulation does not provide any legal certainty, ambitious and concrete results. Although Luxembourg made a negative statement about the proposed regulation, in the voting, they voted 'yes'. Austrian Federal Council was the only country that voted as 'abstain',[90] claiming that the draft legislative act did not comply with the principle of subsidiarity, however, as decisions are usually reached by qualified majority voting in the Council of the European Union, this proposal has accepted by the qualified majority.

---

[90] Council of the European Union (2018) Voting Results https://data.consilium.europa.eu/doc/document/ST-6600-2018-INIT/EN/pdf.

5.4.2 *The Geo-Blocking Regulation*

After the proposed regulation and all the assessments and amendments, the Geo-blocking Regulation has been adopted. This Regulation also has eleven articles, like the proposed one; however, it was developed and amended thanks to the opinions and studies done by the EU Parliament, the Council of the EU, and the European Economic and Social Committee. To mainly outline what has been changed from the proposal:

1. The title of this regulation was amended as both the Parliament, and the Council proposed to add an 'unjustified' word to this topic; this change means that the title has changed from '...addressing geo-blocking...' to '...addressing **unjustified** geo-blocking...'.
2. Article 1 still regulates the objective and the scope of this regulation. Nevertheless, the Geo-blocking Regulation has a different approach than the proposed Regulation to analyse in which situations this Regulation finds application. While the proposed Regulation explained in which situations this regulation should have been applied, the Geo-blocking Regulation only explains the excluded scope of this regulation. Excluded scopes of the Geo-Blocking Regulation are:

   - Purely internal situations,
   - Article 2(2) of the Services Directive -audiovisual services, including cinematographic services, whatever their mode of production, distribution and transmission, and radio broadcasting-,
   - Also, this Regulation shall not affect the rules applicable to the field of taxation, the field of copyright and neighbouring rights, and judicial cooperation in civil matters.

3. In the Geo-blocking Regulation, the geo-blocking practices are explained, and somehow, the geo-blocking has been defined indirectly. Article 1(6) provides the scope of this Regulation in terms of which practises will be considered unjustified for geo-blocking, where a trader in particular:

   - Does not block or limit consumer's access to an online interface
   - Does not redirect consumers to a national version of the interface
   - Does not apply different conditions
   - Accepts payment methods without discrimination.

4. Article 4 was one of the most discussed topics during the legislation process, especially point b of Article 4(2). Hence, this Article regulates the exclusion of copyright-protected works from the scope of the Geo-blocking Regulation. As explained in the previous parts, the main criticism of this Regulation was having a limited scope. Yet, eventually, Article 4 was adopted as it is, without any substantial change. Nonetheless, the change has been done in terms of Article 11, which removes the postponing of enforceability of Article 4(1)(b), as the Council of the EU and the European Parliament agreed to remove the provision. Hence the evaluation article also included a part for the copyright-protected works

(Article 9), and the Commission promised to also evaluate after 2 years from the acceptance of this Geo-blocking Regulation whether or not this regulation shall apply to electronically supplied services, the main feature of which is the provision of access to and use of copyright-protected works or other protected subject matter, in the case *the trader has the requisite rights for the relevant territories*. Furthermore, as part of this evaluation, the Commission promised to evaluate the consequences of the extending the scope of this regulation to the audiovisual services.[91] Nevertheless, the Article or Recitals do not include any provisions regarding the explanation of what is meant by the 'having the requisite rights for the relevant territories'. Therefore, that is not clear which rights and from which countries are needed to clear in order to serve to other countries. This interpretation becomes particularly important, especially in determining when a trader responds to unsolicited customer requests from other Member States, which is crucial for understanding the potential impact of extending the Geo-blocking Regulation. Indeed, in November 2020, the Commission published its first and short-term evaluation report[92] for the Geo-blocking Regulation.

5. Furthermore, Article 6 has been amended, which regulates passive sales as it is discussed before.
6. Additionally, Article 7, which regulates the enforcement of this regulation, also changes a little, as the proposed regulation only provides a penalty applicable for infringements of the provisions of this Regulation, the Geo-blocking Regulation asks the Member States to set out the applicable measures to infringements of the provisions of the Geo-blocking Regulation and ensure that they are implemented as well as with the penalties.
7. Article 11, which regulates final provisions, also includes the postponement of the enforceability of Article 6 (passive sales), and the final provision regulates that: "*Article 6 shall apply to provisions of agreements concluded before 2 March 2018 that are compliant with Article 101 TFEU and with any equivalent rules of national competition law from 23 March 2020.*"

To summarise the geo-blocking regulation:

1. The aim of this regulation is to prohibit discrimination based on customers' nationality, place of residence or place of establishment within the internal market when they try to access goods and services.
2. Types of goods and services are not limited; this Regulation covers all types of goods, including electronically supplied services. On the other hand, this Regulation does not cover copyright-protected electronically supplied services and audiovisual services; however, according to Article 9, this area will be covered by evaluation reports. At the same time, this regulation does not cover financial services, healthcare services, and transportation services.

[91] Statement by the Commission, the Geo-blocking Regulation.

[92] Commission Staff Working Document First short-term review of the Geo-blocking Regulation SWD (2020) 294. (hereinafter will be referred to as the Short-Term Review Report for the Geo-blocking Regulation).

3. The trader:
   - Has to sell to customers without discrimination based on customers' nationality, place of residence or place of establishment.
   - Has to provide the same conditions and should not offer different conditions such as a higher price or if a seller refuses to sell the product in three specific cases, which are:
     - The sale of goods without physical delivery, but if the customer is willing to collect it at the trader's premises or organise delivery himself to his home
     - The sale of electronically supplied services
     - The sale of services provided in a specific physical location
   - Has to allow access to a website.
   - Must not redirect the customer automatically from one version to another, without the consent of the customer.
   - Has to accept payments without discrimination based on customers' nationality, place of residence or place of establishment.
   - Does not have to deliver the goods to the customer's state.
4. To ensure these objectives are met, Member States should designate a body or bodies responsible for the enforcement of the Geo-Blocking Regulation and should take all measures necessary to ensure that they are implemented.
5. Finally, each Member State also designates a body whose job is to provide assistance to consumers in the event of a dispute between a consumer and a trader.

5.4.3 Short-Term Reviews of the Geo-Blocking Regulation

To assess the effectiveness and enforceability of the Geo-blocking Regulation, reviews that should have happened in a short period of time were necessary. Especially as explained above, Article 9 of the Regulation provides a periodic review of this Regulation, and the first review should have been done 2 years from the entry into force of this Regulation. The main aim of this periodic review was to assess the impact of the possible extension of the Regulation's scope to copyright-protected digital products. To that end, the European Commission and the Council of the European Union have published three important studies regarding the possible impacts of the extension of the Regulation to copyright-protected digital products. These studies are:

1. Study on the impacts of the extension of the scope of the regulation to audiovisual and non-audiovisual services giving access to copyright-protected content (The study by VVA et al.), dated 2020.[93]

---

[93] Richard Prooce VVA et al. (2020) European Commission Study on the impacts of the extension of the scope of the geo-blocking regulation to audiovisual and non-audiovisual

2. Report from the Commission and the Commission Staff Working Document on the first short-term review of the Geo-blocking Regulation (The short-term review), dated 30.11.2020.
3. JRC Digital Economy Working Paper 2020–01 on Geo-blocking: A literature review and new evidence in online audio-visual services, by Broocks, A., N. Duch-Brown, E. Gómez-Herrera and B. Martens (The JRC Working Paper on Geo-blocking).

***The study by VVA* et al.** aims to provide an overview of the possible consequences of the extension of the scope of this Regulation. It relies on comprehensive data rather than theoretical economic modelling and the data sourced from various geographical areas in the European Union, each potentially having different demands for digital services. These countries are Belgium, Bulgaria, Estonia, France, Germany, Ireland, Italy, and Poland.[94] To collect this data, the study has conducted a survey with 8000 consumers, stakeholder interviews, desk research, and mystery shopping surveys.[95] These findings will be important points for the final part of this study, where the present author will provide her recommendations for the EU policymakers.

As the Regulation does not explain what is meant by 'having rights in the relevant territories', this study focused on two different scenarios to identify relevant territories where the rights need to be cleared.[96] The first scenario is that the obligations established by the Geo-blocking Regulation would be applicable if the trader possesses the right, either through a licence agreement or as the original rightsholder, to offer the content in the Member State where the customer seeking to purchase the service is located. In the second scenario, if the trader has the relevant rights to disseminate these contents only in the Member States where the trader is actively promoting these services, this would be enough, and the passive sales will be permitted for the area where the customer is seeking access.

This review has done its analysis by dividing sectors into four, which are: audiovisual services, online music, e-books, and finally, games.

The short-term review report from the Commission to the European Parliament, the Council, the European Economic and Social Committee and the Committee of the Regions has been published regarding the first short-term review of the Geo-blocking Regulation in November 2020.

The short-term review looked into (i) the implementation and functioning of the internal market, (ii) the potential costs and benefits of changing the scope of the Regulation, (iii) and finally, the evaluation of extending the scope of the Regulation into other sectors such as audiovisual services and copyright-protected non-audiovisual services. In this part of the study, only the assessment related to audiovisual services and copyright-protected non-audiovisual services will be summarised.

---

services giving access to copyright protected content—Final report. In: Publications Office of the European Union https://op.europa.eu/en/publication-detail/-/publication/4fc70542-223b-11eb-b57e-01aa75ed71a1/language-en (hereinafter will be referred to as the study by VVA et al.).

[94] The study by VVA et al., p. xv.

[95] The study by VVA et al., p. xiv.

[96] The study by VVA et al., p. xv.

In this review, the European Commission made clear the scope of the assessment in terms of copyright aspects, and the Commission pointed out[97]:

(i) Electronically supplied services which require clearing intellectual property rights were excluded from this Regulation. Additionally, audiovisual media services were also subject to different EU legislations, such as the AVMSD.
(ii) This assessment took into account the increasing demand of the consumers, the potential impacts of any extension of this Regulation on consumers, businesses and all the stakeholders in these sectors, and as well as considering any extension provided that the trader has the requisite rights for the relevant territories.

This report aimed to show the results of nearly 2 years of implementation of the Geo-blocking Regulation as well as whether or not this Regulation shall apply to electronically supplied services, the main feature of which is the provision of access to and use of copyright-protected works or other protected subject matter, and audio-visual services, in the case the trader has the requisite rights for the relevant territories. Therefore, this evaluation was necessary to decide on extending the scope of the Geo-blocking Regulation.

The main findings were these:

1. Firstly, the evaluation was supposed to be done by March 2020 according to the Regulation; however, because of the Covid-19 crisis, the report was published in November 2020. Hence, throughout 2020, there has still been a Coronavirus outbreak; the report could be affected by this and during the pandemic. Furthermore, as e-commerce has largely been affected by the Covid-19 crisis and gained more power when compared to traditional commerce, this evaluation report would have changed a lot if it had been done a few months or years later. This issue will be explained in detail in the final part of the study.
2. According to the report, there are some initial positive effects, as blocking access to websites or rerouting consumers to other websites has decreased.

For the copyright-protected content, this review mainly summarises all of the findings presented by the study by VVA et al.; therefore, the main source for this study in terms of the short-term results will be the study by VVA et al., whereas when the review points to a new and important point, the short-term review will also be referenced. As an attachment to the short-term review, the Commission also published a fifteen-page report on the first short-term review of the Geo-blocking Regulation, which mainly summarises the main findings briefly and shows a road map regarding the following steps and legislative interventions if needed.

The JRC Working Paper on Geo-blocking has also tried to analyse the possible results of the extension of this Regulation to copyright-protected digital products by relying on empirical data and literature review. The main aim of this study is to show the new evidence in the context of audiovisual content; therefore, only the findings for the audiovisual sectors of the paper will be referenced.

---

[97] The Short-Term Review Report for the Geo-blocking Regulation: part 2, 3.

In the following part, the present author will summarise some findings presented by these studies. This part will only briefly summarise the findings regarding the potential impact of the extension just to show why the EU has not decided to extend the scope of the Regulation as a result of the first short-term review.

5.4.3.1 Findings from the First Reviews of the Geo-Blocking Regulation: Findings for the Audiovisual Copyright-Protected Services

The audiovisual services market was the largest sector covered in these studies,[98] which means any changes in the Regulation in terms of audiovisual services will have a great impact on the EU. Audiovisual services have been subject to various sector-specific legislation in the EU up to the present date, especially the Services Directive, the Audiovisual Media Services Directive, and the Online Television and Radio Programmes Directive. These directives and other related legislations were and will only be discussed in this study, where these are relevant to the distribution and availability of copyright-protected services.

In this report, it was suggested that in the EU, audiovisual services are usually available in four different business models: (i) free-to-air and pay-TV catch-up services, (ii) TVOD—Transactional Video-on-Demand or pay-per-view services, (iii) SVOD—Subscription Video-on-Demand or streaming and finally (iv) Electronic-Sell-Through (EST) or download to own.[99]

In free-to-air and pay-TV catch-up services, public and commercial broadcasters provide online platforms accessible on multiple devices, and these services offer live channels and on-demand content, including replays of recently aired programs. Transactional Video-on-demand or pay-per-view services function as digital stores utilized by pay-TV operators, broadcasters, retailers, and other online platforms, and users pay per transaction for time-limited access to premium video content such as films, series, and sports events. Subscription Video-on-Demand or streaming services provide unlimited access to a diverse range of titles across genres. Consumers pay a regular fee for streaming premium content like films, series, and sports events. Electronic-Sell-Through (EST) or download to own users can purchase unlimited usage rights for specific video files, accessible through cloud-based or offline storage. Content is acquired through a one-time transaction, ensuring permanent accessibility after purchase.[100]

The study by VVA et al. makes some reference to studies done by the European Audiovisual Observatory regarding audiovisual market research and according to the European Audiovisual Observatory study published in 2018, the financing sources

---

[98] The study by VVA et al., p. 70.

[99] The study by VVA et al., p. 73–74.

[100] The study by VVA et al., p. 73–74.

for the film industry coming from public funding and broadcaster investments, pre-sales funding and producer investments.[101] The study done by VVA et al. points out that the pre-sales have a great impact on distribution and licensing practices since pre-sales funders usually engage in single territory licences or only for a few territories[102] since distribution and showcase of these contents are handled at the national level with local operators.[103] Licensing practices are also very different from the other sectors covered in this study since, in the audiovisual sector, there are usually different broadcasting times, and the licences are usually given in different time windows.[104] As such, for the same audiovisual content, licences are usually distributed in different time windows to different platforms; for example, the same content could be licensed to platform X for pay-TV purposes, while the same content could also be licensed to platform Y for EST/download and physical copies purposes.[105] These differences in the licensing practices and the size of the market make the assessment more complex to provide a straightforward answer in this sector.

The study by VVA et al. also references another study by Oxera and O&O consultants that examines the possible results of lifting geo-blocking practices in 2016.[106] In this study, dated 2016, it is anticipated that larger and richer countries usually have catalogues with numerous options and earlier release dates, while this is the exact opposite for the smaller and poorer countries. This study by Oxera and O&O consultants analysed the potential effects of lifting geo-blocking practices, and it showed that lower-income EU members would be especially disproportionally affected by that change. The study suggests that since locally targeted contents would be affected and the consumer welfare would be lost, in the long term, the consumer would be lost, and that may have an effect on investment, production and cultural/linguistic diversity.

The study by VVA et al. also had some field work and presented some feedback from the industry.[107] The industry stakeholders thought that, with the exclusion of geo-blocking, the prices for the same services would be higher, the consumer choice would be decreased, and there would be less tailored content and less cultural diversity. The prices would be higher since the cost of the pan-European licence would be much more expensive than the territorial ones, and this cost would be shifted to consumers. Related to that, the platforms may afford less content than before, which would result in less consumer choice. Furthermore, especially in lower-income countries, there may be reduced incentives for operators to offer customized content due to limited market size and lower potential for cost recovery. This could result in a dominance of English language content and less tailored content, which would diminish the cultural diversity within the EU.

[101] The study by VVA et al., p. 77.

[102] The study by VVA et al., p. 81.

[103] The study by VVA et al., p. 84.

[104] The study by VVA et al., p. 82.

[105] The study by VVA et al., p. 82–84.

[106] The study by VVA et al., p. 92–93.

[107] The study by VVA et al., p. 97–98.

On the other hand, the JRC Working Paper on Geo-blocking worked on the data provided by Lumiere (2019) and Ampere (2019), and this paper analysed the availability of audiovisual content in the EU. Cross-border availability has been found to be relatively low across the EU, especially for national SVOD platforms.[108] This paper suggests that if the geo-blocking lifted, the smaller platforms would potentially gain more increases in the number of available titles.

In that study, there were different surveys to understand consumer behaviour which would possibly be affected by any extension. This study asked consumers to imagine three specific switching scenarios: In the first example, the offer remains exactly the same, but only the price varies. Not surprisingly, 64% of consumers would switch their audiovisual subscription if the price drop by merely 10% while the offer remains the same. In example 2, the offer provides similar content/catalogue but is intended for users in other countries and may not include the consumers' preferred language, with the price also varying. Almost half (46%) of consumers in the general audiovisual sector are not willing to switch at any price discount if their preferred language is not available. Finally, in the last example, the offer is intended for users in other countries, may not include consumers' preferred language, and may feature limited local/national content, with the price also varying. In this case, 53% of consumers would not be willing to switch if local audiovisual content is limited. As a result of this:

- In the case of Scenario 1, where the trader possesses the right, either through a licence agreement or as the original rightsholder, to offer the content in the Member State where the customer seeking to purchase the service is located, if the same service is available for a lower price, the price-sensitive consumer would switch their subscription with the lower alternative. This would result in an 8% reduction in the average revenue per subscription.[109] At the same time, according to the survey responses from consumers who are not subscribed to any of the SVOD platforms, around 4% would be a member of these platforms after this extension.
- Scenario 2, where the trader has the relevant rights to disseminate these contents only in the Member States where the trader is actively promoting these services and the passive sales will be permitted for the area where the customer is seeking access, would result in more product variety for consumers, and in that case, consumers would also switch their subscriptions to the cheaper versions or the ones which have more content. This also would mean some gross revenue loss as a result of consumer switching, which is expected at 4%.[110] On the other hand, the more attractive subscriptions with more alternative and expensive versions would attract consumers, and as such, the study suggests that an overall slight increase in SVOD would be expected.[111]

[108] JRC report, p. 16.

[109] JRC report, p. 126.

[110] JRC report, p. 131.

[111] JRC report, p. 133.

In the final part of the study by VVA et al., they summarised their expectations regarding the impact of extending the scope of the Geo-blocking Regulation.[112]

- For the pre-sales: The study has used some figures to explain the contribution of pre-sales to cinema productions (see p 161 and 162), and this illustrated that if the budget of the film was low, the pre-sales funding was also low, while high budget films also usually received a high amount of pre-sales contribution. This means any extension of the Geo-blocking Regulation would affect the high- and super-high-budget films in terms of pre-sales contribution.
- The study by VVA et al. suggests that an extension compatible with Scenario 2 would be positive in terms of content variety, yet this would result in complex implications for the audiovisual sectors since consumers would also switch their subscriptions to the cheaper versions or the ones which have more content.
- The study also illustrates its limitations. To start with, the study only modelled SVOD, and other business models have not been explained widely in this study. Secondly, sports have not been modelled separately, which would potentially be very different from the remaining sectors in terms of cross-border demands and live-streaming needs. Finally, the study also did not take into account the possible impact of language differentiations.
- The smaller SVOD providers would be negatively affected as a result of the hypothetical lifting of geo-blocking, yet this study also did not model this potential impact separately.

The short-term review also mainly summarises all of the findings from the study by VVA et al. Apart from the summary, this review correctly points out the Covid-19 crisis and the rapid increase in online consumption.[113] Nevertheless, although this study correctly emphasised the Covid-19 crisis, the review was written in the second half of 2020, and it could not take into account the full effect of this crisis. Yet, it is undeniable that the Covid-19 crisis had a strong and unchangeable effect on online consumption, especially in the audiovisual sectors. The effects of this crisis will be explained in the last chapter of this study, with the more up-to-date data.

5.4.3.2 Findings from the First Reviews of the Geo-Blocking Regulation: Findings for the Non-Audiovisual Copyright-Protected Services

5.4.3.2.1 Findings for the Music Industry

The study by VVA et al. has shared its findings in terms of the music industry, and the main business models for the music industry could be summarised as follows[114]:

---

[112] JRC report, pp. 158–175.

[113] Short-Term Review Report for the Geo-blocking Regulation, p. 86.

[114] The study by VVA et al., pp 181–182.

- Single-song download: With this system, consumers download a song for permanent use and offline use in exchange for a fee. iTunes is one of the most important players in this model.
- Freemium: In this model, the important streaming services usually offer a free version of their service, where only a few songs are available or have fewer features. For the more advanced features, like playing the song that the consumer desires or offline mode, the services usually ask for premium subscriptions. Spotify and Deezer are the most important players to offer freemium subscriptions as of 2023.
- Subscription-based: In this model, subscribers usually have access to all catalogues of songs, and they pay a regular fee to become subscribers. Apple Music and Google Play Music could be given as examples.
- The free advertising-based model mixes audiovisual and music content such as YouTube.

In this study, the main focus was the subscription-based model since one of the most important highlights in this report was that the revenue coming from subscriptions to music services constituted more than half of the total revenue of the music industry.[115]

For the territorial exclusivity, the study presented that the licence distribution almost has no territorial exclusivity, and the same content is usually distributed to multiple streaming services at the same time without exclusivity, even though the rightsholders usually acquire licences on a country basis rather than pan-EU licences.[116] Additionally, the cross-border availability of these contents has been found to be around 73% to 82%.[117]

The short-term review pointed out that geo-blocking practices in the music streaming sector primarily aim to implement price differentiation strategies across different EU Member States, reflecting significant price variations between higher income/demand and lower income/demand countries.[118] As a result of these studies, language is found to be not a substantial factor influencing consumer switching in the music industry.

In Scenario 1,[119] where the trader possesses the right, either through a licence agreement or as the original rightsholder, to offer the content in the Member State where the customer seeking to purchase the service is located, if the same service is available for a lower price, it is anticipated that if the Geo-blocking Regulation's scope is extended, consumers may switch to cheaper versions of the same service due to price differentiation across Member States. This could lead to a substantial 25% reduction in average transaction revenue.[120] The analysis, however, does not consider potential competitive responses or supply-side changes. As a result of this scenario,

[115] The study by VVA et al., p. 178.

[116] The study by VVA et al., p. 188.

[117] The study by VVA et al., p. 188.

[118] Short-Term Review Report for the Geo-blocking Regulation, p. 8.

[119] The study by VVA et al., pp 205–206.

[120] The study by VVA et al., p. 197.

the EU may adopt the approach with uniform pricing across the EU, which may lead to price harmonization but potentially negative overall effects. Mitigation strategies may involve increased price harmonization across countries, possibly leading to higher prices in low-demand countries. Other strategies, such as limiting language interfaces or adapting playlists, could also deter switching to cheaper versions. However, the overall welfare effects of increased price harmonization are uncertain and may have negative implications, depending on the balance between price decreases in high-demand countries and potential price increases in low-demand countries. Scenario 2[121] would also have the same outcome as Scenario 1, where subscribers would switch to cheaper versions of their services. The potential impact on smaller national platforms remains uncertain, requiring further investigation into the specific implications for these players.[122]

5.4.3.2.2 Findings for e-books

According to the study by VVA et al.,[123] usually, non-exclusive licences for e-books are distributed on a territorial basis. Interviews with the stakeholders also showed that the demand for cross-border access to e-books appears to be low, especially when compared to other content services.[124] According to the surveys done by consumers, the study has found that consumers are especially looking for price, language accessibility and local content availability of e-books.[125]

For e-books, there is a significant gap in product availability in different member states; for example, while major markets like the UK and Italy have over 90% availability, Bulgaria, Czechia, and Poland only have around 60%. The extension of the scope of this Regulation has been found to be a solution to this problem.

Alongside that, the study by VVA has found that the price differences across Member States in iTunes' e-book catalogues are generally minor, mostly within ± EUR 0.05. At the same time, some Member States have the application of fixed-price applications for e-books in various Member States, which may result in consumers avoiding this practice in the case of extending the Geo-blocking Regulation.[126] Furthermore, it could be expected that smaller booksellers may experience relatively higher challenges, including increased price pressure and higher administrative costs and could be forced to exit the market.[127]

Under Scenario 1, where the trader possesses the right, either through a licence agreement or as the original rightsholder, to offer the content in the Member State where the customer seeking to purchase the service is located, if the same service is

---

[121] The study by VVA et al., pp. 210, 211.

[122] The study by VVA et al., p. 213.

[123] The study by VVA et al., p. 225.

[124] The study by VVA et al., p. 226.

[125] The study by VVA et al., p. 235.

[126] The study by VVA et al., p. 229.

[127] The study by VVA et al., p. 229.

available for a lower price, since the current licensing practices usually do not on a territorial basis and give the opportunity for cross-border accessibility, no substantial changes would be expected.[128] Furthermore, since the price differentiation between countries is relatively low, the effect on consumer switching for the industry would be expected to be very low in both scenarios.[129] Therefore, the overall expectation in the case where geo-blocking is lifted is that the market would not be dramatically affected by that change because of low demand for cross-border accessibility of e-books from the consumer's side, the importance of the language and the minimal price changes between countries.

5.4.3.2.3 Findings for Games/Software

The study by VVA et al. had some field work, and according to the feedback from the interviews, industry stakeholders agreed that price differentiation between member states was necessary in order to gain more revenue and boost sales in different countries with different affordability.[130] Also, the stakeholders emphasised that the smaller companies usually test the market by making their games available only in a few countries; therefore, if geo-blocking were lifted, these companies would not test the market.[131]

For the licensing practices, the stakeholders also pointed out that licences are already usually distributed EEA-wide, and almost all of the games are identical within all EU countries. As such, the possible impacts of lifting geo-blocking have been found hard to quantify. Also, the stakeholders added the need for compliance costs, such as payment, language, VAT requirements and relevant laws.[132]

This study also made some reference to Eurobarometer surveys, which showed that the demand for cross-border access to video games is considerably low, at around 4%. At the same time, the cross-border availability of the games in Member States was already almost at the desired level; for example, for PC games on Steam, the unavailability of the games across all Member States was only around 3%.[133] Furthermore, the price differentiation from one Member State to another has been found to be minimal.[134] Therefore, the effect on the game sector, extending the scope of this Regulation, would be minimal, according to both studies.

Demand for software also usually depends on the language or localised versions of these services; therefore, according to the short-term review, the cross-border demand is relatively low compared to other sectors.[135] On the other hand, the study

[128] The study by VVA et al., p. 241.
[129] The study by VVA et al., pp. 241–244.
[130] The study by VVA et al., p. 257.
[131] The study by VVA et al., p. 257.
[132] The study by VVA et al., p. 258.
[133] The study by VVA et al., p. 267.
[134] The study by VVA et al., p. 269.
[135] Short-Term Review Report for the Geo-blocking Regulation, p. 52.

by VVA et al. did not model the software and possible impacts on the software industry as a result of the extension separately; therefore, the data and survey were very limited in that regard.

5.4.3.3 Concluding Remarks

The findings from these studies show that extending the scope of the Geo-blocking Regulation would have an impact, either positive or negative, on most sectors. The findings for the potential impact on the music industry usually present possible negative outcomes, whereas for audiovisual services, there could be some potential benefits. Although these studies are quite important in terms of deciding the scope of the Regulation, these assessments usually relied on the data provided between 2015 and 2019. With digitisation and changes in consumption trends, the need for new data and new analysis could easily be supported, and there is a need for a new study that reflects the current trends in online consumption after 2020. The report from the Commission has also emphasised this, and it suggested a new assessment of the full impact of the Covid-19 crisis.[136] Furthermore, this report also suggested a dialogue with stakeholders and another stock-taking exercise in 2022 to decide on the amendments needed for the legislation and any other follow-up measures.[137] The report finally emphasises the importance of copyright licensing practises and copyright law considerations to decide the extension of this Regulation.

5.4.4 Reports and Follow-Up Actions After the Short-Term Review

After the short-term review published in 2020, the Commission and the Parliament have started to follow-up actions and published a few reports. In this part of the study, the actions and reports until May 2026 will be summarised related to the extension of the Regulation.

- Firstly, the EU Commission launched a ***stakeholder dialogue*** in 2021 to discuss and hear industry solutions from the stakeholders on access to and availability of audiovisual content across the EU. The results of this stakeholder dialogue will be explained in the final chapter of the study, since this stakeholder dialogue was proposed as a part of the EU's Media and Audiovisual Action Plan, which plan will be explained in the final chapter of this study.
- ***The European Parliament*** had a plenary debate on 11 March 2021 and the Parliament was subject to parliamentary questions which scrutinise the scope of the Regulation.

---

[136] The study by VVA et al., p. 2.

[137] The study by VVA et al., p. 2.

- In May 2023, the European Parliamentary Research Service published an assessment called ***Implementation of the 2018 Geo-Blocking Regulation in the digital single market***.
- After this assessment, the Committee on the Internal Market and Consumer Protection prepared ***a draft report*** (Rapporteur: Beata Mazurek) in June 2023.
- In July 2023 and October 2023, the opinions of the Committee on Culture and Education and the Committee on Legal Affairs were published, respectively.
- In December 2023, the European Parliament published a ***resolution*** and voted on the extension of this Regulation.
- Finally, in January 2025, the European Commission issued a ***call for evidence*** in relation to the Geo-blocking Regulation and announced that, in connection therewith, it would carry out an evaluation of the Regulation in 2026.

5.4.4.1 The European Parliament's Plenary Debate and Answers to the Scope of the Geo-Blocking Regulation

After the short-term review was published, the Parliament held a plenary debate on 11 March 2021.[138] In this debate, around 30 MEPs shared their opinion regarding the implementation, enforcement and any possible extension of the Geo-blocking Regulation. For the possible extension, the MEPs noted that the Commission would evaluate the current situation with another report until 2022 so that further action could be taken.

To decide on the scope of the Geo-blocking Regulation and have an EU-wide implementation on certain aspects, some questions have been asked to the European Commission by some MEPs. One of the questions that 18 MEPs referred to Parliament was about the inclusion of copyright-protected content in the Geo-Blocking Regulation. The MEPs suggested that in terms of equality, protection of linguistic minorities and cultural diversity, this inclusion could be beneficial. The Parliament again pointed out the stakeholder dialogues and further review would be done until 2022 and suggested that according to these reports, further action would be taken.

5.4.4.2 Implementation of the 2018 Geo-Blocking Regulation in the Digital Single Market Report

In May 2023, after two and a half years from the short-term review, the European Parliamentary Research Service published an assessment prepared by Eckhard Binder with Veronika Juhász.[139] This assessment mainly evaluated the findings

---

[138] European Parliament (2021) 'Sitting of 11-03-2021. In: Europarl. < https://www.europarl.europa.eu/plenary/en/vod.html?mode=chapter&vodLanguage=EN&playerStartTime=20210311-15:39:20&playerEndTime=20210311-16:08:54#.

[139] European Parliament (2023) Implementation of the 2018 Geo-blocking Regulation in the digital single market. In Europarl. https://www.europarl.europa.eu/thinktank/en/document/EPRS_IDA(2023)740255 (hereinafter will be referred as the Implementation Report).

from the short-term review and the important updates regarding the extension of the scope of this Regulation and also explained the follow-up actions done by the EU bodies until May 2023. The summary of the short-term review and follow-up actions have already been presented in this study. Therefore, no further explanations and a summary will be made in that part.

This assessment points out that the short-term review, which was planned for 2 years after the entry into force date of the Regulation, the review was too early because it had to be published without accessing a reasonable amount of data.[140] This present author also strongly agrees with that point since the Member States were not in a hurry to designate a body for enforcement, which resulted in a delay in the implementation of the Geo-Blocking Regulation within the internal market. For example, until the first quarter of 2019, which means after one year, the Geo-Blocking Regulation entered into force, there was no enforcement or supervision available in most Member States. Furthermore, until July 2019, there were still 6 Member States remaining to designate a body for enforcement of the Geo-Blocking Regulation.[141] Therefore, the review could have been done after a reasonable amount of data had been collected over 3 years from all the Member States, as the European Commission's Better Regulation Guidelines recommended.[142]

5.4.4.3 The Draft Report by Beata Mazurek

In June 2023, Rapporteur Beata Mazurek prepared a draft report regarding the implementation of the Geo-blocking Regulation in the digital single market. This report started with a summary of the initial findings of the short-term review. After this brief summary, the Rapporteur explained her position in that regard.[143]

The Rapporteur suggested[144]:

- To analyse a broader legislative framework and access to cross-border transactions.
- Evaluation of the strengthening of the right to 'passive sales.'
- Full application and enforcement of the Geo-blocking Regulation.
- To see the organic evolution of the audiovisual business sector, which met consumer expectations, as happened in the music industry, since the inclusion of the scope of this Regulation would harm the complex nature of this creative sector, especially in terms of licensing practices and copyright law considerations.
- (The Commission should) To provide further guidance for Member States on the application of this Regulation with reference to the Services Directive.

[140] Implementation Report, p. 4.

[141] Short-Term Review Report for the Geo-blocking Regulation, p. 4.

[142] Implementation Report, p. 4.

[143] European Parliament Draft Report on the implementation of the 2018 Geo-blocking Regulation in the digital single market 2023/2019 (INI), 5. (hereinafter will be referred as the Draft Report).

[144] The Draft Report, p. 6.

- To continue analysing the effects of this Regulation since it has not been sufficiently reflected in 2020 reports due to changes in the consumption of digital products with the help of the Covid-19 break and technological advancements.

After these suggestions, on behalf of the Committee on the Internal Market and Consumer Protection, the Rapporteur tabled a motion for a European Parliament Resolution.[145]

5.4.4.4 Opinions of Committees

The Committee on Culture and Education published its opinion[146] in July 2023, and this opinion has been prepared by the Rapporteur Sabine Verheyen. This report has found that the extension of the Geo-blocking Regulation would not bring any substantial benefits to consumers and would bring negative consequences in terms of costs and the number of contents.[147] Also, this report mentioned the importance of the territorial exclusivity of the films in terms of investment.[148] Furthermore, exclusive territorial licences have been found to be beneficial for cultural diversity.[149] Also, the report suggested that the inclusion of audiovisual services in the scope of this Regulation would deter revenue, contractual freedom, distribution and exhibition, and it would create some confusion on compliance with national rules.[150]

The Committee on Legal Affairsalso published its opinion[151] in October 2023 and this report has been prepared by the Rapporteur Karen Melchior. This opinion, different from the opinion of the Committee on Culture and Education, pointed out that cross-border availability of content and licensing in more areas would actually help linguistic minorities.[152] If this availability exists, linguistic minorities will have the chance to watch and access these contents, which are available in their mother tongue.[153]

One interesting thing in this report was that, on Point 14, the report says that: 'Recalls that the Geo-blocking Regulation allows consumers access to online content services in other Member States if the service provider holds the rights for their territories'. However, this statement is not true and is misleading. The Geo-blocking

---

[145] The Draft Report, p. 7.

[146] Opinion of the Committee on Culture and Education on the implementation of the 2018 Geo-blocking Regulation in the digital single market (2023/2019(INI). (hereinafter will be referred to as the Opinion of the Culture and Education Committee).

[147] The Opinion of the Culture and Education Committee, p. 3.

[148] The Opinion of the Culture and Education Committee, p. 3.

[149] The Opinion of the Culture and Education Committee, p. 4.

[150] The Opinion of the Culture and Education Committee, p. 4.

[151] Opinion of the Committee on Legal Affairs on the implementation of the 2018 Geo-blocking Regulation in the digital single market (2023/2019(INI). (hereinafter will be referred to as the Opinion of the Legal Affairs Committee).

[152] The Opinion of the Legal Affairs Committee, p. 7.

[153] The Opinion of the Legal Affairs Committee, p. 7.

Regulation indeed does not allow consumers access to online content services in other Member States if the service provider holds the rights for their territories. For example, if Netflix cleared the right to the series called 'The Crown' in Belgium, but not for in France, a French consumer who lives permanently in France would not be allowed to subscribe and watch this series from Netflix Belgium. This report, most probably, meant the Portability Regulation, which allows consumers to access their subscribed online portable services for a limited period of time when they are temporarily in other EU Member States. Nevertheless, since the Portability Regulation accepts the country-of-origin principle as explained in the previous subtitle, there is no need to clear the rights for other territories. No further explanation, correction or clarification was made regarding Point 14 as of June 2024.

The other suggestions presented by this Committee are also the same as those of the Committee on Culture and Education.

5.4.4.5 Parliamentary Vote in December 2023 and the European Parliament Resolution

The European Parliament published a Resolution[154] on the implementation of the 2018 Geo-blocking Regulation in the Digital Single Market on 13 December 2023 by 376 votes to 111, with 107 abstentions.

The important points from the Resolution regarding the extension of the Regulation are the following:

- The Resolution started with the developments regarding the extension up to date until December, as well as the implementation of geo-blocking and findings from the short-term reviews.
- It also points out the importance of data collection and more analysis, taking into account recent effects on consumer behaviour and market dynamics.
- The need for assessing the effectiveness of passive sales (Article 6) with reference to the competition law has been pointed out.
- Furthermore, the resolution has also accepted that the circulation of audiovisual content and the availability of these contents is not at the desired level now, and there is more to be done to preserve and reflect the richness and diversity of culture in the EU.
- This Resolution also emphasised the need for linguistic minorities to access the contents of their mother tongue.
- The Resolution also pointed out that the use of circumvention tools is very popular to access unauthorised copyright content, therefore, the need for meeting the expectations of consumers would be effective, especially for audiovisual content.

[154] European Parliament resolution of 13 December 2023 on the implementation of the 2018 Geo-blocking Regulation in the digital single market (2023/2019(INI)). (hereinafter will be referred to as the European Parliament Resolution).

- It also emphasised the importance of the stakeholder dialogue in terms of complex value chains and other important factors such as investments, contractual freedom, price stability and expectations of the industry.
- The Resolution also highlighted the findings from the first short-term review of the Geo-blocking Regulation, which suggested that expanding the availability of audiovisual works in response to unsolicited consumer requests, without needing additional licences, could increase cross-border demand for such content. This, in turn, would enhance cultural diversity and allow content to reach new audiences across borders. As a result, the resolution called for further analysis of this approach.
- The Resolution finally pointed out the need for a new and comprehensive consultation with all stakeholders and a new assessment regarding the extension of the scope of this Regulation, which should take into account the recent legislations published by the EU, such as VAT changes, AVMSD, new regulations on cross-border delivery services and many others as well as considering the changes after the Covid-19 pandemic.

After this Resolution, it was official that the EU decided to exclude the copyright-protected digital products from the scope of the Geo-blocking Regulation for now. On the other hand, the Rapporteur Beata Mazurek also pointed out that after more assessment, the need to extend the scope of this regulation should be debated again.[155]

5.4.4.6 Call for Evidence from the Commission

Article 9(1) of the Geo-blocking Regulation provides that by 23 March 2020 and every 5 years thereafter, the Commission shall report on the evaluation of this Regulation. In accordance with this provision, the Commission commenced the preparations for its first review in 2020, as already mentioned, with the consequence that a subsequent review was to be expected in 2025. The latter, however, did not materialise within that year as a completed evaluation; rather, the Commission set the review process in motion in successive stages.[156]

To this end, the Commission first published a call for evidence,[157] which remained open between February and March 2025. Therein, the Commission observed that the Geo-blocking Regulation had applied since December 2018 and that it sought to ensure that both individuals and businesses might enjoy better access conditions to

---

[155] European Parliament (2023) MEPs want to revise EU geo-blocking rules to eliminate remaining barriers In: europarl https://www.europarl.europa.eu/news/es/press-room/20231208IPR15768/meps-want-to-revise-eu-geo-blocking-rules-to-eliminate-remaining-barriers.

[156] Geo-blocking Regulation—evaluation. In: European Commission https://ec.europa.eu/info/law/better-regulation/have-your-say/initiatives/14416-Geo-blocking-Regulation-evaluation_en.

[157] Commission launches evaluation of the Geo-blocking Regulation. In: European Commission https://single-market-economy.ec.europa.eu/news/commission-launches-evaluation-geo-blocking-regulation-2025-02-11_en.

goods and services. The Commission further noted that the initiative would evaluate whether the Regulation had met its objectives.

Thereafter, the Commission launched a public consultation,[158] open from 6 October 2025 to 5 January 2026. The Commission stated that the consultation was intended to gather information on, and insights into, the functioning of the Regulation, and to collect evidence concerning its implementation, application, and enforcement.

As regards the substance of the exercise, the evaluation is intended to assess whether the Geo-blocking Regulation has met its objectives by examining it in the light of the five standard evaluation criteria, namely relevance, effectiveness, coherence, efficiency, and EU added value. The outcome of the evaluation is intended to fulfil the obligation laid down in Article 9 of the Geo-blocking Regulation, which requires the Commission to report on the evaluation of the Regulation to the European Parliament, the Council, and the European Economic and Social Committee. The evaluation covers the period running from 3 December 2018, the date on which the Regulation became applicable, to 31 December 2024, and extends to the territory of the European Economic Area. The publication of this evaluation is anticipated in the second half of 2026, where further discussions on the Regulation's review will take place.

5.5 Conclusion

The Geo-blocking Regulation[159] was indeed very important to solve the unavailability of copyright-protected digital products cross-border, and it was a good opportunity to address this issue by offering a permanent solution. After the Portability Regulation, which tried to solve the digital barriers problem for a limited period of time, the Geo-blocking Regulation and the Portability Regulation were meant to complement each other. At the beginning of the legislative procedure, the key aim was to prohibit geo-blocking throughout the EU and have a reform on this as it can be understood from the early studies mentioned above. Nevertheless, especially with the lobbying,[160] the Commission lost its ambition and very promptly the EU decided to regulate only 'unjustified' geo-blocking and exclude two important topics from the scope of this Regulation: copyright-protected non-audiovisual products and audiovisual products. The copyright gap created lots of critics, and this issue will also be deeply analysed in Chap. 7, where the author will provide some recommendations for the EU policymakers.

[158] Geo-blocking Regulation—evaluation (public consultation). In: Have Your Say https://ec.europa.eu/info/law/better-regulation/have-your-say/initiatives/14416-Geo-blocking-Regulation-evaluation/public-consultation_en.

[159] Just to inform, the Geo-blocking Regulation was also revoked in the UK. For more information please find 'The Geo-Blocking Regulation (Revocation) (EU Exit) Regulations 2019' which can be accessed via: https://www.legislation.gov.uk/ukdsi/2019/9780111183724.

[160] Reda (2020, p. 92).

After its publication, thanks to Article 9, the Geo-blocking Regulation was subject to a very early review in 2020. Although the initial understanding of this Regulation was found to be positive, this review was not very successful in showing the whole picture since countries were reluctant to enforce this Regulation and since the Covid-19 break has changed the industry and consumer behaviour. The potential impact of the Covid-19 break especially for the audiovisual sector will also be explained in Chap. 8 with relevant data.

The other important subject of this review was the potential consequences of extending the scope of this regulation to copyright-protected services. The implementation report and Parliamentary Resolution suggested in December 2023 not to include copyright-protected services in the scope of this Regulation for now, according to the studies published in 2020. As of May 2026, the Geo-blocking Regulation does not apply to copyright-protected digital products, and all recommendations will be provided according to this information in Chap. 8.

References

Berry E et al (2019) Complete EU law: text, cases, and materials, 4th edn. Oxford University Press, Oxford

Broocks et al (2020) Geo-blocking: a literature review and new evidence in online audio-visual services. In: JRC Digital Economy Working Paper 2020-01

Engels S, Nordemann JB (2018) The Portability Regulation (Regulation (EU) 2017/1128): a commentary on the scope and application. JIPITEC 9:179–200

Karmel B (2020) Content portability in the EU: challenges and pragmatic solutions. Eur Intellect Prop Rev 42:414–425

Mylly U-M, Herrero M (2022) Free movement of audiovisual content for benefit of European consumers of culture. IIC 53:1038–1070

Rauer N, Kaase L (2020) Portability regulation. In: Schulze R, Staudenmayer D (eds) EU digital law. Hart Publishing, Oxford, pp 495–590

Reda J (2020) Geoblocking: at odds with the EU single market and consumer expectations. In: Szczepanik P et al (eds) Digital peripheries: the online circulation of audiovisual content from the small market perspective. Springer, Cham, pp 81–100

Schmidt-Kessen MJ (2017) EU digital single market strategy, digital content and geo-blocking: costs and benefits of partitioning the EU's internal market. Colum J Eur L 24:561–576

Shapiro T (2016) The proposed regulation on portability: don't leave home without it. Eur Intellect Prop Rev 38:351–359

Trimble M (2024) The EU geo-blocking regulation: a commentary. Edward Elgar Publishing, Cheltenham

Chapter 6
Territorial Licensing Practices in the Context of Competition Law

Abstract Copyright owners exploit their exclusive rights mainly through licensing, which permits activities otherwise reserved to rightsholders and may be limited geographically, temporally or by the mode of exploitation. Such territorial restrictions can raise concerns under Article 101 TFEU, particularly where they restrict passive sales. The relevance of geo-blocking in this context became evident with the 2015 Pay-TV investigation, where territorial agreements and refusals of unsolicited requests were scrutinised. Subsequent decisions, including Valve and Guess, confirmed that vertical agreements requiring geo-blocking measures are anti-competitive, while FAPL/Murphy clarified that territorial licences are not inherently unlawful but may infringe competition law when combined with additional restrictive provisions. EU rules create a differentiated framework for digital content. The SatCab regime applies the country-of-origin principle for certain broadcasting services; the Portability Regulation allows temporary cross-border access for subscribers. Although the Geo-blocking Regulation excludes copyright-protected digital products, a position reaffirmed in the 2023 review, it remains central to understanding the interaction between geo-blocking practices, territorial licensing and EU competition law.

6.1 Introduction

As mentioned in Chap. 3, copyright owners hold exclusive rights, including the exploitation and transfer of the copyright. The primary methods of exploiting a copyright-protected work are through assignment and licensing. Assignments can be described as a transfer of copyright ownership, allowing assignees to handle the use of the copyright-protected work as they see fit.[1] An assignment must be executed as a written contract to be valid, and it should be written and signed on behalf of the

[1] Bently et al. (2022, p. 325).

F. Cebeci Çorum, *Application of Geo-Blocking to Copyright-Protected Digital Products*, Studies in European Economic Law and Regulation 30,
https://doi.org/10.1007/978-3-032-34507-3_6

assignor.[2] On the other hand, assignments are not very common, especially in the realm of digital copyright, licences are the most basic form of exploitation.[3]

The most common way to permit activities exclusive to the copyright owners is by giving licences. Licences are granted by copyright owners to specific individuals, allowing them to perform certain activities. A licence can be described as permission to do something that would otherwise be prohibited without the copyright owner's consent.[4] Licences can be viewed as permission to undertake specific activities and may be limited geographically, temporally, in terms of specific modes of exploiting the copyright-protected work or restricted by the parties involved, either being non-exclusive or exclusive.[5] On the other hand, these restrictions may be seen as a restriction to competition in the context of Article 101 TFEU. Related to geo-blocking, geographically limited territorial licences were subject to the scrutiny of investigations handled by the EU Commission. Especially the investigations into Pay-TV services and the Valve investigation were relevant and important to assessing the suitability of territorial licences in the context of competition law, which will be later explained in this chapter. Therefore, the compliance of geographically restricted licences with competition law will be an important topic for this study and this section will provide a detailed explanation of the compliance of territorial licences with competition law. To that aim, the general explanation regarding the EU competition law and territorial licences will be provided, and active and passive sales restrictions will be discussed. Subsequently, vertical agreements which includes application of geo-blocking measures will be evaluated under the competition law. In this chapter, collective management organisations and the country-of-origin principle will be briefly explained. Finally, the relationship between the geo-blocking practice, with reference to the Geo-blocking Regulation, and the EU competition law will briefly be analysed. The main aim of this chapter is to show a general grasp of the current competition law problems regarding territorial licences, passive sales restrictions and geo-blocking practice; therefore, only related and important aspects will be briefly mentioned and the relevance of them will be provided.

---

[2] Bently et al. (2022, p. 325).

[3] Bently et al. (2022, p. 325).

[4] Bently et al. (2022, p. 326).

[5] Bently et al. (2022, p. 327).

6.2 Territorial Licences and Competition Law: A Comprehensive Analysis Within the EU Law

6.2.1 Competition Law and Intellectual Property Rights in the EU

The main economic goal of the EU was to create an internal market, where there is a free movement of goods, services, capital and people,[6] as mentioned in Chap. 1. Articles 34 and 35 TFEU ruled that quantitative restrictions on imports and exports shall be prohibited between Member States. On the other hand, Article 36 TFEU provides an exception to these provisions and according to this: *'The provisions of Articles 34 and 35 shall not preclude prohibitions or restrictions on imports, exports or goods in transit justified on grounds of public morality, public policy or public security; the protection of health and life of humans, animals or plants; the protection of national treasures possessing artistic, historic or archaeological value;* ***or the protection of industrial and commercial property****. Such prohibitions or restrictions shall not, however, constitute a means of arbitrary discrimination or a disguised restriction on trade between Member States.'* That provision explains that discriminatory restrictions may be justified if they include the protection of intellectual property.[7] However, according to the second sentence, these restrictions should be proportionate.[8]

As explained in Chap. 2, copyright is a territorial right, like other IP rights. Therefore, the exploitation and the exercise of these rights are also territorial, which could be seen as a partitioning market within the EU. Furthermore, the territoriality of the copyright could also be an excuse and a valid justification for the free movement of goods and services, however, it should not go beyond the protection of copyright owners' rights.[9] If that goes beyond that, the fragmentation of the market could also be regarded as contrary to EU competition rules. To control anti-competitive behaviours within the EU, the TFEU has included two important provisions which are Articles 101 and 102. According to Article 101 TFEU, all agreements between undertakings, decisions by associations of undertakings and concerted practices which may affect trade between the Member States, and which have as their object or effect the prevention, restriction or distortion of competition within the internal market shall be prohibited unless they could fit any of the exemption provided in Article 101(3).[10] Article 102 regulates a provision for the undertakings of a dominant position and

---

[6] This has been explained extensively in the previous chapter.

[7] Pila (2022, p. 537).

[8] Pila (2022, p. 537).

[9] Messina (2021, p. 14).

[10] *The provisions of paragraph 1 may, however, be declared inapplicable in the case of:*
- *any agreement or category of agreements between undertakings,*
- *any decision or category of decisions by associations of undertakings,*
- *any concerted practice or category of concerted practices,*

rules that any abuse by one or more undertakings of a dominant position within the internal market or in a substantial part of it shall be prohibited. This provision does not include any exemptions.

On the other hand, as confirmed in the Deutsche Grammophon case, simply because an agreement includes intellectual property rights does not mean that Article 101 TFEU is inapplicable. Accordingly, especially territorial licences were always scrutinised by the EU to assess whether these licences include anti-competitive practices. Some licence terms may result in excluding some parties from competition.[11] Furthermore, territorial licences may fragment the EU's internal market, and, in each country, there could be different conditions, prices and practices for the same products. These licensing practices may negatively affect the creation of internal market aims and it would be seen as contrary to especially terms provided in Article 101 of the TFEU.

Agreements, practices, or decisions which restrict or prevent competition are regulated under Article 101 TFEU and according to Article 101(1) TFEU if agreements between undertakings, decisions by associations of undertakings and concerted practices affect the prevention, restriction, or distortion of competition within the internal market, these agreements or decisions shall be automatically void. Especially in the case of the following scenarios, as these agreements or decisions would be accepted as *prima facie* prevention, restriction or distortion of competition within the internal market: if the agreement or decision directly or indirectly fixes purchase or selling prices or any other trading conditions; or limit or control production, markets, technical development, or investment; or share markets or sources of supply; or apply dissimilar conditions to equivalent transactions with other trading parties, thereby placing them at a competitive disadvantage; or make the conclusion of contracts subject to acceptance by the other parties of supplementary obligations which, by their nature or according to commercial usage, have no connection with the subject of such contracts. To summarise, according to Article 101(2) TFEU, all the anti-competitive agreements and decisions will be void. On the other hand, Article 101(3) TFEU regulates an exception for anti-competitive restrictions, and it explains that if an agreement, a decision, or a practice which contributes to improving the production or distribution of goods or to promoting technical or economic progress or benefits consumers if they do not impose non-obligatory restrictions on the objective or prohibit for the elimination of competition with respect to a significant portion of the products in question.

In practice, parties are required to do their own assessment to analyse whether or not their agreements or decisions are able to benefit from Article 101(3). However,

---

which contributes to improving the production or distribution of goods or to promoting technical or economic progress, while allowing consumers a fair share of the resulting benefit, and which does not:

(a) impose on the undertakings concerned restrictions which are not indispensable to the attainment of these objectives;

(b) afford such undertakings the possibility of eliminating competition in respect of a substantial part of the products in question.

[11] Pila (2022, p. 591).

the Commission adopted a Regulation on the application of Article 101(3) TFEU to categories of vertical agreements and concerted practices[12] to establish more clear rules for vertical agreements[13] to be included for the application of Article 101(3) to apply and this so-called the Vertical Block Exemption Regulation (the VBER) provides a 'safe harbour'[14] or 'safe heaven'[15] for agreements against the application of Article 101(1) of the TFEU, which prohibits anti-competitive agreements.

6.2.1.1 Selective Distribution in the EU Competition Law

The VBER defines selective distribution in Article 1(1)(g) as a distribution system where the supplier undertakes to sell the contract goods or services, either directly or indirectly, only to distributors selected on the basis of specified criteria and where these distributors undertake not to sell such goods or services to unauthorised distributors within the territory reserved by the supplier to operate that system. The decision to use selective distribution systems has some rationale behind it. Sometimes, the nature of the goods in question could require these kinds of selective distribution systems, especially for luxury goods and complex or technical consumer products.[16] Luxury goods (such as perfumes, cosmetics, or pieces of jewellery) are usually sold under prestigious brand names, and it is important for them to keep their brand image promotive and exclusive.[17] Therefore, manufacturers or suppliers tend to prevent having a negative impact on their brand images and having a selective distribution system could be a crucial point as a marketing strategy.[18] Besides, the increase in selling counterfeit products from the Internet could be another reason to prevent some distributors from selling their branded goods.[19] For complex and technical consumer products (such as computers, televisions or mobile phones), these products usually require pre or after-sales advice or service. Therefore, for the suppliers and manufacturers, having a limited distributor who undertakes specific training regarding these products and who can help the consumers before or after sales is also an important

---

[12] Commission Regulation (EU) 2022/720 of 10 May 2022 on the application of Article 101(3) of the Treaty on the Functioning of the European Union to categories of vertical agreements and concerted practices [2022] OJ L 134. (hereinafter will be referred as the VBER).

[13] Article 1(1)(a) of the VBER defines a vertical agreement as *'an agreement or concerted practice entered into between two or more undertakings each of which operates, for the purposes of the agreement or the concerted practice, at a different level of the production or distribution chain and relating to the conditions under which the parties may purchase, sell or resell certain goods or services'*.

[14] Peers and Barnard (2023, p. 561).

[15] Whish and Bailey (2018, p. 665).

[16] Carloni et al. (2021) p. 56.

[17] Carloni et al. (2021) p. 56.

[18] Commission (2021) Expert report on the review of the Vertical Block Exemption Regulation. In: Europa, p. 7 < https://ec.europa.eu/competition-policy/system/files/2021-06/kd0921156enn_VBER_online_sales.pdf.

[19] Expert report on the review of the Vertical Block Exemption Regulation' (2021, p. 7).

issue.[20] Therefore, with this selective distribution system, suppliers are sure that their products are sold through distributors who convey a particular image or who undertake special obligations such as staff training, after-sale services or brick-and-mortar stores.[21] To summarise, when consumers buy high-quality products, they generally want to get some technical or informational service before, during and after the sale, and suppliers may want trained customer service to promote the brand image. Therefore, suppliers may want to supply high-quality products only to selective distributors to offer a high-quality service with high-quality products and protect an exclusive brand image. Furthermore, this selective distribution system could be necessary if the product requires a specific place to be handled, or specific technical ability or specific premises, such as a minimum number of distributors could be needed in that area, or there could be some requirements from suppliers such as minimum amount of stock or achieving a level of sale. However, this selection of distributors should only be based on non-discriminatory, qualitative criteria to not infringe Article 101 TFEU.

Most of the selective distribution systems do not infringe Article 101 TFEU because these agreements either satisfy the conditions written in Article 101 TFEU or they benefit from the safe harbour created by the VBER by block exemption applicable to the vertical agreements.[22]

To summarise, as e-commerce has created both challenges and opportunities[23] for suppliers, manufacturers, and distributors to protect brand image and prevent free-riding behaviour, usually suppliers or manufacturers tend to use selective distribution systems to control the distribution of products.

6.2.2 Active and Passive Sales Restrictions

In the VBER, active and passive sales have been described as follows: ***'active sales'*** means actively targeting customers by visits, letters, emails, calls or other means of direct communication or through targeted advertising and promotion, offline or online, for instance by means of print or digital media, including online media, price comparison services or advertising on search engines targeting customers in particular territories or customer groups, operating a website with a top-level domain corresponding to particular territories, or offering on a website languages that are commonly used in particular territories, where such languages are different from the ones commonly used in the territory in which the buyer is established; ***'passive sales'*** means sales made in response to unsolicited requests from individual customers, including delivery of goods or services to the customer, without the sale having been initiated by actively targeting the particular customer, customer group or territory,

[20] Expert report on the review of the Vertical Block Exemption Regulation' (2021, p. 6).

[21] Expert report on the review of the Vertical Block Exemption Regulation' (2021, p. 79).

[22] Peers and Barnard (2023, p. 569).

[23] Expert report on the review of the Vertical Block Exemption Regulation' (2021, p. 6).

and including sales resulting from participating in public procurement or responding to private invitations to tender.[24]

Furthermore, Article 4 of VBER contains hardcore restrictions and exceptions. According to this provision, where the supplier operates an exclusive distribution system, the restriction of the territory into which, or of the customers to whom, the exclusive distributor may actively or passively sell the contract goods or services, except:

(i) the restriction of active sales by the exclusive distributor and its direct customers, into a territory or to a customer group reserved to the supplier or allocated by the supplier exclusively to a maximum of five other exclusive distributors;
(ii) the restriction of active or passive sales by the exclusive distributor and its customers to unauthorised distributors located in a territory where the supplier operates a selective distribution system for the contract goods or services;
(iii) the restriction of the exclusive distributor's place of establishment;
(iv) the restriction of active or passive sales to end users by an exclusive distributor operating at the wholesale level of trade;
(v) the restriction of the exclusive distributor's ability to actively or passively sell components, supplied for the purposes of incorporation, to customers who would use them to manufacture the same type of goods as those produced by the supplier…

Territorial restrictions in contracts are usually regarded as a hardcore restriction under the VBER. In this context, the VBER distinguishes between passive sale restrictions and active sale restrictions. Active sale restrictions are usually regarded as normal and expected in order to protect the investment made, and they are not against competition law as also confirmed in the Valve Investigation, which will be explained later in this chapter. On the other hand, passive sale restrictions fall outside the scope of the block exemption, and prohibiting passive sales has been subject to much scrutiny and is often viewed as anti-competitive because this activity provides absolute territorial protection and is regarded as unlawful.[25] That means, any agreement containing restrictions on passive sales will be regarded as a restriction of competition law by object unless it is justified.[26]

In online selling, customers are reaching the sellers/distributors to buy the product, therefore these types of sales are considered passive sales.[27] In online sales, the seller/distributor is answering unsolicited requests coming from the customers, as happens in passive sales. The Commission also found that some agreements related to territorial restrictions online are hardcore restrictions.[28] According to paragraph

[24] Article 2, VBER.

[25] Solek and Blumental (2020, p. 52).

[26] Messina (2021, p. 17).

[27] Solek and Blumental (2020, p. 52).

[28] Communication from the Commission, 'Commission Notice Guidelines on vertical restraints 2022/C 248/01206' [2022] OJ C 248. (hereinafter will be referred as Guidelines on vertical restraints).

206 of the Guidelines on vertical restraints *"In addition to the direct and indirect restrictions referred to in paragraphs (202) to (204), hardcore restrictions specifically relating to online sales may similarly be the result of direct or indirect obligations. Besides a direct prohibition of the use of the Internet to sell the contract goods or services, the following are examples of obligations that indirectly have the object of preventing the effective use of the Internet by the buyer to sell the contract goods or services to particular territories or customers within the meaning of Article 4, point (e) of Regulation (EU) 2022/720: (a) requiring the buyer to prevent customers located in another territory from viewing its website or online store or to re-route customers to the online store of the manufacturer or of another seller. However, obliging the buyer to offer links to the online stores of the supplier or of other sellers is not a hardcore restriction (125); (b) requiring the buyer to terminate consumers' online transactions where their credit card data reveal an address that is not within the buyer's territory..."* will also be hardcore restrictions and will be considered as restriction of competition law by object.

Especially in electronic distribution, consuming copyright-protected products cross-border has significantly increased and the traditional approaches to these matters have become questioned. After the Coditel case, which will be explained later in this chapter from the competition law aspects, the electronic distribution and the territorial nature of the copyright have been questioned in the context of the competition law. As a result of the territorial licences, distributors (or sellers in general) often apply active or passive sales restrictions in order to prevent sales outside of the licensed area.

These restrictions are also related to geo-blocking practices and the Geo-blocking Regulation has also included an article regarding passive sales. The intersection between the Geo-blocking Regulation, competition law and passive sales restriction will be explained later in that chapter with detail.

6.2.3 Territorial Licences for Digital Products and EU Competition Law: Related Investigations and Important Decisions

Territorial licences have been subject to investigations and judicial reviews, particularly concerning digital products. One of the earliest examples of this is the Coditel decision. In that decision, the Court of Justice examined whether territorial licences were compliant with Article 101 TFEU and examined whether these kinds of territorial licences restrict film distribution and distort competition in the film market. Another important step in this area occurred in 2007 when the Commission issued a Statement of Objections,[29] addressing major record companies and Apple. The concern was that agreements between these companies and Apple could restrict music

[29] Memo 07/126 (2007) Competition: European Commission confirms sending a Statement of Objections against alleged territorial restrictions in on-line music sales to major record companies

sales, as consumers could only buy music downloads from the iTunes online store in their country of residence,[30] according to their credit card details.[31] Additionally, in 2011, the CJEU, in the FAPL and Murphy judgment, also assessed the impact of territorial licence agreements containing provisions aimed at preventing the public from receiving broadcasts outside the licensed area within the framework of EU competition law.[32] Following this decision, the Commission has adopted a Statement of Objections on the Pay-TV services, regarding the licensing agreements between Sky UK and Paramount, since the agreements include provisions regarding prohibitions of passive sales. Also, very recently, the Commission opened an investigation and discussed whether geo-blocked steam activation keys restricted the competition and reduced cross-border sales within the EEA states as part of the Valve investigation. Finally, the Guess investigation was also relevant with the geo-blocking practice. These important developments will be explained in detail in the next subsection.

6.2.3.1 The Coditel Decision

The background of this case was also explained in the Chap. 3 part 2.2., therefore no further background information will be provided here. In that decision, the Court asked whether territorial licences are against the EU competition law, particularly Article 101 TFEU. The Court ruled that the characteristics of the cinematographic industry and its markets within the Community, particularly with respect to dubbing and subtitling for different language groups, the potential for television broadcasts, and the system of financing film production in Europe, indicate that an exclusive exhibition licence is not inherently anti-competitive and such a licence, by its nature, does not, in itself, prevent, restrict, or distort competition.[33] On the other hand, the Court made clear that, it was for national courts, where necessary, to ascertain whether the exercise of the exclusive right to exhibit a film imposes artificial and unjustifiable barriers relative to the needs of the industry. They must determine if it leads to fees that exceed a fair return on investment, if the exclusivity period is disproportionately long, and if such practices prevent, restrict, or distort competition within the common market.[34]

and Apple. In: Europa. https://ec.europa.eu/commission/presscorner/api/files/document/print/en/memo_07_126/MEMO_07_126_EN.pdf.

[30] Schwemer (2019, p. 95).

[31] Pila (2022, p. 594).

[32] Schwemer (2019, p. 96).

[33] The Coditel case, para 16.

[34] Ibid, para 19.

6.2.3.2 The Apple Investigation Dated 2007

Apple iTunes's music store includes a library where consumers can purchase music downloads. In 2007, iTunes were promoting these downloads online, and consumers could only purchase these downloads according to the iTunes version of their country of residence.[35] Their country of residence was confirmed according to their credit card details. One of the major UK consumer protection organisations complained that consumers in the UK were subject to higher prices than those in France and Germany.[36] After this complaint, the Commission confirmed that it sent a Statement of Objections to major music recording companies and Apple since these agreements restricted online music sales. The main concern in that situation was the choices of the consumers were restricted and the availability and the price of the music were different in different countries which may constitute an infringement of Article 101 TFEU.[37] Apple announced that they would equalise the prices across countries and after that announcement, the Commission closed the investigation and decided to take no further action.[38]

6.2.3.3 The FAPL and Murphy Judgment

Another important decision was held in the joint cases FAPL and Murphy judgment, in which the Court discussed the territorial restrictions in licence agreements and the result of making these works available to a different public. In the United Kingdom (the UK), the right to broadcast live Premier League (the highest level of league for professional football matches in the UK) matches is distributed by the Football Association Premier League (the FAPL) on a geographically limited basis. To comply with territoriality basis licences, broadcasters are issuing decoder cards, which are subject to the statement that customers are not allowed to use these cards outside of the country. In this judgment, the defendant was the owner of a pub who bought a subscription from Greece since it is cheaper than the UK, and the pub owner made these football matches available in the pub with the Greek subscription. In that judgment, regarding the competition law problem, the Court mainly analysed '*whether the clauses of an exclusive licence agreement concluded between a holder of intellectual property rights and a broadcaster constitute a restriction on competition prohibited by Article 101 TFEU where they oblige the broadcaster not to supply decoding devices giving access to that right holder's protected subject-matter outside the territory covered by the licence agreement concerned*'.[39]

---

[35] Schwemer (2019, p. 95).

[36] Pila (2022, p. 594).

[37] Schwemer (2019, p. 95).

[38] Schwemer (2019, p. 95), Pila (2022, p. 594).

[39] The FAPL and Murphy cases, para 134.

The Court ruled that, according to its case law on intellectual property rights licensing agreements, the mere fact that a rights holder grants a sole licensee the exclusive right to broadcast protected content from a Member State, thereby prohibiting its transmission by others during a specified period, is not sufficient to conclude that such an agreement has an anti-competitive objective.[40] On the other hand, the court suggested that if there is an agreement which creates a border between national markets may also constitute a restriction within the meaning of Article 101.[41] The Court also pointed out that, in following paragraphs,[42] the clause requiring broadcasters not to supply decoding devices for accessing protected content outside the territory covered by the licence agreement is anti-competitive. Additionally, the Court noted that this clause prevents broadcasters from providing cross-border services related to the matches, granting each broadcaster absolute territorial exclusivity and eliminating all competition between broadcasters in this field. The Court observed that FAPL failed to present any economic or legal context justifying that these clauses complying with EU competition rules and therefore do not have an anti-competitive object. Consequently, the Court concluded that these clauses in exclusive licence agreements constitute a prohibited restriction on competition under Article 101(1) TFEU.

The Court mainly pointed out that, exclusive licences are not per se contrary to Article 101(1) TFEU, however in that case, the licensees were required to supply decoders in their respective territories. That means this clause eliminated all competition between broadcasters and this prohibition would be against Article 101 TFEU.[43] This decision was significant in analysing the territorial licences and competition law.

6.2.3.4 The Pay-TV Investigation

In January 2014, the European Commission announced that they would begin formal antitrust proceedings against major US film studios and European Pay-TV broadcasters regarding the agreements between these US film studios and European Pay-TV broadcasters.[44] The main concern in these agreements was whether the provisions in these contracts were preventing the cross-border provision of Pay-TV services by blocking requests and access from across borders. These agreements contain the provisions that prevent accepting unsolicited requests from other countries, and according to the press release published by the EU Commission[45]:

---

[40] The FAPL and Murphy cases, para 137.

[41] Pila (2022, p. 596).

[42] The FAPL and Murphy cases, paras 135–146.

[43] Schwemer (2019, p. 101).

[44] European Commission Press release (2014) Antitrust: Commission investigates restrictions affecting cross border provision of pay TV services. In: Europa https://ec.europa.eu/commission/presscorner/detail/en/IP_14_15.

[45] European Commission Press release (2014) Antitrust: Commission investigates restrictions affecting cross border provision of pay TV services. In: Europa https://ec.europa.eu/commission/presscorner/detail/en/IP_14_15.

> 'The provisions granting "absolute territorial protection" ensure that the films licensed by the US studios are shown exclusively in the Member State where each broadcaster operates via satellite and the internet. These films cannot be made available outside that Member State, even in response to unsolicited requests from potential subscribers in other Member States.'

After this announcement, the Commission published a Statement of Objections in July 2015, stating that these agreements are anti-competitive: '*If the Commission's preliminary position were to be confirmed, each of the companies would have breached EU competition rules prohibiting anti-competitive agreements*'.[46] One of the film studios under these investigations, the UK-based Paramount Pictures, offered some commitments to the Commission[47] and the Commission accepted these commitments, and they became legally binding for five years.[48]

For sure, these commitments affected current licensees, including the Groupe Canal + , since after the Commission's acceptance the provisions requiring the restriction of passive sales were practically abolished.[49] In 2017, Groupe Canal + was granted leave to intervene and brought actions to annul the Commission's decision.[50] Groupe Canal + signed an exclusive licence agreement with the Paramount in France and Groupe Canal + was applying geo-filtering techniques to prevent consumers from accessing these broadcastings outside France. Groupe Canal + claimed that these passive sales restrictions and related clauses *have the effect of favouring cultural diversity without harming competition, whereas abolishing them would lead to a heavier concentration in the cinematographic production sector.*[51] Furthermore, Groupe Canal + suggested that *the inapplicability of the relevant clauses indirectly but unquestionably would affect all the contractual relationships in the sector and lead to the emergence of large-scale licences at EU level that would upset the balance of negotiation to the detriment of EU producers.*[52]

The General Court decided that the purpose of copyright protection is to ensure appropriate remuneration for the rights holder, not the highest possible remuneration through arrangements that exclude any cross-border supply of television broadcasting services and thus entail absolute territorial protection.[53] The Court stated that when agreements concluded by the copyright holder contain clauses that require the holder to prohibit all its contracting partners on the EEA market from making passive sales

[46] European Commission Press release (2015) Antitrust: Commission sends Statement of Objections on cross-border provision of pay-TV services available in UK and Ireland. In: Europa. https://ec.europa.eu/commission/presscorner/detail/en/IP_15_5432.

[47] European Commission Press release, (2016) Antitrust: Commission seeks feedback on commitments offered by Paramount Pictures in pay-TV investigation. In: Europa https://ec.europa.eu/commission/presscorner/detail/en/IP_16_1530.

[48] Pila (2022, p. 597).

[49] Schwemer (2019, p. 116).

[50] Case T-873/16 *Groupe Canal + v Commission* [2018] OJ C 38. (hereinafter will be referred as Groupe Canal + (2018) case).

[51] Groupe Canal + (2018) case, para 29.

[52] Groupe Canal + (2018) case, para 32.

[53] Groupe Canal + (2018) case, para 40.

to geographic markets situated outside the Member State for which it grants an exclusive licence, those clauses confer a contractually specified absolute territorial exclusivity and thereby infringe Article 101(1) TFEU.[54] The Court therefore decided that in such a context, where a licence agreement is designed to prohibit or limit the cross-border provision of broadcasting services, it is deemed to have as its object the restriction of competition. The Court referred to the FAPL case to support this decision.[55] For the cultural diversity claim, the Court stated that this restriction may fall within the meaning of Article 101(3) TFEU.

Groupe Canal + appealed the decision to the Court of Appeal.[56] The Court of Appeal decided that allowing Paramount's contracting partners, including Groupe Canal + , to pursue action in national courts does not sufficiently remedy the impact of the contested decision on their contractual rights.[57] The Court of Appeal concluded that by enforcing Paramount's commitments through this decision, the Commission disregarded the requirement outlined in paragraph 106,[58] effectively rendering meaningless the contractual rights of third parties, including those of Groupe Canal + , in relation to Paramount, thereby violating the principle of proportionality. Furthermore, in that decision, the Court also assessed the passive sales restrictions and ruled that restrictions on passive sales may partition national markets resulting in absolute territorial protection.[59] After these observations, the Court of Appeal annulled the commitment decision.

6.2.3.5 The Valve Investigation

Valve is a technology and software company undertaker and video game developer, and it operates 'Steam', which is a gaming platform where users can download or stream PC video games via the Steam Store. In February 2017, the European Commission opened formal antitrust proceedings[60] against Valve and five video game publishers (which are Bandai, Focus Home, Capcom, Koch Media and ZeniMax) to investigate the bilateral agreements between Valve and these video game publishers.

---

[54] Groupe Canal + (2018) case, para 46.

[55] Groupe Canal + (2018) case, para 48.

[56] C-132/19 P *Groupe Canal + v Commission* [2020] OJ C 131. (hereinafter will be referred as Groupe Canal + (2020) case).

[57] Groupe Canal + (2020) case, para 127.

[58] Ibid, para 106: *As the Advocate General observed in point 123 of his Opinion, when the Commission verifies commitments not from the perspective of whether they are appropriate to address its competition concerns, but also with regard to their effect on the interests of third parties, the principle of proportionality requires that those third parties' rights are not rendered meaningless.*

[59] Groupe Canal + (2020) case, para 97.

[60] European Commission Press release (2017) Antitrust: Commission opens three investigations into suspected anticompetitive practices in e-commerce. In: Europa https://ec.europa.eu/commission/presscorner/api/files/document/print/en/ip_17_201/IP_17_201_EN.pdf.

According to the contractual relationship[61] between Valve and the video game publishers, Valve licenses their technologies and software tools to these publishers so that these publishers can make their games compatible with Steam's platform. Steam activation keys are unique alphanumeric codes,[62] and users buy these codes from outside of Steam so that they can install the games and play on the Steam platform.

These publishers grant a licence to Valve to make available their games via Steam. Valve also provides publishers with 'Steam activation keys' and 'territory control' as part of their digital rights management and anti-piracy services. Valve also imposes a territory control function on their keys so that these games can only be used in certain territories; as such, there is a geographical restriction (geo-blocking) on the use of these keys, and provides them to publishers as part of their requests. Therefore, after the Steam activation key is bought and entered into the Steam platform, this geo-blocking feature checks if this video game can be activated in this territory.[63] As a result of this restriction, these video games could not be activated in any other EEA states other than the states concerned. The European Commission had discussed whether geo-blocked steam activation keys restricted the competition and reduced cross-border sales within the EEA states.

First of all, it has been confirmed that each of the five publishers granted an EEA-wide (if not a worldwide licence) to Valve to disseminate these video games on Steam.[64] Valve claimed that this practice done by Valve Corporation was only the reflection of the non-exhausted copyright regime for video games in the digitally disseminated form. Also, they claimed that when users buy Steam Activation Keys via Steam or outside the Steam platform, they do not own the game; they only acquire a licence to access and play the game on Steam.

The Commission rejected these arguments by stating that:

- If there is a restriction on passive sales, which leads to an absolute territorial restriction, this is the act of partitioning the national market and infringing Article 101 TFEU. The Commission mentioned that 'passive sales restrictions between licensees of the same licensor are hardcore restrictions, hence not exempted by the TTBER,[65] as such restrictions may partition the market and hinder market integration'[66] and 'agreements restricting cross-border sales via geo-blocked Steam

[61] Commission Decision of 20.1.2021 relating to proceedings under Article 101 of the Treaty on the Functioning of the European Union and Article 53 of the Agreement on the European Economic Area 'Cases AT.40413 - Focus Home, AT.40414 - Koch Media, AT.40420 – ZeniMax, AT.40422 – Bandai Namco and AT.40424 – Capcom' C(2021) 75 final, pp 24 – 25. (hereinafter will be referred as the Commission Decision on the Valve Investigation).

[62] Commission Decision on the Valve Investigation, par 25.

[63] Commission Decision on the Valve Investigation, par 29.

[64] Commission Decision on the Valve Investigation, par 89.

[65] Commission Regulation (EU) No 316/2014 of 21 March 2014 on the application of Article 101(3) of the Treaty on the Functioning of the European Union to categories of technology transfer agreements Text with EEA relevance [2014] OJ L 93. (hereinafter will be referred as the TTBER).

[66] TTBER, Article 107.

activation keys which qualifies as a hardcore restriction under Article 4(1)(c) and 4(2)(b) of the 2004 TTBER'.[67]

- Even though copyright infringement may occur because of the non-exhaustion of digital copyright-protected products, the Commission decided that the activity which fragments the national market will infringe Article 101 TFEU by object and the copyright-related problems will not change this observation.
- Finally, it imposed a fine on Valve because Valve has participated in practices which restrict passive sales of video games in the Steam platform within the EEA by imposing geographical restrictions and providing geo-blocked Steam keys.

Valve Corporation has applied to the Court to ask for annulment of the decision.[68] First of all, the Court ruled that the supply of geo-blocked Steam keys restricts parallel imports by making passive sales inadmissible in countries other than those where the geo-blocked Steam keys were purchased.[69] This means it has an impact on Article 101 TFEU and constitutes a restriction of competition by object. The Court also highlighted that the existence of these distribution or licence agreements may harm competition because they include restrictions that result in the fragmentation of the internal market. This would go against the Treaty's objective of achieving a single European market.[70] Furthermore, the Court stated that this decision does not aim to prohibit territorial licences, but the problem lies with the additional measures adopted by the licensor, which make passive sales inadmissible and parallel imports nearly impossible, effectively hindering cross-border sales.[71] The problem here was that the additional measures adopted by the licensor made the sale or use of these video games in other EU countries impossible.[72] The Court also ruled that the adoption of technological measures does not prevent such measures from being scrutinised under Article 101 TFEU when they restrict competition.[73] The Court also again highlighted that competition and copyright laws aim to protect a copyright owner's interests, but they do not grant the right to demand the highest possible remuneration.[74] Copyright law only ensures appropriate remuneration, not the highest possible remuneration. Therefore, if there is market fragmentation to ensure price differentiation aimed at demanding the highest possible remuneration, it will be regarded as anti-competitive. The Court stated that in this case, the geo-blocking of the Steam keys did not aim to protect the publisher's copyright; instead, this technological measure was used solely to eliminate parallel imports to secure the highest possible royalty that could be collected from publishers in certain parts of the EEA.[75] Consequently, the Court

---

[67] TTBER, Article 107.

[68] In Case T-172/21, *Valve Corporation v European Commission* [2023] OJ C 228. ((hereinafter will be referred as the Valve Case).

[69] Valve Case, para 178.

[70] Valve Case, para 179.

[71] Valve Case, para 178.

[72] Valve Case, para 178.

[73] Valve Case, para 198.

[74] Valve Case, para 204.

[75] Valve Case, para 204.

concluded that the Commission's decision was correct, and in this case, the geo-blocked Steam keys constituted a restriction of competition by object under Article 101(2) of the TFEU.[76]

6.2.3.6 The Guess Antitrust Investigation

In June 2017, the Commission launched a formal antitrust investigation into the clothing company Guess's distribution agreements and practices to determine if the company unlawfully limited retailers from engaging in cross-border sales to consumers within the EU's Single Market.[77] In this investigation, it was found that Guess was using the sublicence agreements in which the cross-border sales were prohibited: *"All Advertising by SUBLICENSEE hereunder shall be limited to Advertising and marketing within the Territory and SUBLICENSEE acknowledges and agrees that it has no right to Advertise or otherwise market the Products outside the Territory and is expressly prohibited from doing so."*[78] This practice were confirmed and defended by Guess by saying "*We also want to ensure that their use is limited to their specific territory, e.g. their websites are not shipping guess products outside of their authorized country/territory".*[79]

As a result of this practice, the European Commission has imposed a fine of around €40 million on Guess for violating EU competition rules by preventing retailers from engaging in online advertising and cross-border sales to consumers in other Member States and in the press release, the Commission mentioned the importance of the Geo-blocking Regulation as follow[80]:

> 'Guess' distribution agreements tried to prevent EU consumers from shopping in other Member States by blocking retailers from advertising and selling cross-border. This allowed the company to maintain artificially high retail prices, in particular in Central and Eastern European countries. As a result, we have today sanctioned Guess for this behaviour. Our case complements the geoblocking rules that entered into force on 3 December – both address the issue of sales restrictions that are at odds with the Single Market.'

[76] Valve Case, para 205.

[77] European Commission Press release (2017) Antitrust: Commission opens formal investigation into distribution practices of clothing company Guess. In: Europa https://ec.europa.eu/commission/presscorner/detail/en/IP_17_1549.

[78] Commission Decision (2018) of 17.12.2018 relating to proceedings under Article 101 of the Treaty on the Functioning of the European Union and Article 53 of the Agreement on the European Economic Area 'Case AT.40428 Guess. In: Europa, para 81https://ec.europa.eu/competition/antitrust/cases/dec_docs/40428/40428_1205_3.pdf (hereinafter will be referred as the Commission Decision on the Guess Investigation).

[79] Commission Decision on the Guess Investigation, para83.

[80] European Commission Press release (2018) Antitrust: Commission fines Guess €40 million for anticompetitive agreements to block cross-border sales. In: Europa https://ec.europa.eu/commission/presscorner/detail/en/IP_18_6844.

6.3 Licensing in the EU Copyright Law: Licensing of the Digital Products in Practice

In this part, the author will briefly examine collective management organisations as a licensing practice and after that country-of-origin principle will be mentioned.

6.3.1 Collective Management Organisations

Collective management organisations are very dominant in music industries,[81] and they act as an intermediary between rightsholders and commercial licensees.[82] They mainly possess three main economic characteristics. Firstly, they negotiate and grant licenses for the use of works. Secondly, they monitor usage, enforce rights, and collect royalties. Lastly, they distribute the collected revenues to their members.[83] Collective management organizations generally function as non-profit entities, and they mainly try to maximise the profit for the copyright owners.[84] In 2005, the Commission published a Recommendation on collective cross-border management of copyright and related rights for legitimate online music services. According to this non-binding recommendation, the aim was to grant community-wide licences for the online use of the music; and rightsholders should have the right to entrust the management of any of the online rights necessary to operate legitimate online music services, on the territorial scope of their choice, to a collective rights manager of their choice, irrespective of the Member State of residence or the nationality of either the collective rights manager or the rightsholder.[85] In 2014, the Directive on collective management of copyright and related rights and multi-territorial licensing of rights in musical works for online use in the internal market ('the CRM Directive') was published. This Directive has been established to ensure collective management of copyright works across national borders and also impose some requirements on the collective management organisations that license the online use of musical works on a multi-territorial basis.[86] Involvement and active contribution of the collective management organisations to the cross-border licensing arrangements may be seen beneficial to Digital Single Market and these organisations can take into account to interests of different rightsholders.[87] Therefore, it may be suggested that, taking into account of the DSM Strategy and current competition law provisions, policy intervention in the

[81] Schroff and Street (2018, p. 1308).

[82] Schwemer (2019, p. 43).

[83] Schwemer (2019, p. 43).

[84] Schwemer (2019, p. 44).

[85] Commission Recommendation of 18 May 2005 on collective cross-border management of copyright and related rights for legitimate online music services [2005] OJ L 276, p. 3.

[86] Recital 2 of the CRM Directive.

[87] Schroff and Street (2018, p. 1317).

collective management organisations could actually help cross-border availability of the copyright-protected digital products.[88]

6.3.2 Licensing of Digital Products—the Country-Of-Origin Principle

As explained in Chap. 3, Television Without Frontiers Directive and AVMSD accepted country-of-origin principle to avoid jurisdictional problems, and they will be bound by the jurisdiction of the country *in where their central administration is located and where management decisions are taken on programming or selection of content.*

The SatCab Directive regulates the clearance of rights for online services that are ancillary to the broadcast of specific types of television and radio programmes, and for the retransmission of these programmes.[89] This Directive has included two important provisions regarding the licensing of these programmes first one is the country-of-origin approach, and the second one is the creation of a legal fiction. According to the country-of-origin principle, licensees do not need to clear the rights for all member states; but they only need to clear the rights for the country of their principal establishment.[90] The principle does not apply to subsequent public communications or reproductions of the works contained in the ancillary online service. Due to the unique financing and licensing mechanisms for certain audiovisual works, the principle's scope is limited to specific types of programs, such as news, current affairs, and in-house productions funded by broadcasting organisations. It excludes sports broadcasts and does not apply to licensing these productions to third parties.[91] As it is created in the Portability Regulation, this Directive also creates a legal fiction. According to this, all copyright-related activities will be deemed to occur solely in the Member State in which the broadcasting organisation has its principal establishment according to Article 3. After the Commission's announcement regarding the plan to extend the scope of the SatCab Directive, although lots of studies and consultations have been done to include other types of copyright-protected works, only (a) radio programmes; and (b)television programmes which are: (i) news and current affairs programmes; or (ii) fully financed own productions of the broadcasting organisation were included in the scope of this directive.

The same but limited country of origin principle for the licensing has also been considered in the Portability Regulation, even though the Regulation does not specify

[88] Schroff and Street (2018, p. 1309). The author chooses to keep the explanation short and brief for the collective management organisations since it does not directly related with the aims of this thesis. For more information regarding this, please see: Schroff and Street (2018, p. 1305).

[89] Article 1 of the SatCab Directive.

[90] Zahrádka and Schmücker (2022, p. 6).

[91] Recitals 10–11 of the SatCab Directive.

that directly. In the Portability Regulation, clearing rights from the principal establishment is enough to offer cross-border availability of this content, however for a limited period of time. This regulation and these provisions have been explained in the previous chapter; therefore, no further explanation will be provided for the Portability Regulation.

6.3.3 EU-Wide Licensing Practices for Copyright-Protected Digital Products

In the EU, right now, different sectors have varying levels of EU-wide licensing practices for copyright-protected digital products.

For the video games sector, as explained in Chap. 4, the study by VVA et al. pointed out that, thanks to dialogues with stakeholders, licences are already distributed on an EU-wide basis, and the cross-border availability of the games has been found to be at a good level.[92] Furthermore, thanks to this availability, price differentiation from one Member State to another has been found to be minimal.[93] Therefore, it could be argued that, for the video games sector, EU-wide licensing is already at the desired level, which helps access video games across borders.

For the music sector, although the CMOs are quite active and important in this sector, licensing practices remain mainly on a territorial basis, and EU-wide licences remain elusive.[94] Furthermore, according to the study by VVA et al., rightsholders acquire licences on a country basis rather than EU-wide licences,[95] and the cross-border availability of this content has been found to be around 73–82%.[96]

For e-books, studies found that licences are usually distributed on a territorial basis, since language is an important factor for the demand for cross-border access.[97] Therefore, for the e-books sector, EU-wide licensing practices are still at a lower level.

Finally, for the audiovisual sector, as discussed before, cross-border availability has been found to be relatively low across the EU, especially for national SVOD platforms.[98] For Netflix, distributing content on a territorial basis, although they often have EU-wide licences, especially for Netflix Originals productions, has become a business model to gain more profit and make more reasonable investments, such as making their products available only in certain locations.[99] For Netflix Originals productions, Netflix usually acquires all the distribution rights but chooses to make its products available on a territorial basis to increase profits or avoid complying with

92 The study by VVA et al., p. 258.

93 The study by VVA et al., p. 269.

94 Schroff and Street (2018, p. 1310).

95 The study by VVA et al., p. 188.

96 The study by VVA et al., p. 188.

97 The study by VVA et al., p. 225.

98 JRC report, p. 16.

99 Afilipoaie (2021, p. 307).

certain requirements, such as different legal systems.[100] The same can also be said for Amazon or Disney + original productions.

Until other major platforms emerged, Netflix was almost a monopoly in licensing agreements in Europe and was usually the highest bidder.[101] Nevertheless, with the emergence of Amazon, Disney + , and other platforms, licensing activities became more expensive, and obtaining an EU-wide licence for a single product became more difficult, with only their original productions more commonly securing EU-wide licences.[102] Therefore, today, except for the biggest audiovisual platforms, EU-wide licensing practices are not very common. For Netflix, Amazon, and Disney + , unless they are original productions, they also usually have a hard time obtaining EU-wide licences. Although no publicly available figures are present, stakeholders often mention in dialogues that, as already discussed, obtaining an EU-wide licence is quite costly, and SMEs usually do not have the opportunity to compete with the biggest audiovisual platforms. Therefore, it would not be wrong to point out that EU-wide licensing practices in the audiovisual industry are still not very common and are costlier than in other sectors.

6.4 Geo-Blocking Practice in the Context of the EU Competition Law

6.4.1 The Geo-Blocking Regulation

The Commission pointed out that if geo-blocking measures are implemented through unilateral practises, the EU competition law will not be applicable here, since only the unilateral practices done by the dominant undertakings are subject to scrutiny under the EU competition law according to Article 102 TFEU. These geo-blocking activities may be considered under Article 101 TFEU if these activities were to be based on agreements or concerted practices.[103] Furthermore, these bilateral agreements containing geo-blocking requirements may restrict passive sales and these issues will be dealt with under the competition law.[104] On the other hand, the Geo-blocking Regulation also apply unilateral decisions. The Geo-blocking Regulation includes provisions regarding active and passive sales restrictions in Article 6 and Recital 34 and these provisions explain the relationship between geo-blocking practices and the EU Competition Law.

Article 6 of the Geo-blocking Regulation includes a provision regarding agreements on passive sales and according to that '*Without prejudice to Regulation (EU)*

[100] Afilipoaie (2021, p. 311).

[101] Afilipoaie (2021, p. 308).

[102] Afilipoaie (2021, p. 308).

[103] Messina (2021, p. 15).

[104] Solek and Blumental (2020, p. 52).

No 330/2010 and Article 101 TFEU, this Regulation shall not affect agreements restricting active sales within the meaning of Regulation (EU) No 330/2010 or agreements restricting passive sales within the meaning of Regulation (EU) No 330/2010 that concern transactions falling outside the scope of the prohibitions laid down in Articles 3, 4 and 5 of this Regulation. Provisions of agreements imposing obligations on traders, in respect of passive sales within the meaning of Regulation (EU) No 330/2010, to act in violation of the prohibitions laid down in Articles 3, 4 and 5 of this Regulation shall be automatically void.'

Recital 34 of the Regulation tries to explain and analyse the impact of this Article by stating that '*This Regulation should not affect the application of the rules on competition, and in particular Articles 101 and 102 TFEU. In particular, this Regulation, and specifically its provisions on access to goods or services, should not affect agreements restricting active sales within the meaning of Commission Regulation (EU) No 330/2010 (17). Agreements imposing obligations on traders not to engage in passive sales in respect of certain customers or groups of customers in certain territories are generally considered to restrict competition and cannot normally be exempted from the prohibition laid down in Article 101(1) TFEU. Where, however, such an exemption applies, or where contractual restrictions are not covered by Article 101 TFEU, there is a risk that they could be used to circumvent the provisions of this Regulation. The relevant provisions of such agreements should therefore be automatically void where they impose obligations on traders to act in breach of the prohibitions laid down in this Regulation regarding access to online interfaces, access to goods or services and payment. Those provisions concern, for example, contractual restrictions that prevent a trader from responding to unsolicited requests from individual customers for the sale of goods, without delivery, outside the trader's contractually allocated territory for reasons related to customers' nationality, place of residence or place of establishment.'*

This article and explanation regarding the restriction of passive sales have been seen as the reflection of the general EU competition law.[105] On the other hand, while EU competition law only concerns agreements and concerted practices, the Geo-blocking Regulation also applies unilateral decisions[106] but only vertical agreements will be subject to Article 6 of the Geo-blocking Regulation.[107] Furthermore, horizontal agreements could also contain geo-blocking measures and these measures may be considered under Article TFEU 101.[108]

[105] Picht (2020, p. 250).
[106] Picht (2020, p. 250).
[107] Trimble (2024, p. 112).
[108] Trimble (2024, p. 112).

6.4.2 Horizontal Agreements Including Geo-Blocking Measures

Horizontal agreements can be described as agreements between firms at the same level of the market.[109] These horizontal agreements are subject to Article 101 TFEU which have as their object or effect the prevention, restriction or distortion of competition within the internal market. The European Commission published guidelines on the applicability of Article 101 of the TFEU to horizontal co-operation agreements in 2023.[110] Some restrictions imposed in these horizontal agreements are considered to be hardcore restrictions and they are prohibited, such as price fixing and allocation of market or customers horizontal specialisation agreements[111] or passive and active sales restrictions in horizontal research and development agreements.[112] Geo-blocking activities prohibit both active and passive sales restrictions and can allocate the market and customers, therefore, these horizontal agreements which include geo-blocking measures could be prohibited under these provisions.[113]

6.4.3 Vertical Agreements Including Geo-Blocking Measures

Vertical agreements were defined as an agreement or concerted practice entered into between two or more undertakings each of which operates, for the purposes of the agreement or the concerted practice, at a different level of the production or distribution chain and relating to the conditions under which the parties may purchase, sell or resell certain goods or services in Article 1(1)(a) of the VBER as mentioned before. Article 6 of the Geo-blocking Regulation applies to vertical agreements, therefore, as also confirmed in Valve and Guess investigations, vertical agreements containing geo-blocking measures will be considered as anti-competitive and these agreements will be void.

Furthermore, guidelines on VBER published in 2022 includes a provision for geo-blocking measures and gives reference to the Geo-blocking Regulation. According to this provision: *The protection of exclusively allocated territories or customer groups is not absolute. To prevent market partitioning, passive sales into such territories*

---

[109] Sufrin et al. (2023, p. 723).

[110] Communication From the Commission 'Guidelines on the applicability of Article 101 of the Treaty on the Functioning of the European Union to horizontal co-operation agreements' [2023] OJ C 259/1.

[111] Commission Regulation (EU) 2023/1067 of 1 June 2023 on the application of Article 101(3) of the Treaty on the Functioning of the European Union to certain categories of specialisation agreements [2023] OJ L 143/20, Article 5.

[112] Communication From the Commission 'Guidelines on the applicability of Article 101 of the Treaty on the Functioning of the European Union to horizontal co-operation agreements' [2023] OJ C 259/1, para 111.

[113] Trimble (2024, p. 113).

or customer groups may not be restricted. Article 4, point (b) of Regulation (EU) X applies only to restrictions imposed on the buyer. The supplier may therefore accept restrictions on sales by itself, both online and offline, into the exclusive territory or to some or all of the customers belonging to an exclusive customer group. However, restrictions of passive sales to end users may, in certain circumstances, be void pursuant to Article 6(2) of Regulation (EU) 2018/302 of the European Parliament and of the Council. That means, any vertical agreements containing geo-blocking measures will be subject to both the Geo-blocking Regulation and the Guidelines on VBER.

6.5 Conclusion

In 2015, with the Pay-Tv investigation the term 'geo-blocking' was used for the first time[114] in the context of competition law and the main aim was to investigate these agreements, since as a result of geo-blocking activities, restriction of passive sales and not accepting unsolicited requests were logical consequences. Geo-blocking activities are usually a result of territorial licences in the copyright domain. Therefore, these territorial licences were also under the scrutiny of the EU Commission and the CJEU, especially regarding Articles 101 and 102 TFEU. Related to this, there have been some judicial interventions and the Commission's investigation to assess the territorial licences, passive sales restrictions and geo-blocking activities in the agreements. After the Valve Investigation, both the Commission and the CJEU confirmed that any vertical agreements containing provisions that require geo-blocking measures will be considered anti-competitive. The same understanding was followed in the Guess investigation. This was a very important milestone in that area since this decision also confirmed that these kinds of restrictions will result in a restriction on passive sales and go beyond to protect the interests of the copyright owner.

Restrictions on passive sales are usually considered against competition law and hardcore restrictions. The Geo-blocking Regulation also confirmed that, however, the impact of this Regulation would have been bigger in the copyright law domain since this Regulation also applies unilateral decisions, not only concerted practices and agreements. Yet, this Regulation does not apply to copyright-protected products and as explained in the previous chapter the final review done in December 2023 decided to exclude the copyright-protected digital products from the scope of this

[114] European Commission Press release (2015) Antitrust: Commission sends Statement of Objections on cross-border provision of pay-TV services available in UK and Ireland. In Europa. https://ec.europa.eu/commission/presscorner/detail/en/IP_15_5432. '*US film studios typically license audio-visual content, such as films, to a single pay-TV broadcaster in each Member State (or combined for a few Member States with a common language). The Commission's investigation, which was opened in January 2014, identified clauses in licensing agreements between the six film studios and Sky UK which require Sky UK to block access to films through its online pay-TV services (so-called "geo-blocking") or through its satellite pay-TV services to consumers outside its licensed territory (UK and Ireland).*'

Regulation for now. Furthermore, Article 6 of this Regulation which regulate the passive sales restriction only applies the bilateral agreements and practices.

For the copyright-protected digital products, the impact of the competition law and licensing practices in the context of the geo-blocking practice could be summarised as follows:

- As a result of the SatCab Directive, for the television and radio programmes, the country-of-origin principle will be applicable in terms of licensing practices, for satellite broadcasting, cable retransmission, radio programmes, television programmes which are news and current affairs programmes or fully financed own productions of the broadcasting organisation.
- As a result of the Portability Regulation, for the subscribed video-on-demand service providers, only obtaining a licence from the country-of-origin will be enough to offer cross-border access in the EU for a limited period of time.
- After the FAPL and Murphy judgment, it has been confirmed that territorial licences are not per se anti-competitive, however, other provisions limiting competitivity within the EU may be against Article 101 TFEU.
- After the Pay-TV investigations, it has been pointed out that, provisions restricting passive sales are anti-competitive and in agreements, these provisions should not be included.
- After the Valve and Guess investigations it has been confirmed by both the Commission and the CJEU, that any vertical agreements containing geo-blocking measure requirements are anti-competitive and should not be included. The VBER Guideline published in 2022 also confirms this outcome.
- Finally, although after the final review of the Geo-blocking Regulation, it has been confirmed that copyright-protected products are not included within the scope of that Regulation, this Regulation contains important provisions regarding unilateral decisions and geo-blocking practice. Nevertheless, Article 6 of this Regulation only concerns bilateral agreements and bilateral territorial restrictions. In the case of the extension of the scope of the Geo-blocking Regulation, unilateral practices may be a breach of the Geo-blocking Regulation while they would not be against the EU competition law principles, since unilateral practices are not in the scope of the competition law concerns unless they are applied by the dominant undertakings.[115]

References

Afilipoaie A et al (2021) The 'Netflix original' and what it means for the production of European TV content. Crit Stud Televis 16:304–325

Bently L et al (2022) Intellectual property law, 6th edn. Oxford University Press, Oxford

Carloni F et al (2021) Vertical agreements in the luxury sector. J Eur Compet Law Pract 12:56–64

[115] Picht (2020, p. 253).

Messina M (2021) Geo-blocking and EU competition law in the digital era. In: Lopez Rodriguez AM et al (eds) Legal challenges in the new digital age. Brill, Leiden, pp 13–28

Peers S, Barnard C (2023) European Union law, 4th edn. Oxford University Press, Oxford

Picht PG (2020) The EU Geo-Blocking Regulation from a competition law perspective. J Eur Compet Law Pract 11:244–256

Pila J, Torremans PLC (2022) Seville's EU intellectual property law and policy, 3rd edn. Edward Elgar Publishing, Cheltenham

Schroff S, Street J (2018) The politics of the digital single market: culture vs competition vs copyright. Inf Commun Soc 21:1305–1321

Schwemer SF (2019) Licensing and access to content in the European Union: regulation between copyright and competition law. Cambridge University Press, Cambridge

Solek L, Beyer Blumental E (2020) Geo-blocking at the cross-section between competition law and regulation. Eur Compet Law Rev 41:48–57

Sufrin B, Dunne N, Jones A (2023) Jones & Sufrin's EU competition law, 8th edn. Oxford University Press, Oxford

Trimble M (2024) The EU geo-blocking regulation: a commentary. Edward Elgar Publishing, Cheltenham

Whish R, Bailey D (2018) Competition law, 9th edn. Oxford University Press, Oxford

Zahrádka P, Schmücker R (2022) "We are sorry this video is not available in your country": an ethical analysis of geo-blocking audio-visual online content. J Media Ethics 37:2–17

Chapter 7
Circumvention of Geo-Blocking Practice

Abstract The widespread use of the Internet has normalised instant access to information and digital products, leading users to expect obstacle-free access to all online content. Rightsholders, however, often choose not to make their works available in every territory for various commercial and legal reasons, resulting in the extensive use of geo-blocking measures by traders, distributors and licensees. These restrictions frustrate users accustomed to seamless access and encourage the increasing use of circumvention tools, particularly VPNs, to evade geo-location technologies and other technological protection measures. Such practices raise important questions regarding copyright infringement and user liability. Circumventing geo-blocking to download copyright-protected works clearly infringes copyright, as permanent copies are created; similar conclusions apply to stream-ripping. In streaming scenarios, debates have focused on whether temporary copy and private use exceptions may apply. Judicial attention has also addressed the responsibilities of platforms, with cases such as Grand Production v GO4YOU and Anne Frank confirming that platforms using effective protective measures are not liable for users' reliance on VPNs. Another area of concern is the potential liability of VPN and circumvention-tool providers. Under Article 8(3) of the InfoSoc Directive, rightsholders may seek injunctions against intermediaries, and CJEU case law suggests that such providers could fall within this category. The growing reliance on circumvention tools underscores the need for further analysis. In this chapter, contractual implications are briefly noted, while criminal law aspects are deliberately excluded to maintain a copyright-focused approach.

7.1 Introduction

With the advent of the Internet into our lives, online activities and accessing every product on the Internet has become a straightforward task, and with just one click, people can access these products without any physical effort. Therefore, especially after the Internet, people tend to access every piece of information, content, and product they desire without any obstacles. On the other hand, rightsholders do

F. Cebeci Çorum, *Application of Geo-Blocking to Copyright-Protected Digital Products*, Studies in European Economic Law and Regulation 30,
https://doi.org/10.1007/978-3-032-34507-3_7

not want to make their products available in every country or location due to the numerous reasons as explained in the first chapter. Therefore, the implementation of geo-blocking measures has become a widespread practice among rightsholders, especially traders, distributors, and licensees. However, such geographical restrictions often bother internet users who have become accustomed to easily accessing any product they desire online, prompting them to seek ways to circumvent these restrictions. For this purpose, various circumvention tools, especially VPNs, have been increasingly used, and bypassing technological measures has become quite common and popular among internet users. However, the use of such tools by internet users to access products they would not otherwise have access to and engage in actions such as watching, reading, or saving them raises many questions related to copyright infringement.

In this chapter, the author will initially address geo-location tools, digital rights management and technological protection measures in broad terms and generally describe commonly employed circumvention tools that facilitate the bypassing of these measures. Subsequently, copyright infringement and exceptions to copyright infringement will be briefly explained. Then, the question of whether the circumvention of geo-blocking through the utilisation of circumvention tools constitutes a copyright infringement, as well as the potential liabilities for both users and providers from a copyright perspective, will be addressed with related legislation and case law of the EU. Finally, contractual liability point of view of circumvention tools will also be briefly explained in this chapter.

7.2 Key Terms in the Context of Circumvention of Territorial Restrictions

Internet users see the expression 'this content is not available in your country' in many products, especially in literary, dramatic, musical, and artistic works, such as e-books, videos, music, pictures, and movies (in most of the cases, which are protected by copyright). This means that internet users have faced limitations based on their geographical locations. In practical terms, this limitation can prevent some customers located in Italy from buying digital music that is available to customers in Bulgaria; or prevent a traveller who bought a digital movie from a German provider from watching the end of the movie when they reach France. Furthermore, when a consumer buys an e-book online in Spain, this consumer may not be able to read the book in Hungary. This limitation relies on geo-location technologies, which help physically territorialise the Internet. The basic definition of the geo-location tools was already provided in the first chapter. In this part of the study, firstly, the geo-location tools will be generally described. After that, the definitions of digital rights management (DRM), technological protection measures (TPM), and rights management information (RMI) will be outlined with the help of relevant legislation.

Finally, commonly used circumvention tools for bypassing technological measures employed by the rightsholders will be explained.

7.2.1 Geo-Location Tools

Geo-location tools are integral to online operations, employing various techniques to determine the geographical location of devices. Overall, geo-location tools play a crucial role in enhancing online security, enabling targeted content delivery, and providing users with personalised experiences based on their geographical locations.[1]

At its simplest level, geo-location involves users *self-reporting* their locations, often through drop-down menus,[2] when a user creates an account or opens a website or mobile app and is prompted to select their country, state, or city from a list of options in a drop-down menu. Geo-location technologies help to identify the physical location of the device with the help of unique addresses appointed in individual devices, which are called *IP addresses*.[3] When a user connects to the Internet, the IP address is assigned to the user by the user's Internet Service Provider (ISP).[4] As such, one of the fundamental tools used in geo-location is the IP address, a unique set of numbers assigned to devices for online data exchange,[5] which provides geographically based unique identifiers for internet-accessing devices.[6]

Digital media platforms and other distributors usually rely on IP geo-location because it is cost-effective and easy to implement.[7] When a user sends a request for this platform, website or any other products, this IP number is also sent with this request, and therefore, the server also knows from where the user wants to access this product.[8] These platforms check the IP addresses of these users to be sure that they are trying to access these services from the authorised zone.[9] After the determination of the location, thanks to this IP address, rightsholders may allow or prevent users from accessing this website or product from this location. IP geo-location providers are usually used in firewalls, domain name servers, mail systems, websites and other automated systems.[10]

Additionally, content distributors may rely on hardware with *Global Positioning System (GPS)* capabilities to pinpoint user locations,[11] especially with the prevalence

[1] Dusollier (2012, p. 299).

[2] Hilliard (2015, p. 161).

[3] Hilliard (2015, p. 159).

[4] De-Yolande (2022, p. 90).

[5] Lobato (2019, p. 165).

[6] Weiss (2016, p. 896).

[7] Weiss (2016).

[8] De-Yolande (2022, p. 89).

[9] Lobato (2019, p. 166).

[10] De-Yolande (2022, p. 91).

[11] Lobato (2019, p. 165).

of smartphones.[12] Especially after the emergence of The World Wide Web Consortium (W3C),[13] W3C has standardised geo-location systems, incorporating multiple data sources such as IP addresses, *Wi-Fi and Bluetooth MAC addresses*, *RFID*, *Wi-Fi connection locations*, *GPS*, and *GSM/CDMA cell IDs*.[14] Finally, *geo-coding* further enhances geo-location capabilities by converting textual data like addresses or cities into geographic coordinates, enabling precise location identification.[15]

7.2.2 Digital Rights Management, Technological Protection Measures, Rights Management Information and Geo-Blocking as a Technological Protection Measure

In this part of the study, the definition of Digital Rights Management (DRM) and Technological Protection Measures (TPM) will be presented together with the relevant legislation. After this, some of the technological protection measures tools will be explained. Finally, it will be evaluated whether geo-blocking is a type of technological protection measure.

7.2.2.1 Definitions of Digital Rights Management, Rights Management Information and Technological Protection Measures

Digital Rights Management (DRM) systems have been developed to protect and manage copyright-protected materials in electronic environments.[16] Technological measures which aim to manage the works according to the licensing rights are called digital rights management systems.[17] These systems enforce limitations set by rightsholders, managing access and usage of digital content to safeguard intellectual property rights.[18] DRM could also be explained as software/hardware which protects and manages rules to access and use digital content, such as copyright-protected videos, text, sound or music, etc. enforced by the copyright owners or rightsholders in general.[19] DRM aims to help rightsholders control their digital products and DRM systems are usually designed according to the contractual terms and conditions in

[12] Kra-Oz (2017, p. 386).

[13] For more information please visit: https://www.w3.org.

[14] Dusollier (2012, p. 299).

[15] Dusollier (2012, p. 299).

[16] Dusollier (2012, p. 297).

[17] Dusollier (2012, p. 299).

[18] Finck and Moscon (2019, p. 79).

[19] Finck and Moscon (2019, p. 79).

licence agreements and it operates within the framework of legal regulations and contractual agreements.[20]

DRM is often described as an additional layer of 'paracopyright', supplementing traditional copyright law with technological restrictions.[21] DRM embodies the concept of 'code is law'[22] where digital code regulates behaviour and access to digital content; law intervenes after unwanted behaviours occur, while code directly intervenes in behaviour in advance by preventing it.

DRM technology encompasses two generations.[23] The first generation primarily focuses on limiting content copying to prevent unauthorised distribution.[24] In contrast, the second generation introduces access limitations, such as time-restricted access, device limitations, and restrictions on printing or alteration.[25]

DRM systems utilise technological protection measures and rights management information as critical components to enforce copyright restrictions, and these components include various software and hardware mechanisms aimed at identifying, protecting, and managing IP-protected works in digital form.[26]

In the Grand Production v GO4YOU preliminary application[27] which will be explained in detail later in this chapter, the Opinion of Advocate General (AG) Szpunar also includes the definition and explanation of the DRM as follows: *Digital rights management instruments are commonly used to protect copyright by preventing illegal use (or simply use that the rightholders consider undesirable) of protected works distributed in digital format. They are also used as a tool to manage copyright on such works, making it possible to charge a separate fee for different forms of distribution of the same work, divide the market and apply so-called price discrimination to its different segments, or, finally, charge fees for the content made available on websites.*[28]

International copyright treaties have regulated technological protection measures (TPMs) and rights management information (RMI), which are relevant components of the DRM.[29]

RMI is basically a piece of information regarding the content and the terms and conditions attached to that content.[30] It may be about the licence information or may also be data in a digital music file, which is information about the artist, usage rights, and any other relevant information regarding the intellectual property

---

[20] Finck and Moscon (2019, p. 80).

[21] Finck and Moscon (2019, p. 79).

[22] Kra-Oz (2017, pp 388–389).

[23] Finck and Moscon (2019, p. 78).

[24] Finck and Moscon (2019, p. 78).

[25] Finck and Moscon (2019, p. 78).

[26] Kharb et al. (2023, p. 54).

[27] Case C-423/21 *Grand Production d.o.o. v GO4YU GmbH and Others.* (hereinafter will be referred as the Grand Production v GO4YOU case).

[28] Opinion of the Grand Production v GO4YOU case, para 29.

[29] Finck and Moscon (2019, p. 80).

[30] Finck and Moscon (2019, p. 80).

rights associated with that.[31] RMI has also been described in WCT Article 12(2) like following: '*As used in this Article, "rights management information" means information which identifies the work, the author of the work, the owner of any right in the work, or information about the terms and conditions of use of the work, and any numbers or codes that represent such information, when any of these items of information is attached to a copy of a work or appears in connection with the communication of a work to the public.*' WPPT Article 19(2) has also described the RMI in the context of the phonograms and performers domain, using the same definitions provided above in the WCT.

In the EU Law domain, the definition of the RMI can be found in the InfoSoc Directive, Article 7(2), as follows: '2. *For the purposes of this Directive, the expression "rights-management information" means any information provided by rightholders which identifies the work or other subject-matter referred to in this Directive or covered by the sui generis right provided for in Chapter III of Directive 96/9/EC, the author or any other rightholder, or information about the terms and conditions of use of the work or other subject-matter, and any numbers or codes that represent such information.*'

TPMs can be described as individual technologies that protect the subject matter of copyright-protected work with the help of protection measures; in contrast, DRMs are more complicated and complex protection systems that use contractual, technological, and statutory protection.[32] With the help of TPMs, rightsholders could enforce the conditions written in licence contracts, which may restrict access and use.[33] TPMs allow for restrictions which are used in digital infrastructure to protect and control copyright-protected content.[34]

TPMs have also been regulated in the InfoSoc Directive Article 6, and in Article 6(3) the definition of the TPMs has been provided as follows: '3. *For the purposes of this Directive, the expression "technological measures" means any technology, device or component that, in the normal course of its operation, is designed to prevent or restrict acts, in respect of works or other subject-matter, which are not authorised by the rightholder of any copyright or any right related to copyright as provided for by law or the sui generis right provided for in Chapter III of Directive 96/9/EC.*'

Although both WCT and WPPT have included an obligation for contracting parties to provide adequate legal protection and effective legal remedies against the circumvention of effective technological measures, these treaties did not include any definition of TPMs.

TPMs manage the use of the subject matter of copyright-protected content. These measures can be seen in different formats, such as passwords to access the content, encryption or copy control, limitation of the number of devices for specific copies,

[31] Finck and Moscon (2019, p. 80).

[32] Finck and Moscon (2019, p. 85).

[33] Finck and Moscon (2019, p. 85).

[34] Hilliard (2015, p. 158).

controlling transmission of the information,[35] controlling use, protecting the integrity and authenticity of the information, and tracking the copy.[36]

General acceptance is that there are two categories of TPMs, which are access control measures and other (copy control) measures. In international treaties (such as WPPT and WCT) and legislations (such as the US's DMCA), two categories of TPMs have been regulated; one prevents access to work, and others prevent further copying (reproduction) of these works.[37] On the other hand, the InfoSoc Directive 6(3) regulates the TPM and its categories, and it does not distinguish between these two categories of TPMs,[38] which can be read as follows: *'Technological measures shall be deemed "effective" where the use of a protected work or other subject-matter is controlled by the rightholders through application of an access control or protection process, such as encryption, scrambling or other transformation of the work or other subject-matter or a copy control mechanism, which achieves the protection objective.'* That means where there is a TPM for access control or a protection process, that measure will be deemed an effective protection measure. On the other hand, what makes an effective TPM has not been explained in this Directive.

7.2.2.2 Examples of Technological Protection Measures Tools

There can be different tools of TPMs, and the usage of technological protection measures may vary according to the content, the author, the value of the work, the risk of unauthorised access and the consumer. There are some prominent examples that are usually used as a TPM, such as watermarks,[39] encryption,[40] and rights expression languages (RELs).[41]

Watermarks are mainly technological protections designed to include a message within a file which is difficult to remove.[42] As Fig. 7.1 demonstrates, watermarks may appear in varying degrees of visibility within a digital file.

Watermarks can also be included in the documents/files where there is a need for a licence to obtain this copy. Watermarks can include the IP information regarding the copy, and this is basically used to detect or prevent unauthorised copies of these works.[43]

---

[35] Kharb et al. (2023, p. 55).

[36] Besek (2004, pp 450–451).

[37] Roy and Marsoof (2017, pp 672, 675).
Roy and Marsoof (2017, p. 672).

[38] Roy and Marsoof (2017, p. 676).

[39] Besek (2004, p. 447).

[40] Besek (2004, p. 447).

[41] Finck and Moscon (2019, p. 81).

[42] Finck and Moscon (2019, p. 447).

[43] Finck and Moscon (2019, p. 448).

Fig. 7.1 The figure for watermark, https://en.wikipedia.org/wiki/File:Digital_watermarks.jpg

Encryption can mainly be described as a method of encoding information so that only a limited number of people or limited devices can access and open this information or content.[44] **RELs** are mainly machine-readable expressions of relevant usage rights of that work, which regulate what kind of uses are permitted and forbidden for the content.[45] This technology is basically in use to limit the number of devices, the number of people, the further reproduction and prevent alteration of this work.

Overall, DRM systems play a crucial role with the help of TPM tools in safeguarding intellectual property rights and controlling access to digital content by balancing the interests of rightsholders with the need for content accessibility and protection against piracy.

7.2.2.3 Geo-Blocking as a TPM

As explained in the previous chapters, geo-blocking technology can be used for different purposes. It may be used to direct users to the content which best suits them, such as international editions or products, for localisation of the content, can be used to enforce domestic legislation, such as local safety regulations,[46] to avoid making

---

[44] Finck and Moscon (2019, p. 448). '*A system of encryption is based on algorithms, or formulas. A very basic algorithm might be "shift by n," where each letter used in the message is shifted n spaces (where n is a number from one to twenty-five corresponding to the positions of the remaining letters of the alphabet). For example, if the encryption key is n = 3, the encrypted version of MEET TONIGHT IN PARK would be PHHW WRQLJKW LQ SDUN.*'

[45] Finck and Moscon (2019, p. 81): '*RELs are technical languages that have specific syntax and semantic vocabulary rules for expressing what kind of uses are permitted, forbidden or obligatory. These computer markup languages express a number of permissions such as to stream, copy, delete, modify, embed, execute, export, extract, annotate, aggregate, install, backup, loan, sell, give, lease, play, print, and display in relation to a file. RELs are normally used to express rules contained in the license agreements.*'

[46] Kra-Oz (2017, p. 387).

available pornographic sites in certain locations,[47] national security purposes, for blocking malicious traffic, enforcing price discrimination, location-aware authentication, and fraud prevention.[48] DVD region codes may also be given as an example of an early hardware-based form of geo-blocking.[49] In the copyright context, this technology is commonly used to comply with the contractual terms between the copyright owner and their licensees, and this technology allows copyright owners and licensees to restrict access to the content geographically.[50]

There is a question of whether geo-blocking measures may be a TPM under international treaties and under the InfoSoc Directive. To answer this question, it should be examined whether geo-blocking may fall under the two categories of TPMs: access control measures and copy control measures. Geo-blocking can prevent or restrict access to work which are only available in certain areas on the Internet. The copyright owner or distributor/licensees may lawfully employ geo-blocking in order to prevent other users outside of this area from accessing these works. If geo-blocking has been applied to make content exclusively available in certain countries, then it can be classified as a TPM under access control measures.[51] Geo-blocking can also prohibit further reproduction of these copies, such as downloading or streaming, so geo-blocking could be regarded as a copy-control measure as well rather than only an access control measure.[52] This technology prohibits users from reproducing these works, which is why they can also be regarded as a TPM.[53]

As explained above, in the InfoSoc Directive, there is no distinction between access control and other protection measures in terms of categories of TPMs.[54] Furthermore, there is no definition of effective technological measures as well. In the absence of this definition, geo-blocking may be considered as a TPM falling under DRM, and usually, geo-blocking is accepted as a second-generation DRM tool by the commentators.[55]

In the Grand Production v GO4YOU case, AG Szpunar also described geo-blocking as one of the instruments of digital rights management.[56] In his opinion, he explained this practice as follows: *It involves various protections designed to prevent the use of digital (electronic) content in a manner contrary to the intention of the content provider. Those protections are intended to 'correct' digital data characteristics that are undesirable from the point of view of content providers, namely the ability to produce any number of perfect copies at virtually no cost and to transmit those copies (particularly online) over any distance. With regard to content disseminated*

[47] De-Yolande (2022, p. 88).

[48] De-Yolande (2022, p. 91).

[49] Kra-Oz (2017, p. 387).

[50] Marsoof (2017, p. 101).

[51] Marsoof (2017, p. 101).

[52] Roy and Marsoof (2017, p. 675).

[53] Roy and Marsoof (2017, p. 675).

[54] Marsoof (2017, p. 110).

[55] Kharb et al. (2023, p. 44), Burke (2017, p. 59).

[56] Opinion of the Grand Production v GO4YOU case, para 28.

on the Internet, digital rights management instruments, for instance in the form of geoblocking, can also serve to counter the global nature of this medium, enabling its virtual division into geographic zones, as I mentioned in the introduction. This explanation would also serve as a conclusion of the discussion on whether geo-blocking is a TPM or a DRM in general form. This study also accepts that geo-blocking is a form of a TPM that protects copyright-protected work in digital form.

7.2.3 Circumvention Tools

Territorial limitations annoy customers who want to benefit from a borderless online world, and it results in a form of digital piracy by downloading or accessing content illegally with the help of technological tools.[57] This evasion of geo-blocking can be called cybertravel, circumvention or geo-evasion. In this study, the term for bypassing geo-blocking will be called 'circumvention'. Circumvention of geo-blocking allows Internet users to be seen in different locations other than their actual location with the help of geo-location tools.[58]

Circumvention technologies are the tools which help to remove, circumvent, prevaricate or avoid technologically provided measures[59] and play a role in manipulating IP addresses. There are some circumvention tools used for circumventing territorial restrictions, such as Virtual Private Networks (VPNs), change of Domain Name Servers (DNS) address, Cloud VPN Services, proxies, accessing content with remote access, The Onion Router (Tor) browser, and other methods to access these products with the help of online translation tools, usage of cached pages and archives which will be explained further in that part of the study.

7.2.3.1 Virtual Private Networks (VPN)

VPNs could be described as an encrypted connection method over the Internet, and with this service from a device to a network, a new connection will be established and VPN basically helps the encryption of the Internet traffic and hides the online identity and activity of the user.[60] VPNs establish a private connection between networks,[61] VPNs reroute connections through the use of private networks, and VPNs enlarge these private networks to internet connections that are deemed to connect.[62] With the VPN service, the IP address of the device can be concealed, and at the same time,

---

57 Marsoof (2017, p. 101).

58 Trimble (2012, p. 569).

59 Hilliard (2015, p. 160).

60 Kharb et al. (2023), 50.

61 Kurniadi (2015, p. 22).

62 Hilliard (2015, p. 161).

this VPN service also provides a new IP address for the device.[63] On the other hand, VPN service providers can see the details of internet usage; these VPN providers are the only parties who can see these activities.[64]

For example if a movie is cheaper in Austria than in Sweden; in that case, the VPN service could be used to be seen in Austria, or if the content is not available in Germany, the VPN service could be used to be seen in any other country than Germany.[65] With digitalisation and the enormous increase in digital content consumption, the usage of VPN services has increased rapidly, and free, paid, or subscribed VPN services have become a medium for Internet users. According to the explanation of the EU Vice President for the DSM, Andrus Ansip, one in five Europeans is using VPN to bypass geo-blocking.[66] On the other hand, VPNs can also be used for legitimate purposes, for example, working from home.[67]

Some services have applied measures to block these circumvention tools, especially VPNs.[68] For example, Smart TV users and Blu-ray players could not use VPNs, while BBC iPlayer users were using a VPN to reach this player.[69] According to a report published in 2017, more than 60 million people have accessed the BBC iPlayer by using a VPN outside the UK.[70]

Netflix has had extensive geo-blocking control since 2016.[71] When Netflix was first announced and started to become famous among audiovisual media services, Netflix did not have measures to control illicit activity. Even many Australians used VPNs to access US Netflix between 2010 and 2015 when Netflix was not available in Australia with fake US residential addresses.[72] People were using circumvention tools such as VPNs, Smart DNS proxies, and free browser add-ons to access US-based Netflix service.[73] Between 2010 and 2015, this activity was so common that there were YouTube videos to explain how to geo-evade Netflix.[74] People in Australia and other countries were paying subscription fees, increasing the number of subscribers

[63] Major (2019, p. 13).

[64] Hilliard (2015, p.161).

[65] Berry et al. (2019, p. 485). For more information, please see p 492: '*So how do VPNs circumvent these geolocation services? As explained above, most websites use IP trackers. Once a VPN service is selected, it establishes an encrypted tunnel between a device and a server that is located in another geographic location from the user. The server then creates a new IP address in the foreign country, effectively masking the user's actual IP address. As a result, the user's IP address then appears as if it is from the same country as the server. Thus, if Netflix only allows streaming of Love Island in the United States, a user in Germany can use a VPN to generate a US IP address and stream the otherwise geo-blocked content.*'

[66] Weiss (2016, p. 899).

[67] Kharb et al. (2023, p. 50).

[68] De-Yolande (2022, p. 89).

[69] De-Yolande (2022, p. 96).

[70] De-Yolande (2022, p. 96).

[71] Lobato (2019, p. 163).

[72] De-Yolande (2022, p.163).

[73] De-Yolande (2022, p. 167).

[74] I De-Yolande (2022, p. 164).

to Netflix.[75] Therefore, Netflix gained a better reputation and profit. As such, it was understandable that Netflix did not have any measures to prevent these tools in the first step.[76]

However, during this time, rightsholders were getting worried because of parallel imports and piracy and some concerns have been disclosed through trade papers and tech press.[77] For example, Sony's some e-mails leaked in 2015 and the Sony memo were saying that "Netflix can and should do a much better job geofiltering".[78] Rightsholders also saw circumvention as a problem since subscribers or consumers "stealing" these products from outside their regions was, in a sense, equivalent to illegal downloading and could undermine an orderly digital market.[79] Additionally, because territorial exclusivity could not be guaranteed due to this circumvention, the prices that rightsholders could demand might change and potentially decrease.[80]

After Netflix secured a good level of profit and became a worldwide audio-visual media service provider, Netflix announced an anti-proxy policy in 2016.[81] Netflix issued a press release – 'Evolving Proxy Detection as a Global Service'[82] and informed its users about a new VPN-detection technology, which means they wanted to commit to geo-blocking.[83] Until then, there are very strict and extensive protection measures to prevent the usage of VPNs and other circumvention tools from accessing Netflix.[84] Today, Netflix has an interesting policy, if a user uses VPN, Netflix (usually) understand that and only shows the content that Netflix has a worldwide licence.[85] Nevertheless, unsurprisingly, lots of VPN providers managed to evade Netflix's detection technology today and there are lots of recommendation on the Internet for people to use for Netflix.[86]

[75] De-Yolande (2022, p. 169).

[76] De-Yolande (2022, p. 169).

[77] De-Yolande (2022, p. 169).

[78] De-Yolande (2022, p. 170).

[79] De-Yolande (2022, pp 170–171).

[80] De-Yolande (2022, pp 170–171).

[81] De-Yolande (2022, p. 163).

[82] Evolving Proxy Detection as a Global Service (2016). In: Netflix https://about.netflix.com/en/news/evolving-proxy-detection-as-a-global-service.

[83] Lobato (2019, p. 168).

[84] For more information, please read the chapter 6 of the Lobato (2019).

[85] Watching TV shows and movies through a VPN (2025). In: Netflix https://help.netflix.com/en/node/114701.

[86] Netflix VPN Not Working? How to Beat the Netflix VPN Ban in 2024 (2024). In: Cloudwards https://www.cloudwards.net/how-to-beat-the-netflix-vpn-ban/#:~:text=ExpressVPN%20is%20the%20best%20VPN,you%20watch%20more%20than%20occasionally.

7.2.3.2 Change of Domain Name Servers (DNS) Address and Smart DNS Proxies

Changing the DNS address could be one way of circumventing geo-blocking. To briefly explain the DNS address system, users can connect to websites using user-friendly domain names instead of complex IP addresses.[87] For instance, to access Google, users type domain names like google.com; however, web browsers ultimately communicate using IP addresses. When individuals attempt to access geo-blocked content through tools such as Smart DNS or DNS changers, these tools switch the DNS servers on the user's device from local ones to alternative servers in different countries by tricking the website into believing that the user is in another country.[88] Using these tools ensures that the actual location of internet users remains undisclosed; instead, the tools deceive websites into believing that the user is accessing content from an approved location. Consequently, the IP addresses of internet users remain unmasked, and internet traffic remains unencrypted; only the actual DNS address is concealed. For example, the DNS designation "8.8.8.8" represents one of Google's publicly available DNS servers.[89] These globally accessible DNS servers from Google are a convenient option for users seeking access to Google, irrespective of their geographical location.

There are also DNS Proxy Servers. DNS proxy servers take the requests of the users and pass these requests to a neutral server with the help of the Internet.[90] However, although these services mask your IP address, they do not encrypt your traffic,[91] it is unencrypted, and due to the very high volume of requests, it is relatively slow.[92] Finally, the combined VPN-DNS packages are also possible on the Internet with subscriptions to achieve more complex encryption.[93]

7.2.3.3 Cloud VPN Service

Cloud VPNs are also another type of circumvention tool, which is not the same as VPN services.[94] Cloud VPN is trying to provide a secure and globally accessible VPN service as its primary purpose, and with Cloud VPN, VPN users do not need any VPN infrastructure. Cloud VPN services, such as Google Cloud VPN, use a cloud-based network infrastructure to provide VPN services. With this Google Cloud VPN, there

---

[87] Magnusson et al. (2023, p. 498).

[88] Trimble (2012, p. 602).

[89] Magnusson et al. (2023, p. 508).

[90] Hilliard (2015, p. 161).

[91] Lobato (2019, p. 167).

[92] Hilliard (2015, p. 161).

[93] De-Yolande (2022, p. 96).

[94] Timothy Shim (2023) Alternatives to VPN. In: Web Hosting Secret Revealed https://www.webhostingsecretrevealed.net/blog/web-tools/alternatives-to-vpn/.

is globally accessible VPN access to end users and subscribers via a cloud platform. The user connects to this Cloud VPN via the provider's devices.[95]

7.2.3.4 Proxies

Proxy servers could be considered another option for circumventing territorial restrictions on the Internet since these servers will act like a third party, which stands as a middleman,[96] and it will access the content that actual end users want to access. After reaching the actual content with the help of the proxy servers, these servers will pass this content to end users. This server, the actual end user is trying to access it, will think that the proxy server is the end user.

Private proxies may also be another example of a tool to evade geo-blocking measures. In this method, volunteers provide their machines to other people from other countries who do not want to be seen accessed in their own countries.[97]

When a user seeks to access a web resource, like a website, their request is initially directed to *a web proxy server*.[98] Subsequently, the web proxy forwards the request to the intended server on behalf of the user, obtains the response from the target server, and transmits it back to the user. It is another method to circumvent territorial restrictions, which helps hide or block IP addresses so that this actual IP Address user cannot be detected by a server.[99]

If someone uses *a proxy IP address*, in that system, the user connects to the Internet through a software or website which reroutes the connection by masking the user's IP address and using its own IP address as if the user is connecting to the Internet from a different device in another location.[100] However, these proxies can easily be detected by the websites, and these websites can block access.

7.2.3.5 Accessing Content with the Help of Remote Access Servers

Accessing content with the help of remote access servers could be another way to circumvent geo-blocking and access blocked content. In this way, people can access computers or other technological devices remotely and remote users can access everything as if they are at the same location as the remote computer or other devices. Hence, they can access all the contents which are available at the remote computer or other device location. In this method, since the device is remotely connected to

---

[95] Margaret Rouse (2023) Cloud VPN. In: Technopedia https://www.techopedia.com/definition/30760/cloud-vpn.

[96] Kurniadi (2015, pp 19–22).

[97] Trimble (2012, p. 603).

[98] Kurniadi (2015, pp 19–22).

[99] Kurniadi (2015, pp 19–22).

[100] Trimble (2012, p. 602).

the Internet, actual remote users' identification and their data will be secured.[101] GoToMyPC or LogMeIn could be given as examples of remote access tools.[102] Another example can be 'My Expat Network' (which is known as StreamVPN now); this is a server for people who want to access UK TV programs while located outside of the UK.

Finally, these services can also be used for privacy purposes. There are some tools for people who ask for privacy, such as Anonymiser, and these services reroute users to neutral IP addresses, which do not create any suspicion.[103]

7.2.3.6 The Onion Router (Tor)

Tor is another way to access content regardless of their location since the Tor browser is a web browser used for anonymous use on the Internet. When using the Tor browser, other sites are not allowed to display your identities and geographic locations while surfing the web.[104] As of March 2023, they announced that on their website, their mission is: *'To advance human rights and freedoms by creating and deploying free and open source anonymity and privacy technologies, supporting their unrestricted availability and use, and furthering their scientific and popular understanding.'* To achieve that mission, the provider made Tor free of charge, and they are trying to stop governments and another ISP from learning the Internet user's exact location.[105] To look at how Tor works, when browsing the Internet with Tor Browser, requests are sent to this website over five different servers. All requests sent by the servers are evaluated and then sent to the next server; these requests are repeated in the same way until they gain access to the website.[106] Tor also uses a chain of proxies to protect its users. Because of these formalities, the Internet speed is very low, and websites such as YouTube do not work by default in the Tor Browser.[107]

7.2.3.7 Other Methods to Access Content Which are not Available in Certain Locations

The usage of cached pages and archives could be another tool to circumvent geo-blocking and accessing a 'saved' form of these blocked pages. For example, archive.org has saved billions of saved pages from different times on their webpage.

---

[101] Kaya (2020, p. 99).

[102] Trimble (2012, p. 600).

[103] Trimble (2012, p. 602).

[104] For more information please visit: https://www.torproject.org.

[105] Stuart Dredge (2013) What is Tor? A beginner's guide to the privacy tool. In: The Guardian https://www.theguardian.com/technology/2013/nov/05/tor-beginners-guide-nsa-browser.

[106] Most Frequently Asked Questions. In: TorProject https://support.torproject.org/faq/.

[107] Stuart Dredge (2013) What is Tor? A beginner's guide to the privacy tool. In: The Guardian https://www.theguardian.com/technology/2013/nov/05/tor-beginners-guide-nsa-browser.

Through these kinds of cached pages and archives, if the page that is trying to be accessed has been subject to this process, circumventing blocking could be possible.[108]

Online translation tools could be another way for internet users who try to read some content that is not available in their location.[109] These translation tools, such as Google Translate, offer a translation of a website simultaneously, and the content to be translated is being hold in these translation tools such as in their memory or cached, and this translation is offered from their cached.[110] Therefore, via online translation tools, accessing blocked content could be possible.

7.3 Circumvention as a Copyright Infringement

With the help of circumvention tools, individuals seek to bypass and eliminate territorial restrictions and, in doing so, gain access to desired products. Consequently, this activity resulted in some concerns about the legitimacy of applying these tools to access copyright-protected works that are unavailable in specific locations due to copyright restrictions. Copyright holders usually suggest that the use of VPNs and other circumvention tools is a violation of copyright laws since these products should not be made available in the user's country.[111] Furthermore, the international copyright treaties (such as WCT and WPPT) and EU Directives (notably the InfoSoc Directive) also regulated the results of the bypassing of technological protection measures.

In this part of the study, first of all, the general explanation of copyright infringement will be provided with the possible exceptions for the circumvention activities. Secondly, relevant legislation will be provided in the context of the circumvention of territorial restrictions. Subsequently, the responsibility of the users and the circumvention tool providers will be outlined in the copyright context. Finally, the results of the circumvention of technological protection measures from the contract law perspective will be briefly mentioned. In this study, no explanation regarding the criminal law aspect of the usage of VPNs and other tools to circumvent TPMs will be given since this aspect will require an in-depth analysis to set the whole possible results and it will not have any relation with the outcome of this study.

---

[108] Everyone's Guide to By-Passing Internet Censorship (2007). In: The Citizen Lab, p. 28 https://citizenlab.ca/guides/everyones-guide-english.pdf.

[109] Everyone's Guide to By-Passing Internet Censorship (2007). In: The Citizen Lab, p. 28 https://citizenlab.ca/guides/everyones-guide-english.pdf.

[110] Kaya (2020, p. 99).

[111] De-Yolande (2022, p. 89).

7.3.1 Copyright Infringement and Exceptions

As explained in the previous chapter, copyright protection provides exclusive rights to right owners such as reproduction rights, communication to the public right and distribution rights, as regulated in the InfoSoc Directive Articles 2,3 and 4, respectively. Copyright infringement occurs when someone violates these exclusive rights granted to the author of this protected work by copyright law. On the other hand, to balance the different interests of the rightsholders and users, the InfoSoc Directive have proposed exhaustive lists of exceptions and limitations to certain restricted acts.[112] This means that not all unauthorised uses of these works will fall within the scope of copyright infringement; there may be some defences which permit the use of these copyright-protected works.

Article 5 of the InfoSoc Directive[113] provides numerous optional exceptions and limitations and one mandatory exception (the temporary copy exception) to reproduction, communication to the public and the distribution of these copyright-protected works. In this study, only the temporary copy exception and the private use exception will be explained in the subsequent sub-chapter since other exceptions and limitations will not fit in this context.

All exceptions and limitations are subject to the *three-step test*, which was initially regulated in the Berne Convention 9(2) as a test for the exception of the reproduction right.[114] After the Berne Convention, the TRIPs agreement and WIPO Copyright Treaties also included the three-step test, and all exceptions and limitations should satisfy this test in order to be become permitted use. At the EU Level, the Software Directive and Rental and Lending Directive also regulated this test.[115] Most importantly, the InfoSoc Directive regulated this test, and according to the InfoSoc

---

[112] Recital 31 of the InfoSoc Directive.

[113] *Article 5: Exceptions and limitations.*

1. Temporary acts of reproduction referred to in Article 2, which are transient or incidental [and] an integral and essential part of a technological process and whose sole purpose is to enable:

(a) a transmission in a network between third parties by an intermediary, or.

(b) a lawful use.

of a work or other subject-matter to be made, and which have no independent economic significance, shall be exempted from the reproduction right provided for in Article 2.

2. Member States may provide for exceptions or limitations to the reproduction right provided for in Article 2 in the following cases:

...

(b) in respect of reproductions on any medium made by a natural person for private use and for ends that are neither directly nor indirectly commercial, on condition that the rightholders receive fair compensation which takes account of the application or non-application of technological measures referred to in Article 6 to the work or subject-matter concerned;

...

5. The exceptions and limitations provided for in paragraphs 1, 2, 3 and 4 shall only be applied in certain special cases which do not conflict with a normal exploitation of the work or other subject-matter and do not unreasonably prejudice the legitimate interests of the rightholder.

[114] Article 9 (2) Berne Convention; Articles 10 and 13 TRIPs Agreements.

[115] The Software Directive, Article 6(3); the Rental and Lending Directive Article 10.

Directive Article 5(5), the exceptions and limitations provided in this article shall only be applicable (i) in certain cases, (ii) shall not conflict with a normal exploitation of the work and finally, (iii) shall not unreasonably prejudice the legitimate interests of the rightsholder.

7.3.1.1 The Temporary Copy Exception

The temporary copy exception has been regulated in Article 5(1) InfoSoc Directive, and according to that provision, Member States shall provide an exception for temporary acts of reproduction which are transient or incidental to an integral and essential part of a technological process. For this exception, the sole purpose of the process must be to enable a transmission network between third parties by an intermediary or the lawful use of the work or protected subject matter, and this act must have no economic interest. The InfoSoc Directive have not provided many details regarding this exception, yet the landmark InfoPaq case has provided a very important explanation regarding this exception. In the Infopaq case, the CJEU has set out the five requirements that must be met for the exception to apply,[116] which are:

1. *The act must be temporary.*
2. *The copy of the work must be transient or incidental.*
   - The requirement of being transient has been discussed in the Infopaq case, and CJEU ruled that to be regarded as a transient copy, the duration of this temporary copy must be limited to that necessary for the completion of the process, and the copy should be deleted afterwards without the need of human intervention. In this judgment, CJEU held that cache copies were transient.[117]
   - For the condition of being incidental, the Meltwater case[118] ruled that for a copy to be considered incidental, its existence and purpose must depend on the technological process it integrates.[119] In this decision, the CJEU try to explain incidental copies as follows: '*when an internet user browses the internet, he does not set out to make a copy of the image unless he chooses to download it or to print it out. His aim is to view the content of the website selected. The on-screen copies and the cached copies are therefore merely the incidental consequence of the use of his computer to view a website*'.[120] It may be suggested that incidental copies do not have any significance from the copyright law perspective since they are only depending on the technological process that these copies integrate.[121]

---

[116] The Infopaq case, para54.

[117] The Infopaq case, para 64.

[118] Case C-360/13 *Public Relations Consultants Association Ltd v Newspaper Licensing Agency Ltd and Others* [2014] OJ C 260. (hereinafter will be referred to as the Meltwater Case).

[119] The Meltwater case, para 63.

[120] The Meltwater case, para17.

[121] Karapapa (2020, p. 122).

3. *It must be an integral and essential part of the technological process.*
   - For this requirement to be met, this temporary and transient or incidental copy should be required in the technological process.
4. *The sole purpose of the process must be to enable a transmission network between third parties by an intermediary or the lawful use of the work or protected subject matter.*
   - For this condition, the purpose of this temporary act of reproduction must be done in order to enable internet transmission or to enable lawful use. To decide whether there is a lawful use, the CJEU held that the three-step test should have been applied. According to the three-step test this use should be (i) in certain cases, (ii) shall not conflict with a normal exploitation of the work and finally, (iii) shall not unreasonably prejudice the legitimate interests of the rightsholder.
5. *The act must have no independent economic significance.*

These conditions are cumulative conditions, which means if any of these criteria are not satisfied, there will be a possibility of copyright infringement.[122]

The temporary copy exception and the evaluation of this exception for the temporary access to digital content is especially important in online usage, and further analysis of the act of streaming and the applicability of this exception in that context will be provided in the following part.

7.3.1.2 The Private Copy Limitation

The private copy limitation was regulated in Article 5(2)(b) of the InfoSoc Directive, which rules that Member States may provide a limitation for the reproduction right for the reproductions made by the natural persons for non-commercial purposes and private uses, provided that rightsholders receive fair compensation. Furthermore, this provision rules that if a piece of content is accessible online and is subjected to licensing conditions that limit private copying while also being protected by TPMs, the Directive permits setting aside those limitations.[123] Therefore, if there is a TPM implemented for a work, the user may not benefit from this private copy limitation. Finally, in the Adam BV and others v Stichting case,[124] the Court ruled that only reproductions made from a licensed source will benefit from this exception.[125]

---

[122] The Infopaq case, para 55.

[123] Quintais (2015, p. 70).

[124] Case C-435/12 ACI *Adam BV and Others v Stichting de Thuiskopie, Stichting Onderhandelingen Thuiskopie vergoeding* [2014] OJ C 399.

[125] Adam BV and others v Stichting case, para58.

The CJEU's recent ruling in Stichting de Thuiskopie[126] further refined the scope of the private copy limitation under Article 5(2)(b) of the InfoSoc Directive, this time in the context of subscription-based streaming services. The Dutch collecting societies SdT and SONT sought to impose private copying levies on hardware manufacturers, including HP and Dell, in respect of "offline streaming copies" which are local copies placed by streaming providers on users' devices to enable offline access to music or films. The Court held that such copies fall outside the scope of the private copy limitation, on two cumulative grounds. First, the Court characterised the making available of offline streaming copies as an act of communication to the public under Article 3(1) rather than a reproduction under Article 2, on the reasoning that subscribers access the work itself (rather than a specific copy under their control) at a place and time of their choosing. Since Article 5(2)(b) applies only to reproductions, the limitation could not be invoked. Second, and in the alternative, the Court reasoned that even if such acts were classified as reproductions, the private copy limitation would still not apply: the copy is made by the streaming provider rather than by the natural person, the source of the copy is held by the provider, and the user neither has technical control over the copy nor lawful access to its source independently of the service. Crucially, the encryption and app-based restrictions implemented by streaming providers qualify as TPMs within the meaning of Article 6(3) of the Directive, ensuring that the rightsholder retains control over the work and can block access at any time. Consistent with the logic already embedded in Article 5(2)(b), that TPMs displace the private copy limitation, the Court concluded that no compensable harm arises where the rightsholder retains technological control and has authorised the copy through a licence.

7.3.2 Circumvention of Technological Protection Measures in the Relevant Legislation and in the Case Law of the EU

7.3.2.1 Circumvention of Technological Protection Measures in the Relevant Legislation

As explained above, rightsholders may consider applying technological protection measures for their works in a digital form in order to protect their work from unlawful uses.[127] Especially in the audiovisual sector, the practice of geo-blocking is not only about the protection of copyright, but it may also be seen as a business model, and rightsholders may use this practice for fragmentation of the market, increasing more revenue, tailoring the content to maintain cultural and linguistic diversity.[128]

[126] Case C-496/24 *Stichting Onderhandelingen Thuiskopievergoeding and Stichting de Thuiskopie v HP Nederland BV and Others* (CJEU, 16 April 2026).

[127] Armstrong (2008, p. 1).

[128] Kharb et al. (2023, p. 48).

On the other hand, these kinds of restrictions could frustrate users, and these users may seek ways to circumvent these measures with the help of the circumvention tools, which have also been explained above. Unsurprisingly, the usage of these tools and bypassing technological protection measures have been subject to judicial and legislative considerations. Circumvention of TPMs and its results have been regulated both in WIPO treaties and the InfoSoc Directive.

WCT Article 11 and WPPT Article 18 regulate that all contracting countries should provide adequate legal protection and effective legal remedies against the circumvention of effective technological measures. Furthermore, the InfoSoc Directive Article 6(1) regulates that *Member States shall provide adequate legal protection against the circumvention of any effective technological measures, which the person concerned carries out in the knowledge, or with reasonable grounds to know, that he or she is pursuing that objective.*

The InfoSoc Directive also obliges Member States of the EU to provide effective protection against the circumvention of TPM and anti-trafficking of circumvention devices and services.[129] However, this makes no further explanation regarding what constitutes adequate and effective legal protection against the circumvention of these protection measures. Furthermore, Article 8 of the InfoSoc Directive[130] also obliges Member States to impose appropriate sanctions and remedies in the case of copyright infringement.

7.3.2.2 Circumvention of Technological Protection Measures According to the Case Law of the EU

In July 2021, the CJEU was asked to clarify how the communication to the public under Article 3 of the InfoSoc Directive should be interpreted in cases where effective geo-blocking measures are implemented by content providers but are still circumvented in the Grand Production v GO4YOU case. This was a very important preliminary request in this field because for the first and only time as of July 2024, the CJEU were asked to clarify the results of the circumvention of geo-blocking measures. This decision will be explained in detail.

---

[129] Gasser and Girsberger (2004, p. 9).

[130] *Article 8 Sanctions and remedies.*

1. Member States shall provide appropriate sanctions and remedies in respect of infringements of the rights and obligations set out in this Directive and shall take all the measures necessary to ensure that those sanctions and remedies are applied. The sanctions thus provided for shall be effective, proportionate and dissuasive.

2. Each Member State shall take the measures necessary to ensure that rightholders whose interests are affected by an infringing activity carried out on its territory can bring an action for damages and/or apply for an injunction and, where appropriate, for the seizure of infringing material as well as of devices, products or components referred to in Article 6(2).

3. Member States shall ensure that rightholders are in a position to apply for an injunction against intermediaries whose services are used by a third party to infringe a copyright or related right.

Secondly, another important decision regarding the involvement of the circumvention tools to bypass geo-blocking has been held by the Dutch Courts related to the copyright infringement claim on Anne Frank's works in 2022.[131] The Anne Frank decision will also be explained in this chapter in detail.

7.3.2.2.1 The Grand Production V GO4YOU Case – the Opinion of Advocate General

The Serbian company Grand Production produces entertainment TV programs, and GO4YU has a licence for programming television stations, which are retransmitted on the Internet and their streaming platform is accessible from Serbian territory and outside of it.[132] The company GO4YU only have a licence to retransmit online within the territory of Serbia and Montenegro, the entertainment programs licenced by the Grand Production; they impose geo-blocking for the Internet users who are trying to reach this Internet outside the territory of these two states.[133] Nevertheless, with the help of VPNs, some internet users managed to circumvent geo-blocking and access and watch GO4YU content outside of Serbia and Montenegro.[134] Furthermore, Grand Production claimed that between 30 April 2020 and 15 June 2020, their entertainment programmes were freely accessible in Austria thanks to the streaming platform of the company GO4YU without geo-blocking.[135] Grand Production asked for an injunction against GO4YU because of performing an act of communication to the public in Austria, and Grand Production also claimed that geo-blocking measures were circumvented via VPN.[136] After some interim injunctions applications, the case was before the Supreme Court of Austria, and the Supreme Court decided to stay the proceedings and asked CJEU to clarify how communication to the public under Article 3 of the InfoSoc Directive should be interpreted in that case.[137]

The AG started their analysis to accept territorially restricted rights on the Internet because of the territorial nature of all laws. Accordingly, the AG stated that there is a need to resolve the contradiction between the global nature of the Internet and the territorially limited rights, and he stated that this contradiction could be resolved in two ways: either by 'territorialising' the Internet with the help of geo-blocking or having a global level of regulation for the activities carried out on the Internet.[138] Accordingly, the AG has started to analyse whether there is a communication of these

[131] C/13/710961/ KG ZA 21-1010 IHJK/MV *Anne Frank Fonds v Anne Frank Stichting, Koninklijke Nederlandse Akademie Van Wetenschappen, Vereniging Voor Onderzoek En Ontsluiting Van Historische Teksten* (2021) (hereinafter will be referred as the Anne Frank Case).

[132] Opinion of the Grand Production v GO4YOU case, paras 8–9.

[133] Opinion of the Grand Production v GO4YOU case, para 11.

[134] Opinion of the Grand Production v GO4YOU case, para 11.

[135] Opinion of the Grand Production v GO4YOU case, para 12.

[136] Opinion of the Grand Production v GO4YOU case, para 13.

[137] Opinion of the Grand Production v GO4YOU case, para 16.

[138] Opinion of the Grand Production v GO4YOU case, para 2.

works to the public by the operator of this streaming platform if users circumvent geo-blocking by using VPNs.[139]

The AG stated that if a rightsholder or licensee has rights limited to a specific territory and uses technological protection measures to prevent internet users from accessing content outside of these areas, in that case, the rightsholder will not be held liable for the act of communication to the public if their users circumvent this measure via VPN, provided that the rightsholder has not intentionally implemented ineffective measures.[140] The AG further stated that when the copyright holder applies technological protection measures to restrict access outside the areas where they have obtained this right, it could be understood that the copyright-protected works are intended to be accessible only to individuals accessing the content protected by the specified region. Therefore, it could be argued that the rightsholder does not have the intention to communicate this work to the public in other regions.[141] From a circumvention perspective, the AG also stated that there are no fully effective technological protection measures today; every measure could be circumvented or violated.[142] Therefore, the streaming platform will not be liable for the act of communication to the public; however, if internet users try to circumvent this blocking via a VPN, these internet users could perform an act of communication to the public instead of the streaming platforms, which imposes technological protection measures.[143]

The outcome of this decision would be very important in that area since, for the first time, the CJEU was asked to explain the responsibility of the platforms in the case of circumvention of geo-blocking activities. Yet, in January 2023, the Supreme Court of Austria informed the Court that it was withdrawing its request for a preliminary ruling.[144]

The opinion of the AG is quite important as well because it directly explains the provider of the platform's responsibility in the context of the usage of circumvention tools for bypassing geo-blocking. The study also agrees that, for copyright-protected works, if these platforms implement effective (which are not intentionally ineffective) geo-blocking measures, they should not be responsible for the usage of circumvention tools as well. As AG correctly stated, the breach (circumvention) techniques are always one step ahead of security (TPM) techniques,[145] therefore, there is no fully effective technological protection for copyright-protected works.

[139] Opinion of the Grand Production v GO4YOU case, para 27.

[140] Opinion of the Grand Production v GO4YOU case, para 44.

[141] Opinion of the Grand Production v GO4YOU case, para 36.

[142] Opinion of the Grand Production v GO4YOU case, para 38.

[143] Opinion of the Grand Production v GO4YOU case, para 41.

[144] Removal Order of the President of the First Chamber of the Court of 13 February 2023, OJ C 422.

[145] Removal Order of the President of the First Chamber of the Court, para 38.

7.3.2.2.2 Anne Frank's Works - the Court of Amsterdam Decision

Anne Frank kept a diary about her life while in hiding under Nazi persecution, and she died in 1945. After her father, Otto Frank, inherited the copyrights on her work, the Anne Frank Fonds (AFF Fund) was founded by him.[146] In about 60 countries, including Belgium (the so-called Public Domain (PD) countries), the Fund no longer has those copyrights. Anne Frank Foundation, which is an independent foundation from the Fund, made a statement in 2021 that, as a result of their scientific research, the works of Anne Frank will be accessible through a www.annefrankmanuscripten.org domain. At the same time, this work would not be available online in the Netherlands, because in the Netherlands, the copyright to a number of texts by Anne Frank has not yet expired.

In the press release, the Foundation also included a Copyright statement:

'Copyright

Because the copyright in a number of Anne Frank texts has not yet expired in the Netherlands, part of the research, such as the transcripts of Anne Frank's diaries, has taken place in Belgium. The online edition cannot be viewed in the Netherlands. In about sixty countries where this is possible under copyright, such as in Belgium, Germany and the Netherlands Antilles, this edition is accessible to everyone online: www.annefrankmanuscripten.org. *Through geo-blocking, availability is limited to those countries. Later, an English version of this edition will also be accessible in the countries where this is copyrighted.*

The online publication is provided by the Association for Research and Access of Historical Texts (…).' (unofficial translation)

The Foundation stated that on that website, they will be using geo-blocking technology in order to limit availability to those countries.[147] After this press release, the Anne Frank Foundation initiated preliminary proceedings before the district court of Amsterdam. The Anne Frank Foundation basically claimed that the geo-blocking practice used by the Foundation is not sufficient since geo-blocking is very easy to circumvent, including via a VPN connection and usage of a VPN connection is widespread and not illegal.

The Dutch court rejected the copyright infringement claim on Anne Frank's work because the Court ruled that no technical measure is perfect, and there is no other better way than geo-blocking to restrict access on a territorial basis. The Court also

---

[146] Jan Jacobi (2022) Dutch court rejects copyright infringement claim on Anne Frank's works due to geoblocking. In: IPKat https://ipkitten.blogspot.com/2022/02/dutch-court-rejects-copyright.html.

[147] In their statement, they also explained that:

"If the website is visited from the Netherlands, the notice follows:

Access denied.

(…).

We are sorry…

This website is not accessible from your country.

The scientific online edition of Anne Frank's manuscripts cannot be made available in all countries for copyright reasons." (Unofficial translation).

referenced the big companies like Amazon, Netflix and Disney, pointing out that these major companies also impose geo-blocking as a technological measure when they want to restrict access to copyright-protected material. The Court finally ruled that the defendants have done everything reasonably possible to block access to the website from the Netherlands, at least sufficiently complicate and discourage it, which means they do not communicate these works in the Netherlands. For that reason, the Court concluded that there was no copyright infringement in the Netherlands.

Following this, the claimant in the main proceedings brought an appeal. In those circumstances, the Supreme Court of the Netherlands (Hoge Raad der Nederlanden) decided to stay the proceedings and to refer the following questions to the CJEU for a preliminary ruling[148]:

1. whether, in order for a work published on the internet to be regarded as a 'communication to the public' in a particular country, it must have been specifically directed at the public of that country;
2. whether, even where access has been blocked by means of geo-blocking, a communication to the public may nonetheless be said to take place in the blocked country where the block can be circumvented by tools such as a VPN, and whether the adequacy of the technical measures taken is relevant to that assessment;
3. whether, where circumvention of the block by means of a VPN constitutes a communication to the public, that communication may in law be attributed to the person who published the work online, and whether the interposition of a third-party service provider alters that outcome.

For the answers to these questions, on 15 January 2026 AG Rantos delivered his Opinion. With regard to the first question, the AG concluded that Article 3(1) of the Copyright Directive does not require that, in order for the publication of a work on a website to be classified as a 'communication to the public' in a given country, it must have been specifically directed at the public of that country. Expressly referring to Szpunar's Opinion in the Grand Production case, AG Rantos endorsed the view that, where geo-blocking has been applied by the rightsholder, the protected content is to be regarded as directed only at persons situated within the geographic area determined by the rightsholder and in which access is not blocked, and that, accordingly, no communication to the public can be deemed to take place in other areas.

As regards the second question, Rantos discussed whether, where the geo-blocking measure can be circumvented through tools such as a VPN, a communication to the public may nonetheless be said to occur in the blocked country, and whether the adequacy of the technical measures taken is relevant to that assessment; on this point, he underlined that no security measure is absolutely incapable of being breached.

He considered that the ease of the unlawful tools or methods enabling users to circumvent the geo-blocking measure is one of the factors to be taken into account in the assessment, but that, as long as effective and up-to-date protective measures have been applied, the defendants cannot be held liable for the unlawful acts of third

---

148 Opinion of Advocate General Szpunar in Case C-507/17 Google LLC v Commission nationale de l'informatique et des libertés (CNIL) [2026].

parties. In this framework, according to Rantos, in respect of a website on which copyright-protected content is published, and which is subject to an effective geo-blocking measure, it cannot be concluded that a 'communication to the public' takes place in the country in which that content is protected.

As regards the final question, Rantos stated that, even assuming that the circumvention of the geo-blocking measure, thereby rendering the work accessible online in the blocked country, were to give rise to a communication to the public, where a user located in a country in which access to the work is blocked makes use of a VPN or similar service in order to overcome that block, the service provider in question cannot, under the relevant provision, be held liable for the user's acts, save where that service provider actively encourages such unlawful use for the purpose of providing access to the protected work in that country.

The Anne Frank case is significant in that it brings to light the CJEU's approach to, and assessment of, geo-blocking measures. Indeed, in the earlier Grand Production v GO4YU case, the Austrian Supreme Court, which had made the reference for a preliminary ruling, withdrew its request, with the result that the CJEU had no opportunity to rule. Accordingly, if it is decided on the merits, the Anne Frank case will be the first in which the CJEU's approach to this issue can be seen.

Within the Anne Frank case, AG Rantos's Opinion contains several important points. First, according to Rantos, for an act of 'communication to the public' to exist it is sufficient that the publication in question has afforded an indeterminate number of persons the possibility of accessing protected documents to which they did not previously have access. Whether those persons have in fact obtained access, and whether the publication was specifically directed at a particular public, are not decisive. In this framework, it should be noted that taking accessibility as the criterion for classifying an act as a 'communication to the public' runs parallel to the approach of AG Szpunar, who had previously delivered the only Opinion in the geo-blocking context.

A second point is that the VPN-related assessments, which remained limited in AG Szpunar's Opinion in Grand Production v GO4YU, were likewise addressed within a narrow framework in AG Rantos's Opinion. As regards the liability of the VPN provider, Rantos confined himself to the assessment that, where a user in the country in which access is blocked makes use of a VPN or similar service in order to circumvent the geo-block, the service provider cannot be held liable for the user's acts unless it actively encourages the unlawful use aimed at obtaining access to the protected work in that country. That said, another notable aspect of the Opinion is that the matter is addressed, at least in part, from the perspective of human rights and freedom of expression, and that Rantos expressly refers to this dimension at various points. In this framework, the Opinion makes clear that the interpretation of Article 3(1) of the Copyright Directive must give weight not only to the rightsholder's exclusive right but also to freedom of access to information, and that a fair balance must be struck here. In particular, the claimant proposed that the work not be published in full, or that the protected documents be made only partially accessible; it further proposed a limited access model akin to library computer terminals, or a subscription-based access system protected by a username and password. Rantos considered that these closed access models, while strengthening copyright protection, would seriously restrict the access to information of users in the public-domain countries. These assessments are highly valuable, since they may enable the tension between freedom of expression and copyright to be subjected to a detailed examination by the CJEU as well. The present author also agrees with that decision, which has almost the same outcome as the opinion of the Grand Production case. As long as the effective geo-blocking measures are applicable by the platforms, then these platforms will not be responsible for any possible copyright infringement claim resulting from the VPN or other circumvention tools usage. Finally, it must be noted that AG Opinions are not binding, and the CJEU may therefore reach a different conclusion in its final judgment. Nevertheless, it is hoped by the present author that the CJEU will rule on the merits of this matter and provide a more detailed assessment, particularly as regards the liability of VPN providers and their users and, in the context of fundamental rights and freedoms, the fair balance between copyright and freedom of expression and information.

7.3.3 Circumvention as a Copyright Infringement – an Analysis

Since intellectual property rights are territorial, the rightsholders are usually given territorial licences which are limited to one or some countries, and licensees are usually obliged to impose geo-blocking measures to restrict access, download or streaming of these products. Furthermore, territorial licences are also be distributed by the rightsholders to gain more profit or any other business strategies. In that case, if a person circumvents geo-blocking via VPN services or other ways and reaches the contents which are not available in her actual location, there is a very important question needs to be answered: could accessing, streaming, or downloading online while using cybertravel tools lead to copyright infringement by reproduction of copyright works or communication to these works to the public?

As explained above, the Opinion of the Grand Production case and the decision for the Anne Frank case held that users who bypass TPMs would be regarded as responsible for the copyright infringement claims. In that part, the study will discuss whether end users could be responsible for using circumvention tools to access copyright-protected works. Firstly, the digital content sharing and accessing types will be explained, then accessing TPM-protected copyright-protected works with the help of circumvention tools would amount to infringement of reproduction, and communication to the public rights will be discussed. Finally, the responsibilities of circumvention tools providers will be outlined in the copyright context.

7.3.3.1 Digital Content Sharing and Accessing Types

To decide whether VPN services and other cybertravel tools to circumvent geo-blocking technology amount to an infringement of reproduction rights, digital content sharing and accessing types should also need to be explained: what is downloading, streaming, and stream-capturing/stream-ripping.[149]

i. ***Downloading*** involves the permanent copy of the work, initiation, reception and saving of data transferred from a remote system or server.[150]
ii. ***Streaming***, on the other hand, does not involve a permanent copy of the copyright-protected works, and it could be explained as follows: *"a method of transmitting data packets so that the earlier packets can be reassembled and processed before the entire file is downloaded, allowing for immediate display or playback"*.[151] In the streaming process, to stream copyright works, only a part of it will be loaded into the device buffer, and the data packets will be automatically removed from the device buffer once end users stop streaming.[152] At the same time, streaming could be divided into two subcategories, which are on-demand or interactive streaming and noninteractive streaming.[153]
    - In *on-demand or interactive streaming,* digital content is stored on a central server, allowing users to access the content whenever they wish, such as for watching movies or streaming music. This type of streaming enables users to control playback functions, including fast-forwarding, playing, and re-watching the content.[154]
    - In *noninteractive streaming*, these contents are only accessible at specified times, such as live sports and concerts.[155]
iii. ***Stream-capturing or stream-ripping*** is used by a software tool to save and capture data from streaming contents in order to have a permanent copy of these contents.[156]

7.3.3.2 Infringement of the Reproduction Right by Circumventing Technological Protection Measures

As outlined before, according to Article 2 of the InfoSoc Directive, the rightsholder has the exclusive right over their works to authorise or prohibit direct or indirect, temporary or permanent reproduction by any means and in any form, in whole or in

---

[149] Liang (2020, p. 802).
[150] Quintais (2017, p. 140).
[151] Quintais (2017, p. 140).
[152] Liang (2020, p. 799).
[153] Liang (2020, p. 799).
[154] Liang (2020, p. 801).
[155] Liang (2020, p. 801).
[156] Quintais (n 854, p. 141).

part. Any unauthorised activity will be regarded as prima facie copyright infringement unless it fits into the scope of the exceptions and limitations.

In the case of downloading with the help of circumvention tools, the work will be downloaded to the device of the user, and there will be a permanent copy of that work. Hence there is a permanent copy of the copyright-protected work; the user will not benefit from the temporary copy exception. Furthermore, since people who use circumvention tools accessed these works from unlicensed areas (which are not made available in certain locations), therefore the private copy exception will not be applicable in that case. That means, in the case when people use circumvention tools to circumvent technological restrictions and download these works, there will be an infringement of reproduction right under the InfoSoc Directive Article 2.

Determining copyright infringement in the case of streaming is not as straightforward as it is in the case of downloading because, in this type of digital dissemination, the access method involves creating a temporary copy of the work rather than a permanent one. To decide whether the streaming act infringes the copyright by creating a temporary copy, the defence of temporary copy exception under Article 5 (1) of the InfoSoc Directive should be considerable. As explained above, for the applicability of the temporary copy exception, the CJEU has set out the five requirements that must be met for the exception to apply in the Infopaq case, which are:

1. The act must be temporary.
2. The copy of the work must be transient or incidental.
3. It must be an integral and essential part of the technological process.
4. The sole purpose of the process must be to enable a transmission network between third parties by an intermediary or the lawful use of the work or protected subject matter.
5. The act must have no independent economic significance.

To apply these five requirements to streaming, firstly, it could be arguable this *act is temporary* because there will not be any permanent copy of the work as a result of the streaming act and only a part of it will be loaded into the device buffer and the data packets will be automatically from the device buffer once end users stop this act. Therefore, the first condition could be considered as met.

For the second condition, in streaming, copies are transient and incidental; hence existence and purpose must depend on the technological process it integrates, and the duration of this temporary copy is limited to that necessary for the completion of the process, and the copy is deleted afterwards without the need of human intervention.[157] Therefore, the second condition is also met.

For the third condition, this temporary, transient or incidental copy is an integral and essential part of the technological process; hence, in the streaming act, keeping copies in RAM in order to stream that content is integral and essential.[158] Therefore, the third condition is also met.

---

[157] Quintais (n 854, p. 141).

[158] Liang (2020, p. 806).

To answer the question about whether the fourth condition is met, there is a need to check the recitals of InfoSoc Directive, namely Recital 33, which points that:

> To the extent that they meet these conditions, this exception should include acts which enable browsing as well as acts of caching to take place, including those which enable transmission systems to function efficiently, provided that the intermediary does not modify the information and does not interfere with the lawful use of technology, widely recognised and used by industry, to obtain data on the use of the information. **A use should be considered lawful where it is authorised by the rightholder or not restricted by law.**

According to this Recital, although there is an inclusion of acts of caching within this exception, it clearly states that the act should only be considered lawful where it is authorised by the rightsholder or not restricted by law. This question has been asked to the CJEU in the Brein v Filmspeler decision,[159] where the Court had the opportunity to discuss the application of the temporary copy exception to where a temporary reproduction was made by an end user during the streaming of the copyright-protected work from a third-party website which work is offered without the authorisation of the rightsholder. The CJEU ruled that since the streaming of the content was not authorised by the rightsholder, there was no lawful use in this context. Therefore, if there is a TPM and this content is not made available by the rightsholder in that particular location, the usage of circumvention tools to evade this restriction and accessing and streaming this content will not benefit from the 'temporary copy defence' under this Directive since there is no lawful use.[160] Another important decision was held in the so-called the FAPL and Murphy judgment, and this decision was already summarised in the previous chapters. In this part of the study, only the circumvention part of this case will be explained. In this decision, the CJEU discussed the temporary acts of reproduction defence under Article 5(1) of the InfoSoc Directive and held that the act might benefit from this exception. This act was found to fulfil the conditions laid down in Article 5(1) of the InfoSoc Directive since this copy is a temporary, and transient or incidental copy, and there is a lawful use of the work because there is a lawful subscription.[161] Finally, the Court held that since these reproductions are not capable of generating an additional economic advantage going beyond the advantage derived from mere reception of the broadcasts at issue, there is no economic significance of this act.[162] Therefore, the Court ruled that this act fulfils the condition set in Article 5(1) and Article 5(5) as well, and the act may be carried out without the authorisation of the copyright holders concerned.[163]

---

[159] Case C-527/15 *Stichting Brein v Jack Frederik Wullems* [2017] OJ C 27. (hereinafter will be referred as the Filmspeler case).

[160] Paragraph 72 of the Filmspeler Case: *Article 5(1) and (5) of Directive 2001/29 must be interpreted as meaning that acts of temporary reproduction, on a multimedia player, such as that at issue in the main proceedings, of a copyright-protected work obtained by streaming from a website belonging to a third party offering that work without the consent of the copyright holder does not satisfy the conditions set out in those provisions.*

[161] The FAPL and Murphy cases, para176.

[162] The FAPL and Murphy cases, para177.

[163] The FAPL and Murphy cases, para178.

Furthermore, according to the Berne Convention 9(2), the exceptions and limitations provided in this article shall only be applicable in certain cases, shall not conflict with a normal exploitation of the work and finally, shall not unreasonably prejudice the legitimate interests of the rightsholder. Therefore, accessing and streaming with the help of the circumvention tools to these protected contents with TPMs will conflict with a normal exploitation of the work,[164] and as such, these exceptions and limitations will not be applicable to these scenarios.

Finally, since there is also a permanent copy of the copyright-protected content, in case of stream capturing or ripping act for the copyright-protected works, there will be an infringement of reproduction right.

7.3.3.3 Infringement of Communication to the Public Right by Circumventing TPMs

Infringement of communication to the public right under Article 3 of the InfoSoc Directive by making available contents by circumventing restrictions also needs to be considered in that chapter. Unsurprisingly, the CJEU has also discussed in several cases to decide on whether these individual acts constitute an infringement of the communication to the public right under the InfoSoc Directive Article 2.

The judgment ruled in the VG Bild-Kunst v Stiftung case[165] in 2021 has a particular interest in that manner since it discusses whether framing thumbnails in circumvention of a TPM was an act of communication to the public. Stiftung Preußischer Kulturbesitz (SPK) is the operator of the Deutsche Digitale Bibliothek (DDB), a German digital library. SPK wanted to have a licence agreement with VG Bild-Kunst (VBK - which is a collecting society) for the use of the works in the thumbnails form.[166] However, VBK wanted to have this agreement on the condition that SPK

---

[164] Rosati (2023, p. 141). '*In compliance with these standards— notably strict interpretation of exceptions and limitations— private copying must be understood as excluding reproductions from unlicensed sources. This conclusion is also compliant with Article 5(5): holding otherwise, ie accepting that reproductions for private uses may be made from an unlawful source, would in fact encourage the circulation of unlicensed works and inevitably reduce the volume of sales or of other lawful transactions relating to the protected works. This would be contrary to exceptions and limitations not being in conflict with a normal exploitation of the work and not unreasonably prejudicing the legitimate interests of rightholders.*'

[165] Case C-392/19 *VG Bild-Kunst v Stiftung Preußischer Kulturbesitz* [2021] OJ C 270. (hereinafter will be referred as VG Bild-Kunst v Stiftung case).

[166] VG Bild-Kunst v Stiftung case, para10: '*The DDB website contains links to digitised content stored on the internet portals of participating institutions. However, as a 'digital showcase', the DDB itself stores only thumbnails, that is to say smaller versions of the original images of the subject matter. When the user clicks on one of those thumbnails, he or she is redirected to the page concerning the particular subject matter on the DDB website, which contains an enlarged version of the thumbnail concerned, with a resolution of 440 by 330 pixels. When that enlarged thumbnail is clicked on, or the 'magnifying glass' function is used, a further enlarged version of the thumbnail, with a maximum resolution of 800 by 600 pixels, is overlaid by means of a 'lightbox'. Further, the 'Display object on original site' button contains a direct link to the website of the institution providing the subject matter, either to its home page or to the page relating to that subject matter.*'

uses TPMs to prevent third parties from framing these thumbnails.[167] SPK thought that this condition was unreasonable, and under copyright law, VPK was obliged to grant these licences without any condition requiring SPK to implement such technological measures.[168] SPK brought an action against VPK, and when the case was before the Federal Court of Justice, the Court asked the following question to the CJEU for a preliminary ruling: '*Does the embedding of a work – which is available on a freely accessible website with the consent of the right holder – on the website of a third party by way of framing constitute communication to the public of that work within the meaning of Article 3(1) of Directive 2001/29 where it circumvents protection measures against framing adopted or imposed by the right holder?*'.[169]

The CJEU has said 'yes' to this question – by stating framing by circumventing TPMs could actually infringe the communication to the public right. The Court ruled that to ensure legal certainty and the effective operation of the Internet, copyright holders cannot restrict their consent without implementing effective technological measures as defined in Article 6(1) and (3) of the InfoSoc Directive.[170] Without such measures, determining whether a copyright holder intends to object to the framing of their works can be challenging, especially for individual users. Consequently, in such scenarios, embedding a copyright-protected work through framing on a third-party website, which is freely accessible to the public with the authorisation of the copyright holder on another website, constitutes an act of 'making that work available to a new public'.[171]

These decisions are of great importance in that area, yet these activities are quite common, especially in the last few years. For example, lately, especially in sports broadcasts, some works requiring membership or purchase are being streamed live on various platforms using certain technologies. For example, to watch a Premier League match, one needs to subscribe to certain sports channels.[172] However, some important football matches can be streamed by some users on X (previously known as Twitter) or other platforms, and some individuals can follow the football match without subscribing the channel of the original licence holders of these competitions. It can be seen as a new form of circumvention of TPMs. Indeed, in the very near future, the author strongly expects that, national courts or the CJEU will be asked to decide on this matter. However, the outcome of this referral is quite predictable, especially when looking at previous decisions regarding unauthorised communication to the public. Content published without the rightsholder's consent will amount to copyright infringement.

There is also a possibility of discussing the responsibility of online content-sharing platforms under the DSM Directive Article 17. According to this provision, online

---

[167] VG Bild-Kunst v Stiftung case, para 11.

[168] VG Bild-Kunst v Stiftung case, para 12.

[169] VG Bild-Kunst v Stiftung case, para 18.

[170] VG Bild-Kunst v Stiftung case, para 46.

[171] VG Bild-Kunst v Stiftung case, para 55.

[172] Broadcast Schedules. In: Premier League < https://www.premierleague.com/broadcast-schedules.

content-sharing service providers, such as YouTube, X, Facebook, etc., are required to have authorisation from the rightsholders when these platforms give the public access to copyright-protected works uploaded by their users. Therefore, in these scenarios, the responsibility of the online content-sharing platforms will also need to be discussed. This Article was one of the controversial and debated provisions in the DSM Directive, even the Republic of Poland claimed that this article limiting freedom of expression and applied for annulment of this rule to CJEU.[173] Nevertheless, the Court confirmed that this provision does not conflict with the CFR Article 11 and decided not to annul this article.

According to Article 17 of the DSM Directive, when someone makes available copyright protected works on their platform:

- Firstly, an online content-sharing service provider shall therefore obtain an authorisation from the rightsholders,
- Users should also show that they are not acting on a commercial basis or where their activity does not generate significant revenues.
- When no authorisation form granted, the platform should demonstrate that either (i) made best efforts to obtain an authorisation, (ii) made best efforts to ensure the unavailability of specific works and other subject matter for which the rightsholders have provided the service providers with the relevant and necessary information; and in any event, (iii) acted expeditiously, upon receiving a sufficiently substantiated notice from the rightsholders, to disable access to, or to remove from their websites, the notified works or other subject matter, and made best efforts to prevent their future uploads. Otherwise, online content-sharing service providers shall be liable for unauthorised acts of communication to the public, including making available to the public, of copyright-protected works and other subject matter.

That means, as a result of the DSM Directive Article 17, online content-sharing platforms such as YouTube, X, Facebook, could also be regarded as responsible for copyright infringement when their users make available other's copyright-protected works in these platforms. This liability regime is also very important from the circumvention point of view.

7.3.3.4 Responsibilities of Circumvention Tools Providers

In this section, it will be discussed the question of whether VPN (and other circumvention tools) providers can be considered responsible for copyright infringement, especially for helping in the dissemination of these works to the public.

According to the InfoSoc Directive Article 8(3), *Member States shall ensure that rightholders are in a position to apply for an injunction against intermediaries whose services are used by a third party to infringe a copyright or related right.* Under this provision, it is important to analyse whether VPNs and other tools would be regarded

[173] Case C-401/*19 Action for annulment under Article 263 TFEU* [2019] OJ C 270.

as intermediaries.[174] In the LSG v Tele2 judgment,[175] the CJEU has provided a definition for intermediaries which are access providers which merely provide users with Internet access without offering other services or exercising any control over the services which users make use of.[176] According to this judgment, it may be argued that since VPNs and other tools are providing access, they can be regarded as intermediaries.[177] As such, in the case of copyright infringement, the responsibility of these providers will also need to be discussed. About that subject, the InfoSoc Directive Recital 59 clearly suggests forwarding an injunction against the intermediaries as can be seen as follows: '*In the digital environment, in particular, the services of intermediaries may increasingly be used by third parties for infringing activities. In many cases such intermediaries are best placed to bring such infringing activities to an end. Therefore, without prejudice to any other sanctions and remedies available, rightholders should have the possibility of applying for an injunction against an intermediary who carries a third party's infringement of a protected work or other subject-matter in a network.*' According to this provision, in case of copyright infringement, VPN providers could also be regarded as liable and rightsholders can apply for an injunction against them.

Furthermore, according to the Article 2 (1)(e) of the Conditional Access Directive,[178] illicit device is defined as any equipment or software designed or adapted to give access to a protected service in an intelligible form without the authorisation of the service provider. Therefore, these VPN providers can also be regarded as an illicit device according to this directive and activities which manufacture, import, distribution, sale, rental or possession for commercial purposes of illicit devices may be regarded as infringing according to Article 4 (1)(a).[179]

Apart from this issue there are some advanced scenarios that the CJEU may address in the future. For example, could VPN (or other tools) providers be asked to restrict access to copyright-infringing, especially TPM-protected, content?[180] Or, may the Court also be asked in the future to what extent the platform operator can be held directly liable for the users' VPN (and other tools) usage, especially if

[174] Roy and Marsoof (2017, p. 675).

[175] Case C-557/07 *LSG-Gesellschaft zur Wahrnehmung von Leistungsschutzrechten GmbH v Tele2 Telecommunication GmbH* [2009] ECR 2009 I-01227. (hereinafter will be referred as LSG v Tele2 case).

[176] LSG v Tele2 case, para 30.

[177] Roy and Marsoof (2017, p. 675).

[178] Directive 98/84/EC of the European Parliament and of the Council of 20 November 1998 on the legal protection of services based on, or consisting of, conditional access [1998] OJ L 320.

[179] Trimble (2024, p, 46).

[180] Tatiana Synodinou (2023) AG Szpunar's Opinion in Grand Production: "Grande première" for the VPN legal saga in the context of geoblocked streaming. In: Kluwer Copyright Blog https://copyrightblog.kluweriplaw.com/2023/02/28/ag-szpunars-opinion-in-grand-production-grande-premiere-for-the-vpn-legal-saga-in-the-context-of-geoblocked-streaming/.

their platform has 'intentionally ineffective geo-blocking or other TPMs'?[181] These questions are open to interpretations, and no direct provision or decision has shaped this area so far. In the future, it is likely that the CJEU will also deal with these kinds of requests. This study will not discuss these scenarios specifically, but the author believes that setting these question marks is particularly important for the future studies and looking forward in this field.

7.3.4 Contractual Liability in the Case of Circumvention of TPMs

In most of the streaming or video-on-demand platforms, TV hubs or any other types of platforms that could be used to access online content, there are some terms and conditions for use, and in most of them, there is a specific provision for circumventing territorial restrictions measures, and if there is the usage of circumvention tools, there will be a breach of contract[182] and terms of use these services. Some of the terms from the most used platforms could be found like the following:

i. Terms of Use for ITVX and ITV Hub[183]: *The Service uses "geo-blocking" measures to prevent you from accessing the Service from outside the Territory. This is necessary for us to comply with the terms of our broadcast and content licences. You agree not to attempt to access, and not to attempt to circumvent the geo-blocking measures to access the Service from outside the Territory.*
ii. Terms of Use for the BBC's digital services[184]: *Accessing content from outside the UK that you aren't allowed to, or helping others do the same. For example: using a VPN service so you can watch BBC iPlayer when you're outside the UK.*
iii. Netflix Terms of Use[185]: 4.*6. Except as explicitly authorized by us, you agree not to (ii) circumvent, remove, alter, deactivate, degrade, block, obscure or thwart any of the content protections or other elements of the Netflix service, including the graphical user interface, any advertising or advertising features, copyright notices, and trademarks;*

[181] Eleonora Rosati (2022) AG Szpunar advises CJEU to rule that streaming platforms are not liable (unless they have intentionally applied ineffective geo-blocks) if their users use VPNs' In: IPKat https://ipkitten.blogspot.com/2022/10/ag-szpunar-advises-cjeu-to-rule-that.html.

[182] Trimble (n 27, p. 49).

[183] Terms of Use for ITVX. In: ITV https://www.itv.com/terms/articles/itvhubonlineterms.

[184] Terms of Use for the BBC's digital service. In: bbc.co.uk < https://www.bbc.co.uk/usingthebbc/terms-of-use/.

[185] Netflix Terms of Use. In: Netflix Help Centre https://help.netflix.com/legal/termsofuse.

iv. Disney + Subscriber Agreement United Kingdom[186]: *3.b.you may not and agree not to i. circumvent or disable any content protection system or digital rights management technology used in connection with the Disney + Content...*
v. Amazon Prime Video Terms of Use[187]: *4. k. General Restrictions. You may not (i) transfer, copy or display the Digital Content, except as permitted in this Agreement; (ii) sell, rent, lease, distribute, or broadcast any right to the Digital Content; (iii) remove any proprietary notices or labels on the Digital Content; (iv) attempt to disable, bypass, modify, defeat, or otherwise circumvent any digital rights management or other content protection system used as part of the Service; or (v) use the Service or Digital Content for any commercial or illegal purpose.*
vi. YouTube Terms of Service: *You are not allowed to: circumvent, disable, fraudulently engage, or otherwise interfere with the Service (or attempt to do any of these things), including security-related features or features that: (a) prevent or restrict the copying or other use of Content; or (b) limit the use of the Service or Content...*

These licence agreements are also clear that these services do not let circumvention access the content offered on their platform. That means circumvention of these restrictions to access content will also be against the terms and conditions of these platforms, and circumvention of these restrictions may result in contract law liability as well.

On the other hand, it is important to discuss whether these provisions may be included considering the Portability Regulation, since this regulation ruled that provisions which prohibit cross-border portability of online content services or limit such portability will be unenforceable.[188] Therefore, it may be suggested that these contractual limitations will not be in line with the provision provided in the Article 7, therefore these will be unenforceable.[189] The author believes that not all of the provisions mentioned above would be unenforceable due to Article 7 of the Portability Regulation. Only provisions that restrict cross-border portability would be deemed unenforceable. This means the author suggests that any provision preventing cross-border access should be considered unenforceable. However, a provision that prohibits the use of circumvention tools would remain applicable.

---

186 Subscriber Agreement. In: Disneyplus https://www.disneyplus.com/en-gb/legal/subscriber-agreement.

187 Amazon Prime Video Terms of Use. In: Prime Video https://www.primevideo.com/help?nodeId=202095490&view-type=content-only.

188 Article 7(1) of the Portability Regulation: *Any contractual provisions, including those between providers of online content services and holders of copyright or related rights or those holding any other rights in the content of online content services, as well as those between such providers and their subscribers, which are contrary to this Regulation, including those which prohibit cross-border portability of online content services or limit such portability to a specific time period, shall be unenforceable.*

189 Trimble (2019, p. 494).

7.4 Conclusion

When people cannot access products legally, they try to access them illegally. For the geo-blocking measures as a TPM, when users encounter them, they try to find a way to evade them. Circumvention tools, especially VPNs, are serving this aim, and they help users to circumvent geo-blocking measures by mainly seem to locate elsewhere. Nevertheless, these measures were subject to lots of scrutiny, particularly from the copyright infringement point of view, the discussion was very intense.

First of all, if someone circumvent geo-blocking measures with the help of circumvention tools, and download the copyright-protected products, it was found clear that since there is a permanent copy of that work this act will infringe copyright. This situation is the same for the stream-ripping. In the case of streaming, since there is a temporary copy of the work as a result of this act, the possibility of the applicability of temporary copy exception and the private use exception were discussed.

Another important discussion in the circumvention was to discuss the responsibility of the platforms in case of circumvention of the geo-blocking measures. In the Grand Production v GO4YOU case and in the Anne Frank case the courts were asked to clarify the responsibilities of the platforms in the context of circumvention of the geo-blocking measures. In both cases it was decided that as long as platforms use effective measures, they will not be responsible for the usage of VPN and other circumvention tools.

The other important question mark in this circumvention debate was the responsibility of the circumvention tools providers in the case of copyright infringement. According to the InfoSoc Directive Article 8(3), rightsholders may also ask for an injunction against intermediaries in the case of the copyright infringement. Since VPNs and other tools are providing access, they can be regarded as intermediaries as a result of the decision ruled by the CJEU, VPN and other tools providers may also be asked for an injunction. Nevertheless, this present author strongly advises more studies regarding the responsibility of the circumvention tools providers, since the mass use of these tools are becoming particularly important day by day and for the copyright owners, the results are getting more serious especially from the remuneration perspective.

Finally, the study mentioned the contractual liability of the circumvention tools usage very briefly, and chose not to mention the criminal law liability of the circumvention tools usage since the criminal law perspective of this debate would be substantial and may require substantive analysis. Therefore, to keep this research solely from the copyright law perspective, criminal law aspects were excluded.

References

Armstrong TK (2008) Fair circumvention. Faculty Articles and Other Publications, Paper 143, pp 1–50

Berry K (2022) "This content is unavailable in your geographic region": the United States' and the European Union's implementation of anti-circumvention measures. Vand J Transnatl Law 55:485–528

Berry E et al (2019) Complete EU law: text, cases, and materials, 4th edn. Oxford University Press, Oxford

Besek JM (2004) Anti-circumvention laws and copyright: a report from the Kernochan Center for Law, Media and the Arts. Colum J Law Arts 27:385–519

Burke T (2017) Jumping the wall: geoblocking, circumvention and the law. Univ West Aust Law Rev 42:56–68

De-Yolande MH (2022) The circumvention of geo-blocking and copyrights infringement. Open J Soc Sci 10:88–105

Dredge S (2013) What is Tor? a beginner's guide to the privacy tool. The Guardian. https://www.theguardian.com/technology/2013/nov/05/tor-beginners-guide-nsa-browser

Dusollier S (2012) DRM at the intersection of copyright law and technology: a case study for regulation. In: Brousseau E, Marzouki M, Méadel C (eds) Governance, regulation and powers on the internet. Cambridge University Press, Cambridge, pp 297–317

Finck M, Moscon V (2019) Copyright law on blockchains: between new forms of rights administration and digital rights management 2.0. IIC 50:77–108

Gasser U, Girsberger M (2004) Transposing the Copyright Directive: legal protection of technological measures in EU Member States. Berkman Publication Series 10:1–31

Hilliard C (2015) Evaluating the legitimacy of geo-location circumvention in the context of technical protection measures. Queen Mary J Intellect Prop 5:157–182

Karapapa S (2020) Exhaustion of rights on digital content under EU copyright: positive and normative perspectives. In: Aplin T (ed) Research handbook on intellectual property and digital technologies. Edward Elgar Publishing, Cheltenham, pp 483–505

Kaya MB (2020) Internet hukuku. Yetkin, Ankara

Kharb D et al. (2023) Circumvention of geo-blocking measures in audio-visual sector: related copyright issues. NTUT J Intellect Prop Law Manag 12:44–60

Kra-Oz T (2017) Geoblocking and the legality of circumvention. IDEA 57:385–430

Kurniadi DD (2015) The difference between using proxy server and VPN. SISFORMA J Inf Syst 2:19–22

Liang M (2020) Copyright issues related to reproduction rights arising from streaming. J World Intellect Prop 23:798–814

Lobato R (2019) Netflix nations. New York University Press, New York

Magnusson J et al. (2023) A second look at dns qname minimization. In: Goos G, Hartmanis J (eds) Passive and Active Measurement. Springer

Major T (2019) Parallel importing and the blurred lines of the digital age: the implications of avoiding the geo-block. Victoria University of Wellington Legal Research Paper No. 37/2020

Marsoof A (2017) Geo-blocking and virtual private networks: a comparative discourse in copyright law. WIPO–WTO Colloq Pap 2017:101–114

Quintais JP (2015) Private copying and downloading from unlawful sources. IIC 46:66–92

Quintais JP (2017) Copyright in the age of online access: alternative compensation systems in EU law. Kluwer, Alphen aan den Rijn

Rosati E (2023) Copyright and the Court of Justice of the European Union, 2nd edn. Oxford University Press, Oxford

Rouse M (2023) Cloud VPN. Techopedia. https://www.techopedia.com/definition/30760/cloud-vpn

Roy A, Marsoof A (2017) Geo-blocking, VPNs and injunctions. EIPR 39:672–680

Shim T (2023) Alternatives to VPN. Web Hosting Secret Revealed. https://www.webhostingsecretrevealed.net/blog/web-tools/alternatives-to-vpn/

Trimble M (2012) The future of cybertravel: legal implications of the evasion of geolocation. Fordham Intell Prop Media & Ent LJ 22:567–657

Trimble M (2019) Copyright and geoblocking: the consequences of eliminating geoblocking. Scholarly Works 2019:476–502

Trimble M (2024) The EU Geo-Blocking Regulation: a commentary. Edward Elgar Publishing, Cheltenham

Weiss CA (2016) Available to all, produced by few: the economic and cultural impact of Europe's Digital Single Market strategy within the audiovisual industry. Colum Bus L Rev 2016:877–923

Chapter 8
Recommendations for Geo-Blocking of Copyright-Protected Digital Products for the EU Policy-Makers

Abstract This chapter examines whether policy intervention is required to address the exclusion of copyright-protected digital products from the Geo-blocking Regulation and evaluates how such intervention should be structured. The discussion considers recent data on cross-border availability within the EU and weighs the interests of key stakeholders, including consumers, rightsholders, distributors and policymakers, with the aim of identifying a balanced and proportionate solution that supports the objectives of the Digital Single Market. Fifteen recommendations are proposed to address the identified shortcomings. The preferred approach combines a country-of-origin mechanism with an obligation on distributors to accept unsolicited requests (passive sales) from Member States in which they do not hold a licence, supported by a legal fiction deeming access to occur solely in the actively targeted Member State. To implement this model, several amendments to the Regulation are suggested: removing the exclusion of copyright-protected electronically supplied services from Article 4(1)(b); introducing a new Article 4a establishing rules on licensing and localisation for digitally supplied copyright works and audiovisual services. Complementary amendments include defining "untargeted regions" in Article 2 and adapting Article 6 to ensure that contractual restrictions conflicting with Articles 3, 4, 4a and 5 are rendered void. This approach is presented as the most effective means of enhancing cross-border accessibility while maintaining an appropriate balance between consumer interests and rightsholders' legitimate expectations.

8.1 Introduction

This chapter will focus on the author's perspective regarding the necessity for policy intervention in relation to the Geo-blocking Regulation. Specifically, it will explore whether such intervention is needed, and if so, the reasoning behind it and the manner in which it should be implemented. The author will present the most recent data concerning the availability and cross-border accessibility of copyright-protected digital products within the European Union, providing a comprehensive overview of the current landscape.

F. Cebeci Çorum, *Application of Geo-Blocking to Copyright-Protected Digital Products*, Studies in European Economic Law and Regulation 30,
https://doi.org/10.1007/978-3-032-34507-3_8

Furthermore, the author will seek to identify the most balanced approach to addressing these issues by considering the perspectives of various stakeholders involved in this complex discussion, including consumers, rightsholders, distributors, and policymakers. The author's analysis will aim to ensure that the proposed solutions respect the diverse interests of these groups while promoting the goals of the single market within the EU.

In addition, the author will put forward fifteen distinct recommendations intended to address the challenges identified throughout the analysis. Following this, the author will present what she believes to be the most effective option, based on her assessment of the evidence and stakeholder considerations, and will propose targeted amendments to the Geo-blocking Regulation to better facilitate equitable access to copyright-protected digital products across Member States. The chapter will ultimately argue for a balanced reform that fosters both consumer rights and the legitimate interests of copyright holders, seeking to advance the European Union's digital single market objectives.

8.2 Is There a Need for a Policy Intervention?

The Geo-blocking Regulation was proposed following the announcement of the DSM Strategy, as explained in Chap. 4, which was introduced in 2015. Much of the supporting data came from research conducted in 2016 and 2017, which played a crucial role in shaping the final version of this legislation. When comparing the findings from that period to today's trends, it is clear that digital product consumption has seen a significant increase. As explained in Chap. 4, the Geo-blocking Regulation includes a review clause to assess its scope and impact on various stakeholders. In 2020, the first reports were published related to this review. Furthermore, just a very short time after the Geo-blocking Regulation was published, the Covid-19 pandemic occurred between March 2020 and summer 2022. As a result of this pandemic consumer habits across the EU underwent significant changes. Thus, relevant data on these shifts will be presented in this part of the study, and the discussion will focus on whether the Geo-blocking Regulation should be amended in light of the new consumption patterns that emerged during this period.

Most notably, Article 9[1] and the Recital 37[2] of the Geo-blocking Regulation includes a provision stating that the Commission should prepare a report to assess and propose amendments if deemed necessary. As already discussed in this study, in 2023, the European Parliament and other institutions held discussions on the reports from 2020. These institutions decided not to propose any amendments regarding the inclusion of electronically supplied services, the main feature of which is the provision of access to and use of copyright-protected works or other protected subject matter, and audiovisual services. Although Article 9 states that the first review will focus on assessing the scope of the Regulation, particularly its application to copyright-protected digital products, Recital 37 indicates that Regulation should be regularly evaluated with a view to proposing amendments when necessary. This creates some confusion as to whether only the first review will focus on the scope of the Regulation or if subsequent reviews will also address the Regulation's scope. In the 2023 meetings held by the European Parliament, the Resolution concluded by stating that more data will be needed in the next review to analyse the inclusion of audiovisual and non-audiovisual copyright-protected services in this Regulation. As a result, it is expected that subsequent reviews will also focus on the scope of the Regulation, with more detailed analysis provided in future assessments. As such, an important question arises for the next review, which is planned for 2026: Is there a need for policy intervention? Should any amendments to the Geo-blocking Regulation be proposed as part of the Article 9(2) of this regulation? The author of this study strongly believes that there should be a policy intervention in this regard and the Geo-blocking Regulation is in the need for some amendments accordingly and include electronically supplied services, the main feature of which is the provision of access to and use of

---

[1] Article 9 (1) '*By 23 March 2020 and every 5 years thereafter, the Commission shall report on the evaluation of this Regulation to the European Parliament, the Council and the European Economic and Social Committee. In doing so, the Commission shall take into account the overall impact of the Regulation on the internal market and cross-border e-commerce, including, in particular, the potential additional administrative and financial burden for traders stemming from the existence of different applicable regulatory consumer contract law regimes. That report shall, where necessary, be accompanied by a proposal for an amendment of this Regulation, in light of legal, technical and economic developments.*

(2)The first evaluation referred to in paragraph 1 shall be carried out, in particular, with a view to assessing the scope of this Regulation, as well as the extent of the prohibition laid down in point (b) of Article 4(1) and whether this Regulation should also apply to electronically supplied services the main feature of which is the provision of access to and use of copyright protected works or other protected subject matter, including the selling of copyright protected works or protected subject matter in an intangible form, provided that the trader has the requisite rights for the relevant territories.'

[2] *Recital (37) This Regulation should be regularly evaluated, with a view to proposing amendments where they are necessary. Such evaluations should take into account the overall impact of this Regulation on the internal market and on cross-border e-commerce. The first evaluation should concentrate on assessing the possible extension of the prohibition of different general conditions of access to electronically supplied services, including those the main feature of which is the provision of access to and use of copyright protected works or other protected subject matter, provided that the trader has the requisite rights for the relevant territories. It should also analyse whether the scope of this Regulation should be extended to services falling outside the scope of Directive 2006/123/EC, taking due account of the particularities of each of those services.*

copyright-protected works or other protected subject matter, and audiovisual services within the scope of this regulation. The author would like to justify her opinion as follows:

Firstly, the European Commission and other institutions put considerable effort into analysing media, audiovisual, and other forms of media consumption in the EU following the publication of the Geo-blocking Regulation. Their research revealed significant findings, indicating that after the regulation was introduced, there were changes in consumption patterns, consumer demand, and the availability of digital products.

Secondly, shortly after the Geo-blocking Regulation was published, the world experienced the significant impact of the Covid-19 pandemic, which brought about major changes in consumer demand and production. There was a notable increase in digital consumption, which altered consumer trends and had a profound effect on the industry.

Furthermore, European studies have often underestimated the importance of accessing home country content. Many people wish to access products from their home country but are unable to do so, because they live abroad. Some people also want to access other country's own products they have a specific interest in a country's culture or language. This highlights that consumers are not solely driven by price, as content availability, especially content produced in their home country, is crucial, according to recent studies. Therefore, any impact on the cross-border availability of products within the EU should be evaluated with this in mind. The author of this study also believes that there has been insufficient analysis of the potential positive shift in consumer behaviour regarding the cross-border availability of services or products. For instance, some individuals might be willing to pay more to access their preferred version of a product, or others may seek out exclusive items only available in specific countries.

The author of this study is also asking for a change to the Geo-blocking Regulation, as she believes it would align with the Digital Single Market Strategy. This change would enable better access to cross-border products and allow European products to move more freely across borders, ultimately benefiting the European Union's economy.

Another key aspect the author of this study highlights is the belief that eliminating geo-blocking could significantly contribute to preserving human rights, promoting cultural diversity, and protecting linguistic minorities.

Since 2016, as discussed in the circumvention chapter, even platforms like Netflix were not employing geo-blocking measures to prevent cross-border access to their content. This indicates that the use of geo-blocking has increased over the past 6 years, parallel to the rising demand for access to digital products. This created several challenges for both consumers and distributors of digital products. As a result, the issue of geo-blocking in relation to audiovisual products and copyright-protected non-audiovisual products became a key concern.

The author of this study also believes that Article 6 of the Geo-blocking Regulation, which addresses passive sales, should be reconsidered in light of recent decisions related to territorial licences and competition law concerns. This provides a strong basis for re-evaluating and potentially amending the Geo-blocking Regulation.

Moreover, the current Geo-blocking Regulation is having a minimal impact, which raises concerns.

To create a more comprehensive and effective regulation, the author of this study strongly believes that amendments are necessary. She intends to elaborate on her views in greater detail in this chapter.

8.2.1 Six Years of the Geo-Blocking Regulation: Changes in Consumption, Consumer Demand, and Availability of Digital Products

The EU Institutions conducted several studies to assess the consumption and availability of digital products and the trend in consumer demand. To begin with, in December 2020, the Commission published a communication on the Media and Audiovisual Action Plan, aimed at transforming the industry by facilitating easier access to products and improving the availability of cross-border content throughout the EU. This Communication proposed that initiating a stakeholder dialogue on the availability and accessibility of digital products across the EU would be a valuable step (the Stakeholder Dialogue). The second suggestion was to create a report to analyse media trends, with the aim of implementing appropriate policy interventions based on the findings of these reports (The European Media Industry Outlook). After these reports were released, in July 2024 the Commission published a staff working document addressing the impact of the geo-blocking regulation and the progress made in further reducing cross-border barriers. In this part, all these reports will be briefly summarised, focusing specifically on studies related to the availability and accessibility of copyright-protected digital products across borders throughout the EU.

8.2.1.1 The Communication from the Commission: Media and Audiovisual Action Plan

In December 2020, the Commission has published a communication called 'Europe's Media in the Digital Decade: An Action Plan to Support Recovery and Transformation'.[3] Main aims of this Communication have been outlined as (i) recovering audiovisual and media companies by providing liquidity and financial support, (ii) transforming industry by helping the twin transitions of climate change and digitisation in the context of global competition, and finally (iii) enabling more innovation in

[3] Communication From the Commission 'Europe's Media in the Digital Decade: An Action Plan to Support Recovery and Transformation' COM (2020) 784 final. (hereinafter will be referred as Communication on Europe's Media).

the sector and empowering citizens to access content more easily and take informed decisions.[4] To that aim, the Communication prepared an action plan containing ten different subjects and provided a timeline for this.[5] Action plans regarding only the availability of audiovisual content will be explained in this part.

This Communication, first of all, explained the importance of the audiovisual industry and news media sectors in the context of keeping citizens informed and entertained especially during the Covid-19.[6] The need for the correct information and the demand for the films, series or videogames were also increased in this period, according to the Communication. Although the cinema sector and production industry negatively affected during this period, the Communication suggested that, during the pandemic online platforms were positively affected since they gained more subscribers and attention.[7] The Communication very importantly confirmed that it was clear with the pandemic, the traditional media industry struggled to adopt to online market.

This Communication also very importantly admitted that in the audiovisual sector, the market fragmentation is problematic. This Communication compared the European films and the US films, found out that US films are available in more countries even within the EU. Furthermore, it was also pointed out that European media players are noticeably smaller than the US competitors.[8] The Communication suggested that audiovisual companies in the EU should not only consider their national markets but also take into account the whole European continent. Finally, it was correctly pointed out that policy response is necessary in order to thrive cultural diversity, to benefit from information, along with the media and artistic freedom.[9] To achieve these aims, one of the action plans outlined in the Communication was unleashing innovation through a European media data space and encouraging new business models (Action 4) by creating a report to analyse media trends (European Media Industry Outlook).[10] Furthermore, launching a dialogue with the audiovisual industry towards a broader availability of audiovisual content across the EU (the stakeholder dialogue) was also regarded another important action plan (Action 7) in this field. European Media Industry Outlook report published in May 2023, while the stakeholders dialogue planned for between November 2021 to December 2022. The summaries of these dialogues were also published in the Commission's website.[11]

---

[4] Communication on Europe's Media, p. 4.

[5] For more information regarding the action plan, please visit Communication on Europe's Media, pp 22–23.

[6] Communication on Europe's Media, p. 1.

[7] Communication on Europe's Media, p. 2.

[8] Communication on Europe's Media, p. 2.

[9] Communication on Europe's Media, p. 3.

[10] Communication on Europe's Media, p. 11.

[11] Access to and availability of audiovisual content across the EU (2025). In: Shaping Europe's digital future https://digital-strategy.ec.europa.eu/en/policies/access-and-availability-audiovisual-content (hereinafter will be referred as the Stakeholders Dialogues).

8.2.1.2 The Stakeholders Dialogue

The first meeting of the Dialogue on access to and availability of audiovisual content across the EU was scheduled for November 2021. The main objective of these meetings was described as finding industry-driven solutions to enhance consumers' access to audiovisual content and increase its availability within Member States.[12] The goals of the Dialogue included identifying concrete measures to improve the circulation of audiovisual works, making a more diverse range of audiovisual content available online in each member state, and exploring potential solutions to enhance the discoverability of audiovisual content online.[13] In the first meeting, the growing demand for cross-border access to audiovisual content was discussed, comparing the periods between 2015 and 2019. It was evident that this demand had significantly increased over the past 4 years, rising from 8 to 15%.[14] As a result of the first meeting, the Commission requested concrete ideas to enhance the availability and access to audiovisual content. It was suggested that these ideas would be discussed in the upcoming meetings.[15] The second meeting took place just roughly two weeks, after the first one. In this meeting, stakeholders discussed ways to encourage the production of audiovisual works that could appeal to a broader audience across the EU, as well as strategies to improve the distribution and discoverability of these works throughout the EU.[16] As a result of this meeting, the Commission reminded all stakeholders to come up with concrete answers and potential solutions to these questions.[17] In the third meeting there were no significant development regarding the dialogue either.[18] In the final meeting, the Commission discussed the written contributions submitted following the first three meetings from the stakeholders.[19] Even though the Commission made significant efforts to encourage the improvement of the circulation of audiovisual works and consumer access to cross-border audiovisual content, representatives of the audiovisual industry were very reluctant to propose any concrete ideas regarding their business practices, particularly those related to the licensing of rights and the distribution of works across the EU.[20] The representatives argued that there is already a wide availability of audiovisual content across the EU, so they believed there was no need for any significant changes to the current market practices.[21]

---

[12] The Stakeholders Dialogues, the first meeting presentation.

[13] The Stakeholders Dialogues, the first meeting presentation.

[14] The Stakeholders Dialogues, the first meeting presentation.

[15] The Stakeholders Dialogues, the first meeting summary.

[16] The Stakeholders Dialogues, the second meeting summary.

[17] The Stakeholders Dialogues, the second meeting summary.

[18] The Stakeholders Dialogues, the third meeting summary.

[19] The Stakeholders Dialogues, the final meeting summary.

[20] Commission Staff Working Document on the impact of the Geo-blocking Regulation and progress in further reducing cross- border barriers SWD (2024) 196 final, p. 36. (hereinafter will be referred as the SWD on the impact of the Geo-blocking Regulation (2024)).

[21] SWD on the impact of the Geo-blocking Regulation (2024, p. 36).

Regarding the circulation and distribution of audiovisual works, one of the initial suggestions was to ensure that publicly funded films are available on video-on-demand platforms. This would involve introducing a requirement for publicly funded films that have unsold territories after twenty-four months to be made available on verified video-on-demand streaming platforms on a non-exclusive, revenue-sharing basis.[22] Furthermore, it was suggested that cross-border access to transactional video-on-demand services from unlicensed territories could be allowed. Rightsholders would have the option to offer access to audiences in these unlicensed territories through customised TVOD services, supported by public funding and supplemented by private investment.[23] It was also proposed to provide cross-border access to out-of-commerce films by designating older films or those without an active producer as out-of-commerce, allowing them to be made available through a cultural heritage organisation.[24] In this consultation, representatives of consumer associations, especially linguistic minorities expressed their support for the idea of enabling cross-border access to audiovisual content and services where such content or services are not available in the consumer's country.[25] On the other hand, representatives of the audiovisual sector argued that this proposal would undermine the industry's sustainability, and they refrained from engaging in any discussion on this matter.[26] Making publicly funded films available on video-on-demand platforms after a certain period, offering cross-border access to video-on-demand services from unlicensed territories, and providing cross-border access to out-of-commerce films through cultural heritage organizations will also be discussed further in this chapter as potential solutions.

8.2.1.3 European Media Industry Outlook

As part of the Media and Audiovisual Action Plan, the Commission published a report in 2023 titled *Consumer Survey on Consumer Behaviour and Preferences Related to the Consumption of Audiovisual Entertainment Content*.[27] The primary aim of this report was to assist the Commission's services in preparing the Media Industry Outlook[28] report which will help the future policy interventions thanks to its data. This report aimed to analyse consumer habits, preferences, and motivations regarding the consumption of audiovisual content. Online surveys were conducted across fifteen EU Member States, with data collected between July and August

[22] The Stakeholders Dialogues, the final meeting presentation.

[23] The Stakeholders Dialogues, the final meeting presentation.

[24] The Stakeholders Dialogues, the final meeting presentation.

[25] SWD on the impact of the Geo-blocking Regulation (2024, p. 35).

[26] SWD on the impact of the Geo-blocking Regulation (2024, p. 35).

[27] European Commission 'Consumer survey on consumer behaviour and preferences related to the consumption of audiovisual entertainment content: final report', (2023). (hereinafter will be referred as the Consumer survey on the audiovisual consumption).

[28] Commission Staff Working Document 'European Media Industry Outlook' SWD (2023) 150 final. (hereinafter will be referred as the Media Industry Outlook).

2022, involving over 15,000 interviews.[29] This data was crucial for analysing trends in audiovisual consumption, and main findings are as follows:

- This study compared the frequency of using audiovisual viewing services with data from 1 year ago and found that the highest growth was in SVOD and AVOD, while the biggest decline was in cinemagoing.[30]
- This study also explored the reasons why people subscribe to SVOD services, with EU consumers primarily citing factors such as ease of use, a wide variety of high-quality films and series, and the availability of content that aligns with their preferences. Furthermore, when the study asked why consumers subscribe to a new video streaming service, they indicated that the main reason was the availability of a wide variety of films or series to choose from, with an attractive price being another key driving factor.[31]
- Additionally, when the study asked how consumers discover and choose audiovisual content, they responded that they typically search for films or series within categories/ genres offered by the platforms, or they are watching the recommendations that their friends or family made.[32]
- The study also revealed that four out of five EU consumers watch films from the US, and nearly the same number applies to those who watch films or series from their home country. Additionally, seven in ten EU consumers are watching films or series from other EU countries. The study also asked which countries EU consumers would like to see more films from, and three out of ten European consumers expressed a desire to watch more films from other European countries.[33] Seven out of ten EU consumers also indicated that they are likely to watch movies or series coming from other European countries, which demonstrates that consumers are quite open to watching content regardless of the language or country of origin.
- This study revealed a growing interest in subscription streaming services, as nearly six in ten EU consumers indicated that they are planning to replace their TV subscriptions with streaming services. Additionally, more than half of EU consumers expressed a preference for watching new films at home, using streaming services or TV, rather than going to the cinema, even if the cost of watching at home were the same as the price of a cinema ticket.[34]
- More than one third of EU consumers also noted that they plan to use SVOD services more frequently next year than they did this year.[35]

This research was very crucial to see the trends in consuming audiovisual content across the EU. The European Media Industry Outlook which was published in May

[29] Consumer survey on the audiovisual consumption, p. 3.

[30] Consumer survey on the audiovisual consumption, p. 5.

[31] Consumer survey on the audiovisual consumption, p. 6.

[32] Consumer survey on the audiovisual consumption, p. 7.

[33] Consumer survey on the audiovisual consumption, pp 7–8.

[34] Consumer survey on the audiovisual consumption, p. 24.

[35] Consumer survey on the audiovisual consumption, p. 28.

2023 also analysed the data from the consumer survey as well as analysing market trends for video games and news media industries.

For the audiovisual sector, the Outlook highlighted that younger consumers are driving the demand for change, as they have distinctive consumption habits. They tend to favour online or virtual spaces over traditional television or cinema theatres.[36] Interestingly, the research also indicated that non-EU players are adapting their business models and content offerings to align with consumer needs and trends, for example, they provide lower subscription fees, often through ad-supported options.[37] The study also mentioned AVOD, which refers to advertisement-based video-on-demand services, and FAST, which stands for free ad-supported streaming television services[38] and suggested that the FAST version could be a good opportunity for the EU industry.

Although this report includes a good level of research on the video games and news media industries, it lacks specific studies on the consumption, availability and accessibility of these products across borders in the EU. Most importantly it could be pointed out that video games sector was found to be the fastest-growing sector, especially after the Covid-19 pandemic,[39] and this sector was found to be dominated by non-EU countries, particularly Japan, China, and the United States.[40]

The report suggested that such research will be conducted over time to continuously monitor trends and recommend the best policy changes.[41]

8.2.1.4 The Commission Staff Working Document on the Impact of the Geo-Blocking Regulation and Progress in Further Reducing Cross-Border Barriers (2024)

In July 2024, the European Commission published a staff working document on the impact of the Geo-blocking Regulation and the progress made in further reducing cross-border barriers. In this report, the Commission examined the key outcomes of the Geo-blocking Regulation's impact, particularly in relation to e-commerce practices, and in the aftermath of the Covid-19 pandemic. Additionally, the Commission reviewed other studies and research mentioned in this chapter and the Geo-blocking Regulation section, including the first short-term review, European Parliament's resolution dated December 2023, consumer surveys, the European Media Outlook report, and stakeholder dialogues. For audiovisual content, the Commission summarised all relevant documents and research. According to this Document, the Commission is exploring ways to gather further evidence on consumer demands and seeking new business ideas to enhance access, distribution, and promotion of audiovisual content

36 Media Industry Outlook, p. 5.

37 Such as Disney; for more information, please see Media Industry Outlook, p. 19.

38 Consumer survey on the audiovisual consumption, p. 13.

39 Consumer survey on the audiovisual consumption, p. 4.

40 Consumer survey on the audiovisual consumption, p. 57.

41 Consumer survey on the audiovisual consumption, p. 4.

across the EU. The Commission also plans to continue discussions with industry stakeholders to improve the distribution of EU works throughout the region, as part of the Media and Audiovisual Action Plan.[42] Finally, the Commission concludes its report by stating that the European Parliament and other relevant EU organisations and institutions will review the latest evidence, consumer demands, and industry insights, and will take the most appropriate measures once the reviews will be held.[43]

8.2.2 *The Covid-19 Pandemic and the Increased in the Digital Consumption*

The Covid-19 pandemic is a worldwide outbreak caused by the severe acute respiratory syndrome coronavirus 2 (SARS-CoV-2), a highly infectious disease.[44] This disease was declared a pandemic in March 2020, and more than 3 years later, in May 2023, the World Health Organization (WHO) announced that it no longer be regarded as global emergency. During this 3-year period, many countries chose to implement strict measures, such as closing their borders to other nations or shutting down public spaces where people could gather. In particular, countries opted to close cinemas, shopping malls, and other public venues to better manage society and slow the spread of the disease. This meant that people were required to stay at home and manage their work and daily lives from within their homes. As a result, the virus was not just a physical and infectious threat; it also became a psychological challenge for many.[45] People often felt isolated and experienced fear and anxiety about the virus and its impact. As a result of this isolation and the lockdown, people experienced feelings of loneliness, boredom, and even anger.[46] To cope with these negative emotions, people sought ways to entertain and inform themselves, such as watching movies online or tuning into TV channels, either online or through their televisions, to easily access accurate information.[47] As people spent more time at home, there was a significant rise in domestic media consumption.[48]

WIPO conducted a study to assess the impact of the Covid-19 pandemic on the creative industries.[49] The report pointed out that the pandemic had a significant

---

[42] SWD on the impact of the Geo-blocking Regulation (2024, p. 37).

[43] SWD on the impact of the Geo-blocking Regulation (2024, p. 37).

[44] Emergencies. In: World Health Organization https://www.who.int/europe/emergencies/situations/covid-19.

[45] Dadouh and Aomari (2022, p. 4436).

[46] Dadouh and Aomari (2022, p. 4437).

[47] Dadouh and Aomari (2022, p. 4437).

[48] Mikos (2020, p. 31).

[49] Marilena Vecco et al. (2022) The impact of the COVID-19 pandemic on creative industries, cultural institutions, education and research In: WIPO https://www.wipo.int/edocs/mdocs/copyright/en/wipo_cr_covid_19_ge_22/wipo_cr_covid_19_ge_22_study.pdf (hereinafter will be referred as the WIPO study on the impact of the Covid-19).

effect on the functioning of cultural and creative markets, particularly on the global cross-border activity of digital cultural content.[50] This unprecedented time brought challenges for people, leading to new consumption habits and the emergence of a new normal. Many platforms capitalised on this shift, introducing innovations and significantly increasing their subscriber base during this period.[51] Streaming platforms such as Netflix, Amazon Prime Video, Disney + , and others strengthened their positions as a result of the pandemic.[52] According to a survey conducted, 27% of people increased their streaming activities during the pandemic to watch and access digital content and Netflix increased their subscribers by 25 million in the first half of the 2020.[53]

Notably, this shift in consumption patterns was not limited to the initial lock-down period according to studies. Data from 2021 indicated that there was still a high level of consumption on digital streaming platforms, which is higher than before, suggesting that the pandemic has permanently altered viewing habits, with this change likely becoming the new normal.[54] The data presented in the European Media Outlook also confirmed this observation.

The pandemic clearly highlighted the importance of digital tools and transformed the business practices of many companies. They sought innovative ways to boost digital consumption and adapted their distribution methods, moving away from the traditional tools used before the pandemic.[55] The pandemic opened up new opportunities for artists, leading to diverse forms of digital consumption for different groups with varied interests. For example, musicians began hosting live concerts through their online accounts to connect with fans and followers, while also attempting to recoup some of the revenue lost during the lockdown period.[56] Again, publishers began releasing more e-books than usual because physical bookstores were closed. They needed to recoup their investments and generate revenue through alternative means.[57] It is undeniable that Covid-19 has transformed the way cultural products are consumed, how entertainment is enjoyed, how research is conducted, how education is delivered, how books are read, and how films are watched.[58]

During this period, there was a greater need for people to consume cultural products, especially for those living outside their home country who were unable to return when they wish due to travel restrictions. Furthermore, with most activities outside the home being restricted, people had more time to spend on leisure activities at home. As a result, they watched more movies or consumed more online content and felt the need to learn new things. Many used this time to pick up new skills, such

[50] WIPO study on the impact of the Covid-19, p. 7.

[51] Lopez-Orosco et al, (2023, p. 23).

[52] WIPO study on the impact of the Covid-19, p. 7.

[53] Mikos (2020, p. 31).

[54] WIPO study on the impact of the Covid-19, p. 11.

[55] WIPO study on the impact of the Covid-19, p. 22.

[56] WIPO study on the impact of the Covid-19, p. 15.

[57] WIPO study on the impact of the Covid-19, p. 20.

[58] WIPO study on the impact of the Covid-19, p. 47.

as learning languages or reading more books. As a result, the need for accessing digital products across borders became a significant issue during this period. The increase in consumption, which had not been anticipated when the Geo-blocking Regulation was being prepared and legislated, created new consumption patterns. People now had a greater need for cross-border access to digital products. Therefore, the expectations outlined in the staff working documents and other studies no longer accurately reflected the current realities of society. As the 2022 WIPO study suggested, the increased consumption trend was becoming the new normal, which was supported by findings in the European Media Industry Outlook and other studies conducted by various scholars. These studies clearly showed that people were becoming increasingly reliant on streaming platforms and other digital platforms that distribute copyright-protected audiovisual and non-audiovisual products. According to these studies, it is expected that the number of subscribers to these platforms will continue to grow in the near future. Therefore, taking into account of the substantial increase in consumer trends especially after the Covid-19 break, the author of this study thinks that the Geo-blocking Regulation should undergo some amendments to address this consumption.

Although the Geo-blocking Regulation reviews based on Article 9(2) in the European Parliament took place in 2023, they were based on studies conducted in 2020 by the European Commission and other relevant departments. This means that the studies and surveys used did not reflect the increased consumption trends and the growing demand for cross-border access. Therefore, it is crucial to analyse the situation using more recent studies that accurately capture the current trends and needs for cross-border access to these products, based on up-to-date data. The author strongly argues that if the data had been collected in more recent years, the consumer perspective would be entirely different, with a much greater emphasis on consumption of copyright-protected digital products and on the need for cross-border access to products than outlined in the 2020 studies. This argument is supported by studies conducted by WIPO, the European Media Outlook, and other current research, which reinforce the author's position.

Data from various important studies, conducted by both formal and informal organisations and research groups, clearly shows a significant increase in the consumption of digital products, a trend likely to continue in the future. For example, according to the survey done by the European Media Outlook, 37% of the consumers are expected to use more SVOD services in the next year, while 53% of the consumers are expecting to use almost the same.[59] That means, the need for access products cross-border will increase. As a result, the issue of geo-blocking of digital products will become even more prominent, and the traditional copyright framework and solutions established in 2018 will no longer be sufficient to address this growing problem.

[59] Media Industry Outlook, p. 21.

8.2.3 *The Importance of the Accessing Home Country's Products*

The short-term review, along with studies related to it, particularly focused on analysing the potential impact of including copyright-protected products. These studies aimed to assess consumer trends that could be influenced by the availability of audiovisual and non-audiovisual products across borders.

First of all, the short-term review assessed consumer trends that could be influenced by the availability of subscriptions to SVOD services across all countries. As discussed in Chap. 4, the short-term review focused on different scenarios to understand consumer responses to price and content changes. The surveys revealed that while 64% of consumers would switch if the price dropped by 10% for the same offer, 46% would not switch at any price discount if their preferred language was not available, and 53% would be unwilling to switch if local content was limited. Although these studies primarily focused on the potential loss of consumers, assuming that people would prefer the cheaper versions, these results may also prove that consumers are not solely driven by price; the availability of content from their home country is also a crucial factor, as also demonstrated in the European Media Outlook studies.[60] The survey conducted by the European Media Outlook shows that, the content from the US and from the home country are the most appealing ones while choosing something to watch.

Another aspect of the comprehensive analysis of consumers' subscription switching should be the potential positive change in the number of subscriptions these platforms may experience. As explained in Chap. 4, the short-term study suggests that more appealing subscriptions, including more premium and alternative options, would likely draw consumers, leading to a slight overall increase in SVOD subscriptions. For instance, the Croatian version of Netflix is two euros cheaper than the Romanian version. However, Romania offers approximately 1,300 exclusive content items on its Netflix platform, which is only available in the Romanian version of Netflix.[61] If users switch from the Romanian version to the Croatian one, they will lose access to those 1,300 exclusive items. Therefore, an average consumer would consider this carefully before making a decision.

For the music industry, as explained in the Chap. 4, the short-term review found that the cross-border availability may lead consumer choosing the cheaper options and 25% reduction in average transaction revenue may be expected. Again, in that case, consumers would lose to access their desired version in order to pay less. Attractive prices would attract consumers and consumers may choose the cheaper versions, however, music from their mother language or languages that desired would be equally attractive.

---

[60] Media Industry Outlook, p. 24.

[61] Iordache (2021, p. 9).

For the e-books sector, the short-term review highlighted a significant disparity in e-book availability across different member states, with the extension of this Regulation identified as a potential solution. Price variations in iTunes' e-book catalogues across Member States are minimal, generally within a range of ± EUR 0.05. Furthermore, the e-books sector, unsurprisingly, has been regarded as the most language-sensitive sector, and cross-border access demand is relatively low compared to other sectors. Therefore, it could be argued that if cross-border availability exists for such products, people living in other Member States who do not have access to books from their home country, or people who know or want to learn the language of a specific country, may want to access these products. This cross-border availability would be very useful for academics or students who want to access a specific country's publications while conducting research. As such, cross-border availability of e-books may actually result in an increase in revenue for copyright holders or distributors and may help users legally access desired products.

The short-term review indicated that demand for cross-border access to video games is low, approximately 4%, while availability across Member States is already high, and price variations between Member States are minimal, and extending the Regulation would have little effect on the gaming sector. Similarly, cross-border demand for software remains relatively low due to the need for language or localised versions. That means, the same comment with the e-books sector can also be made; the desire to switch their version to other countries' version in the case cross-border availability exists, could come from people living in other Member States who do not have access to games or software from their home country, or people who want to access specific country's exclusive products. As such, cross-border availability of games and software may actually result in an increase in revenue for copyright holders or distributors and may help users legally access desired products.

Another point in this regard is that some people may even be willing to pay more, to access their preferred version of content, whether it's available in their home country or a country whose culture or language they want to learn. Furthermore, another group of people may also wish to access exclusive platforms that are only available in certain countries, such as some platforms limited to Scandinavian and north European countries[62] or German-speaking regions.[63] These individuals may want to access these services if cross-border availability were to exist. Therefore, the author of this study strongly believes that viewing this issue solely from the narrow perspective that assumes cross-border availability will lead to a shift towards cheaper versions of services is misleading. As previous studies, such as the European Media Outlook, suggest, this may not be true in many cases. One key factor is the preference for products from home countries, and just because some

[62] For example, Viaplay is only available in Sweden, Norway, Denmark, Finland, Iceland, Latvia, Lithuania, Estonia, Poland, the Netherlands, the UK, the US and Canada. Please see: Viaplay https://www.viaplaygroup.com/brands/viaplay#:~:text=Available%20in%20Sweden%2C%20Norway%2C%20Denmark,kids'%20most%2Dloved%20animation%20and.

[63] For example, RTL + is only available in Germany, Austria, Switzerland and Hungary. Please see: Wikipedia 'RTL + ' https://en.wikipedia.org/wiki/RTL%2B.

services are slightly cheaper in certain regions does not mean people will automatically switch to the cheaper but not familiar ones. On the contrary, some may opt for the more expensive versions simply because cross-border availability allows them legal access. Additionally, some individuals will become new subscribers to exclusive platforms that operate only in specific countries. Nevertheless, this perspective was overlooked during the short-term reviews conducted by the European Commission and other institutions. This area was neglected, and the author of this study strongly recommends gathering concrete data to show the potential consumer benefits from cross-border availability, allowing for a more thorough analysis of the economic impact of such a change. This would also enhance the reports assessing the feasibility of the change and could potentially prompt industry stakeholders to take action in this regard. Approaching the discussion from this angle and understanding content availability and the increased demand for accessing home country or other desired country's' digital product become key points that needs to be considered when debating whether a policy intervention is necessary. This issue was not given much attention in earlier discussions, particularly in the short-term review. However, this aspect could influence the course of the debate, and the outcomes of any feasibility studies conducted.

8.2.4 The Digital Single Market Strategy and Cross-Border Access to Digital Products

Alongside with all of these, the cross-border unavailability of digital products contradicts the concept of establishing a digital single market within the EU. The author of this study strongly supports this view, which was also discussed in the first chapter of this study. The EU has been attempting to address the issue of territorial IP rights in the digital realm and aimed to resolve the cross-border unavailability of copyright-protected products within the EU. However, with the exclusion of copyright-protected digital products from the Geo-blocking Regulation, the EU did not fully achieve this goal. The Digital Single Market strategy, which consists of three pillars, had its first pillar focused on providing better access across the EU. In the Digital Single Market, consumers should benefit from e-commerce without facing unjustified discrimination. To eliminate barriers to cross-border transactions and support both consumers and businesses, the Commission introduced an action plan to tackle these issues, with ending geo-blocking being a key priority for the EU. Yet, with the exclusion of copyright-protected digital products from the scope of this Regulation, the EU has not been able to fulfil its promise of better access within the Union. The author of this study strongly believes that geo-blocking remains a significant obstacle to achieving a fully functioning digital single market.

Thanks to the European internal market, EU citizens are free to move between different Schengen member states without the need to apply for a visa or undergo border checks within the EU. People are not denied the right to purchase certain copyright-protected products in tangible form in different countries, regardless of their nationality, place of residence, or place of establishment. However, in the online world, they are often denied access to these products in digital form due to their nationality, place of residence, or place of establishment. They can also freely carry DVDs, books, and other copyright-protected materials in tangible form while they are crossing borders. Yet, when it comes to intangible items, such as digital products, cross-border access is restricted, creating an imbalance between the treatment of tangible and intangible goods. This inequality between tangible and intangible forms highlights the potential need for new policy interventions to address and eliminate such disparities.

Preserving the Digital Single Market is particularly important, especially when considering the economic aspects of this debate. For example, the three major audiovisual services operating in the EU, Netflix, Disney + , and Amazon Prime Video, are US-based platforms. These platforms have been particularly successful because, when they were first established in the US, they benefited from a true digital single market with potential access to over 340 million consumers.[64] This allowed them to grow their businesses domestically, providing them with the economic strength to expand their cultural products into other territories such as the EU, where they not only increase their content reach but also gain further economic advantages. If EU-based platforms had access to a more integrated Digital Single Market with a larger consumer base, they too would have the opportunity to grow and expand their businesses across countries, just as their US competitors have. The author of the study argues that EU consumers and platforms should also benefit from a fully established Digital Single Market within the EU. This would enable EU stakeholders to expand and strengthen the audiovisual and other industries, ultimately contributing to the economic growth of the European Union.

8.2.5 Preserving Human Rights, Cultural Diversity and Linguistic Minorities

Geo-blocking can be seen as a significant barrier to accessing information available online, which was also discussed in Chap. 1. As a result, it may infringe upon the freedom of expression and access to information. Furthermore, geo-blocking could hinder the promotion of cultural products and the ability to access cultural content online. This is especially problematic for vulnerable groups, such as linguistic minorities, language learners, people living outside their home countries for short or long periods, or individuals who seek to explore and engage with other countries' cultures. Geo-blocking can undermine the EU's aim of promoting cultural diversity and supporting European culture. The most recent official report in Parliament

[64] U.S. and World Population Clock. In: United States Census Bureau https://www.census.gov/popclock/.

also acknowledged that linguistic minorities and other vulnerable groups are disproportionately affected by geo-blocking.[65] The report emphasised that more efforts are needed to preserve and promote the cultural availability of these products, particularly for linguistic minorities. Additionally, it stressed the importance of ensuring these groups have better access to content produced in their home countries. In the stakeholders' dialogue, consumer associations also highlighted this issue of geo-blocking and called for greater efforts to improve access to these products.[66] However, no further actions or discussions have taken place since. The author of this study believes this presents a valuable opportunity to consider the need for new policy interventions and amendments to promote the cross-border availability of digital products on the internet.

The AVMSD aimed to regulate and promote cultural diversity within the EU. It regulates that audiovisual media services, including on-demand services, must ensure that at least 30% of their catalogues consist of European works. The goal was to support the production and distribution of European content by guaranteeing a minimum share in catalogues and giving it sufficient prominence.[67] According to a new report published by the European Audiovisual Observatory, the three platforms, Netflix, Amazon Prime Video, and Disney + , account for 85% of the viewing time on subscription video-on-demand platforms in Europe.[68] When looking at the viewing time for all works, 61% is spent on US content, 8% on other international works, and 8% on UK productions. Only around 22% of the total viewing time is dedicated to EU-produced works.[69] These data indicate that EU works are not widely consumed, with US content dominating the audiovisual sector. One reason for this could be that consumers are not as familiar with EU-produced content. For example, there is no single EU-based audiovisual platform that operates across all countries. Additionally, cross-border availability of EU products is limited. If a French consumer wants to watch a Belgian-produced show, they can only access the version licensed for distribution in France or adapted for the French market. They have no option to access the Belgian version of the platform and view the content in the Belgian version. As the study from the European Media Outlook suggests, one of the main factors influencing people's choice of products is recommendations from friends or family. However, if their friends or family do not have access to these products and are unfamiliar with content produced outside their home country,

---

[65] Opinion of the Legal Affairs Committee, p. 7.

[66] The SWD on the impact of the Geo-blocking Regulation (2024, p. 35).

[67] Recital 35 of the AVMSD '*Providers of on-demand audiovisual media services should promote the production and distribution of European works by ensuring that their catalogues contain a minimum share of European works and that they are given sufficient prominence.*'

Article 13 of the AVMSD '*Member States shall ensure that media service providers of on-demand audiovisual media services under their jurisdiction secure at least a 30% share of European works in their catalogues and ensure prominence of those works.*'

[68] European Audiovisual Observatory 'SVOD Usage in the European Union' (2023) https://rm.coe.int/SVOD-usage-report-in-the-eu-2023-december-2023-c-grece-and-j-a-tran/1680af0850.

[69] SVOD Usage in the European Union (2023). In: European Audiovisual Observatory, https://rm.coe.int/SVOD-usage-report-in-the-eu-2023-december-2023-c-grece-and-j-a-tran/1680af0850.

they cannot recommend it. On the other hand, US-based productions are widely distributed across both the US and most EU countries, making it easier for people to access and share recommendations with friends and family.

On the other hand, some argue that geo-blocking actually promotes cultural diversity and supports local cultural products by reducing competition from international content. It also helps home country's product since people will need to consume them more.[70] For instance, during discussions on the Geo-blocking Regulation proposal, a Member of the European Parliament suggested that if Hollywood productions were geo-blocked, EU consumers would turn to European products, giving them more visibility and a better chance to be consumed and promoted.[71] However, the author of this study disagrees with that perspective. She strongly believes that cultural diversity is about learning from different cultures, backgrounds, and beliefs. Culture includes creative expressions such as visual arts, music, dance, literature, and other forms of artistic expression.[72] This means that accessing creative products, which are most likely protected by copyright, is also essential for being part of a culture. The EU is culturally diverse and within the EU, as mentioned before, there are around 60 regional or minority languages, spoken by around 50 million people. In the EU, preserving cultural and linguistic identity, respecting diversity, and having a shared cultural heritage are crucial.[73] In Article 22 of the CFR, the Union has committed to respecting cultural, religious, and linguistic diversity. To maintain this culturally diverse union, the most important action is to ensure the existence and exchange of culturally different services and products within the union and to encourage their consumption. For people benefiting from free movement within the EU, whether for education, health, work, or other reasons, accessing cultural products in their own language is an important issue. At the same time, it is also very important for language learners and those with a specific interest in other cultures to access and benefit from the cultural productions of other countries.

With the increase of consumption online, cultural and creative products, such as movies, songs or books, are increasingly being made available in digital formats. While the principle of exhaustion allows physical copies of these products to circulate freely within the European Union, their digital counterparts are subject to more restrictive copyright rules, with licences territorially limited to one or more member states. Copyright restrictions of this sort are commonly enforced through geo-blocking practices and restrict the availability of digital products, in line with existing copyright licences. This may significantly impact the ability of anyone exercising their rights to access cultural and creative content that responds to their cultural, religious or linguistic identity or their desire to be included in that culture.

---

70 Synodinou (2020, p.147), Zahrádka and Schmücker (2022, p. 10).

71 Felix Reda (2016) How We Can End Geoblocking in the EU. In: YouTube, https://www.youtube.com/watch?v=MF8k5ooc4mw.

72 Definition of the 'culture' from Britiannica: can be found at: https://www.britannica.com/topic/culture.

73 Magdalena Pasikowska-Schnass (2016) Regional and minority languages in the European Unio. In: Europarl https://www.europarl.europa.eu/EPRS/EPRS-Briefing-589794-Regional-minority-languages-EU-FINAL.pdf.

If cross-border availability were implemented, people would have the opportunity to explore other countries' cultures, traditions, languages, and beliefs. For those living outside their home country, cross-border access would make it easier for them to stay connected with their own culture, language, and traditions. This would be particularly valuable for preserving minority languages, allowing people to access content in their native language. In this way, the EU's goal of promoting cultural diversity would be achieved.

8.2.6 *Increase in the Technological Protection Measures Usage and Online Piracy Since the Proposal*

The issue of geo-blocking has become more significant in the last 6 years since the Geo-blocking Regulation was introduced, particularly for copyright-protected digital products. For example, Netflix began applying geo-blocking measures after 2016, and as digital consumption trends have surged, with more people using platforms like Netflix, the problem of geo-blocking has grown increasingly important. Therefore, when compared to the situation in 2016 and 2017, when the Geo-blocking Regulation was first proposed, the issue of geo-blocking appears much more serious today.

Another key aspect to consider is how geo-blocking influences piracy and the increase in circumvention of geo-blocking measures. When people have no legal means to access these products, they often choose to access them illegally. As discussed in Chap. 6 with the Grand Production case and the Anne Frank case, no geo-blocking or any other technological protection measures is completely airtight. These measures can always be bypassed, meaning that individuals determined to access such products may find illegal ways to do so. This puts copyright holders and distributors at risk of not being properly compensated and remunerated for their products, as people may access them without paying or providing the appropriate remuneration to the rightsholders. Recent studies indicate that the primary driver of piracy is the unavailability of a product, rather than its price.[74] This suggests that when products are accessible, many people are willing to pay and legally obtain them. This means that, rather than paying a considerable amount to online circumvention tools, users could legally access the products, allowing copyright holders to be fairly remunerated. This suggests that for both consumers and copyright holders, eliminating piracy and providing legal options to purchase, access, view, download, or stream digital products online would be mutually beneficial.

Another perspective on the use of TPMs is that they can sometimes lead to disproportionate outcomes. For example, as discussed in Chap. 5 of this study, traditional copyright law includes exceptions such as the private use exception and the temporary copy exception, which individuals can benefit from in certain cases without infringing copyright. In the context of tangible items, people can often claim these

[74] Zahrádka (2020, p. 195).

exceptions. However, in digital copyright law, when websites or interfaces implement TPMs, users are often prevented from exercising these rights, even for private use or temporary copy purposes. For example, they cannot copy, print or read certain copyright materials when they are protected with the TPMs. This could be suggested that geo-blocking should be regulated in a way that prevents any disproportionate impact on users.

The author of this study suggests that, rather than seeking technological solutions and attempting to provide geo-blocking as a protection for licensed works, it would make more sense to offer all users legal access to these products while ensuring appropriate fees are paid to rightsholders. Therefore, the author argues that the Geo-blocking Regulation should be amended accordingly.

8.2.7 Bilateral Agreements Containing Geo-Blocking Measures Are Against Competition Law

Considering the recent decisions by the CJEU and the European Commission concerning competition law investigations into territorial restrictions in licensing agreements, such as Valve investigation, the current trend shows that bilateral agreements imposing geo-blocking restrictions on distributors are viewed as contrary to the principles of competition law as discussed in Chap. 5. This raises the possibility that unilateral geo-blocking activities, especially those prohibiting passive sales, could also be scrutinised under competition law, particularly Article 6 of the Geo-blocking Regulation. Therefore, it is worth considering whether there is a need to include copyright protected audiovisual and non-audiovisual products within the scope of the Regulation. Therefore, the author of this study suggests thoroughly reviewing Article 6 of the Geo-blocking Regulation to determine if there is a better provision available and whether any changes to it are necessary regarding the passive sales aspects.

8.2.8 The Minimal Impact of the Regulation

As it could be understood from reports published by the EU Institutions, the current form of this Regulation has had minimal impact to promote Digital Single Market in the EU, meaning it is not effectively solving the problem due to its very limited scope. There are numerous gaps in the Geo-blocking Regulation, including those related to financial services, transport services, healthcare services, and, most notably, the copyright gap. Since the primary aim of this study is to evaluate whether the Geo-blocking Regulation should include copyright-protected digital products within its scope, the other gaps will not be explored in detail. As can be understood from the legislative process, the primary goal was to create a regulation that addressed the issue of geo-blocking for copyright-protected products as well. The initial intention behind this Regulation was to tackle all forms of geo-blocking, not just a narrow aspect of the problem. However, due to lobbying efforts and opposition from key players, particularly in the audiovisual industry, it was ultimately decided to exclude copyright-protected services from the scope of this Regulation. This demonstrates that even in 2016, the Commission was aware of the issue regarding the cross-border unavailability of copyright-protected products and sought to create a single European market in the EU.[75] However, despite these efforts, the problem has persisted and even intensified over time. This clearly indicates that the issue deserves careful consideration for potential policy intervention in this area. As highlighted in the Digital Single Market Strategy, the primary goal of this Regulation is to improve access to products across the EU, both online and offline. Therefore, the author believes the Regulation should have had a greater impact and should include copyright-protected digital products within its scope.

Another important development in this field was the Portability Regulation as also explained in the Chap. 4 in detail. This Regulation aims to regulate the accessibility of portable online content services, lawfully provided in their Member State of residence, for subscribers temporarily present in another Member State. Under this Regulation, subscribers can access and use these services when they are temporarily outside their Member State of residence. This Regulation prevents geo-blocking for travellers, short-term migrants, and tourists, and as of 2020, only approximately just 0.5% of the EU population, have benefited from this Regulation, as discussed in the relevant chapter. In practice, the service providers made their content available in other member states as part of this Portability Regulation for only around 4–5 weeks. Therefore, the Regulation provides a temporary solution which only affects a very limited part of the EU citizens. As such, the author of this study strongly suggests finding a permanent solution for the problem of unavailability of digital products cross-border.

8.2.9 Conclusion

Although the author gives respect and understands arguments in favour of geo-blocking, which were thoroughly explained in the first chapter, she believes that due to the reasons outlined, the Geo-blocking Regulation requires intervention. Some amendments should be proposed in order to include copyright-protected digital products to the scope of this regulation. In that regard, the most important question to be asked is what kind of amendment should be proposed. This issue is such a complex area since lots of different stakeholders and interests are at stake. Therefore, the

[75] Marketa Trimble (2018) The European Union Anti-Geoblocking Regulation Isn't the End of the Anti-Geoblocking Battle. In: Technology & Marketing Law Blog https://blog.ericgoldman.org/archives/2018/03/the-european-union-anti-geoblocking-regulation-isnt-the-end-of-the-anti-geoblocking-battle-guest-blog-post.htm.

author strongly believes that before suggesting any amendments or policy interventions, it is essential to consider the various interests at stake, those of copyright holders, users, and distributors supplying these products to users. Therefore, the next section of this chapter will focus on outlining these different interests and will seek to find the most appropriate and balanced solution, giving due consideration to each party's concerns.

8.3 The Balance Between the Interests of Copyright Holders, Users, and Distributors

After outlining the context and providing a thorough analysis of why the Geo-blocking Regulation should be amended, this section of the study aims to highlight the different interests involved in this debate. This part will focus solely on summarising the various interests at stake, as they have already been discussed in detail in earlier chapters. Therefore, it will briefly explain why each party holds different interests and freedoms, and how they defend their respective positions. Following this summary, the author will present key points to consider for achieving the most balanced approach. This will be particularly important from the aspect of the striking the fair balance between the copyright and the other competing interests.

This study will try to find a fair balance between the copyright holders, users and other rightsholders – in this chapter other rightsholders will be considered as distributors, since they usually acquire the rights to circulate copyright-protected products.

8.3.1 The 'Fair Balance' Between the Copyright and Other Competing Rights According to the Judgments of the CJEU

Under the Article 17(2) of the CFR, intellectual property shall be protected. On the other hand, this is not an absolute right and can be restricted for the public interest according to the Article 17(1). Furthermore, According to Article 52(1) of the CFR[76] the proportionality principle should be respected while proposing any limitation to fundamental rights. Therefore, from the copyright law perspective, when there are other competing rights are at stake as happened in the geo-blocking practice; such as freedom of expression, right to access culture, non-discrimination and freedom to

[76] Article 52(1) of the CFR: '*Any limitation on the exercise of the rights and freedoms recognised by this Charter must be provided for by law and respect the essence of those rights and freedoms. Subject to the principle of proportionality, limitations may be made only if they are necessary and genuinely meet objectives of general interest recognised by the Union or the need to protect the rights and freedoms of others.*'

conduct business, an important question may arise: what is the fair balance between the copyright and other competing rights in the case of finding a proportionate solution to geo-blocking problems? In that part of the study, the author will briefly mention the most important cases which discuss the fair balance between the copyright and other competing rights. This analysis will be brief as the primary objective here is to examine the CJEU's general approach on this issue and to apply this approach when developing solutions for the geo-blocking problem. As such, to avoid unnecessary details, which are not integral to geo-blocking debate, background information of the cases will not be provided, unless they are useful to emphasise a point.

CJEU tried to find a fair balance between the copyright and other competing rights especially since the last two decades, with the introduction of the InfoSoc Directive and the CFR. Nevertheless, it will not be wrong to set out just in the beginning of this discussion is that there is no proper definition, rules or conditions which explains what requires a 'fair balance' in the competing interests.[77] In the opinion of the AG Szpunar's in Funke Medien case,[78] the AG stated that a case-by-case analysis would be useful in the assessing fair balance between copyright and other fundamental rights.[79]

The InfoSoc Directive included some provisions regarding the fair balance. Fair balance should be set out by reassessing the new electronic environment, as stated in Recital 31 of the InfoSoc Directive as follows: '*A fair balance of rights and interests between the different categories of rightholders, as well as between the different categories of rightholders and users of protected subject-matter must be safeguarded. The existing exceptions and limitations to the rights as set out by the Member States have to be reassessed in the light of the new electronic environment...*' Recital 3 of the InfoSoc Directive also requires that there should be a free movement of four freedoms within the internal market with respect to the law of property, freedom of expression and the public interest. Additionally, a fair balance between these interests and freedoms should be set out. Furthermore, under the Recitals 2,3 and 62 of the DSM Directive, the modernisation of the copyright laws should not compromise the high level of protection for the copyright holders.[80] Furthermore, Recitals 9 and 10 also regulates that copyright holders should receive appropriate reward for the use of their work.

To help achieve a finding a fair balance and uniform application of copyright and other competing fundamental rights, CJEU has played an important and central role

---

[77] Garben (2020, p. 1928).

[78] Opinion Of Advocate General Szpunar in Case C-469/17 *Funke Medien NRW GmbH v Bundesrepublik Deutschland* [2018].

[79] Opinion Of Advocate General Szpunar in Case C-469/17 *Funke Medien NRW GmbH v Bundesrepublik Deutschland* [2018], para 31: '*Any balancing of copyright against fundamental rights which goes beyond merely interpreting the provisions of copyright law, an exercise on the borderline between the interpretation and application of the law, must therefore, in my view, be carried out having regard to the circumstances of each individual case. That case-by-case approach enables the principle of proportionality to be applied as accurately as possible, thereby avoiding unjustified interferences with both copyright and fundamental rights.*'

[80] Pila and Torremans (2019, p. 318).

in this debate. To start with, in the Metronome decision,[81] which is given before the InfoSoc Directive, the Court ruled that the right to property, form part of the general principles of Community law and ruled that these freedoms are not absolute can be restricted.[82] In the Laserdisken decision,[83] the Court also accepted that the intellectual property rights are part of the right to property.[84]

In the Promusicae case[85] the CJEU a ruled that Member States must take into account the fair balancing between fundamental rights while transposing directives and do not interpret their national laws which would be contrary to general principles of the Community law, such as the principle of proportionality.[86] The CJEU also discussed fair balance and principle of proportionality in the Sky Österreich case, which case was mentioned before in the context of the freedom to conduct business aspects of this debate. In that case, the Court ruled that principle of proportionality requires that measures should not exceed the limits of what is appropriate, should not be disproportionate and should be necessary.[87]

In the Painer case,[88] and later again, in the Deckmyn case[89] the CJEU also confirms that exceptions provided in the InfoSoc Directive seek to achieve a fair balance between rights and interest of the authors, and rights of users.[90] In the GS Media case[91] the Court mentioned the objectives of the InfoSoc Directive which are the high level of protection for the authors but also providing the fair balance between competing rights and interests, in particular their freedom of expression and of information, safeguarded by Article 11 of the CFR, and of the general interest.[92] Nevertheless, the Court did not point out what constitutes fair balance between right to property, namely copyright, and freedom of expression.

---

[81] Case C-200/96 *Metronome Musik GmbH v Music Point Hokamp GmbH* [1998] ECR 1998 I-01953.

[82] Case C-200/96 *Metronome Musik GmbH v Music Point Hokamp GmbH* [1998] ECR 1998 I-01953, para21.

[83] Case C-479/04 *Laserdisken ApS v Kulturministeriet* [2006] ECR 2006 I-08089.

[84] Case C-479/04 *Laserdisken ApS v Kulturministeriet* [2006] ECR 2006 I-08089, para65.

[85] Case C-275/06 *Productores de Música de España (Promusicae) v Telefónica de España SAU* [2008] ECR 2008 I-00271.

[86] Case C-275/06 *Productores de Música de España (Promusicae) v Telefónica de España SAU* [2008] ECR 2008 I-00271, para68.

[87] Sky Österreich case, para50.

[88] Case C-145/10 *Eva-Maria Painer v Standard VerlagsGmbH and Others* [2011] ECR 2011 -00000.

[89] Case C-201/13 *Johan Deckmyn and Vrijheidsfonds VZW v Helena Vandersteen, Christiane Vandersteen, Liliana Vandersteen, Isabelle Vandersteen, Rita Dupont, Amoras II CVOH and WPG Uitgevers België* [2014] OJ C 189.

[90] Painer case, para132; Deckmyn case, para26.

[91] Case C-160/15 *GS Media BV v Sanoma Media Netherlands BV and* Others [2016] ECR 2016-00000.

[92] Case C-160/15 *GS Media BV v Sanoma Media Netherlands BV and* Others [2016] ECR 2016-00000, paras 30–31.

In 2019, three important judgments provided by the CJEU which were referred by the Federal Court of Justice of Germany. In the Funke Medien case[93] the Court pointed out that the high level of protection for authors should be established and at the same time proper functioning of the internal market should be safeguarded.[94] In that case, the Court also gave reference to Deckmyn case and reminded that under the Recital 31 of the InfoSoc a fair balance between different fundamental rights should be provided.[95] In the Spiegel Online case[96] the Court was asked to clarify whether using the work without the authorisation of the rightsholder be justified for the purposes of reporting current events and informatory purposes.[97] In that case, the Court mentioned the principle of proportionality and rules that *use of the protected work must not be extended beyond the confines of what is necessary to achieve the informatory purpose.*[98] In that case, the Court ruled that in the case of protection of the freedom of the media, under the purpose of press and to inform the public,[99] use of a protected works to report current events may not require a prior request for authorisation from the author of that work.[100] In the Pelham case[101] the CJEU also mentioned the fair balance between fundamental rights, but in that case the freedom of the arts was in question. In that decision, the Court pointed out that a balance must be struck between copyright and other rights; such as freedom of arts, freedom of expression, which includes freedom to take part in the public exchange of cultural, political and social information and ideas of all kinds.[102] In that case the Court, very importantly, discussed whether sound sampling could be regarded form artistic expression, which is covered by the freedom of arts and decided that sampling constitutes a form of artistic expression and covered by the freedom of the arts.[103] The Court ruled that when a new work, this sample is unrecognisable to the

---

[93] Case C-469/17 *Funke Medien NRW GmbH v Bundesrepublik Deutschland* [2019] OJ C 382.

[94] Case C-469/17 *Funke Medien NRW GmbH v Bundesrepublik Deutschland* [2019] OJ C 382, para 50.

[95] Case C-469/17 *Funke Medien NRW GmbH v Bundesrepublik Deutschland* [2019] OJ C 382, para 51.

[96] Case C-516/17 *Spiegel Online GmbH v Volker Beck* [2019] OJ C 392.

[97] Case C-469/17 *Funke Medien NRW GmbH v Bundesrepublik Deutschland* [2019] OJ C 382, para 60.

[98] Case C-469/17 *Funke Medien NRW GmbH v Bundesrepublik Deutschland* [2019] OJ C 382, para 68.

[99] Case C-469/17 *Funke Medien NRW GmbH v Bundesrepublik Deutschland* [2019] OJ C 382, para 72.

[100] Case C-469/17 *Funke Medien NRW GmbH v Bundesrepublik Deutschland* [2019] OJ C 382, para 74.

[101] Case C-476/17 *Pelham GmbH and Others v Ralf Hütter and Florian Schneider-Esleben* [2019] OJ C 347.

[102] Case C-476/17 *Pelham GmbH and Others v Ralf Hütter and Florian Schneider-Esleben* [2019] OJ C 347, para 34.

[103] Case C-476/17 *Pelham GmbH and Others v Ralf Hütter and Florian Schneider-Esleben* [2019] OJ C 347, para 35.

ear it should not be regarded as 'reproduction'; since such an acceptance would be against to meet the fair balance between copyright and other rights.[104]

Apart from these decisions, as discussed in Chap. 3, the Court also recognises the supremacy of the internal market over the copyright holders' interest, as confirmed by the Membran and the Patricia cases, especially in the creation and application of the exhaustion principle. Finally, as a result of their intellectual creations, copyright holders are expected to be fairly remunerated. According to recent decisions by the CJEU, such as the Valve case, the Group Canal + case, and FAPL and Murphy cases this remuneration should be equitable, meaning that it should reflect a fair, standard level of compensation rather than the maximum possible profit.

Recently, the ECtHR delivered its judgment in the case of Safarov v. Azerbaijan, as explained in the Chap. 3. The Court held that the domestic court failed to provide legal reasoning regarding the applicability of a copyright exception in the present case, thereby violating the State's positive obligations to protect the copyright of its citizens under Article 1 of Protocol No. 1 of the ECHR. With this judgment, the ECtHR confirmed that intellectual property rights fall within the scope of Article 1 of Protocol No. 1, which governs the right to the peaceful enjoyment of possessions. Accordingly, the Court affirmed that States have a positive obligation to take appropriate measures to protect property rights, including intellectual property rights. Therefore, states should provide necessary measures to protect the intellectual property rights of the authors.

To summarise, the CJEU does not have any uniform application or guidance to show the creation of a fair balance between the copyright holders' interests and other competing interests. On the other hand, latest decisions and provisions of the CFR and InfoSoc Directive shows that none of these freedoms are absolute and can be restricted. Therefore, in that part of the study, the author will try to show the concrete interest and expectations of each party in this debate and try to find a fair balance between the copyright and other competing rights, under the principle of proportionality.

8.3.2 The Copyright Holders Interest in the Geo-Blocking Debate

Copyright is one of the fundamental forms of personal property right, and as part of this, copyright holders wish to maintain control over their licensing practices and how their works are exploited. They seek the freedom to decide how to use their intellectual creations, which countries they want to operate in by choosing to make their products available in certain locations. This means that copyright holders expect their property rights to be safeguarded, their freedom to manage their rights to be respected, and that they should receive fair remuneration for their work.

---

[104] Case C-476/17 *Pelham GmbH and Others v Ralf Hütter and Florian Schneider-Esleben* [2019] OJ C 347, paras 36–37.

In the stakeholders' dialogue, The Society for Audiovisual Authors (SAA) expressed support for improving the availability and exploitation of audiovisual works across the EU by exploring solutions that uphold fair and proportionate remuneration for authors and respect the territoriality of rights, which they see as fundamental to the European audiovisual licensing model.[105] The Federation of European Screen Directors, (FERA) also emphasised the need for full implementation and respect of the European copyright framework, particularly in relation to authors' moral and economic rights.[106]

According to the opinions of the scholars,[107] if geo-blocking were eliminated, copyright holders might be forced to make their works available across the entire EU, which could pose challenges for them. They may have valid reasons for not granting licences in certain territories, such as plans to release the works later, or even choosing not to make them available at all due to associated risks. These risks could include logistical challenges, language requirements, or the potential exposure to personal jurisdiction and legal obligations in multiple countries. Furthermore, if their works were to be made available across the entire EU or on a global scale, copyright holders might feel compelled to adapt their works to meet globally accepted standards, which could place pressure on them and potentially have a negative impact on their creativity. On the other hand, it could be argued that, from a remuneration perspective, copyright holders often lose potential income due to the unavailability of these products legally, as users bypass geo-blocking measures and access them illegally without providing any payment.

Moreover, the costs of production and other expenses related to the creation and distribution of copyright-protected works often rely heavily on pre-sales funding.[108] This means that investors typically provide funding before the product is sold to consumers. As a result, copyright holders need to be mindful of this, as investors usually assess which kind of products in which territories or countries will best serve their interests, carefully weighing the pros and cons of their investment. If territorial exclusivity is removed, copyright holders could be disproportionately and negatively affected, as investors might become hesitant to make future investments.[109] Therefore, any recommendations or offer for changes to the Geo-blocking Regulation must consider these factors and remain attractive to investors.

In summary, the author of this study suggests that, from the perspective of copyright holders, the solution to the unavailability of digital products should meet the following criteria:

---

[105] Territoriality and release windows in the European audiovisual sector (2023). In: European Audiovisual Observatory p. 49. https://rm.coe.int/iris-plus-2023-02en/1680abd676.

[106] European Audiovisual Observatory, 'Territoriality and release windows in the European audiovisual sector' (2023, p. 51).

[107] Trimble (2019, pp 496–500).

[108] Zahrádka and Schmücker (2022, p. 10).

[109] POLITICO Europe (2016) 'Copyrights and Wrongs: Making a Single Market for Digital Content Work'. In: YouTube https://www.youtube.com/watch?v=qL5LSpEPDPQ.

- This solution should not disproportionately affect the copyright holders' property rights or their freedom to manage their intellectual creations.
- This solution should ensure that copyright holders are fairly compensated.
- After the amendments of the Geo-blocking Regulation, copyright holders should not be in the risk of losing investors.
- Finally, this solution should minimise or eliminate any risks associated with the removal of geo-blocking.

8.3.3 Users Interests in the Geo-Blocking Debate

As discussed in Chap. 1 and this chapter, geo-blocking issues disproportionately affect those who need cross-border access to products the most, such as linguistic minorities, immigrants, travellers, and individuals seeking to access diverse content. From their perspective, restricting access could be viewed as a violation of their freedom of expression and their right to receive information without borders, and it may also be seen as undermining the protection of cultural diversity within the EU.

This issue was also raised during the stakeholder dialogue, where consumer associations emphasised that linguistic minorities and other vulnerable groups require cross-border access to products. They stressed the need for measures to enhance the availability of these products for such groups. Furthermore, during debates on the evaluation of the Geo-blocking Regulation, the European Union acknowledged this problem, particularly for linguistic minorities and vulnerable groups. They highlighted the importance of doing more to preserve and reflect the EU's cultural diversity and richness, noting that linguistic minorities need access to products in their native languages.

As highlighted by the surveys from the European Media Industry Outlook, consumers have made it clear that they primarily want access to products from their home country, along with US content. Additionally, many consumers indicated that they plan to subscribe to and use video-on-demand platforms more frequently in the future. One of the main reasons for selecting these services is the combination of attractive pricing and the availability of content they find most appealing. In the stakeholder dialogue COMMUNIA[110] proposed to enable passive sales across the member states since consumers should have the right to access content available in other member states when it is not available in their own.[111] This proposition will be discussed in the possible recommendations part in more detail.

[110] About. In: COMMUNIA Association, https://communia-association.org/about. '*COMMUNIA is an international association incorporated under Belgian law that advocates for policies that expand the Public Domain and increase access to and reuse of culture and knowledge. It acts as a network of like-minded activists, researchers and practitioners based in Europe and the United States who seek to limit the scope of exclusive copyright to sensible proportions that do not place unnecessary restrictions on access and use.*'

[111] Stakeholder dialogue to improve cross border access to audiovisual content (2021). In: COMMUNIA Association, https://communia-association.org/2021/10/22/stakeholder-dialogue-to-improve-cross-border-access-to-audiovisual-content/.

Furthermore, while distributors and copyright holders have the right to choose the markets in which they operate and make their products available, users do not have the same freedom.[112] They cannot choose the market in which they wish to purchase products or subscribe to a platform. This imbalance is an important consideration from the perspective of users.

Therefore, the author of this study suggests that it would be accurate to recognise geo-blocking as a significant issue for users, and from the user's perspective, any solution should address these key factors:

- Their freedom of expression and their right to cultural diversity should be protected.
- The solution should ensure improved cross-border access to digital products.
- Furthermore, the solution should not compromise attractive pricing or lead to significant price differentiation within the EU.

8.3.4 Distributors Interests in the Geo-Blocking Debate

Distributors, such as platforms, websites or on-demand services, have also different interests in the geo-blocking debate. First of all, as evidenced from the stakeholders dialogue, distributors were generally reluctant to engage or propose reasonable solutions to this issue because they are satisfied with the current market situation. They argue that the market is built upon existing licensing practices and geo-blocking measures. Consequently, they suggest that any changes to this regulation could negatively impact the functioning of the market, making them hesitant to support significant modifications.

Secondly, as discussed throughout the dissertation, geo-blocking is often seen as a business strategy and a standard method for generating revenue. It allows companies to fragment the market into different territories, enabling them to maximise profits through price differentiation and by adjusting conditions and languages. This practice ultimately allows businesses to gain greater benefits from the market. As a result of freedom to conduct business, distributors may sometimes have legitimate reasons to enter into agreements with specific parties in certain countries, and they can exercise this freedom to implement geo-blocking.

Importantly, some distributors argue that if geo-blocking is removed and EU-wide or global licences are required, it could negatively impact market competitiveness. Larger distributors may be able to meet the costs, while small and medium-sized enterprises could be forced out of the market, leading to negative economic consequences. This could also mean that if geo-blocking is removed and EU-wide or global licences become necessary, the cost of these licences would significantly increase, leaving only a few distributors able to remain in the market.

---

[112] Zahrádka (2020, p. 196).

In the stakeholder dialogue, the representative of the audiovisual industry emphasised the importance of a voluntary approach, where the industry or the audiovisual platforms themselves could offer solutions according to their will.[113] Nevertheless, the author of this study disagrees with and does not recommend such a voluntary approach, as it tends to be vague and lacks clear enforcement mechanisms. She believes that such an ambiguous solution would likely create confusion for both consumers and the industry, proving ineffective in addressing the needs for cross-border access to copyright-protected digital products in the Digital Single Market.

Many unions, including audiovisual platform unions, have called for the exclusion of copyright-protected products from the Geo-blocking Regulation. As of January 2024, over 700 audiovisual companies have signed this petition, advocating for the exclusion of these products to safeguard the EU's cultural diversity, linguistic minorities and current businesses.[114]

Therefore, the author of this study suggests that these essential elements should be incorporated into an ideal solution for amending the Geo-blocking Regulation:

- First of all, the solution should not interfere with the freedom to conduct business, allowing companies to decide freely in which markets and regions they wish to operate.
- Additionally, it should not disrupt the normal functioning of the market by imposing disproportionate costs, nor should it have a significant negative impact on the market overall.
- Finally, the solution should take into account small and medium-sized enterprises, larger market players, and smaller distributors, ensuring that it does not disproportionately affect any of them. It should promote a well-functioning competitive market across the EU.

8.3.5 Conclusion

Geo-blocking is commonly used by rightsholders, becoming a routine aspect of daily life and the normal way of accessing digital products. As a result, this issue has many different dimensions, with various stakeholders, copyright holders, users, and distributors, each having their own interests in the debate. As discussed here and in the first chapter of this study, all parties involved have their own perspectives, each grounded in the rights associated with their freedoms. Users argue for their freedom of expression, the right to receive information, and the promotion of cultural diversity. Copyright holders view copyright as part of their property rights, believing they have

[113] SWD on the impact of the Geo-blocking Regulation (2024, p. 36).

[114] Vote for Culture in the European Parliament INI Report on the EU Geo-blocking Regulation (2024). In: Unic-cinemas https://www.unic-cinemas.org/fileadmin/12_JAN_2024_UPDATED_FILM_AV_SECTOR_Geoblocking_Joint_Statement_FINAL.pdf.

the right to manage it. Distributors, on the other hand, rely on the freedom to conduct business, asserting that they should be free to decide how they run their operations.

On the other hand, none of these freedoms are absolute. According to Article 10(2) of the ECHR, the right to freedom of expression and access to information can be subject to specific formalities, conditions, restrictions, or penalties when necessary to protect the rights of others, as outlined in the first chapter. In that chapter, the author also discussed the fair balance between copyright and other competing rights. Finally, regarding the freedom to conduct a business, the CJEU has clarified that it is not an absolute right. Restrictions may be imposed on the exercise of this freedom, as long as those restrictions align with objectives of general interest pursued by the European Union and do not result in disproportionate or intolerable interference, undermining the essence of those rights, as discussed in Chap. 4.

Additionally, when examining the rulings of the CJEU, the court typically recognises the supremacy of the internal market and bases its decisions accordingly. This issue is also explored in greater detail in Chap. 3. Therefore, the author of this study suggests that any recommendations should support the proper functioning of the internal market and promote the development of the digital single market, which is also in line with the new electronic environment.

The next part of this chapter will be dedicated to recommendations for the EU Policy makers. Before these recommendations, the author would like to summarise the basic elements of perfect recommendation which serve the needs of all parties as follows:

1. The recommendation should not disproportionately affect the copyright holders' property rights or their freedom to manage their intellectual creations.
2. The recommendation should ensure that copyright holders are fairly remunerated.
3. The recommendation should not put copyright holders in the risk of losing investors.
4. The recommendation should minimise any risks associated with the removal of geo-blocking which would have negative impact on the copyright holders.
5. The recommendation should ensure that user's freedom of expression and their right to cultural diversity should be protected.
6. The recommendation should ensure improved cross-border access to digital products.
7. The recommendation should help providing attractive pricing and should not lead significant price differentiation within the EU.
8. The recommendation should not interfere with the freedom to conduct business.
9. The recommendation should not disrupt the normal functioning of the market by imposing disproportionate costs, nor should it have a significant negative impact on the market overall.
10. The recommendation should promote a well-functioning competitive market across the EU by taking into account all distributors in the market.
11. The recommendation should help the promotion of the digital single market.

Following these key points, the author intends to propose several options in the next part of the study and evaluate the most balanced approach for copyright holders, users, and distributors within a fully functioning internal market, by using the proportionality assessment.

8.4 Recommendations

In this section of the study, the author will present potential recommendations that have been suggested either by scholars, previous studies, or by the author herself. These recommendations will be critically assessed, with their pros and cons thoroughly analysed. Ultimately, one or some of the options will be selected as the most suitable solution, and the author will propose amending the regulation accordingly.

8.4.1 Option 0: Proposing no Changes to the Geo-Blocking Regulation

The first option could be to propose no changes concerning the inclusion of copyright-protected products. This was the recommendation made in the Resolution published by the European Parliament in December 2023. The Resolution argued that geo-blocking for copyright-protected products is an important tool for preserving cultural diversity.[115] It noted that the reviews conducted before the Covid-19 pandemic were based on pre-pandemic data, and there is currently insufficient information to assess the impact since then.[116] Additionally, the resolution warned that including copyright-protected products under the Geo-blocking Regulation could lead to significant revenue loss, jeopardise investment in new content, and undermine contractual freedom. It could also reduce cultural diversity in content production, distribution, promotion, and exhibition. Moreover, such inclusion could limit distribution channels and potentially increase prices for consumers.[117] Finally, the Resolution recommended that the Commission propose tangible solutions for consumers, particularly for those living in cross-border regions or belonging to linguistic minorities.[118] It also suggested that, should any changes occur, audiovisual services and distributors should properly adapt their business models to the new rules while ensuring the preservation of cultural diversity and content quality.[119] The resolution further recommended conducting regular mystery shopping exercises and full assessments

[115] European Parliament Resolution, p. 4.

[116] European Parliament Resolution, p. 4.

[117] European Parliament Resolution, p. 8.

[118] European Parliament Resolution, p. 9.

[119] European Parliament Resolution, p. 9.

based on up-to-date data.[120] Consequently, due to these considerations, the Resolution officially advised against making any changes to the Geo-blocking Regulation, as also discussed in Chap. 3.

Conversely, the author of this study does not support this solution for the reasons outlined in that chapter, especially in Sect. 8.2 with great detail. The author firmly believes that the current market needs, along with the demands from users and the potential benefits of these changes, may necessitate adjustments in the Regulation. Therefore, this option may not be regarded as the best choice for this study.

8.4.2 Option 1: Accepting the Unified EU Copyright Law

Another recommendation could be the adoption of a unified EU copyright law.[121] This approach could eliminate the disparities between national copyright laws, thereby removing the need for territorial fragmentation within the EU market. With a single copyright framework across all member states, there would no longer be a requirement for territorial restrictions, which could help resolve the geo-blocking issue. Consequently, geo-blocking would no longer be necessary for these products. Nevertheless, as discussed in more detail in Chap. 2, the unification of EU copyright law can only be viewed as a long-term project. The European Union has been working towards greater harmonisation of copyright law since the 1980s, but it is evident that full unification and harmonisation is a complex and challenging task.

Since unifying the EU copyright law is a highly complex and challenging task that would require significant changes to the current EU acquis, and given the extensive time it would take, the author acknowledges that while this approach could indeed address the geo-blocking issue from a copyright law perspective, it is not a practical recommendation. The changes required would affect multiple pieces of legislation. Therefore, the author does not recommend this option as a solution, as the focus of this study is on proposing amendments for the Geo-blocking regulation, not a complete overhaul of the EU copyright law.

8.4.3 Option 2: Requirement of Community-Wide Licences

Another recommendation in this area could be to impose an obligation on copyright holders to distribute their works EU-wide, requiring them to provide EU-wide licences to distributors.[122] In this way, there would be no need to apply geo-blocking to these products, as all distributors would have the option and licence to distribute the works in any EU country. Although this solution would allow users to access these

[120] European Parliament Resolution, p. 10.

[121] Trimble (2019, p. 500).

[122] Trimble (2019, p. 500).

products in every EU country without the need for geo-blocking or the negative impacts associated with it, it could have some adverse consequences for copyright holders and distributors.

First of all, copyright holders would be required to operate in every EU country, obligating them to make their products available across the entire region. As previously discussed, this could pose challenges for copyright holders, as they would need to navigate different legal systems and languages. Compliance with various requirements in each EU country could lead to additional costs and economic drawbacks. Moreover, as mentioned earlier in this chapter, this could also impact the intellectual creativity and originality of the works that copyright holders are distributing. Furthermore, some argue that adopting this approach could negatively impact cultural diversity and hinder the promotion of cultural products in the EU.[123]

Secondly, the cost of EU-wide licences could increase, leading to potential negative effects for both copyright holders and distributors. For copyright holders, there is a possibility that fewer distributors would be willing to purchase EU-wide licences. For distributors, only a selected few major companies would likely be able to afford such licences, which could disproportionately affect SMEs as well as new start-ups. This could push these smaller players out of the market, leaving only major distributors active in the EU. Ultimately, this would harm market competition within the EU.

As such, due to the reasons outlined here, the author of this study does not recommend this option as a viable solution to the geo-blocking issue. The potential harms to both copyright holders and distributors make this approach unsuitable.

8.4.4 Option 3: The Imposition of an Obligation on Distributors to Provide Copyright-Protected Products at the Request of Consumers for an Additional Fee

Another recommendation in this area could be to impose an obligation on distributors to provide copyright-protected content or services at the consumer's request, provided that the consumer pays a legitimate additional fee for the product.[124] This recommendation could be viewed as a reflection of the Digital Single Market in the EU, where consumers should have the right to access copyright-protected products across the European Union under the same general conditions.[125]

In her article, Synodinou suggested that this model would require compulsory licensing approach in the copyright law and taking some inspiration from the FRAND

[123] Synodinou (2020, p. 147).

[124] Synodinou (2020, p. 147).

[125] Synodinou (2020, p. 147).

patent law licensing model[126] may be suggested.[127] In her article, she suggested that 'fair and reasonable terms' may refer not only to licensing rates but also to preventing anti-competitive behaviour, which could be unlawful in the market.[128] Additionally, there should be equitable remuneration for copyright holders, ensuring they receive a fair price for their work. The 'non-discriminatory principle' may imply that licensors must treat all licensees equally and if there are any differences in price or other licensing terms, there should be clear and justified reasons for those variations.[129] Finally, she suggested that in the upcoming evaluation of the Geo-blocking Regulation, this approach could be considered as one of the potential options to take into account.[130]

On the other hand, the current author has some reservations about this suggestion. First, compulsory licensing and obliging the distributor to provide products cross-border, even with users paying an appropriate fee to the copyright holders, could lead to similar outcomes as accepting community-wide licences option, which discussed in Option 2. Secondly, considering the current system of especially audiovisual services, which is dominated by streaming platforms, determining an appropriate fee for individual content or an entire catalogue could present challenges. For example, as of July 2024, the French version of Netflix offers a catalogue of approximately 7,000 titles,[131] with users paying around €11[132] for the basic plan. This illustrates how determining a fair fee for individual content could be a complex and challenging task. Although adopting this option could provide additional remuneration for copyright holders and facilitate cross-border access for users, however, since this approach may significantly alter the current structure of the industry and existing business strategies, the author does not support it. The author believes that such a major change to the current licensing system could create problems for the industry and lead to numerous negative outcomes for all stakeholders involved. Therefore, this option will not be accepted as one of the potential solutions for this study.

---

[126] Licensing on fair, reasonable and non-discriminatory terms – for more information please see Synodinou (2020, p. 148).

[127] Synodinou (2020, p. 148).

[128] Synodinou (2020, p. 149).

[129] Synodinou (2020, p. 148).

[130] Synodinou (2020), p. 150).

[131] Countries with most content available on Netflix worldwide as of July 2024 (2024). In: Statista https://www.statista.com/statistics/1013571/netflix-library-size-worldwide/.

[132] Netflix raises prices again in UK, US and France after password crackdown brings in more subscribers (2023). In: Euronews https://www.euronews.com/business/2023/10/19/netflix-raises-prices-again-in-uk-us-and-france-after-password-crackdown-brings-in-more-su#:~:text=However%2C%20it%20still%20is%20a,10.99%20and%20€19.99%2C%20respectively.

8.4.5 *Option 4: Recommended Solutions in the Stakeholder Dialogues*

In the stakeholder dialogues, several recommendations were made regarding potential solutions to the geo-blocking issue for copyright-protected products. One suggestion was to offer cross-border access to TVOD services from unlicensed territories. In this approach, rightsholders would have the option to provide access to audiences residing in unlicensed territories which products rely on a mix of public support and private investment. The goal of this recommendation was to make products available in countries where no other licensing agreements had been signed, thereby offering access to these products in unlicensed territories.

Another option was to make publicly funded films available on medium-demand platforms after a certain period of time. This option aimed to make publicly funded content more accessible across the EU, ensuring that more products would be available in countries where such publicly funded works are produced.

Finally, it was suggested that older films or films without an active producer be declared out of commerce and made available through cultural heritage organisations. This option, proposed by audiovisual representatives in the stakeholders' dialogue, aimed to improve cross-border access to out-of-commerce films.

Although the author of this study recognises that these recommendations could have a positive impact in certain cases, they are too limited in scope and not comprehensive enough to provide a fully effective solution to the problem. As a result, the author does not recommend these options as viable solutions for addressing the geo-blocking of copyright-protected products or for amending the Geo-blocking Regulation.

8.4.6 *Option 5: Language Exclusivity Instead of Territorial Exclusivity*

Another important recommendation in that area provided by Hugenholtz and Poort[133] in their article, which suggests licensing in the basis of language exclusivity instead of territorial exclusivity. In this system, distributors receive licences based on language versions. For example, a broadcaster based in Germany might acquire an exclusive licence to broadcast a movie that is dubbed or subtitled in German.[134] Only this version would be broadcasted across the EU, while other language versions could still be licensed to other broadcasters and distributed throughout the EU. In their article, this option was proposed to eliminate territorial exclusivity and avoid a territorially fragmented market.[135] They highlighted that the EU is a culturally diverse union with

---

[133] Hugenholtz and Poort (2020).

[134] Hugenholtz and Poort (2020, p. 180).

[135] Hugenholtz and Poort (2020, p. 181).

many official languages and regional minority languages spoken by approximately 40 million people. As a result, they believed this could be a beneficial option for individuals who wish to access content in their native language.

On the other hand, the article also acknowledged some potential negative outcomes of this approach. Firstly, they suggested that focusing exclusively on certain languages could negatively impact smaller languages, as fewer audiences may be interested in content available in those languages.[136] English could become the preferred option for licensing, leading to more producers creating content in English, further marginalising smaller languages. Furthermore, it was also acknowledged that there are risks with this option, as advancements in artificial intelligence and other technologies could allow users to modify dubbed or subtitled versions of products, reducing the practical effectiveness of language-based exploitation.[137] Additionally, this could lead to a focus on cheaper versions of these options, with users relying on such tools to change the language of the content.

The author of this study also recognises these negative outcomes and wishes to emphasise that such licensing practices could significantly transform the industry, potentially leading to substantial losses in the sector. For example, for audiovisual platforms, this shift could disrupt established business models and affect revenue streams. Especially for SVOD platforms like Netflix, rather than having country-specific versions like Netflix France, we might see versions like Netflix French or Netflix German in the future. This indicates that such changes could have a significant impact on the industry. Therefore, the author of this study does not recommend this option as a potential solution to the geo-blocking issue for copyright-protected digital products.

8.4.7 Option 6: A New Copyright Exception for Cultural Goods and Services

Another suggestion in that area could be creating a new exception that allows users to access their cultural products without infringing copyright, viewing access to cultural diversity as a legitimate right.[138] If consumers are unable to access their cultural products, geo-blocking could be deemed illegitimate, granting users a moral right to access their cultural diversity and creating an exception for this purpose.

This option could be particularly beneficial for individuals seeking access to cultural products and for linguistic minorities. However, it may lead to practical confusion. For instance, what types of products would qualify as cultural products? Would this include products published in a native language, those depicting cultural history, or products representing the country of origin? For example, Emily

[136] Hugenholtz and Poort (2020, p. 182).

[137] Hugenholtz and Poort (2020, p. 182).

[138] Zahrádka and Schmücker (2022, p. 14).

in Paris[139] sparked an increase in tourism in France after its release on Netflix. However, it is an American TV series about an American woman temporarily living in Paris. Despite its American origin, it could be considered a cultural product since it showcases various cultural views of Paris and includes French-speaking characters, incorporating cultural elements. Furthermore, in this context, for example, products published in English could be considered cultural products for many people, as a large number of individuals speak English, and it is the official language of the EU. These types of confusion could lead to practical imbalances, making it unlikely that this approach would adequately address the geo-blocking issue. Therefore, the author does not recommend creating an exception for accessing cultural products in the EU.

8.4.8 *Option 7: Accepting Digital Exhaustion*

Accepting digital exhaustion as a solution to the geo-blocking problem could also be considered a potential recommendation. Digital exhaustion was thoroughly explained in Chap. 3, so the author will not elaborate it here further. As discussed in Chap. 3, the author strongly believes that adopting a balanced approach to digital exhaustion would be preferable. With the support of technology, an exception to this principle could be highly effective and is indeed necessary to align with the digital environment and the evolving copyright law. However, accepting digital exhaustion would only address the issue of geo-blocking for digital products that are downloaded or owned on a permanent basis, as discussed also Chap. 3. This is because, if digital exhaustion were to be established, there would be no need for applying geo-blocking measures. Once the copyright holders exercise their exclusive right to distribute the content, their distribution rights would be exhausted, and they would no longer have the option to impose any further restrictions on the content's distribution. While the author believes that digital exhaustion could resolve the geo-blocking issue for these products, it would only provide a partial solution.[140]

Additionally, as explained in this chapter and throughout the study, the author aims to recommend changes to the Geo-blocking Regulation. The digital exhaustion principle falls under different legislation, such as the InfoSoc Directive or the DSM Directive. Therefore, the author does not recommend including the digital exhaustion principle in the Geo-blocking Regulation. Firstly, it is not suitable for this particular regulation, and secondly, it would only offer a partial solution to the problem.

---

[139] Netflix's 'Emily in Paris' and 'Lupin' drive tourism, says French film center (2024). In: Le Monde with AFP (https://www.lemonde.fr/en/france/article/2024/01/18/netflix-s-emily-in-paris-and-lupin-drive-paris-tourism_6443181_7.html#:~:text=Tourism-,Netflix's%20'Emily%20in%20Paris'%20and%20'Lupin'%20drive%20tourism,by%20France's%20national%20cinema%20body.

[140] To the author's best knowledge, as of July 2024, this is the first time this recommendation has been made by anyone.

8.4.9 Option 8: Accepting the Country-Of-Origin Approach

Another recommendation in this area could be adopting the country-of-origin approach for the distribution of copyright-protected digital products.[141] This would mean that clearing the rights in the country where the distribution originates would be sufficient to offer cross-border access to copyright-protected products. Therefore, clearing rights from other countries where the distributor is not actively promoting these works will not be necessary. This approach has already been accepted in the SatCab Directive and the Portability Regulation for the distribution of such products as already discussed in the previous chapters. If this option were accepted, distributors would only need to obtain a licence in the country-of-origin where distribute the product. They could then distribute the product across borders without the need to purchase EU-wide licences. This could also be a better option than requiring an EU-wide licence, which would be very costly and could negatively impact smaller players in the market, ultimately harming competition. Adopting the country-of-origin approach would help mitigate these issues. Nevertheless, this option may not be effective as a stand-alone solution. If distributors were allowed to actively sell their products across borders by obtaining a licence from just one country, it could lead to issues with licensing practices, licence pricing, and could cause disruption in the sector. Therefore, the author suggests that while adopting the country-of-origin approach, as seen in the SatCab Directive and the Portability Regulation could be a good option, it should be complemented by other provisions and not used as the sole solution for copyright-protected products under the Geo-blocking Regulation.

8.4.10 Option 9: Allowing Passive Sales of Copyright Protected Digital Products

Another recommendation in this area could be to include copyright-protected services within the scope of Article 6 of the Geo-blocking Regulation and ensure that passive sales of these products are not restricted.[142] This would mean that consumers from untargeted territories could access these products, and distributors would be required to accept unsolicited requests to their products from those untargeted regions. This option could be beneficial in ensuring a remuneration for copyright holders instead of using circumvention tools while also improving cross-border access to digital products in the online world. For these reasons, it could be considered a viable option, nevertheless, this option could also lead to legal uncertainties, such as determining the applicable law or other requirements. Distributors, copyright holders, or consumers might find themselves in a difficult position regarding compliance with various legal obligations. To avoid this negative outcome, introducing a legal fiction similar to that

---

141 Zahrádka and Schmücker (2022, p. 16).

142 POLITICO Europe (2016) 'Copyrights and Wrongs: Making a Single Market for Digital Content Work'. In: YouTube https://www.youtube.com/watch?v=qL5LSpEPDPQ.

in the SatCab Directive and Portability Regulation could be a viable solution. This approach will be discussed in more detail in the recommended option.

8.4.11 Option 10: Freedom to Use Circumvention Tools

Another suggestion was to introduce an exception allowing the use of circumvention tools to bypass geo-blocking measures in order to access copyright-protected products, where the content is not available in the user's country of residence.[143] This option was officially recommended by the Australian Productivity Commission, which proposed amending the Copyright Act to clarify that it is not an infringement for consumers to bypass geo-blocking technology. They also advised that the government should avoid entering into any international agreements that would prohibit or restrict consumers from circumventing geo-blocking measures. Nevertheless, this option was not accepted by policymakers, as they believed that geo-blocking measures could, in some cases, be justified.[144] Additionally, they noted that circumvention technology may not be user-friendly for many individuals. As a result, they recommended finding more user-friendly and appropriate solutions to address the geo-blocking issue.

Apart from these, the author of this study believes that allowing circumvention could result in injustice for copyright holders and distributors. If geo-blocking measures become ineffective and circumvention tools are widely used by consumers, several issues could arise. Firstly, rather than ensuring appropriate remuneration for copyright holders, payments would instead go to VPN and other circumvention tools providers and copyright holders may lose remuneration for their intellectual creations. This practice could also disrupt business strategies, as widespread circumvention would render geo-blocking measures ineffective. This would ultimately undermine the purpose of geo-blocking, making the practice obsolete. Additionally, as demand for VPNs and other circumvention tools increases, their prices may rise. This could create further complications, including cybersecurity concerns. Consequently, policymakers may soon face the need to address the growing problem of circumvention tools in a more comprehensive way. Therefore, the author of this study does not recommend this option as a viable solution for addressing the geo-blocking issue related to copyright-protected products.

---

[143] Yu (2019, p. 519).

[144] Yu (2019, p. 521).

8.4.12 *Option 11: Prohibition of Geo-Blocking After the Sale of the Product or Subscription*

One suggestion could involve introducing a prohibition on geo-blocking after the sale of a product or once a subscription has been made.[145] It could be proposed that consumers should have the right to continue accessing content after purchase or subscription, without the removal of downloaded content or blocking of services for the duration of the paid period. This option could be justified by arguing that, after purchasing an e-book or downloading a product, geo-blocking measures may restrict access if you change countries. While someone was in a legal position to purchase these products when they made the agreement with the provider in their original country, moving to a different country, temporarily or permanently, can result in those products becoming unavailable. This situation can create problems and lead to a sense of injustice, as they are being denied access to content they legally paid for. Many subscriptions are on a monthly basis, so this measure would ensure continued access during that period. When subscribing to these services and paying for products, users enter into a legally binding agreement, which includes various terms and conditions that they accept upon payment. However, often when users change countries, their subscription may be rendered void, or their downloaded content may be gone. Also, users were already subject to this agreement and its terms, just as if they were still using the products in their country of origin.

This issue was addressed, in part, by the Portability Regulation, which aimed to handle the problem for paid subscriptions to online portable content provider services. However, the same problem persists for products like e-books or downloaded content, which are not covered under this Regulation. Yet, the main criticism of the Portability Regulation is its limited scope, meaning that only a small portion of EU citizens can benefit from its provisions. Offering a solution for products other than portable online content services could be a step in the right direction. However, this approach might still face criticism for its limited scope, as only a small portion of citizens would benefit from it. Furthermore, as discussed in the digital exhaustion option (Option 7), this approach would only address the issue for products that have already been downloaded, or people can access them for a limited period of time, meaning the scope would remain very limited. Additionally, people who have never been in a specific country may wish to purchase products available in other countries, but they would still be excluded from this solution. As a result, cross-border availability would remain below the desired level. For these reasons, the author of this study does not recommend this option as a viable solution.

---

[145] To the author's best knowledge, as of July 2024, this is the first time this recommendation has been made by anyone.

8.4.13 Option 12: Using Blockchain Platform

Blockchain can be described as an open, distributed ledger technology and database that allows users to record and track transactions exchanged over a peer-to-peer network.[146] The modern concept of blockchain was designed by an individual or group known as Satoshi Nakamoto, introduced in their paper titled 'Bitcoin: A Peer-to-Peer Electronic Cash System'. In blockchain technology, thanks to the algorithmic designs, all data is stored across multiple devices, creating complete copies of the database on each one.[147] This decentralized system is why blockchain has become particularly significant in cryptocurrency, allowing users to make peer-to-peer payments without the need for a central authority. Because blockchain technology is decentralized, with no central authority, it raises uncertainty about jurisdiction and which laws apply to transactions carried out on the platform.[148] This lack of clarity can lead to confusion in legal matters.

In the most modern form of blockchain platforms, smart contracts have been established with the help of Turing-complete programming languages.[149] These smart contracts are typically pieces of code that generate transactions when certain predefined conditions, are met. For example, if a user pays a specified amount, ownership of a piece of product could be transferred to that user. Moreover, the legal status of smart contracts remains unclear, which can lead to uncertainty about their enforceability and create confusion regarding their legal validity in different jurisdictions.[150] Using blockchain to access copyright-protected products in exchange for fee remuneration for copyright holders, facilitated by smart contracts, could be considered a promising solution to the geo-blocking problem.[151] First, blockchain operates on a decentralised platform, meaning there is no central authority or territorial restrictions, unlike traditional systems. As such, the concept of territories, which is central to geo-blocking, does not exist in blockchain. Furthermore, specific legal frameworks could be developed exclusively for blockchain, making this approach a viable option for addressing geo-blocking issues. Secondly, using blockchain could serve as a reliable method to ensure that copyright holders automatically receive remuneration when users access copyright-protected products. The payment would be made directly to the rights holder, eliminating intermediaries and ensuring transparency in the transaction.[152] For example, Revelator[153] can be cited as a blockchain startup that aimed to distribute music on the blockchain platform and ensure that artists receive

---

[146] Hauck (2021, p. 18).

[147] Finck and Moscon (2019, p. 90).

[148] Hauck (2021, p. 21).

[149] Bodó, et al., p. 316.

[150] Bodó, et al., p. 316.

[151] To the author's best knowledge, as of July 2024, this is the first time this recommendation has been made by anyone.

[152] Hauck (2021, p. 35).

[153] The revelator platform can be accessible through: https://www.revelator.com.

remuneration directly through the same platform.[154] Finally, blockchain technology is highly resilient to hacking or cybersecurity issues, as every transaction is validated by the previous or the next user, ensuring the integrity of the system.[155] This structure helps maintain security and transparency, allowing for the data to be assessed and verified across the platform. This makes circumvention tools very ineffective in that option.

On the other hand, although blockchain could provide a promising solution to many issues related to copyright law, particularly in addressing geo-blocking, there are still some challenges to consider. Firstly, blockchain is not a particularly user-friendly or widely known technology that everyone can use without difficulty. It remains a tech-savvy option, and in today's world, it is unrealistic to expect that everyone will understand how blockchain works, how to access products through it, or how to make a payment on a blockchain platform. Secondly, although blockchain has been around for many years, as of 2024, there are still numerous ambiguities regarding the legal challenges associated with it. These include the legal status of smart contracts, payments, and issues related to jurisdiction, applicable law, and other legal uncertainties surrounding blockchain technology. Finally, the blockchain platform is not very user-friendly, particularly in terms of speed and ease of access to products. It is not as fast or convenient as other payment methods, like credit cards or similar services.[156] Although the author believes that blockchain could become a significant option in the near future, as of 2024, due to the reasons mentioned, the author does not recommend a blockchain-based approach for the Geo-blocking Regulation. This recommendation is not only user-unfriendly and legally complex, but it would also require significant changes to how users, audiovisual and non-audiovisual services, platforms, and copyright holders operate. Therefore, such a comprehensive solution is not considered practical for addressing the geo-blocking issue, as the author aims to suggest a solution specifically focused on the Geo-blocking Regulation, without overly broad or disruptive changes.

---

[154] For more information: *An example for using distributed ledger technology in this way is the music blockchain startup Revelator, working with the music recognition service BMAT and the Finnish music collecting society Teosto. The application "Artist Wallet" enables the payment of performance royalties to composers for radio airplay. BMAT runs a music recognition service that uses fingerprinting technology to identify songs being played on various platforms. Revelator maintains a blockchain platform based on Ethereum. The smart contract architecture is designed to enable accurate real-time splits of rights holders' royalty positions, providing enhanced visibility for clearance and settlement of royalty transactions. Payments are automatically distributed to all the stakeholders at the same time. Revelator sends queries to BMAT every two hours. When BMAT returns "play data" for one of the compositions involved in the prototype, Revelator deposits a transaction on its Original Works platform through a smart contract that determines which rights holders get paid and how much. Payments are made in Original Works tokens. The rights holders will be able to convert those tokens to the paper currency of their choice once the project reaches that stage. This system enables near-real-time payments for public performances of musical works instead of the conventional scheme of payments, for example 45 days after the end of each quarter.*

[155] Finck and Moscon (2019, p. 101).

[156] Hauck (2021, p. 21).

8.4.14 Option 13: Accepting a Sector-By-Sector Solution

Another recommendation in this area could be to provide a sector-by-sector solution, meaning only addressing specific sectors, such as offering a solution for the audiovisual industry or the e-books sector, while leaving other sectors outside the scope of the Geo-blocking Regulation.[157] Based on the findings of recent studies on the demand for accessing audiovisual services, e-books, music, and videogames, as discussed in the first section of this study and in Chap. 4. Furthermore, the short-term review of the Geo-blocking Regulation and the study on the potential consequences of extending its scope to audiovisual and non-audiovisual copyright-protected products, different sectors show no significant changes in demand or outcomes and therefore, the author believes there is no need to differentiate between sectors or exclude some from the scope of the regulation. Although some studies or articles focus solely on the audiovisual sector as a potential area for changes to the Geo-blocking Regulation, when considering the results of the latest studies, it can be argued that including all types of audiovisual and non-audiovisual copyright-protected services within the scope of this regulation would not cause any significant harm. For the e-book sector, it has been found that demand for cross-border access is particularly low, but the price differences between EU countries are also minimal. In the video games sector, cross-border availability is already at a good level, with very little price variation between countries. While the music sector is expected to be more affected than the e-book and video game sectors, the price differences between countries in this sector are also minimal. Additionally, cross-border demand for specific versions in the music sector could potentially lead to revenue gains as a result of this change. Therefore, the author does not support offering a partial solution to this issue and strongly believes that geo-blocking for copyright-protected digital products should be addressed comprehensively. A potential solution should benefit all sectors effectively.

8.4.15 Option 14: Providing an International Solution Through Berne Convention or WIPO Copyright Treaties

Another potential solution could be implementing an international approach to address geo-blocking comprehensively, incorporating it into key copyright treaties such as the Berne Convention or the WIPO Copyright Treaties.[158] This would be particularly beneficial for countries like Australia, which face significant geo-blocking challenges and often pay higher prices for digital services and products. Nevertheless, the author of the study acknowledges the difficulties and challenges

[157] To the author's best knowledge, as of July 2024, this is the first time this recommendation has been made by anyone.

[158] To the author's best knowledge, as of July 2024, this is the first time this recommendation has been made by anyone.

in proposing a global solution to geo-blocking issues. Supporters of geo-blocking measures would likely be even more prominent on a global scale. For example, offering products globally would result in numerous legal challenges, such as complying with different countries' laws, addressing language requirements, and managing consumer-related issues, which could lead to litigation or other complications, as well as logistical problems. Additionally, this could negatively impact intellectual creativity, as authors may feel pressured to create works that cater to a global audience, potentially limiting their creative freedom. Furthermore, the territoriality of copyright law could pose additional challenges to prohibiting geo-blocking on a global scale, even though the Berne Convention and WIPO Copyright Treaties aim to create some level of harmonisation across countries. A higher degree of harmonisation would be necessary to enforce a global prohibition on geo-blocking. Given that this is already a complex issue within the EU, the author believes that achieving a global solution would be extremely difficult. Therefore, she does not support this kind of proposal.

8.5 The Recommended Solution: Option 8+ Option 9+ Creating Legal Fiction

The author of this study proposes a combined approach for potential amendments to the Geo-blocking Regulation.

First of all, the author wants to make a point in the 'requisite rights for the relevant territories' debate. Article 9(2) of the Geo-blocking Regulation includes a provision which stays that '*provided that the trader has the requisite rights for the relevant territories.*' As mentioned before, the term 'requisite rights for the relevant territories' are neither defined nor explained in the Geo-blocking Regulation or any other subsequent publications. The study by VVA et al. analysed two potential scenarios in that case and according to second scenario if the trader has the relevant rights to disseminate these contents only in the Member States where the trader is actively promoting these services, this would be enough, and the passive sales will be permitted for the area where the customer is seeking access. The author of this study will assume that having requisite rights for the relevant territories is understood under the Scenario 2, which allows passive sales. Under this assumption:

First, the author recommends including copyright-protected digital products within the scope of the Geo-blocking Regulation by adopting a country-of-origin approach for licensing practices concerning these digital products. Second, the author suggests prohibiting agreements that restrict passive sales across the Union and require distributors to accept unsolicited requests from consumers in untargeted regions. In this manner, distributors will not actively sell or make their products available cross-border, for example they will not use new interfaces to adjust the language or offer location-based content in the untargeted territories, but they would also not be permitted to geo-block them. Furthermore, adopting a legal fiction specifically for copyright-protected digital products, similar to that used in the Portability Regulation, would help avoid unnecessary legal complications arising from conflicts of law, jurisdictional issues, or potential litigation.

The author of this study believes that this proposal will provide a fair balance between copyright holders' rights, freedom of expression, freedom to provide services, freedom to conduct business and, non-discrimination and right to be a part of the culture and cultural diversity. This recommendation does not disproportionately interfere with copyright holders' property rights or their freedom to manage their intellectual creations, as they retain the right to choose the countries in which they wish to operate and determine how their rights are made available to the public. It will ensure that copyright holders are fairly remunerated, as users will have the option to purchase these products legally instead of paying a fee to VPN providers and illegally access these copyright-protected products. This recommendation will not put copyright holders at risk of losing investors, as the author anticipates that it will not significantly disrupt the industry. It also minimises risks associated with the removal of geo-blocking, which could otherwise have a negative impact on copyright holders, by creating a legal fiction.

Furthermore, user's freedom of expression and their right to cultural diversity will be protected, since with that way the right to receive and impart information will be protected while accessing cultural products will be easier for the users. This approach will improve cross-border access to digital products, since with the inclusion of the copyright-protected digital products to the Geo-blocking Regulation, users will have the right to access products available in the EU. The author anticipates that this approach will not undermine attractive pricing or cause significant price differentiation within the EU.

From the distributors' point of view, this recommendation will respect the freedom to conduct business. It will not disrupt the normal functioning of the market by imposing disproportionate costs, nor will it have a significantly negative impact on the market overall. It will promote a well-functioning competitive market across the EU by considering all distributors, ensuring that smaller players are not pushed out due to disproportionate licensing costs.

This recommendation finally will support the development of the Digital Single Market by ensuring better access to digital products.

The author, therefore, believes that this option represents the most balanced solution for all parties involved which also respect principle of proportionality. The following section will propose specific amendments to the Geo-blocking Regulation.

8.6 Recommendations for Changes to the Geo-Blocking Regulation

First of all, the author suggests removing the part 'other than services the main feature of which is the provision of access to and use of copyright protected works or other protected subject matter, including the selling of copyright protected works or protected subject matter in an intangible form' from the Article 4(1)(b). Furthermore, she also suggests changing Article 1(3) as follows:

This Regulation does not apply to the activities referred to in Article 2(2) of Directive 2006/123/EC, ***other than audiovisual services.***

Finally, the author suggests including a provision for licensing and localisation, for the copyright-protected digital products as follows:

Article 4a

Licensing and Localisation of Access to Copyright-Protected Electronically Supplied Services and Audiovisual Services

When making electronically supplied services, main feature of which is the provision of access to and use of copyright protected works or other protected subject matter, and audiovisual services available to users, the distributor must obtain a licence from the Member State in which they are actively engaged in active sales. The trader will be obliged to accept unsolicited requests from consumers in untargeted regions in a non-discriminatory manner.

For the purposes of this Regulation, the act of providing access to electronically supplied services, main feature of which is the provision of access to and use of copyright protected works or other protected subject matter, and audiovisual services to a consumer, including access, purchase, streaming, and use of those products by the user, shall be deemed to occur solely within the Member State where the trader is actively selling.

Related to this recommendation, the author suggests including the definition of untargeted regions as follows:

Article 2

Definitions

…

(19) Untargeted regions should be understood as Member State(s) in where the trader has not a licence for the electronically supplied services, main feature of which is the provision of access to and use of copyright protected works or other protected subject matter, and audiovisual services to actively market and promote these.

The author also recommends changing Article 6 as follows:

Article 6

Agreements on *Passive* Sales

1. Without prejudice to Regulation (EU) No 330/2010 and Article 101 TFEU, this Regulation shall not affect agreements restricting active sales within the meaning of Regulation (EU) No 330/2010 or agreements restricting passive sales within the meaning of Regulation (EU) No 330/2010 that concern transactions falling outside the scope of the prohibitions laid down in Articles 3, 4, **4a** and 5 of this Regulation.
2. Provisions of agreements imposing obligations on traders, in respect of passive sales within the meaning of Regulation (EU) No 330/2010, to act in violation of the prohibitions laid down in Articles 3, 4, **4a** and 5 of this Regulation shall be automatically void.

References

Bodó B et al (2018) Blockchain and smart contracts: the missing link in copyright licensing? Int J Law Inf Technol 26:311–336

Dadouh A, Aomari A (2022) Audiovisual consumption in lockdown context: research paths. Int J Soc Sci Hum Res 5:4436–4442

Finck M, Moscon V (2019) Copyright law on blockchains: between new forms of rights administration and digital rights management 2.0. IIC 50:77–108

Garben S (2020) Fundamental rights in EU copyright harmonization: balancing without a solid framework: Funke Medien, Pelham, Spiegel Online. Common Mark Law Rev 57:1909–1928

Hauck R (2021) Blockchain, smart contracts and intellectual property: using distributed ledger technology to protect, license and enforce intellectual property rights. Legal Issues Digit Age 2:17–41

Hugenholtz PB, Poort J (2020) Film financing in the Digital Single Market: challenges to territoriality. IIC 51:167–186

Iordache C (2021) Netflix in Europe: four markets, four platforms? A comparative analysis of audio-visual offerings and investment strategies in four EU states. Televis New Media 23:1–22

Lopez-Orosco LA et al (2023) Analysis of digital data consumption of video streaming platforms during COVID-19. In: Lopez-Orosco LA et al (eds) Mobile computing and sustainable informatics. Springer, Cham, pp 23–36

Mikos L (2020) Film and television production and consumption in times of the COVID-19 pandemic: the case of Germany. Balt Screen Media Rev 8:30–34

Pila J, Torremans P (2019) European intellectual property law, 2nd edn. Oxford University Press, Oxford

Synodinou TE (2020) Geoblocking in EU copyright law: challenges and perspectives. GRUR Int 69:136–150

Trimble M (2019) Copyright and geoblocking: the consequences of eliminating geoblocking. Scholarly Works 2019:476–502

Trimble M (2024) The EU Geo-Blocking Regulation: a commentary. Edward Elgar Publishing, Cheltenham

Yu PK (2019) A hater's guide to geoblocking. B U J Sci Technol Law 25:507–529

Zahrádka P (2018) Geo-blocking: protection of author's rights, of cultural diversity, or of an outdated business model? Annu Rev Law Ethics 26:191–208

Zahrádka P (2020) The Czech and Slovak audiovisual market as a laboratory experiment for the Digital Single Market in Europe. In: Szczepanik P et al (eds) Digital peripheries: the online circulation of audiovisual content from the small market perspective. Springer, Cham, pp 101–124

Zahrádka P, Schmücker R (2022) “We are sorry this video is not available in your country”: an ethical analysis of geo-blocking audio-visual online content. J Media Ethics 37:2–17

Chapter 9
Conclusion

Abstract This concluding chapter synthesises the findings of the present study and addresses its principal research question, namely whether electronically supplied services the main feature of which is the provision of access to and use of copyright-protected works or other protected subject matter, together with audiovisual services (collectively, copyright-protected digital products), ought to be brought within the scope of the Geo-blocking Regulation in the forthcoming review mandated by Article 9 thereof. Drawing upon the preceding analysis of the justifications underlying geo-blocking practices, the territorial nature of copyright law, EU harmonisation efforts, the principle of exhaustion and its potential digital extension, the existing acquis on cross-border availability, in particular the Portability Regulation and the Geo-blocking Regulation, the enforceability of territorial licensing arrangements under competition law, and the copyright-law implications of circumventing geo-blocking measures, the chapter concludes that the current exclusion can no longer be justified in light of the increased cross-border demand observed in the wake of the Covid-19 pandemic and ongoing technological developments. On this basis, the chapter advances fifteen policy recommendations and identifies a combined approach as the most balanced solution for the upcoming review: the application of the country-of-origin principle to copyright-protected digital products, coupled with an obligation upon distributors to respond to unsolicited requests from unlicensed territories (passive sales), and complemented by a legal fiction designed to shield both distributors and consumers from undue legal complications. It is submitted that this approach reconciles consumer demand with the legitimate interests of rightsholders without requiring substantial alterations to existing market strategies, and aligns with the recent case law of the CJEU on fair balance and the principle of proportionality. The chapter further urges the European Commission to gather updated data covering recent years, particularly the post-Covid-19 period, in order to inform any prospective reform.

F. Cebeci Çorum, *Application of Geo-Blocking to Copyright-Protected Digital Products*, Studies in European Economic Law and Regulation 30,
https://doi.org/10.1007/978-3-032-34507-3_9

9.1 Conclusion

The Geo-blocking Regulation was introduced by the European Union to support the Digital Single Market within the EU's internal market. Its primary goal was to remove barriers, eliminate cross-border restrictions, and improve accessibility to digital products, making access easier than before. On the other hand, electronically supplied services, main feature of which is the provision of access to and use of copyright protected works or other protected subject matter, and audiovisual services were excluded from the Geo-blocking Regulation. This means that distributors are still allowed to apply geo-blocking measures to such products, leaving their cross-border availability unchanged. This exclusion persists despite the growing demand for these products over the past five years, particularly due to the impact of the Covid-19 pandemic and advancements in technology. The Geo-blocking Regulation contains a specific provision (Article 9) that requires regular reviews of its scope and its impact, particularly in relation to the potential inclusion of copyright-protected services within its scope, to determine whether such inclusion would be appropriate.

This study aimed to analyse and critically assess the necessity of including copyright-protected digital products within the scope of the Geo-blocking Regulation. To analyse and decide on this matter, this study first focused on the geo-blocking discussion and the possible justifications for geo-blocking practices. It aimed to present the entire debate surrounding geo-blocking, particularly emphasising the territorial nature of copyright law. Given the reliance on territorial licensing, geo-blocking activities have often been considered justified. To better illustrate the territorial nature of copyright law and its relationship with geo-blocking activities, this study examined the territoriality of copyright law and the responses to this territorial characteristic within the EU's internal market. The first response discussed was the harmonisation of EU copyright law, and the second was the acceptance of the exhaustion principle. This study specifically focused on the concept of digital exhaustion, evaluating the potential of adopting such a principle in the digital domain. It suggested that adopting digital exhaustion could effectively address geo-blocking issues for products that are permanently acquired in the digital sphere. With the aid of technology, digital exhaustion could help resolve geo-blocking concerns for products that users have permanent access.

Following the discussion on the territorial nature of copyright law, this study shifted its focus to the current EU legislation concerning the cross-border availability of copyright-protected digital products within the EU. It aimed to identify potential gaps and critically examine the primary criticisms of these legislations, particularly those Portability Regulation and the Geo-blocking Regulation. The Portability Regulation has often been criticised for its limited impact on cross-border availability, as only a small percentage of EU citizens can actually benefit from it. The regulation aims to allow subscribers to portable online content services to access their subscribed platforms when temporarily present in another Member State, outside of their country of residence. The primary criticism of the Geo-blocking Regulation is the exclusion of copyright-protected digital products from its scope. This exclusion significantly narrowed the scope of the regulation. Despite its original goal of creating a borderless space within the EU, where consumers could fully benefit from the Single Market, the final draft of the Geo-blocking Regulation fell short in addressing the cross-border unavailability of digital products within the EU.

After outlining the current EU legislation and the existing framework for cross-border availability of the copyright-protected digital products, this study focused on territorial licensing practices within the EU, discussing their legality, particularly in the context of competition law concerns. Based on the latest investigations and decisions by the European Commission and the CJEU, the current trend indicates that licensing agreements containing provisions mandating geo-blocking measures are not permitted and have been found to infringement of competition law. Following these significant decisions, it was determined that any vertical agreement containing geo-blocking measures might be in violation of competition law. This marked an important step in defining the limits of geo-blocking practices in relation to competition law concerns.

Geo-blocking activities have also led users to circumvent measures applied by distributors or rightsholders aimed at enforcing geo-blocking, especially when users are either not permitted to access these products legally or are only able to access them under less favourable conditions. Consequently, another chapter of this study focused on the potential outcomes of circumventing geo-blocking measures within the context of copyright law and discussed the possibility of the application of the temporary copy exception under the circumvention scenario.

Finally, based on this information, the study explored whether there is a need to include digital products within the scope of the Geo-blocking Regulation. To address this question, the final chapter examined the latest data from various studies and considered the different balances required to tackle the geo-blocking issue effectively. Furthermore, this study proposed fifteen different recommendations and selected two of them as a combined approach to serve as a potential recommendation for extending the Geo-blocking Regulation in the upcoming review planned for 2026. According to this recommendation, the study first suggests applying the country-of-origin principle to copyright-protected digital products while not actively marketing and promoting them in countries where they do not acquire a licence. However, the regulation should require distributors to respond to unsolicited requests from unlicensed territories, obligating them to respond passive sales. Additionally, to mitigate any potential legal complexities, the study recommends implementing a legal fiction to protect both distributors and consumers from unnecessary legal complications. The author believes that this approach would allow the Geo-blocking Regulation to meet both consumer demand and the interests of rightsholders without necessitating substantial changes in market strategies and business plans. Therefore, the author considers this approach to be the most balanced solution and in line with the latest decisions provided by the CJEU in the context of fair balance and principle of proportionality. Furthermore, the author strongly recommends gathering more up-to-date data, particularly for the period between 2020 and 2024, to better understand the increased demand for cross-border access to copyright-protected digital products, a trend already indicated by several studies. As such, the author urges the European Commission to collect up-to-date data to provide more precise and effective solutions to the geo-blocking issue.

MIX
Papier aus verantwortungsvollen Quellen
Paper from responsible sources
FSC® C105338

If you have any concerns about our products,
you can contact us on
ProductSafety@springernature.com

In case Publisher is established outside the EU,
the EU authorized representative is:
Springer Nature Customer Service Center GmbH
Europaplatz 3, 69115 Heidelberg, Germany

Printed by Libri Plureos GmbH
in Hamburg, Germany